EMERSON'S PROTÉGÉS

EMERSON'S PROTÉGÉS

Mentoring
and Marketing
Transcendentalism's
Future

David Dowling

Yale UNIVERSITY PRESS
New Haven & London

Copyright © 2014 by David Dowling.

Yale University Press books may be purchased in quantity for educational, business, or promotional use. For information, please e-mail sales.press@yale.edu (U.S. office) or sales@yaleup.co.uk (U.K. office).

Set in Galliard and Copperplate type by IDS Infotech, Ltd.
Printed in the United States of America.

Library of Congress Cataloging-in-Publication Data
Dowling, David
Emerson's protégés: mentoring and marketing transcendentalism's future / David Dowling
        pages   cm
    ISBN 978-0-300-19744-0 (alk. paper)
    1. Emerson, Ralph Waldo, 1803–1882—Influence. I. Title.
PS1638.D69 2014
    814'.3—dc23   2013046759

A catalogue record for this book is available from the British Library.

This paper meets the requirements of ANSI/NISO Z39.48-1992 (Permanence of Paper).

10 9 8 7 6 5 4 3 2 1

FOR MY PARENTS, R. OAK AND MARY S. DOWLING

CONTENTS

Acknowledgments

One particularly imaginative call for papers issued by the Emerson Society inspired the research that expanded until it became this book. I am indebted to Susan Dunston, the program chair at the time, for conceiving the powerful and evocative topic of "Emerson as Mentor" and accepting my work on Emerson and Fuller for presentation on the American Literature Association panel. My earliest efforts at framing the book came under the roof of longtime friends Matt and Laure McConnell, who generously opened their Colorado mountain home to me the following summer. The serene rural high country—punctuated by Wagnerian Rocky Mountain thunderstorms—afforded an ideal setting for full immersion into the world of transcendentalism.

The archival research for this book would not have been possible without the assistance of the staff at Harvard's Houghton Library and the John Hay Library at Brown University. The expert advice of prominent Emerson scholars was also essential. Wesley Mott deserves special recognition for providing meticulous feedback on the manuscript; his loyal support and guidance were invaluable. My deep appreciation goes to Ronald Bosco, David Robinson, and Meg McGavran Murray for their detailed readings of the manuscript. Robert D. Richardson, Laura Dassow Walls, Robert D. Habich, William Rossi, Philip Round, Bruce Rhonda, and Joel Myerson all encouraged this project. My debts also extend to Patrick Chura, whose innovative work on vocation and the commercial world emboldened me to pursue an understanding of Emerson as a worldly and connected critic.

Ed Folsom, who attended my presentation on Fuller that became the first chapter of this book, has been a pillar of support along with Brooks Landon. My career from the beginning owes much to their loyalty and generosity. Martin Bickman and A. Robert Lee continue to be model mentors of the highest order. I wrote much of this book with their examples in mind. For their professional handling of the manuscript, I owe a debt of gratitude to Yale editors Eric Brandt and Phillip King, both of whom made the publication process smooth and pleasurable. Trading notes on the life and work of Margaret Fuller at the Melville Society conference in Rome with John Matteson, a Pulitzer Prize–winning scholar surging at the height of his powers, was an uncommon privilege.

The students of my University of Iowa courses were essential to the development of this research, offering fresh perspectives, challenges, and innovations. John Beatty of the fall 2011 course "Emerson's Disciples" deserves acknowledgement for his powerful commentary on transcendentalism's political and spiritual manifestations in the contemporary world. I am also indebted to Brittany Suson, who became an existential counterpart to the historical study of intellectual apprenticeship through her research on Margaret Fuller that I had the privilege to advise. To these and all my students who made this project burn bright, thanks and shine on.

Finally, this book would not have been possible without the vital influence of my wife, Caroline Tolbert, a source of joy and strength. Her distinguished scholarship on the frontier of politics and the digital world continues to open new paths for my understanding of the correspondence between media history and our twenty-first century. Our children, Jacqueline, Eveline, and Edward, will always inspire me with their vast capacity for imagination and adventure. You have taught me more than you will ever know; we will continue to explore the world together.

Abbreviations

CEC   *The Correspondence of Emerson and Carlyle*, ed. Joseph Slater (New York: Columbia University Press, 1964).

CS   *The Complete Sermons of Ralph Waldo Emerson*, 5 vols. to date, ed. Alfred J. von Frank et al. (Columbia: University of Missouri Press, 1989–92).

CW   *The Collected Works of Ralph Waldo Emerson*, 10 vols., ed. Alfred R. Ferguson, Joseph Slater, Douglas Emory Wilson, and Ronald A. Bosco (Cambridge: Harvard University Press, 1971–2013).

EL   *The Early Lectures of Ralph Waldo Emerson*, 3 vols., ed. Robert E. Spiller, Stephen E. Wicher, and Wallace E. Williams (Cambridge: Harvard University Press, 1959–72).

JMN   *The Journals and Miscellaneous Notebooks of Ralph Waldo Emerson*, 16 vols., ed. William H. Gilman, Ralph H. Orth, et al. (Cambridge: Harvard University Press, 1960–82).

L   *The Letters of Ralph Waldo Emerson*, 10 vols., ed. Ralph L. Rusk and Eleanor M. Tilton (New York: Columbia University Press, 1939, 1990–95).

TN   *The Topical Notebooks of Ralph Waldo Emerson*, 3 vols., chief editor Ralph H. Orth, volume editors Susan Sutton Smith et al. (Columbia: University of Missouri Press, 1990–94).

W   *The Complete Works of Ralph Waldo Emerson*, 12 vols., ed. Edward Waldo Emerson (Boston: Houghton Mifflin, 1903–4).

EMERSON'S PROTÉGÉS

INTRODUCTION

Embodying "The Newness"

In a fit of unbridled exuberance, Ralph Waldo Emerson sang out praise for what he deemed at the time the greatest achievement of his young poet apprentice, Henry David Thoreau. "Sympathy," he insisted, was so much better than the other contributions in the July 1840 debut number of the *Dial* that it should have been set in larger type to reflect its significance, since the poem was "good enough to save a whole bad Number" (*L*, 2:311). Emerson wanted his star pupil front and center on this new stage to provide him with a bold introduction commensurate with this "beautiful poem" of "the purest strain & the loftiest, I think, that has yet pealed from this unpoetic American forest" (*JMN*, 7:230–31). This was the promising youth Emerson had hoped would emerge, not only as the messiah for a beleaguered condition of American poetry, but also as the creative engine for his new journal. He was promoting not only a star pupil, but the *Dial*, a literary enterprise in defiance of the meek pieties and safe moralism of the reform writing spreading throughout the new republic. The journal should be bold, like its young poets, he urged Margaret Fuller. "Let them print the word *Dial* in strong black letters that can be seen in the sunshine. It looks cautious now, pale face, lily liver." As a vehicle for promoting his young apprentice, Emerson wanted more youthful swagger and audacity in a periodical "broad and great" and even "a little *bad*. The first number is not enough to scare the tenderest bantling of conformity" (*L*, 2:311).[1]

At the time Emerson wanted a venue visible and bold enough to properly stage the introduction of his best young poet, Thoreau, and his best

Ralph Waldo Emerson (Courtesy Concord Free Public Library)

product, "Sympathy." Years later, however, he would direct his disciple to throw his poetry into the fire.[2] Thoreau no longer publicly pursued a poetic career from that point on, unlike Walt Whitman, whose early endorsement from Emerson could not be rescinded, much to Emerson's chagrin. For Whitman, Emerson's initial exuberant praise—"I greet you at the beginning of a Great Career"—functioned like a barbaric yawp in its own right for the young poet (*L*, 8:446). The phrase offered itself as an ideal marketing slogan perfectly suited to the project of promotion and publicity, attached as it was to the name of the most important writer of his generation, whose support virtually guaranteed winning elite educated audiences. Emerson's letter became a kind of carte blanche for the enterprising self-promoter infamous for writing many of his own best reviews and including his own phrenological chart within select editions of *Leaves of Grass*. Whitman brandished Emerson's golden words throughout the literary marketplace, emblazoning them in gilded script on the spine of the 1856 edition of *Leaves*. He also submitted Emerson's complete letter to the *New-York Tribune*, the antebellum equivalent of a modern press release.[3]

What prompted Whitman to covet Emerson's endorsement so obsequiously was a charismatic and stirring oration titled "The Poet," which Emerson delivered in New York City, and which was published later in 1844. Walter Whitman, whose alter ego of the larger-than-life poet figure of *Leaves of Grass* had yet to be born, was in the audience at the time and pounced at Emerson's resounding call for a poet to break the shackles of convention and boldly lead America into a democratic golden age. American materials abound, Emerson urged in what now looks like an imitation of Whitman's signature pluralistic catalogues of the nation's characteristic democratic features. Emerson proclaimed, "We have had no genius in America, with tyrannous eye," such as the one Whitman would cast on the masses crossing Brooklyn ferry, "which knew the value of our incomparable materials, and saw in the barbarism and materialism of the times, another carnival of the same gods whose picture he so much admires in Homer." One can imagine Whitman's reaction as he heard Emerson illustrate that "yet unsung" carnival of "our logrolling, our stumps and their politics, our fisheries, our Negroes, and Indians, our boasts, and our repudiations, the wrath of rogue, and the pusillanimity of honest men, the northern trade, the southern planting, the western clearing, Oregon, and Texas." If "America is a poem in our eyes," Whitman was acutely responsive to how "it will not wait long for metres," as he would break into song (in "Song of Myself," "Song of Occupations," and elsewhere) in a free verse to match the rough-hewn democratic character of his subjects (*CW*, 3:22).[4]

The look and feel of "The Newness," as many were calling the transcendentalist movement in Concord, was crucial to Emerson. He knew that if the unique cultural perspective of his enclave was to have a life beyond the narrow confines of his Boston suburb, then it was necessary to engender young talented writers to carry the torch. Whitman never studied under Emerson, yet potentially could have, given the elder's propensity for recruiting aspiring authors into literary apprenticeships under his guidance. Publicity for transcendentalism, as Emerson understood it, required fresh new talent to expand the reach of the fledgling *Dial*. Emerson, however, was quick to withdraw access to his publicity machine from opportunists like Whitman who understood its power to launch the careers of his new recruits.[5] Critics have long observed that Emerson did not typically maintain enthusiasm toward his mentoring projects.[6] Caleb Crain builds on and refines William Moss's older description of Emerson's pattern of warming hope and cooling disappointment toward the promising youths that entered his life.[7] Crain identifies more precisely three stages of "seduction, adoption, and rebuff."[8] In the case of Thoreau's poetry career, for example, it is telling that in 1874 Emerson's *Parnassus*, an anthology of what in his view were the greatest poems of all time, excluded "Sympathy," which had seduced Emerson into a white heat decades earlier, and includes no Whitman at all.[9] But "rebuff" was never so absolute in other instances. Notable exceptions such as Emerson's relationships with Samuel Ward and Margaret Fuller instead show an enduring mutual respect and admiration between mentor and pupil, as in the case of the landscape painter Christopher Cranch, who began his career yearning to become Emerson's idealized poet figure of his inspirational writings.

This book picks up where older research on Emerson's protégés has left off, providing a deeper explanation of the professional fates of those in whom Emerson invested generous time, energy, creativity, and capital for their literary success. I build on discussions of the impact of those relationships as put forward by Christina Zwarg, who details the reciprocal intellectual influence of Fuller's feminism and Emerson's self-reliance in *Feminist Conversations*, and Crain, who sorts out the problematic romantic entanglements of Ward and Fuller in light of their relationships with Emerson.[10] Expanding on Crain's *American Sympathy*, the most recent work to dissect the social matrix of the Concord circle, this book explores the broader and richer historical context of the literary market that mitigated the material consequences of these writers' careers. Emerson's professional guidance and advocacy on their behalf in the publishing world amended and even contradicted his aesthetic, literary, and moral counsel expressed in his letters, lectures, and published works. Through his alternating and overlapping roles as mentor, marketer, editor, and promoter, Emerson profoundly shaped the careers that defined the transcendentalist movement, ranging from those of the now canonical Margaret Fuller and Henry David Thoreau to the lesser known Christopher Pearse Cranch and Samuel Ward, and the reckless romantic poets Jones Very and Ellery Channing (the younger). Usually discussed in isolation in single-author biographies, or in the case of Ward, named only in glancing reference to the movement, I draw out the human interest of the lives shared under Emerson's influence.[11] The dramatic stories of their apprenticeships appear within the conceptual framework of the social role of literary vocation in transcendental authorship, the most frequently addressed subject in Emerson's own writing at the time.[12] With all the critical attention to Emerson's relationships, little has been written about his tutelage of figures like Newcomb, Ward, and Ellen Sturgis Hooper. Each apprenticeship under Emerson that occurred from roughly 1837 to 1842 propelled the protégé's long-term personal and professional life. My profile of Thoreau, for example, explores his seldom-discussed training under Emerson to become a professional poet. Forgotten aspects of such well-known authors as Fuller and Thoreau are thus brought to light next to lesser-known transcendentalist figures to reveal their shared circumstances of the curious position—tumultuous, vexing, exhausting, and inspirational—of training under Emerson.[13] These profiles also detail the material effects of Emerson's vocational ideals to render an aggregate portrait of his signature method and style of patronage, which has received little critical attention.

Central to this study is the concept of genius, both as a philosophical ideal that fascinated Emerson, and as the framework by which he selected his apprentices. Emerson's subjects, all of whom he deemed geniuses of various sorts, led quicksilver lives that unfolded like dynamic fictional narratives. The infinitude of each unique creative mind initially captured Emerson's mystical imagination because, like literary art itself, it seemed as if it could "never be 'described,'" as Frederic Jameson notes, "in the textbook sense of the word insofar as it is never static and will never sit for its portrait." Genius, as embodied by Emerson's closest followers, contained its own inherent truth rooted in the mystical concept of the exceptional mind. When his apprentices did sit for their portraits, as it were, for close examination and description in the textbook sense, Emerson felt pressure to impose his judgment "from outside by subjective fiat" leading to his disenchantment. Like Bertolt Brecht's defamiliarization effect, the concept of "genius" ceased to be a "natural and thus inevitable and eternal" construct at some point in each relationship, when he realized that their minds could be actively cultivated along with their literary reputations. Toward the end of each apprenticeship, we find Emerson pragmatically advocating his charges according to the assumption that their works and careers were "the results of human action," which included a network of supporting literary intermediaries, that "could therefore be changed by other human beings."[14]

Emerson's mystical view of genius succumbed to the demystifying realization of his own involvement in the construction of his promising youths, especially in his own coauthorship of their careers. Genius repeatedly appeared in this constructed demystified commercial form to Emerson, the most glaring of which was Whitman's use of his endorsement. Emerson leapt at mentoring projects, only to be disillusioned precisely by the constructedness of literary fame, by its reliance on patronage, privilege, and power and revelation of the arbitrary assignation of value as intrinsic and organic. Emerson actively worked to maintain his belief in genius as an unmitigated force of nature. As each relationship developed and the exigencies of economic necessity and the literary market intervened, "genius" shifted and slipped, became unstable and contested despite his attempts to institutionalize it (as in his "Verses of the Portfolio" from 1840, for example, a redefinition of poetic value designed to include unfinished verse by Ellery Channing) or domesticate it (by having Thoreau live with him, among other instances). This book describes the results of Emerson's efforts, both professionally and personally, to accommodate and to carve out a space for the genius he intuited in his chosen apprentices. At stake in his investment in the genius of each disciple was nothing less than the veracity of arguably the most essential tenet of his transcendentalist philosophy.

Bronson Alcott heavily influenced Emerson's antiauthoritarian pedagogical approach to his circle of young geniuses, a method that aimed not "to bring men to me, but to themselves," pronouncing it a failure due to "impurity of insight if it did not create independence," as he wrote in his journal (*JMN*, 14:258). Interestingly, Emerson aligns pure insight here with pure pedagogy, refusing to separate the two. He measured the value of his insight in direct proportion to the independence it nurtured in his protégés, just as he measured the success of his own literary production in the autonomy it inspired in his readers and lecture hall audiences. As a mentor, Emerson was disgusted more with himself than with his pupils, such as when he discovered them aping him. In Thoreau, for example, he noticed "my own [thoughts], quite originally drest." Habitually read as Emerson's disappointment in Thoreau, the mentor in this case is instead more upset with himself for imparting "impurity of insight [that] did not create independence" in the young apprentice (*JMN*, 8:96).

Such self-blame in failing to nurture independence echoes Alcott's radical reversal of authority in his Temple School, in which his method of classroom management overturned the era's norm of corporal punishment by demanding that disruptive students flog him for failing to engage their attention in the lesson.[15] As Lawrence Buell notes, "More than any other major writer, Emerson invites you to kill him off if you don't find him useful. This makes him one of the most unusual authority figures in the history of western culture, the sage as anti-mentor."[16] In terms of Emerson's guidance of aspiring professional authors in the literary marketplace, this pedagogy proved particularly problematic. Where is the authority of a mentor such as Emerson who maintains that the only obedience required of a pupil "is an obedience to a secret impulse of an individual's character" (*CW*, 2:149)?

Emerson's insistence on liberating his protégés from his authority met further complications in light of economic transformations in the literary market. For most of his followers, winning an apprenticeship with Emerson was both a commitment to an informal aesthetic education and a radical rejection of conventional and safer established vocational options. Some construed joining forces with the Concord sage as a statement of defiance against the surging free market economy that had proven unstable and untrustworthy in the late 1830s. Yet the primary objective for most was a professional literary career in this tenuous and duplicitous capitalist context. Thus "vocation" forms a part of this book's framing device of the "market" (and its myriad monetary and gift economies), because professional identity is inextricably bound to and conditioned by the periodical press and publishing industry where careers would be determined. The turbulent, shifting economy in the years after the Panic of 1837 made things particularly difficult for Emerson's protégés. The market had been booming and was thus rife with new opportunities, given the expansion of print culture into distant regions via new railroad distribution networks that were amply supplied by new steam-powered printing press technology. But the competition was fierce, and the heart of the five-year depression following the economic crisis coincided exactly with the youth movement sparked by *Nature* (1836) and the Harvard Divinity School Address (1838). The question of value, both moral and monetary, was at the core of the economic crisis, which was precipitated by Andrew Jackson's reaction to the skyrocketing inflation brought by the closure of the Second Bank of the United States. Responding to the cultural climate of "speculation fever" in which fraudulent land claims were being sold with state bank notes, Jackson promptly ordered the acceptance of hard currency, or "specie" payments in gold and silver, at banks. The economy collapsed in response, as the run on banks ruined a record number of financial institutions, escalating unemployment to what was then an all-time high. The age of speculation fever—its rampant fraudulence, debt, and counterfeit currency—incited President Jackson's response to this aberration in the development of capitalism at the height of the market revolution.

In the aesthetic realm, Emerson was equally alarmed by the fraud at the heart of the Panic, and lashed back at the avaricious culture behind the economic crisis. Both were reacting, as so many others had at the time, to the instability of bureaucracies and institutions concomitant to these early stages in the development of modernity. With the security of institutional structures of the bank system so severely shaken, Jackson's withdrawal of trust in the abstract currency of the bank note parallels Emerson's contempt for the compromised vocational purpose and eroding professional identity that enabled such corruption. Jackson's radical reform of the banks is thus the political and economic analogue of Emerson's reform of vocation, both of which robustly overturned accepted standards of value to purify an increasingly corrupt system. Though well intended, Jackson's measures inadvertently damaged the economy at large, whereas Emerson's response morally enlightened the nation to the corrupt underpinnings of its capitalist development, while beckoning a cadre of idealistic thinkers to join the epicenter of America's most important intellectual movement before the Civil War. But their establishment in the literary world was predicated on their development through a career channel, however alternatively figured, which must inevitably pass through the financial networks of the growing publishing industry.[17]

Thoreau would voice his ironic reformulation of speculation fever in *Walden* by posing as something of a miner for spiritual gold of the transcendental variety. In living deliberately, his metaphors explicitly invoke digging deep "till we come to a hard bottom and rocks in place, which we can call *reality*," the mother lode of real value, whose exact worth is detectable by a device he imagines called a "Realometer." "I would mine and burrow my way through these hills," he writes, searching for the most profitable seam like a speculator in California gold: "I think that the richest vein is somewhere hereabouts; so by the divining rod and thin rising vapors I judge; and here I will begin to mine."[18] Indeed, most of Emerson's disciples also were engaging in their own intellectual and spiritual form of speculation fever, rejecting the standard system of vocational currency for alternative riches, the true gold, found in self and nature. Interestingly, as economic institutions became more volatile, such alternative modes of value as Thoreau's became more desirable. Once the vulnerability of taken-for-granted institutions like banks suddenly became exposed, modernity's more pervasive materialism and hollow institutions came into view, offering itself for critique by the transcendental circle. Emerson's protégés thus focused their attention on how "the background of social action . . . becomes less reliable, more open to negotiation, culturally thinner, and increasingly an object of reflection," as Arnold Gehlen explains the development toward modernity. Then, as Bryan Turner articulates Gehlen's purview, "the foreground expands," and "life is seen to be risky and reflexive" in precisely the ways that Thoreau dramatized in his antiinstitutional speculation for transcendental gold. "The objective and sacred institutions of the past recede," like the Second Bank of the United States and the Harvard Divinity School, "and modern life becomes subjective, contingent, and uncertain," giving rise to "a world of secondary or quasi-institutions." Such secondary institutions, really *anti*-institutions, included

Thoreau's system of deliberate living (which he catches himself institutionalizing at the end of *Walden* and thus chooses to leave behind), and the unaccredited Emerson college at Concord specializing in creative writing for the production of transcendental literature.[19]

The historical period was thus marked by a set of forces that encouraged the eruption of an unprecedented youth movement in response to Emerson's idealistic liberal romantic refiguring of vocation. This was a time when many were professionally suffering from the economic repercussions of the Panic of 1837. Despair was associated with capitalism, yet Emerson insisted that a life of letters was not only possible in America, it was imperative to combat the rampant materialism behind the economic crisis. The history of Emerson's rise to fame and his efforts to embody "The Newness" with a fresh crop of promising youths in the late 1830s aids in understanding the cultural context that created and conditioned each of their unique paths toward a coveted apprenticeship with Emerson.

"Emerson Mania"

The struggle to embody "The Newness" in a fresh young writer was not a simple case of Emersonian idealism colliding with the realities of untapped potential in what was mostly a cadre of wayward eccentric individualists. Particularly troubling to Emerson's mentorship method was his romantic predilection toward literature, both from the perspective of writer and reader, that held that one must always yield to snap judgments and first impressions of subjects. He always warned against thoroughly analyzing books, for example, and instead believed they should only be used for what they might offer the reader, since "what another sees and tells you is not yours, but his." As in judging the poetic aptitude of his promising youth, Emerson felt that in reading, "often a chapter is enough. The glance reveals what the gaze obscures."[20] His approach toward writing, particularly in his journal and individual essays and lectures, also thrived on first impressions and sheer improvisational celerity. "Lecture on Love tomorrow night. 40 pages is the rule, and I count now but 21 finished," he wrote his brother in December 1838 at the height of his popularity among collegians (*L*, 2:177). Emerson's journal of patchwork impressions speaks to his fear, as Richard Poirier astutely observes, "that he might block and therefore forever lose some momentary partial conviction, simply because he wants instead, and impossibly, to discover a formula that will express fully whatever is going on inside him."²¹ To judge the power of character, which was Emerson's main function in identifying his literary progeny, was a task as partial and fleeting as a poetic subject's essence. For in the identities of those potential progeny, like the snowstorm Emerson described in his journal and set into verse, he knew "better than to claim any completeness in my picture. I am a fragment and this is a fragment of me," as he states in "Experience" (*CW*, 3:47). Conscience and intuition were sacrosanct faculties of the individualist's human soul that formed the cornerstone of transcendental thought. If Emerson could let his soul guide his impressions of the written word and the natural world with such smashing results in his lectures and poetry, he felt justified in relying on such radically subjective impressions in his judgment of young literary talent.

Compounding the difficulty of accurately, if not objectively, judging their potential was the heady optimism and sheer enthusiasm of the many young scholars who courted Emerson. His swagger and defiance voiced in the Harvard Divinity School Address and philosophical depth in the pages of *Nature* were totally unmatched in New England at the time. At thirty-five years old in 1838, Emerson was at the height of his powers, and any bright young graduate looked upon his endorsement and patronage longingly. He could simultaneously make one's career through the sheer power of his celebrity and take one's thinking, writing, and spirituality to new heights. Under his patronage and genius, economic concerns for a professional career could vanish and aesthetic visions could soar. He embodied the Newness, and the new generation of thinkers flocked to this messianic force that desecrated the temple (not only at the Harvard Divinity School but in his own abandonment of his ministry) and spoke to dazzled onlookers with uncommon wisdom and authority. His moral perfectionism, far from excessively pious and prim, was cloaked in the radicalism of one who had called for the layout and typeface of *Dial* to evoke the outlaw spirit, and to look "*bad.*"

Promising youths eager to win an apprenticeship under Emerson flocked. The transcendental youth movement called "Emerson mania" by one reviewer ignited in the late 1830s, burning with Emerson's radical fervor of moral self-reliance and intellectual independence from European models.

Emersonian transcendentalism was particularly popular among college students in the late 1830s, anticipating with rich irony Thoreau's hold on rebellious undergraduates of the countercultural movement during the late 1960s and early 1970s. Christopher Cranch, one of Emerson's "many readers and admirers amongst the youth of our universities," which included students in England by the late 1840s, defended against the common charge that transcendentalism was nothing more than a youthful novelty.[22] Detractors claimed it reeked "of the too enthusiastic reception which young and fresh spirits are apt to give to new views." Over a century later, college audiences of the play *The Night Thoreau Spent in Jail* echoed the Emersonian youth movement by rallying around the antiwar implications of the doctrine of civil disobedience penned by Emerson's most famous pupil. In language we might mistake for the rhetoric of a sixties-era activist, Cranch responded in 1841 to allegations of wild-eyed liberalism and overexuberance by calling them "the superficial charges of stiff barren conservatives."[23]

Emerson had his detractors, especially in the summer of 1838 following his Harvard Divinity School Address famously indicting the corpse-cold doctrine of conservative Unitarianism, yet very few were under thirty. Beleaguered with controversy, Emerson welcomed support from youthful enthusiasts that included the nineteen-year-old Caroline Sturgis, Samuel Ward at twenty-one, Anna Barker, twenty-five, and Margaret Fuller, twenty-eight. Cranch, Thoreau, Very, Channing, and Charles King Newcomb ranged in age from eighteen to twenty-five. Classmates of Very at Harvard, Ward and Channing were best friends at the preparatory Round Hill School in Northampton and were inseparable, and even sat together at their graduation. Until Emerson became his mentor, no one was closer to Channing than Ward; it was Ward who originally sent Channing's poems to Emerson. This cohort gravitated toward Emerson directly from the halls of higher education. Harvard Divinity student William Dexter Wilson, for example, explained in a letter to Emerson in 1838 the extent of the former minister's popularity among the student body and eventually invited him to address the graduating class. Two years later, Emerson regarded the best of this youth movement as "my contemporaries [who] have risen very much in my respect, for within that period, I have learned to know the genius of several persons who now fill me with pleasure & hope," as he explained to Cranch (*L*, 7:374).

Legions of young writers responded to Emerson's call for new authors, whether in the guise of the intellectual he fashioned in "The American Scholar" or the new romantic poet he incarnated in "The Poet." Works like "The Poet" drew new literary talent, which in turn rallied the youth movement for "Emerson mania." Although instances occurred in which Emerson appeared the innocent celebrity stalked by admirers both bizarre (as in the disturbing eccentricities of Very and Newcomb) and aggressive (as in the amorous Caroline Sturgis), he was largely responsible for placing himself in such high demand. Contact with him promised at least to provide a spark of creative inspiration. At most, it might grow into an intimate mentorship, and eventually a close personal relationship. Emerson mobilized members of the younger generation with literary inclinations otherwise stuck in professions that prevented them from realizing their full creative potential. He not only gave voice to their aspirations, he also insisted that they consummate their dreams. This was not perfunctory lip service to community building through the prioritization of the arts and literature in American society. Encouragement for youth to abandon their chosen professions, most of which were prone to soul-killing specialization—particularly in clerical training, legal apprenticeships, and training to take over the family business—repeatedly drove the conclusions of his lectures and essays on vocation. "I look in vain for the poet whom I describe," he beckoned, drawing them out with the irresistibly liberating proposition that "the world is full of renunciations and apprenticeships, and this is thine" (*CW*, 3:21). Between 1837 and 1876, Emerson wrote no fewer than twelve essays on the topic of literary vocation under the broad categories of the scholar's role in society and poetic inspiration. He engaged this subject in his writings and lectures more than any other during his entire career. His fascination with the subject traces back to his earliest days in the ministry, as he had given sermons on the topic of finding one's calling no fewer than seven times by 1832.[24] Would such intellectual immersion in vocation make him the ideal mentor and patron? Would his theories therefore be especially potent in guiding the careers of his apprentices?

Emerson's dedication to the topics of professional identity and vocational purpose combined with his characteristic vaulting optimism in a way that left him inundated with solicitors for his patronage, particularly in the wake of the Harvard Divinity School Address of 1838. At this time, the parlor of Bush, Emerson's Concord residence, was often crowded with legions of barefooted and bearded aficionados not unlike Melville in 1841 whose lawyer brother seized this jobless long-haired free spirit and enlisted him with a whaler. Emerson's wife, Lidian, received such visitors with a "feeling of horror." The scholar's role, the prime subject of Emerson's life work, always worked toward the ideal, yet had the effect of actively courting this very real demographic, many of whom, as they would for John Lennon and J. D. Salinger in the next century, wound up on his doorstep. "Waldo's menagerie," as Elizabeth Hoar called them, consisted of zealots of all stripes, including reformers engaged with issues of "War, Slavery, Alcohol, Animal Food, Domestic Hired Service, Colleges, Creeds, and now at last Money also."[25] Those who struck him as rebels without a cause he dispatched for their pointless resistance to "their spirited and unweariable assailants," suggesting they "must pass out of use or must learn a law" (*JMN*, 7:115). But in others he saw potential despite their appearing "perchance disagreeable; their whole being seeming rough and unmelodious, but have a little patience" (*JMN*, 7:155).

Certainly Channing, Thoreau, Newcomb, and Very, at least in their early careers, might have fit the profile of Waldo's menagerie. Emerson had called for a "new-born bard of the Holy Ghost" in the Divinity School Address and received a cast of characters as colorful as they were professionally unstable (*CW*, 1:90). Others who grew close to Emerson and received his generous wisdom and patronage were more scholarly and stable. These included the well-to-do art collector and continental traveler Ward, and the Goethe scholar, Fuller, who saw through pretentious radicals and sycophants among her contemporaries—even calling out the toadyism of Goethe's biographer—as readily as Emerson had. Ward and Fuller were also the most professionally grounded and career savvy of Emerson's promising youth. Ideologically, Fuller was one of few who sided with Emerson in rejecting George Ripley's invitation to help establish Brook Farm, the alternative agrarian utopian community. Emerson's exit from Brook Farm shows that he was never afraid of disaffiliation, especially from something that was beginning to look and feel like an institution. While Fuller renounced Brook Farm, Charles Newcomb, Emerson's protégé and close friend of Fuller's, was one of its staunchest supporters and residents of longest standing. Emerson's promising youths, therefore, represented a wide variety of temperaments, as well as stances toward transcendentalism, aesthetics, and social reform. But they all shared the privilege of Emerson's audience for a limited yet intense phase when they embarked on careers in the world of letters. This was a venture tenuous enough without the mantle of transcendentalism, whose stock in the literary market was problematic since the coterie, though widely recognized, bewildered and angered a significant portion of the American readership.

Emerson, it should be noted, did not uniformly accept all solicitors of his support for their various cultural enterprises. Nor did all solicitors elicit such a carefully considered and measured refusal as the one Emerson presented to Brook Farm founder George Ripley in December 1840.[26] Sylvester Graham, for example, health food guru and inventor of bran bread made from unsifted flour eventually known as Graham crackers, struck Emerson as absurd. Pseudo-revolutionaries like Graham could never carry the torch, since such a "poet of branbread & pumpkins" runs up against "a limit to the revolutions of a pumpkin, project it along the ground with whatever force soever." Those who failed to meet Emerson's standard for the ideal revolutionary poet, or at least show a spark of potential for reaching it, were dispatched with aplomb. Emerson constantly found himself in the position of judging the poetic power and cultural impact of visions pitched to him by visitors and well-wishers. As for Graham, his "is not a winged orb like the Egyptian symbol of dominion, but an unfeathered, ridgy, yellow pumpkin, & will quickly come to a standstill" (*JMN*, 7:120). Emerson's dismissal is telling not only of his often-overlooked dry humor, but also of the two essential dimensions of aesthetic appeal and political power he believed inhered in the ideal poet, a revolutionary in both cultural and political senses, much as Whitman had internalized it.

Career crisis—his own and those he precipitated in the younger generation—is at the heart of the Emersonian credo that attracted so many youths. His definitions of "poet" and "scholar" remained consistent throughout his career. He repeatedly envisioned the ideal author as critically vigorous, alert to the spiritual condition of his contemporary culture, and fearlessly independent in his views. This latter point forms a crucial issue in my treatment of each of his protégés in this book. Indeed, the paradox inherent in each of Emerson's mentorships was his emphasis on independence, which threatened to undercut his professional and pedagogical authority. For their learning to be successful, both aesthetically and professionally, it was essential that his pupils did not become pale reflections of himself. Such an emphasis on self-reliance proved problematic in each of the lives of his apprentices, as my individual case studies show. Emerson's approach, which measured success by the degree to which his subjects showed originality, was a reaction to his own Unitarian apprenticeship under the well-meaning yet tradition-bound conservative Reverend Henry Ware, Jr.

Before his apprenticeship with Ware, Emerson's sense of vocational rebellion had been brewing from the moment he took his first teaching job after graduating from Harvard. His complaint in his journal at the time reflects his privileging of several key principles he would later dedicate his life to, in opposition to a clearly defined set of flaws he believed were intrinsic to conventional occupational pursuits. "Now I'm a hopeless school master just entering upon years of trade to which no distinct limit is placed," in a kind of limbo of onerous tasks like those carried out for eternity by the sinners in Dante's *Inferno*. He lamented "toiling through this miserable employment even without the poor satisfaction of discharging it well." The passage is striking for the way it lays the groundwork for the scores of lectures and essays he later wrote assailing pointless labor with no distinct limit, and the corrosive moral effects of such miserable employment. The answer, as he would refine and articulate in "The American Scholar," the Divinity School Address, and "The Poet," lies in a professional identity rooted instead in the pride associated with being a poet and a romantic collegian: "Then again look at this: there was a pride in being a collegian, & a poet, & somewhat romantic," precisely the features he called for in the Harvard graduating classes (*JMN*, 1:129–30). Emerson attached great significance to the fact that he was named the poet of his graduating class, even though six others had been offered and turned down the distinction. As Lawrence Buell notes, "to be a poet was a youthful dream and role he intermittently indulged. 'Scholar' was his usual self-descriptor. Poet he would have liked to be; scholar he never doubted that he was."[27] By the late 1830s, that unfulfilled poetic ambition fed his desire to bring a proud romantic collegian into the world of poetry and teach him to soar. Thus a preponderance of the figures I examine (Thoreau, Cranch, Channing, and Very) were initially tutored by Emerson with the intention of transforming them into the embodiment of the Newness in its loftiest ideal in which the poet stood for much more than verse-maker. As Robert D. Richardson explains, Emerson "used the word to take in what we now mean by 'writer,' and his essay 'The Poet'" argues that "expression is a basic human need and is the fundamental function of literature."[28] He was loath to say it explicitly, but the blending of the category of poet into writer also implied a merging into the new context of the literary market in which writing increasingly took place during the antebellum era.

Emerson thus had a long history of romantic urges to rebel against conventional vocational roles by the time he clashed with Ware's rearguard conservatism. Thomas Carlyle, whose works Emerson was so instrumental in publishing in American editions that he was dubbed "Carlyle's editor," explained his break simply as a matter of Emerson growing tired of the subject of " 'Jesus,' &c" (*CEC*, 371). The problem more precisely derived from Emerson's obvious distaste for giving sermons; by comparison, he relished the comparative freedom of the lyceum lecture and poetry. "A sermon, my own, I never read with joy, though sincerely written; an oration, a poem, another's or my own, I read with joy," he confessed in his journal. Is it that in "the first species of writing we cannot banish tradition, convention, & that the last is more easily genuine?" he asked rhetorically (*JMN*, 7:68). Emerson always felt that goodness, if it is worth anything, should have an edge to it; the formal constraints of the sermon allowed for no edge. "I hate goodies. I hate goodness that preaches [because it] undoes itself," he explained, condemning controlled conventionality. Such preaching made for an "odious religion that watches the beef & watches the cider in the pitcher at table, that shuts the mouth hard at any remark it cannot twist nor wrench into a sermon." Paradoxically, "Goodies make us very bad" in their attempt to do us good, a point vigorously corroborated by Nathaniel Hawthorne's assault on his Puritan ancestry in so much of his fiction. "We will almost sin to spite them. Better indulge yourself, feed fat, drink liquors, than go strait laced for such cattle as these" (*JMN*, 7:31).

Ware insisted on more biblical textual evidence and analysis in his sermons, to which Emerson responded by citing chapter and verse first, and then proceeding with his own thoughts. The trouble for Emerson lay not just in the lack of control he had over his material, but that its dedication "to Goodness, to Duty" and "domestic obligation and observance" interfered with his access to "Beauty . . . the spirit that flies with hilarity and delight." He would not be associated with "Duty and Divinity" that "shun demonstration, & do retreat into silence" (*JMN*, 7:68). Emerson's reference to domesticity in this passage of his journal is telling of his debacle with Ware, who objected most strenuously to Emerson's refusal to recognize an anthropomorphic God, especially one figured according to the benevolent patriarch revered and worshiped from hearth to pulpit in antebellum America. Ware's rejoinder to Emerson appeared as a pamphlet titled *The Personality of the Deity*, a transcript of his sermon delivered in September 1838. Obeying God, Ware argued, was the same as "affectionate subjection to a Parent" rather than fearful "obedience to command." This attempt to restore the patriarchal authority of the Unitarian God armed Ware with the sentiment of domesticity: "Take away the Father of the universe, and, though every ordinance remain unchanged, mankind becomes but a company of children in an orphan asylum."[29] God the father was a misleading cultural construct tantamount to demagoguery, Emerson argued in the Divinity School Address, that denied the divine within us all. Along with several other blasphemies that incited the fury of conservative Unitarians (discussed in the Very chapter), Emerson discredited and deconstructed in one stroke not only the God that so many worshiped, which was rooted in the secular yet equally sacrosanct cult of domesticity—Catherine Beecher's *Treatise of Domestic Economy* (1846) being the canonical text—he also dismissed the core value of paternal guidance in the culture's understanding of mentorship. This would pose a serious dilemma for Emerson once his break from the church was complete and he began directing literary apprenticeships. His promising youths had been culturally conditioned to assume the role of child in obedience to authority figures, especially in their formal educational experience.

Further troubling the social role Emerson was to play for his disciples was the fact that his own departure from the church was also an entry into the world of professional writing in the capitalist literary marketplace, unprotected by the institutional conditions and controls that Harvard University or the Unitarian Church offered. Thus patronage and mediation with the publishing world that involved agency and promotion were also demanded of Emerson. Had his promising youths been acolytes to his senior pastor, their relationships would have been much simpler indeed, for the Unitarian Church would have controlled and conditioned the dynamics of their learning and his teaching without the edgy and fraught challenge of navigating an unforgiving, yet potentially profitable, literary marketplace. If Emerson would not play the role of God the father for his pupils, he would also not neglect his followers in the name of self-reliance either. Instead, he adopted something closer to his role as "Carlyle's editor," as he negotiated the publication of books by Cranch, Very, Channing, Thoreau, and Fuller.[30] He also made aggressive use of his own *Dial*, and of the *New-York Tribune*, run by loyal transcendentalist advocate and promoter Horace Greeley, to accommodate their shorter works in the periodical press.

Ware had envisioned his role as something of a parent, and he was indeed quite kind and caring toward Emerson even during the Divinity School Address controversy. (Andrews Norton presented himself as more of an arch-nemesis to Emerson.) Emerson on the other hand tended to see his pupils, though of the younger generation, as his contemporaries. He rebelled not only against a profession that insisted on stripping him of his intellectual authority by demanding he conform to the conventions of the sermon. He also resisted the alienating and awkward arranged visits required of his pastoral work, which led him on at least one occasion to counsel the wrong person with the same last name of the one he sought. Such experiences directly fed his writing on the importance of authenticity in interpersonal relationships (however complicated by the economy of gifts and favors as he discusses in the essays "Friendship," "Love," and "Gifts"). He dreaded the many institutionally mandated encounters he was subjected to, not unlike some of the parties he regretted hosting at Bush. During his clerical apprenticeship, one arranged pastoral visit to a grizzled Revolutionary War veteran on his deathbed spoke volumes to how ill suited the young minister was to his calling. Not knowing how to proceed, Emerson noticed an array of medicine bottles next to the bed and began talking about glass making to fill the void. Though in the final throes of death, Captain Greene could sense Emerson's incompetence. "Young man," he said, "if you don't know your business, you had better go home."[31]

"Born with Knives in Their Brain"

The knife in Emerson's brain was that he knew too well what his pastoral business was, and refused to carry it out. It is therefore not by coincidence that the professionally wayward critically astute "young men," as he described them decades after the youth movement of the late 1830s, were "born with knives in their brain, a tendency to introversion, self-dissection, anatomizing of motives. The popular religion of our fathers had received many severe shocks from the new times." His disciples delivered many of them. His followers, along with "Modern Science," would "destroy the pagan fictions of the Church" in this pivotal "religious revolution."[32] Beyond the controversy it raised over miracles (Emerson found miracles omnipresent especially in nature) and revealed or "historical Christianity" (which Emerson faulted for its neglect of the sanctity of the Holy Spirit within), the fallout surrounding the Divinity School Address focused on youth and its future. Emerson was deemed dangerous because he was redefining the graduates' vocational options, significantly liberating them from the accepted standards the Unitarian ministry and their culture at large had inculcated in them. Emerson's antimaterialism struck at the heart of capitalism, to borrow from Frederic Jameson's analysis of law in Hegel's *Phenomenology*, threatening to "destroy the concept of law rather than offer the chance of formulating some new ones" in the eyes of Norton and Ware. Instead, he was replacing it with "the 'law of the heart,' an inner frenzy having to do with individuality and universality," by rescuing the individual from "the hands of a suprahistorical Law that seem more like a big Other."[33] Emerson's own early hatred of teaching stemmed from this desire to defy the church's complicit authority with free market capitalism to enforce conformity to expected vocational paths. Many felt that he was developing a cultlike following, charismatically seducing the innocent and God-fearing collegians to follow him down the road to perdition. Edward Taylor, the pastor of the Seaman's Bethel whom Melville immortalized in *Moby-Dick* (1851), defended Emerson against such allegations by noting, "it may be that Emerson is going to hell, but of one thing I am certain; he will change the climate there, and emigration will set that way."[34] Given the influx of followers, it would seem that he indeed made the climate far more temperate.

Emerson recollected in 1867 that although outsiders believed a conspiratorial army of such satanic transcendentalists existed, and "that there was some concert of *doctrinaires* to establish certain opinions and inaugurate some movement in literature, philosophy, and religion . . . the supposed conspirators were quite innocent." Emerson could speak with authority here, as his relationships with many grew into the most intimate of his life. "I suppose all of them were surprised at this rumor of a school or sect," or cult even, Emerson said in an attempt to distance himself from the very real revolutionary visions in the language of his lectures, the most hostile and strident of which were his first two.[35] "Religion," delivered in 1837, along with "Holiness" the following year provided the materials for *Essays: First Series* (1841). Though less polished and celebrated than the Divinity School Address, these were far more vitriolic. "Nowhere does the radicalization of Emerson's religious thought come out more pugnaciously than in . . . those lectures," Buell observes.[36] Thus, before the Divinity School Address, Emerson had already been heating up his rhetoric of the "influx of the Divine Mind into our mind," advocating an unmediated connection to the Universal Being, and heretically placing the Bible on the same plane as other sacred texts such as "Shaster, Zendevesta, Orphic Verses, Koran, and Confucius" that share in this single "core of all religions."

With more visibility, these lectures might have posed an even greater threat to Emerson's opponents, since they so deliberately assaulted conventional vocation: "quit the whole world and take counsel of the bosom alone" (*EL*, 2:87, 86, 95). This admonition also surfaces in "Spiritual Laws," from *Essays: First Series*, in a passage that demonstrates Emerson's habitual blending of spirituality and profession. His attack on received notions of goodness is first couched as a question of religion, of the individual right to "the choice of my constitution; and that which I call heaven," which rapidly transforms into an issue of occupational choice. One's life work he considered sacred, for "the action which in all my years tend to do, is the work for my faculties." For work to be sacred it must be individually chosen through authentic inner intuition. Thus "we must hold a man amenable to reason for the choice of his daily craft or profession. It is not an excuse any longer for his deeds that they are the custom of the trade. What business has he with an evil trade? Has he not a calling in his character?" (*CW*, 2:82). To an artistically inclined recalcitrant romantic like Ellery Channing, for example, this sentiment was irresistible.

Equally radical is Emerson's Man Thinking, from "The American Scholar." Touted as society's greatest treasure, Man Thinking should not be allowed to escape or hide, but must be placed front and center. As for fear, "Let him look into its eye and search its nature, inspect its origin . . . he can henceforth defy it and pass on superior. The world is his who can see through its pretension." His language is nothing short of revolutionary, and even militantly so. "See it be a lie, and you have already dealt it its mortal blow" (*CW*, 1:64).

Man Thinking, significantly, is a man of action, a trope that is repeated in *Representative Men*. This would prove ironic given how Thoreau enjoyed donning the self-effacing image of idler in *Walden*, a pose reflective of the dearth of publications he produced during his career. Channing, perhaps his best friend besides Emerson, was officially listed in the Concord census one year as a "do nothing," despite Emerson's willingness to collaborate with him on a volume for publication called *Concord Walking*, to which he even promised to contribute prized segments of his valuable journal.[37] Others among Emerson's disciples, like Fuller and eventually Thoreau, would be more socially and politically active, especially in their respective advances on behalf of feminism and civil disobedience. These promising youths therefore were not in concert, as Emerson correctly recalled, and thus hardly could be called a cadre of ideologues. Instead they were a constellation of thinkers outshining the dark cultural effects of convention and formality.

After drawing them in, Emerson was faced with the question of how to lead these youths with knives in their brains. As my case studies show, he was directive and deeply involved in their growth. Yet Emerson was particularly averse to pedantry, and instead inspired by example. His method was to facilitate an educational environment to inspire growth, usually through a series of readings he carefully recommended, as in the case of Fuller and Ward. He did not dote over the development of their writing as he did with his poet apprentices. As mentor, Emerson reached high moments of exultation, often made possible by his own financial and editorial assistance, or direct advocacy in the literary market. Through his mentoring and marketing of his promising youths, we are afforded a glimpse of Emerson riding the highs and lows, the triumphs and dejection of fresh careers in the making. When he was at his most exasperated, like a parent stunned at the recalcitrance of his offspring, it often appeared that he had little patience for the painstaking process of tutoring. Channing responded to Emerson's displeasure with the mechanical flaws of his and Jones Very's poetry by claiming that spelling is dictated by the spirit, to which Emerson asked in a letter to Elizabeth Hoar, is "the poetic inspiration amber to embalm and enhance the flies and spiders? As it fell in the case of Jones Very, cannot the spirit parse and spell?" (*L*, 2:331). He took great pains to edit Channing's coarse unfinished verse, to buoy the unmoored and gargantuan fits of romantic inspiration Very was capable of, to channel the artistic knowledge of Cranch and Ward into transcendental visions, and to steer the omnivorous and insatiable reading of Fuller toward a viable career in the mass literary market of New York City and beyond.

Commercial concerns inevitably intervened in each apprenticeship. Emerson pursued popularity in his own career, and was of vital assistance in securing profits for his friend Carlyle's American publications by fiercely protecting him from pirates.[38] In 1826, he worried that "little is yet done to establish my consideration among my contemporaries and less to get a memory when I am gone." "I confess the foolish ambition to be valued," he wrote, actively resisting "vulgar hunger" and instead adopting a "refined appetite" (*JMN*, 3:15). Two years after leaving the ministry, his ambition was even more explicit: "Were it not a heroic adventure in me to insist on being a popular speaker?" (*JMN*, 4:315). Was Emerson's profit motive therefore more important to him than the welfare of his pupils? Was he socially responsible? Certainly his opponents, such as Andrews Norton, suggested he was a dangerous spellbinder manipulating undiscriminating admirers. Norton linked Emerson's corrupting influence on youth to his desire to win "a degree of fame in this country" through "antic tricks" and "an over-excited and *convulsionary* style" to "deceive his hearers."[39] Emerson's advice to young scholars, however, was not reckless romanticism (though the madness of Jones Very at least anecdotally supports that claim), but idealism balanced with what Richard Teichgraeber calls "a realistic assessment of the historical possibilities for putting such values into practice."[40] Putting definitive practical limits on his zeal, Emerson in effect cautioned his followers in "Man the Reformer": "I do not wish to push my criticism on the state of things around me to that extravagant mark, that shall compel me to suicide, or to an absolute isolation from the advantages of civil society" (*CW*, 1:155).

Emerson redefined the social role of the public intellectual in America, specifically to move it away from religious discourse and toward philosophy and poetry. Serial fiction dominated the antebellum periodical press at the time, as witnessed by the popularity of Harriet Beecher Stowe and Fanny Fern. It was that gap between religious discourse and popular fiction that Emerson wished to bridge with philosophically ideal yet socially relevant writings. One could be socially connected and work to "find a way of seeing daily market pursuits themselves as sites of individual self-expression," as Teichgraeber notes, and in so doing "to cheer, to raise, and to guide men," according to "The American Scholar" (*CW*, 1:62).[41] This advocacy of the market as a place wherein one *can* find self-expression combines with Emerson's sense of transcendental authorship, equivalent to today's "public intellectual" who engages the most powerful mechanisms of mainstream mass communication to engender his or her ideals. Emerson's lectures on the lyceum circuit and Fuller's writings for the *New-York Tribune*, for example, fulfilled precisely this function.

Emerson Learning, Learning Emerson

Each protégé taught Emerson something new. Born to be educated, Emerson once proclaimed that he would never graduate, and thus he embraced his charges for what they could add to his understanding of the world. He became a most eager pupil of Very's mad spirituality, of Ward's knowledge of painting, of Fuller's mastery of German language and literature, of Thoreau's ecological and practical wisdom, of Channing's verbal wit, and of Cranch's visual artistry. Of Newcomb he even said, "his mind was far richer than mine" (*TN*, 3:55). Emerson clearly relished being surrounded by such vibrant minds and drew from their energy to suffuse his own work with the vigor that made it famous.

With the exception of Fuller, all of Emerson's followers profiled in this book began their apprenticeships with the ambition of becoming Emerson's ideal romantic revolutionary poet. All but Channing would change course. Cranch wrote the poetry of a repressed painter, Very that of a future preacher, Thoreau a budding naturalist, and Ward an art critic. Channing's

was a satirist's poetry for the most part, and remained that way. All vacillated in their professional identities. Even Channing began in law, and
tried his hand at farming, before settling into a life of writing verse.
Migration into related authorial occupations in the publishing world did
not satisfy him, as his stint with Greeley's *Tribune* attests.

This book offers a typology of the Emersonian protégé. How did they
enter Emerson's world? What initially attracted Emerson to them? How
was his alternative theology pivotal in their career decisions? If Emerson
had been a university faculty adviser, his placement rate of graduate
students, as it were, would be instantly called into question, a red flag for
any incoming students seduced by his great mind but also worried about
professional and economic necessity in the long run. Yet my goal here is
to give Emerson the credit that he deserves for inspiring so many members
of the younger generation. He "has been denied proper credit for his
responsiveness to his star pupil, Henry David Thoreau," Buell points out,
as well as a host of dynamic individualists, who should not be deemed
uniform failures.[42] I also want to be frank about Emerson's shortcomings
as a mentor and literary agent, linking those limitations specifically to his
philosophical understanding of friendship, a concept that has been the
subject of critical concern in William John Rossi and John T. Lysaker's
recent edited volume, *Emerson and Thoreau: Figures of Friendship* (2010).
I also highlight Emerson's strengths as an adviser—reclaiming the power,
for example, he saw in Newcomb's "Dolon," a work routinely dismissed
given the rapid departure of its author from the Concord circle—and in
the process reanimate antebellum Concord to humanize the promising
youths that have so frequently been referred to in the aggregate, and flatly
depicted as zealous enthusiasts with little professional aptitude. Ward and
Newcomb, whose stories are seldom told compared with those of Jones
Very's and Ellery Channing's financial disasters, went on to lucrative careers,
and maintained their connection to the arts. Ward amassed an impressive
art collection, funded by his equally impressive foray into business following
his Concord years. He was eventually recognized as a prominent patron
of the arts, and today his name appears among the original founders in the
marble entry of the Metropolitan Museum of Art.

Probing the fates of Emerson's apprentices not only yields insight into
Emerson himself and the applicability of his philosophy to mentorship and

literary agency, but also provides a fuller picture of the socially diverse and colorful blend of figures that populated the Concord scene. In addition to the standard cast of the Alcotts, Emersons, Thoreau, Fuller, and brief glimpses at Hawthorne, these minor figures more than filled out an undifferentiated background of supporting roles. Indeed, they drove the very social dynamic of the Concord circle because they represented the transcendentalist future Emerson and others doted over and communed with, cared for and coddled, inspired and promoted. They were at various stages Emerson's muse for his innumerable essays and lectures on vocation and his most intimate friends. Together, the protégés make up an aggregate profile of Emerson, each representing a different side of him. Concord indeed supported these writers, upheld them, and tolerated their idiosyncrasies, which at times proved vexing and downright exasperating. Emerson judged his young projects sometimes too severely and at others he nurtured virulent strands of authorial self-perception, as in the case of Jones Very. The image of Concord this book aims to convey is thus diverse and populous, at once defying stock portraits and monolithic definitions of this literary circle by bringing to light its more intriguing stories of professional development under the most important writer of the generation.

Emerson has taught so many of us so much that it is important to look back on those he quite deliberately taught during his life, and measure their successes and failures, both aesthetically and professionally. He thrived on the future, as his disarmed hilarious half-grin in daguerreotypes with children attest, as much as he despised excessive reverence for the past, especially in the tyrannical authority of received tradition as "The American Scholar" and his other works reveal. In *Walden*, Thoreau echoes this love of newness in his reverence for morning work and his spite toward older generations, calling into question how much he can learn from them, and dismissing their wisdom as useless. This was a genuine youth movement driven toward consciousness-raising experimentation of all sorts, from the enlightening effects of intense meditation on nature to the alternative lifestyles of Thoreau's deliberate living at Walden, and the utopian community at Brook Farm. The transcendentalists sought everything new, from social arrangements to women's roles to religion. The total commitment to the new was also visible in the reimagination of education through Alcott's Temple School, and the concept of capital, especially as demonstrated in Thoreau's "Economy."

These last two categories are particularly important to the conceptual frame for this book. The new orientation toward education as student-centered and noncoercive together with new understandings of capital as antimaterialistic and anticonsumerist were compelling at a time when the market began to take over so many social functions, as the transition from agrarian to mass production took hold. For as much as these new conceptions of education and capital provided such profound critiques of conventional authoritarian pedagogy and free market enterprise at the time, they also proved quite problematic as a basis for aspiring transcendentalists to develop financially profitable and philosophically significant careers. The challenge to forge both materially satisfying and socially progressive careers tested the dialectical richness of the transcendental ethos, the limitations of its individualism, and the boundaries of its doctrine. Indeed, the pressure on Emerson to move beyond simple cheering support for Concord's promising youths, a role so natural and consonant with the transcendental commitment to newness, into professional advocacy and career guidance brought the greatest challenge of all: commercial survival.

In some cases, as with Fuller, that tension proved fruitful. In others, such as Thoreau, it professionally did not. Others reflect more varied results. Christopher Cranch's sketch parody of his mentor as transparent eyeball in the forest embodies a flip, somewhat recalcitrant schoolboy's caricature of his overbearing schoolmaster, ironically a role Emerson himself avoided and detested in others. Cranch's discomfort toiling under Emerson's outsize and nearly inhuman philosophy, as the proportions and physical features of his sketch show, speak to his strain under Emerson's tutelage. Jones Very, quite oppositely, took the transparent eyeball's vacated ego as an invitation, if not a command, which he dutifully obeyed, transforming himself into a vessel of the Holy Spirit.

Cranch's art has had attention in the form of an edited book, but his poetry has been neglected, especially in conjunction with his ties to Emerson. Newcomb continues to be an enigma not well situated into the culture of Emerson's promising youth that ranged from the unsavory of "Waldo's menagerie" to the divine of his "new born bard," embodied variously, but short lived, by Very, Channing, and Thoreau. William Moss's original study of Concord's failed poet-seers that inspired this book touches on an oddity in the history of transcendentalism that demands further inquiry. Was Emerson capricious in his hot-and-cold treatment of his pupils, as Moss suggests? Was he incompetent as a mentor or marketer of budding careers? Or are the protégés themselves to blame for their myriad failures in their careers as authors? The case studies that follow illustrate how Emerson's pupils were far more successful than Moss and others since have assumed; many reinvented themselves because of inner truths they learned in pursuit of their initial authorial ambition under Emerson. Rather than remaining for the duration of their post-Emerson careers utterly silent or wholly ineffectual, they landed on their feet like Emerson's image of a New England farm boy who tries all trades self-reliantly. Although these disciples did not fully realize the ideal revolutionary poet Emerson had wished them to become (much as he himself never could), and although they shared a gradual distancing from Emerson in the long run, they learned valuable advice from him that helped direct them, with few exceptions, toward fulfilling and, for some, profitable autonomous careers. In all cases, Emerson did not leave a trail of tears in his wake as he sailed through the lives of the younger generation of transcendentalists. Rather, he dislodged them from otherwise unexamined vocational identities, forcing them out of the comfortable existence of the professions laid out for them, either by family, custom, or greater cultural expectation. Authorship freed them to explore creative sides of themselves that they likely did not know existed.

If poetry or cultural criticism did not fit, they eventually would find their way in other venues. Jones Very went on to a career as a minister, and he extracted huge benefits from his work under Emerson, as his now available sermons bear out. Very's spiritual crisis and insanity stand as the most extreme example of the immediate fallout of Emerson's projects, but Very's relative stability in a vocation ideally suited to him echoes that of Christopher Cranch. Approaching transcendentalism as poet, Cranch could write himself into existence as a painter through the guidance of Emerson. The volatile and abrupt ending of Thoreau's poetic career directed him toward nature writing and social criticism, which would eventually drive *Walden*, his magnum opus. Fuller's departure from Concord and success in New York City with Horace Greeley was directly supported by Emerson, whose mentorship in her case was pointed more toward the pragmatics of reform that matched her role as author for the mass periodical press. Ellery Channing stands as the only one of Emerson's projects who considered poetry the primary vocation for the duration of his life. Though he met his break from Emerson with as much or more pain than any pupil with the exception of Thoreau, he never reinvented himself professionally, and continued his life as a poet with mixed results. Though a kindred spirit in many respects to Channing, Thoreau showed greater responsibility in supporting his family late in his career by reentering the lyceum circuit.

In the following, Part I includes chapters on Fuller and Thoreau, the two most recognizable figures of this study. The first weighs the effect of Emerson's tutelage on Fuller's journalism career, while the second focuses on the perils of Thoreau's experience as poet in training. Part II explores the visual art connection to transcendentalism with examinations of Cranch's and Ward's relationships with Emerson, the former a practitioner, and the latter a critic, historian, and collector. The final section examines the reckless romantics, Channing, Very, and Newcomb, who went to the outer edge of Emerson's vocational paradigm, testing the limits of its liberalism. The epilogue offers a glimpse at the relatively unknown Emersonian protégé Ellen Sturgis Hooper, perhaps the darkest visionary of Concord's pantheon of young geniuses. However peripheral a role history has relegated Newcomb and Hooper, their relationships with Emerson are profoundly revealing of his struggle to face his own darkest guilt and fear. Newcomb's "Dolon," written after the loss of Emerson's son Waldo, and Hooper's revelation of the sobering underside of transcendental ecstasy were especially effective in drawing out this seldom-glimpsed side of Emerson. It is to Margaret Fuller, one of Hooper's admirers and the very best literary critic of her generation, that we now turn.

PRIZED PROGENY

1

EMERSON'S HERO: MENTORING

MARGARET FULLER

Of the three Emerson protégés who ventured into the antebellum New York City literary market to launch their careers, only Margaret Fuller would emerge an unqualified success. Ellery Channing and Henry Thoreau squandered a series of opportunities with contacts arranged by Emerson. In contrast, Fuller became a celebrated literary editor and columnist for the *Tribune* while living in New York. Even from abroad, her dispatches from revolutionary Italy became America's primary source of information about the war. So how could her protracted and engrossing apprenticeship under Emerson—a transcendentalist philosopher and metaphysician labeled abstract and incomprehensible to the point of irrelevance by detractors— have contributed, if at all, to her success? Or was her socially engaged reform writing and support of the Italian revolution a form of rebellion against him? Did she finally become such a powerful voice in American literature and journalism despite, rather than because of, Emerson's influence?

The historical condition of newspaper writing and antebellum publishing frames this chapter's twofold emphasis on Fuller's work with Emerson on the *Dial*—during which he helped promote and publicize her career—and on the importance of her Emersonian mentorship in laying the foundation for her subsequent success in the world of New York City journalism. From 1836 to 1839 Fuller played the role of adoring young scholar to Emerson's renowned mentor. Then from 1839 to 1840 during her *Dial* editing years she made a concerted move toward professionalization that would serve

Margaret Fuller (Courtesy Concord Free Public Library)

her eventual transition to Horace Greeley's *Tribune*. The principle of self-reliance and the critique of institutional corruption, materialism, and social injustice at the core of Emersonian transcendentalism equipped her with an outlook ideally suited to her position as literary editor. The trajectory of her career corresponds with Emerson's pattern of enthusiasm, adoption, and judgment of his protégés. His relationship with Fuller would end not in disappointment, but in his eventual acceptance of her for the fully realized and accomplished professional she became. She achieved her success primarily through the periodical press, flourishing in both the *Dial* and the daily newspaper world of the *Tribune*.[1]

Fuller's professional development occurred in the context of the revolution of authors' salaries in antebellum America, particularly in newspapers and magazines. She took the ethical role of writing and editing for the periodical press to be saddled with monumental responsibility for the shaping of the nation's moral principles. In *Papers on Literature and Art*, she illustrated such power and concomitant moral responsibility given the surges in print production and mass distribution of reading for an expanding populace more literate and solvent than ever before. Forgery is the controlling image in the lines she quotes from Cornelius Mathews to highlight the potential for corruption in journalism, reflecting her anxiety about mounting materialism in the culture, a trend encompassing authorship as seen in the revolutionary salaries paid by Robert Bonner, *New-York Ledger* editor-publisher and consummate capitalist. "A dark-dyed spirit he, who coins the time,/ To virtue's wrong, in base disloyal lies,/ Who makes the morning's breath the evening's tide/ The utterer of his blighting forgeries." Commitment to the powers of good, which was embodied by Fuller's own progressive feminism and criticism of corrupt government institutions, is poetically captured by Matthews in an image of journalist as heroic truth speaker: "To know the instant and to speak it true/ Its passing lights of joy, its dark sad cloud/ To fix upon the unnumbered gazers' view," unflinchingly facing the White Whale–like mass audience of readers, "is to thy ready hand broad strength allowed."[2]

Teaching philosophical independence was Emerson's primary objective as mentor. It was a role well suited to his agency and guidance through the perilous waters of the increasingly competitive literary market. Despite his efforts, many of Emerson's promising youths—those "many extraordinary young men who never ripened, or whose performance in actual life was not extraordinary," as he describes in "Heroism"—failed as professionals (*CW*, 2:153). It might appear that he did not provide the right scaffolding for their success in the publishing industry. But many of his disciples other than Fuller resisted his generous assistance in the market. He usually began by publishing their work in the *Dial* and referring them to his publisher, James Munroe. Munroe's marketing prowess, however, was so abysmal that one of his authors, Alexander Hill Everett, complained in 1846, "Munroe did not seem to me to be doing quite so much as he might to get my book into circulation. Would it not be wise to have some placards placed at the windows of shops where it is sold, and perhaps have it advertised more freely?"[3]

But the *Dial* and Munroe were not Emerson's only resources. Among the many book publications he arranged, his protégés' work appeared with Ticknor and Fields (Thoreau), Carey and Hart (Christopher Cranch), Little, Brown and Company (Ellery Channing and Jones Very), James R. Osgood and Company (Channing), and Cupples, Upham and Company (Channing). Emerson was of course the reason Greeley had all but given carte blanche to his protégés to publish with his *Tribune*. But none capitalized on Emerson's assistance like Fuller. Her access to the *Dial* she turned into an editorship; her access to Greeley she turned into a permanent staff position, the first held by a woman.

Fuller believed that commercial considerations and the market were always already integral facets of authorship, transcendental or otherwise. She resisted the Brook Farm experiment in communal living because it pretended to escape commercial culture altogether. "I doubt they will get free from all they deprecate in society," she predicted, foretelling much of the financial anguish that befell the knot of dreamers Nathaniel Hawthorne would satirize in *The Blithedale Romance*.[4] Elizabeth Peabody was also aware of the apparent contradictions between the pursuit of professional authorship and the transcendentalist denunciation of trade. She commented that "when commerce seemed about to be *reformed out*, I had come to Boston on my first commercial enterprise, to which some collateral circumstances conspired to open a prospect of success in obtaining the means of subsistence."[5] Peabody apparently appreciated the irony of fighting against the tide of the market at the very moment of her entrance into it. Fuller had always viewed authorship as an economically grounded enterprise. Writing was among the many professions she would pursue, initially out of need to support her family following the death of her father. In *Women in the Nineteenth Century*, Fuller would emphasize the importance of women entering the public world to fulfill their professional potential. Emerson was instrumental in enabling Fuller to adapt transcendental authorship to the market, mainly because his dialectic on commerce was large enough to accommodate earnest aggressive free market enterprise.

Emerson mentored Fuller at a time when print culture was rapidly burgeoning into an early form of what we now recognize as "mass culture." Instead of reflecting a neat, static division between high and low culture, the literary market was in the process of radically subdividing into a multitude of dynamic overlapping readerships. Despite his misgivings voiced in *Walden*'s "Reading" toward the popular prose fiction of the story papers, Thoreau had also observed in his journal that print culture sorted itself not into literary and popular categories, but into an array of highly specialized markets for literature. Emerson similarly noted "the library of the present age had become an immense miscellany" in which it seemed that "every opinion old and new, every hope and fear, every whim and folly has an organ."[6]

Transcendentalist authorship appears in greater alliance with this developing mass literary market than we may have supposed, especially in light of Emerson's contention that "it is handsomer to remain in the establishment better than the establishment, and conduct that in the best manner." Emerson originally made this statement in the context of denouncing the narrow interests of specialized reformers who have "become tediously good in some particular but negligent or narrow in the rest; and hypocrisy and vanity are often the disgusting result" (*CW*, 3:154). Such reformers typify the market's increasing specialization that had conspired to turn men into extensions of their tools, a condition embodied by "the tradesman [who] scarcely ever gives an ideal worth to his work, but is ridden by the routine of his craft" (*CW*, 1:53). Rather than suggesting no work should be done in the market, a charge typically directed at Thoreau, Emerson asserted that an "ideal worth" should be attached to one's vocation, as he urged in the famous passage of "The American Scholar." Professional writing should thus avoid the "penny wisdom," the "soul destroying slavery to habit" that makes "literature become frivolous" in Emerson's view (*CW*, 1:89–90). Thus profound implications emerge for remaining in the establishment of the commercial world and improving upon it. Fuller pursued exactly this objective in her position at the *Tribune*, refusing "to make a sally against evil by some single improvement, without supporting it by a total regeneration," such as the universal education of the masses she advocated (*CW*, 3:154). Emerson did not of course passively comply with the logic of surplus capitalism, but was acutely aware of the market's capacity to embody his most valuable principles of self-reliance and radical individualism. Escapist consumerism he clearly rejected, but a preponderance of his writing is saturated with economic language to describe his spiritual quest for the Universal Being. He commonly reformulated the ordinary language of the market so that descriptions of self-culture appear in financial terms. His intention in doing so was not always ironic or satirical. Transcendentalists, he believed, should meet the commercialization of letters more imaginatively than with summary disapproval. The instruments of production for mass culture, according to Emerson, should be utilized in the most liberal sense to humanize social values, conventions, and the institutions that perpetuate them, a belief evident in his theory of newspapers. In this way Emerson believed that, without succumbing to narrow sectarian squabbling, the periodical press might be harnessed by a transcendental author like Fuller to reach the masses with its salient social criticism.[7]

Emerson looked to the market to overcome "the worst feature of the double consciousness" produced by the mind-body dualism of transcendentalism. He located this problem in how "the two lives, of the understanding and of the soul, which we lead, really show little relation to each other; never meet and measure each other; one prevails now, all buzz and din; and the other prevails then, all infinitude and paradise; and, with the progress of life the two discover no greater disposition to reconcile themselves" (*CW*, 1:213). Bringing the reflective world of infinitude and paradise "to meet and measure" the "buzz and din" of the market meant synthesizing the ideal and the real, the insular Concord coterie and the teeming urban center, a union he knew from his own success on the lecture circuit contained tremendous power. Further, he felt that the free market allowed individuals to pursue wealth, and that government institutions should not interfere with the process. We should not envy the possessions of the wealthy, he argued, but admire their independence, freedom, and capacity to use capital to realize the ideal. "Wealth brings with it its own checks and balances. The basis of political economy is non-interference. The only safe rule is found in the self-adjusting meter of demand and supply. Do not legislate," he wrote, echoing Adam Smith's laissez-faire philosophy. The liberalism of Emersonian self-reliance drives this notion of the free market, which can be utilized for higher purposes than crass consumerism.

Indeed, for the wily entrepreneur, "power is what they want, not candy. Is not then the demand," rather than the material end, "to be rich legitimate?" With such a capacity to accommodate for the market, transcendentalism's otherwise sharp criticism of commerce thus was not entirely to blame for the professional failures of so many Emerson disciples.

Fuller embodied Emerson's sense that "commerce is a game of skill, which every man cannot play, which few men can play well," a game that demands "probity and closeness to the facts." Her transcendentalist training rooted in this commitment to higher truths resonated through her conception of authorship, which, Emerson held, "add[s] a certain long arithmetic" of spiritual significance rather than the narrow pursuit of profit for its own sake. Indeed, Emerson's vision of how "the laws of nature play through trade" encouraged Fuller's entrance into the market. "Open the doors of opportunity to talent and virtue and they will do themselves justice," he affirmed, for in a "free and just commonwealth, property rushes from the idle and imbecile to the industrious, brave, and persevering" (*CW*, 6:56). Emerson's vision of transcendentalism did not just make concessions or adjustments to accommodate itself to the tastes of a mass audience. That vision could only claim social relevance if it was dedicated to reimagining the market's potential to spread the curious Concord gospel, which Emerson himself so successfully did through his lectures, and which Thoreau attempted in his New York City gambit. In Fuller, Emerson found his best disciple to realize that objective.

The Accidental Mentor

Beginning with their correspondence in 1836–39, Emerson adopted "a tone of mentor—encouraging and challenging [Fuller] to increase her efforts in writing" at a time when she appears to have had "little influence" over Emerson, according to the standard critical view.[8] This was no one-way conversation, however, but a mutually enriching association. Further, much has been made of Emerson's quarrels with Fuller in his essays "Friendship" and "Love." A great deal of praise for Fuller (and disdain for Thoreau) as promising pupil, however, is expressed in "Heroism," "Manners," and the correspondence. Fuller and Emerson's relationship, though tumultuous, was reciprocally inspirational, and her first two years of work under him were extremely consequential in setting her on the path toward success with Greeley's *Tribune*, the very position that eluded both Channing and Thoreau. Her chemistry with Emerson during those pivotal two years enhanced Fuller's training and better prepared her to adapt transcendental authorship to the literary marketplace of New York. Thoreau's poetic apprenticeship, on the other hand, left him feeling profoundly incompatible with the commercial context of the antebellum publishing industry. Inspired by Emerson's fiery individualism, Fuller developed a fearless critical voice. Her pragmatic understanding of the authorial role rooted in social and political activism won her prestige in the largest and most rapidly growing literary market. Perhaps most important, she understood the connection between writing and the market the way Emerson had.

Emerson's enthusiasm for Fuller, eventuating in his adoption of her as a protégé, is evident in his essay "Heroism." The piece suggests that he truly supported her, as it is overflowing with enthusiasm and encouragement for female intellectual and spiritual development. Not only are his references to Sappho, Marie de Sévigné, and Madame de Staël closely associated with Fuller.[9] The tone of the passage also reveals the ebullient and lofty idealism, indeed bright hopes for the future, he was harboring at the time for her development. Emerson's style of mentorship with all of his protégés typically began with such exuberance. In "Heroism," he heralded the powers intrinsic to women and urged them to bloom into heroic proportions. A closer look reveals that "the maiden" he imagines in the essay is continually cast as pupil to the motivating mentor of his narrative voice. Speaking of women in the aggregate, he exhorts them to fulfill their potential and soar despite the culture's inherent resistance to women's professional growth. "The fair girl who repels interference by a decided and proud choice of influences," namely the prodigious literary ones Emerson himself had introduced to her, "so careless of pleasing, so willful and lofty, inspires every beholder with some what of her own nobleness." Emerson himself was among those beholders inspired by Fuller, especially in a pattern of reciprocal influence and intellectual growth between mentor and student. Emerson remade his protégé, who had notoriously atrocious eyesight and posture, into an intellectual hero by effectively straightening her sloping shoulders, stooped head, and squinting eyes, imagining her "walk[ing] serenely on her way, accept[ing] the hint of each new experience" with an "erect soul" and a sharp focus on "all the objects that solicit her eye." Though armed with considerable power, she was still a neophyte with "a new and unattempted problem to solve," unmistakably poised in the role of pupil to "learn the power and the charm of her new born being" (*CW*, 2:153).

The intellectual growth of the maiden-as-Fuller's "new born being" in "Heroism" hinges on her capacity to access the wealth of her self-knowledge independently. Emerson's extreme emphasis on independent development as the bedrock of self-culture is reflected in his role as inspired observer assessing her strengths and measuring precisely what she has yet to learn. His role is the antithesis of the coercive pedant here. Emerson's antiauthoritarian approach toward mentorship prompted Lawrence Buell to label him the "Anti-Mentor" in his recent biography. Refusing to coerce any of his literary disciples, Emerson was acutely aware of the implications for political tyranny inherent in the role of pedant depositing knowledge into his pupils so that they might faithfully render it upon demand. Such training and conditioning to reknit minds in the mentor's image was of course anathema to self-reliance. A paradoxical tension therefore surfaced in his own disciples' propensity to reconstruct themselves into intellectual replicas of him or any other prophet.

By winter 1839, when her rigorous intellectual training with Emerson began in earnest, Fuller was still playing the role of eager young scholar, but beginning to show signs of emergent professional autonomy. Toward the end of the initial stage of their correspondence, Fuller began to push back against Emerson's authority, if not outright defy it. She registered disappointment, for example, at missing one of Emerson's lectures. He had canceled a scheduled lecture for the stated reason that he had not slept the night before, an excuse Fuller playfully rebuffed while aligning herself with him as an intellectual. "Imagine my indignation: lost a night's rest!" she gasped with mock exasperation, challenging his credentials as a true romantic author: "As if an intellectual person ever had a night's rest; one too of that sect who are supposed to be always 'Lying broad awake.'"[10] His modest reply was that she did not miss much, as he satirized his own commodification of his philosophy into the neat little boxes of "Human Life in Ten Lectures or the Soul of man neatly done up in ten pin-boxes exactly ten" (*L*, 2:179). Interestingly, Emerson would later call attention to the limitations of his own powers as a mentor when he sarcastically chided "the sudden schoolmasters who have short methods & teach the art of life in 'six lessons.'" His comment here laments the limited communication of isolated pinbox forms—the conversation, the letter, the lecture, the article, the book. Instead, he suggests they bide their time with each other, and even savor it, trusting that they might converge and exchange "a look through your telescope or you one through mine;—an all explaining look. Let us float along through the great heavens a while longer and whenever we come to a point whence our observations agree, the time when they did not will seem but a moment" (*L*, 2:349). Though Emerson was candid that the art of life was impossible to teach and be learned by Fuller or anyone else in six discreetly packaged installments—whose contemporary analogue is visible in the myriad online or recorded lectures that festoon today's market—he persisted in his ongoing efforts to mentor Fuller with abiding faith in their momentary convergence.

Fuller's powers of critical observation, which distinguished her from most of her peers at the time, reached a crucial turning point in June 1839, six months into her serious training under Emerson. By then, his encouragement had built the powers of her mind to exceed her own capacity to express it, at least comfortably so. The input was nearly overwhelming at this stage. Careful to acknowledge his praise from an earlier letter in which he wrote, "I know that not possibly can you write a bad book or a dull page, if you only indulge yourself and take up your work somewhat proudly" (*L*, 2:197), Fuller replied, "I heartily thank you for your encouraging word about my work and I pray you always to encourage me whenever you can. But in truth," she continued, "I find much more done for me than I expected. To arrange with discretion," to organize the rising tide of literature she was consuming mostly at Emerson's encouragement, "rather than to divine will be my task." Here she seems intent on using her reading not just as a stimulus or model for her own creative works, but as a sophisticated frame of reference explicitly driving the writing itself. Indeed, *Summer on the Lakes* and *Woman in the Nineteenth Century* are distinguished by their rich allusions to literary, historical, and cultural sources reflective of her role under Emerson as omnivorous bibliophile. In this June 1839 letter, she expressed a preference for documentary literary research and not "to divine," Emerson's approach that left sources off the page and relegated to nascent sparks of inspiration behind his insights, which otherwise appear to have emerged pristine and without any origin beyond his own mind. However illusory, Emerson's image of authorship as the unmitigated expression of the individual utterly without influence appears in his strident intellectual declaration of independence from European models in "The American Scholar." Indeed, this particular exchange marks a critical juncture in which Fuller developed her own authorial self-definition distinct from Emerson. She was establishing her penchant for rigorous, thorough engagement with secondary sources in a way that both clashed with his mercenary reading process and confirmed the influence of her six-month mentorship, which had encouraged her reading in world philosophy, literature, and art. Sounding like an archival historian, Fuller voiced her preference for systematically sorting and assembling her sources for her writing—"I find daily new materials and am at present almost burthened by my riches"—rather than flying through them randomly, even manically, as Emerson did with his own readings, only to turn away from them at the moment of utterance.[11]

Fuller's Professional Development

By January 1840, Fuller's association with Emerson had transformed from pupil to *Dial* editor. One letter speaks to her transition toward managing the Concord periodical, concerns for which had now blended with her intellectual conversations with Emerson. The letter begins with her in the role of editor squarely on the business of the *Dial*, suggesting "to sell the Journal by merit rather than subscription," and ends in the voice of a pupil. Like a good student, she shares the comments on Shakespeare she had penciled into a notebook. The substance of that insight, however, reveals significant growth beyond a pupil's role, as it speaks volumes of her critical awareness of writing for a mass market and attendant emergence into professional authorship. The springboard of the insight also reflects the pupil's application of the master's theory, in this case one derived from Schlegel, a translator of Shakespeare, and Swedenborg, whose concept of "correspondence" between the facts of physical reality and spiritual phenomena were also the sources of the

"Language" section of Emerson's *Nature*. But in Fuller's hands they bring new meaning to her expanding notion of audience, which was keeping pace with the nation's rapidly growing sea of readers.

In *Much Ado About Nothing*, Benedick solicits Don Pedro's ear in a conspiratorial whisper: "Old Signior, walk aside with me. I have studied eight or nine wise words to speak with you, which these hobby horses must not hear." Fuller seized on the phrase "hobby horses" and reflected on the public nature of professional authorship for a mass audience. "To write for hobby horses," to her, meant addressing "all audiences assembled in hall of state, saloon, or lecture-room." "Is it not this term," she continued, "and none other, which must ever after being once acquainted with it, rise in the mind, on each day's intercourse with the world?" Her question deftly moved from her tone of a German translator's fascination with lexical choice to a richer, more seasoned overlay of transcendentalist "intercourse with the world," with the realities of the ever expanding mass readership in the antebellum literary marketplace populating "hall of state, saloon, or lecture-room."[12] The tone here appears disparaging of the masses, but at once breaches social boundaries by mixing tavern patrons with political and intellectual elites. Fuller realized the daunting challenge of reaching a democratic audience riddled with radically diverse political interests, philosophical theories, and prejudiced palaver. The *Dial* never reached such a broad audience, whereas the *Tribune* ostensibly already had when Fuller took her position there.

By the fall of 1840, Fuller was asserting her independence from her mentor more stridently. She was showing clear signs of departing from the role of pupil and emerging as an equal force to be reckoned with. The sparring and fruitful discord that created this tough-minded individualistic journalist presented a crisis, but by no means a debilitating one, in their relationship. In response to Emerson's cold distance, she cited his own principle of mentorship premised on free exchange and open challenge for mutual growth. "But did not you ask for a foe in your friend? Did not you ask for a 'large formidable nature'?" she asked, quoting his own words back to him. "But a beautiful foe, I am not yet to you,"[13] she wrote, insinuating that she had not ascended to the "beautiful enemy, untamable, devoutly revered" he defines in "Friendship" (*CW*, 2:124). She is irked in part by constantly being judged, if not pedantically or coercively instructed, thus far in her apprenticeship. But what she is uncomfortable with—the judgmental scrutiny of her expression, interests, and character in place of an affectionate sympathy—became a defining feature of her position as staff writer and literary editor of the *Tribune* in the unrelenting glare of the public eye. Indeed, such scrutiny under Emerson functioned to make her market ready. "He weighs and balances, buys and sells you and himself all the time," she complained.[14]

But such treatment prepared her for the incessant judgments of the highly discriminating, and buying, readership. Blind to these benefits, Fuller was only aware that Emerson violated his own assertion in "Gifts" that "I like to see that we cannot be bought and sold." As such, she was enacting a key moment common (and almost inevitable) in long-term mentorships in which the student becomes painfully aware of the mentor's self-contradictions. Fuller was sensitive to being reified in a mentor-protégé relationship. She was careful not to absorb his advice without loving him personally. Love was a key ingredient in the best working relationships, according to Emerson. "They eat your service like apples and leave you out. But love them," as he indeed loved her, and "they feel you and delight in you all the time" (*CW*, 3:96). By this time Fuller had outgrown the role of young apprentice and was asserting herself as a colleague and burgeoning literary professional in her own right. Emerson's reply was something of a character defense in which he asserted that he attracted friends despite himself. Undermining his own authority as her mentor, Emerson offered that he in fact was in debt to her and others "who show me a stroke of courage, a piece of inventive wit . . . or a pure delight in character" (*L*, 2:341).

Emerson appears to have been reversing ground on an earlier letter to Fuller that she must have read with her heart in her throat. In that letter, he wrote that "I now understand your language better . . . though still I see not into you & have not arrived at your law." Replying to a letter currently not extant, the transcendentalist in Emerson praises her for a "certain willfulness and not pure acquiescence which seems to me the only authentic mode," in order to purge the mentor in him. He had maintained in his journal that traditional notions of mentorship at the time, especially the directive didactic models, did not resonate with him. "I lament that I find in me no enthusiasm," he wrote, "no resources for the instruction and guidance of the people when they shall discover that their present guides are blind." He then confesses that such a view on "Education is cold, but I *should perhaps affect a hope I do not feel were I bidden to counsel it.*" In voicing his disdain for formal education, especially the theatricality of the public pledges filling the lecture halls and press of antebellum New England "not to drink wine, not to drink ink, not to lie, not to commit adultery . . . not to use the sword and bullet," Emerson was revealing a deep distrust in his own authority as a mentor (*JMN*, 7:239). Perhaps we can account for much of his success in mentoring Fuller precisely because he did not initially think of his early relationship with her in those terms. In the early stages of their correspondence he certainly did not "affect a hope" because he was "bidden to counsel it," but instead appears wholly unaware of the profound instruction and guidance he was providing her. He was teaching her despite himself as a kind of accidental mentor. Self-consciousness spooked him from his powers as teacher, just as it had bridled the forward momentum of the Brook Farm experimental reform community.[15] The hilarity of their exchange the previous July (1840) had tapered considerably, as tensions were brewing over the debut issue of the *Dial*. The stress of launching the journal to a less than spectacular reception took its toll emotionally and physically on Fuller, who described this period as "a terrible season of faintness and discouragement" that wracked her with violent headaches.[16] Emerson acknowledged their differences, figured as a Chinese wall. The stunning statement of ultimate separation inherent in student-mentor relationships followed: "whoever lives must rise and grow . . . I am willing to see how unsuccessfully I make out a case of difference and will open all my doors to your sunshine and morning air" (*JMN*, 7:336–37). Remarkably, evolution toward difference and separation, and even the realization of the error in his own thought, he embraces here as a moment of mutual growth and enlightenment.

Emerson's letters empowered Fuller to become a feminist force in the literary market. Their mutual enthusiasm for Swedenborg emphasized women's power as latent, systematically repressed, and thus potent to produce a lasting effect in the professional world. He mentioned the historical significance of women's role noted by Edward Gibbon in *The Decline and Fall of the Roman Empire* to shed light on the current predicament of women, whose "*latent* and beneficent state of this wild element" he particularly highlighted. Charles Fourier's contention in *The Theory of the Four Movements* (1808) that the strength of a nation should be measured by the livelihood of its women[17] also appears to be operative in Emerson's statement that "we are not content with brightest loveliness until we discern the deep sparkle of this [revolutionary] energy which when . . . outraged flashes up into a volcano jet, & outdares, outwits, & outworks man" (*L*, 2:345).

At this stage Emerson was acutely aware of the unique position of power Fuller held as the *Dial* editor. As the volcanic imagery attests, he openly wondered where it would lead. Emerson was also fully aware that his young apprentice was building her authority directly through him, for he could plainly see in her correspondence her hunger for *Dial* suggestions and contributions from Emerson. With a sense of urgency exceeding his own and anticipating her deadline-driven work for the *Tribune*, she exhorted them to "make haste to print all the good things we have, lest both editor and publishers tire of their bargain at the end of the year." Her ambition to feed the far-flung masses with the *Dial* sought to move the insular journal beyond the confines of the Concord circle. Indeed, her vision had her "more interested in the Dial, finding it brings meat and drink to sundry famishing men and women at a distance from these tables."[18] As publisher to her editor, Emerson provided the materials she requested, such as poetry by Henry Moore, Charles Emerson, and Ellery Channing, in addition to his own "Essay on Art." He even acquiesced to playing the "poor devil author" in response to her sharp criticism of that piece, stepping even further away from his old role as mentor. "I was a little ashamed to learn that I must verily face it in print," he confessed (*L*, 2:372). Hence a new era in their relationship dawned when Fuller could pass judgment on *Emerson's* writing. Fuller expressed anxiety about her emergence into this jostling and bruising marketplace and its attendant "hobby horse" audience. In this publishing world, she found "something obviously wrong in this attempt to measure one another, or one another's act."[19] She lamented her new editorial position, sensing the inherent violence in it. Fuller was feeling the pressure of the literary market in her editorial role, which exposed her to the brutality of constantly measuring one another—between publisher-editor, editor-contributor, and contributor-reader assessments—that governed the business of its daily operations.

A Platform for "This Athletic Soul"

With so many failed promising youths, how did Fuller spring into the publishing world of New York City with such alacrity, an overnight success so sudden it seemed fated?[20] Emerson played a role in it, and not just as adversary. Many have been quick to point out his allusion in the *Memoirs of Margaret Fuller Ossoli* to a "crisis" in their relationship, which appears unproblematically corroborated by his essay "Friendship." Yet Emerson's misgivings toward Fuller in "Friendship" alone—often coupled with his complaints about her tendency to collect friends and wear them like "a necklace of diamonds about her neck" and regard herself as a "rather mountainous ME"—does not negate her influence upon him.[21] *Memoirs* might even be reconsidered in this light as Emerson's attempt to market Fuller to her posthumous readership, a work designed simultaneously to commemorate and promote her. (Ellery Channing would similarly market and memorialize Thoreau in his biography that immediately followed his friend's death.) Buell recently observed that "Fuller was the best case he could possibly have chosen from among his circle of acquaintances as the exemplar of friendship, both in lived experience and in her philosophy of criticism, which defines the critic as 'companion and friend.'"[22] Even Emerson's essay "Friendship" honors Fuller because it holds her to the same lofty standards to which he held himself. Often overlooked in that piece is his rather unflattering rendition of himself as cold, distant, and all too willing to use others to feed his intellectual hunger. His flattering portraits of her are extensive and rich by contrast to these misgivings that found their way into his work. Beyond "Heroism," his essay "Manners" also portrays her as the ideal self-reliant American woman.

Given this level of support, the tension that did arise in their relationship was fruitful and indeed aided in Fuller's professional success. Emerson's desire to nurture her independence fueled her feminism, which enabled her transgression into the public sphere. She then joined forces with the popular press, which she heralded as the "only efficient instrument" for educating the masses on moral and social reform issues.[23] Indeed, her career embodied the ideal scholar as an agent of action Emerson envisioned in "American Scholar," one not bookish and insular, but armed with potent political power. With the *Tribune*, she became that transcendental scholar.

The *Tribune* article that illustrates this best is "Our City Charities," which takes the reader on a Dante-esque tour of the appalling squalor and suffering of the Bellevue Alms House, the Farm School, the Asylum for the Insane, and Penitentiary on Blackwell's Island. The piece embodies the best of her socially responsive writing for the *Tribune*, as it deftly uses transcendental principle to undergird her social reform. Fuller laments the commodification of the human spirit, a signature transcendentalist stance, in her description of "the Farm School, where the children show by their unformed features and mechanical movements that they are treated by wholesale."[24] Her solution calls for "a more intelligent public attention" to obviate "such an evil incident to public establishments" like these, urging the nonpartisan selection of officials for not only the Farm School, but the asylum, alms house, and penitentiary. Emerson's contempt for partisan squabbling that impedes true humanitarian reform by the cowardly asso-ciation of individuals "to the section to which we belong" receives similar emphasis in his essay "The Transcendentalist." In it, he distances the Concord circle from narrow partisan thinking by flatly declaring, "there is no such thing as a Transcendental *party*" (*CW*, 1:205). Political corrup-tion and compromised morals form Emerson's target here. Likewise, Fuller complains that these institutions are too often "made the sport of political changes," giving way to flagrant corruption and surpassing that of London and Paris. Fuller's writing for the *Tribune* was equally adept at exposing corruption. She painted its more lurid scenes in moving portraits of "high poetical interest," which she then justified, "for such bane [i.e., this insti-tutional corruption] as is constantly poured into her veins demands powerful antidotes."[25]

The most powerful antidote at her disposal was her subtle literary eye that could render a portrait of suffering poetic in order to attract "intel-ligent public attention." Such an effect appears in Fuller's striking image of a woman she spotted while touring the asylum. Seated laconically in the corner of her cell with a shawl folded around her head and chest like a nun's habit, the woman incessantly chanted an insane litany, for "She was a Catholic who became insane while training to be a Nun." Fuller carefully draws her educated readership toward the woman as "a figure from which a painter," rather than say P. T. Barnum, "might study for some of the most consecrated subjects." In this manner, the woman is not a dehumanized object from which we are to shrink in revulsion, but is portrayed in a way that solicits the reader's belief in her potential for recovery through the transcendental conviction that the divine resides in all. Artistic vision persists in a brutal industrial condition every way contrary to it, as the divine is evident in the otherwise pallid guise of the deranged former nun through "her eyes large, open, fixed and bright with a still fire."[26] Emerson underwrote such journalism because he was of the firm belief that "such a truth speaker is worth more than the best police and worth more than the laws of governors; for these do not always know their own side, but will back the crime for want of this very truth speaker to expose them. That is the theory of the newspaper," embodied by Fuller's professional practice, "to supersede official by intellectual influence."[27]

Emerson's investment in the moral potential of the periodical press indicates how effective Fuller's transcendental training was for her *Tribune* writing. Fuller's preparation under Emerson encouraged her to embrace journalism as a means by which to realize the full moral potential of transcendental authorship. She would call into question rampant institutional corruption and social ills with the precision and fearlessness, if not the acerbic sarcasm, that saturate Thoreau's *Walden*, for example. The origins of her best newspaper writing and fruitful New York career are rarely traced back to Concord, however. Instead, critics frequently cast her successful emergence into the public limelight as an escape from the provincial insular Concord coterie and its attendant solipsistic contemplative life, with her boldly bursting through the limits imposed on female professional development. Emerson often plays the villain in this master narrative, as scholars have usually pointed not only toward the "Friendship" and "Love" essays for evidence of their strife, but also Emerson's mention of a crisis in their relationship in her *Memoirs*, in addition to the further corroborating evidence of the chafing tension between "Free Hope" and "Self Poise" in *Summer on the Lakes* that allegorized their growing hostilities.[28] Such arguments emphasize the strife in the correspondence to support the dramatic tale of her emergence into New York's literary market as a clean break from the patriarchal tyranny of Emerson.[29]

Tension obviously existed in the relationship, but what this pattern of explanations for her New York success misses is precisely the value of Emerson's effectiveness in training her not only as a transcendental thinker, but also as a viable competitor in the market for young authors. David Robinson, one of the few who have argued against the grain of this critical commonplace, has called *Woman in the Nineteenth Century* not so much a parting shot at Concord and Emerson in particular, but "a translation of the transcendental idealism into the social and political realm and . . . an exemplary bridge between romantic philosophy and social reform."[30] The insight can be usefully modified to support my argument that her move to New York and success there was a realization of that transcendental idealism, and proof, more specifically, that Emerson's articulation of it in the role of mentor could culminate in the success of a young transcendental author. Indeed, Fuller, more than any of Emerson's protégés, proves that transcendentalists could make a living in the intensely commercial mass market dominated by the popular story papers, abolitionist pamphlets, and special interest journals of the largest urban center in America. The key to this success was a curious and often volatile cocktail of advice, encouragement, dialogue, and fruitful tension in the most successful transcendental mentorship, professionally speaking, if not the most famous, in literary history.

Fuller's success in New York is partially explained by the fact that she came to transcendentalism at precisely the moment it became an international phenomenon, aided by the publicity machine that was Elizabeth Peabody and her bookstore at 13 West Street in Boston. The eclectic clientele of Peabody's shop, along with the richly diverse and worldly offerings on her shelf, attest to how "despite an inward trajectory, the intellectual synergy of the Transcendentalists struck off cosmopolitan sparks," made so not only by Henry "Germanicus" Hedge, the namesake of the original literary circle that would later call themselves the Transcendental Club, but by Fuller herself, whose immersion into Goethe had her seriously contemplating writing his full-scale biography for American readers.[31] Dante, Beethoven, George Sand, and the other German romantics came to Concord primarily through Fuller's influence. This cosmopolitan climate was necessary for her success in the literary market. In this rich and stimulating environment, her feminist thinking grew under the wing of Emerson. His combination of a commitment to truth and sophisticated exposure to world literature reciprocally stimulated a relationship that made her an ideal critic, providing her with a sensibility consonant with the periodical press's more successful authors. Although she wasn't as well read as Fuller, Fanny Fern had distinct transcendentalist leanings, especially in her liberal progressive feminism, commitment to individualism, and her deep distrust of the rampant materialism taking over the leisure classes of New York City.[32]

Far from the received image of Fuller refusing to leap from the deck of her sinking ship and swim to safety on Fire Island in 1850, she was a survivor with a gritty resourcefulness that she learned from supporting her family upon the death of her father. Such optimism is present in Emerson's own writing, whose pride in her resiliency is echoed in his admiration in "Self-Reliance" of "a sturdy lad from New Hampshire or Vermont, who in turn tries all the professions, who *teams it, farms it, peddles*, keeps school, preaches, edits a newspaper . . . and so forth, in successive years, and always, like a cat, falls on his feet, is worth a hundred of these city dolls" who fall on hard times "in the cities or suburbs of Boston or New York and are disheartended and complaining the rest of their lives" (*CW*, 2:43). The competitive fire in Emerson exudes a bravado to match Melville's exhortation of Americans to produce their own Shakespeare in "Hawthorne and his Mosses," only Emerson is wagering on his "sturdy lad from New Hampshire" to defeat the urbane gentry of New York at their own hard-scrabble capitalist game. His appetite and intensity here are hardly those of a detached and contemplative philosopher indifferent to the competitive market. Instead, his passion suggests how he urged Fuller on through the powerful application of self-reliance to the literary marketplace.

Emerson's tutelage of Fuller resulted in a distinct fearlessness and resiliency echoed in the New England lad's ongoing professional self-reinvention that interestingly included "keeping school" and "editing a newspaper," positions in which Fuller engaged with the full support and encouragement of her mentor, as their correspondence bears out. When she joined the *Tribune* staff, Greeley noted that her contributions were distinguished "by a directness, terseness, and practicality, which are wanting in some of her earlier productions." Indeed, this boldness can be traced to Emerson's commitment to truth speaking at all costs, even to the offense of the Harvard Divinity School administration, which did not ask for another lecture from him for thirty years after he stunned the newly minted graduates by accusing them of practicing corpse-cold Unitarianism. "Is it the truth? Is it such as the public should know?" were her steadfast and abiding concerns over any fastidious fuss about the decorative effect of her language, according to Greeley.[33] Exposing hypocrisy as Emerson had in his Harvard Divinity School Address, Fuller was committed to calling out social injustice at all costs, particularly in *Tribune* pieces on race, poverty, prison, and asylum reform.

Fuller became the "finished man" that, by the end of his career, Emerson had convinced himself he could not develop. Perhaps due to gender, or perhaps due to his sense of her as a friend first and a protégé second, Emerson was blind to his own accomplishment of influencing Fuller's professional success, the single exception among "So many promising youths, and never a finished man!" Christopher Cranch, Henry Thoreau, Jones Very, and Ellery Channing (the younger) apparently did not qualify (*CW*, 1:209). "Writing and speaking what were once novelties, for twenty five or thirty years," the elderly Emerson groused, "and not now one disciple" (*JMN*, 14:258). His aversion to conformity and his ardent support of independent growth in young talent led him to regard his lack of followers as an ironic source of pride. His dearth of disciples was matched only by the conspicuous absence of professional successes among them, with the exception, of course, of Fuller. More than any of his other projects, he had fully invested in her literary professionalism to the extent that he entrusted the editing of the *Dial* to her, a gesture that speaks to how he distinguished her from the others as both possessing skills more readily adaptable to the business of literature, and thriving at the nexus of the periodical market. Indeed, his endorsement of her editorial competence suggests that he regarded her as the most capable of his protégés to flourish in the business of letters. (He appointed Thoreau as interim *Dial* editor only for an abbreviated stint of a few months.) To him, she possessed an aptitude for literary commerce anticipating precisely the capitalist condition in which the *Tribune* operated. Like Fern, here was a woman "with the courage and skill to cut heads off which were not worn with honor" and to call "the act by its name" (*JMN*, 14:307).

Emerson acknowledged her ferocious work ethic, one he felt was better suited to the deadline-driven life of a journalist than the slow Thoreauvian machinations of a transcendental author. "The facility with which she assumed stints of literary labor, which veteran feeders of the press would shrink from . . . I have often observed with wonder," Emerson recalled, likely alluding to a letter in which she defended that work ethic.[34] Replying to his accusations of recklessness, she insisted, "I do not domineer over myself, but unless I were sure of dying, I cannot dispense with making some exertion, both for the present and for the future," indicating how much he had underestimated her endurance and how deeply ingrained literary productivity was to her sense of self.[35] She responded on one occasion with disgust at her friend Charles Newcomb's response to illness. "Charles Newcomb has been passing three or four days with me. He is wretchedly ill. I think he may die, and perhaps it would be well, for I doubt if he has strength to rise above his own doubts and fears," she explained, appalled at his mental weakness. "Oh how I thank Heaven that I am made of firmer fiber and more resolute mind. No sharp pain can debilitate like this vacillation of mind," she declared. Such psychological fortitude is evident in her capacity to bear a child while working on the front lines of the Italian Revolution in 1849, to serve as the top war correspondent to the United States, and to write her magnum opus on the event, a work that would have placed her at the pinnacle of American letters had it not been tragically lost at sea.[36] She took seriously the maxim that although pain may be inevitable, suffering is optional.

Indeed, such endurance and immersion in the craft is supported by her clear-eyed erect depiction in "Heroism" and image in the *Memoirs* of "this athletic soul [that] craved a larger atmosphere than it found."[37] She yearned for the expansive New York literary market. Emerson noted that she "lived at a rate so much faster than my own" in a life more attuned to the rhythms of the urban center than Concord.[38] Often overlooked in Emerson's portrait of Fuller in the *Memoirs* is the way in which not only her approach toward literary production but also her attributes of character point toward her aptitude for New York journalism. She emerges as fully engaged socially, possessing a playful wit that incited his own reflexive laughter, one so raw and authentic it startled him. Whereas Thoreau's archly dry humor tended to distance rather than attract the mass audience with its eccentricity, Fuller's candor flowed with an "incredible variety of anecdotes," according to Emerson. He found her "the readiest wit to give an absurd turn to whatever passed; and the eyes, which were so plain at first, soon swam with fun and drolleries, and the very tides of joy and superabundant life," an attribute indispensible for producing a vigorous and engaging mainstream editorial column.[39]

The *Tribune* "Star" Rises

Fuller was personable, putting her interlocutors at ease, drawing surprising confessions and pent-up stories from them in a way that "disarmed the suspicion of recluse scholars by the absence of bookishness," a high compliment from Emerson, given his diatribe against bookishness in "The American Scholar."[40] Indeed, Emerson's description of Fuller in society also serves as an apt depiction of her powers as a writer. With a distinctly mass appeal that transgressed age, gender, and social class boundaries, her "honeyed tongue" could hold "children, and old people, men of the world, and sainted maids." Though undeniably "rich and entertaining," she could express not just sensational effect or "flowers and music," but "broadest good sense" of substantial wisdom. Businessmen went to Fuller for such philosophical sustenance. One lady recalled that "the moneyed men, the manufacturers, and so on, knowing that they will have small interest in Plato . . . approach Margaret with perfect security for she could give them bread that they could eat."[41]

This side of Fuller runs counter to Horace Greeley's early complaints about her romantic approach to authorship. Greeley explained the lesser-known demands of authorship for the periodical press in contrast to the commonly known romantic one: "That the writer should wait [for] the flow of inspiration, or at least the recurrence of elasticity of spirit and relative health of the body, will not seem unreasonable to the general reader; but to the inveterate hack-horse of the daily press, unaccustomed to write at any time, on any subject, and with rapidity . . . the notion of waiting for a brighter day or happier frame of mind, appears fantastic and absurd." Emerson and Greeley both complained about Fuller's sense of authorship, but from opposite perspectives. Emerson feared for her health, believing that she seriously compromised her physical well-being with such intense literary labor. "I foreboded rash and painful crises," he wrote, "and had a feeling as if a voice had cried, *Stand from under!*" He worried that her "high and happy moments" of exuberant literary exultation would crash on the rocks of "lassitude and pain." Greeley contrastingly found Fuller to be a languid and pampered aesthete when she began working for him. Despite natural disparities in their literary climates, Greeley's depiction of Fuller proved less accurate than Emerson's. Her rapid adjustment to the demands of journalism shows that her temperament and skills were readily adaptable to this new mode of authorship. Greeley did not tutor Fuller to adapt to the rigors of the *Tribune*, so much as Emerson's training predisposed her toward making the transition from "essays in the Dial" that were "more elaborate and ambitious [to] reviews in the Tribune [that] are far better adapted to win the favor and sway the judgment of the great majority of readers," as Greeley explained.[42]

The Fuller-Emerson correspondence reveals that Fuller did not so much curtail or suppress her Concord training in order to achieve such a winning reception with readers. A crucial dynamic of those letters suggests that Emerson encouraged an unselfconscious experimental voice in Fuller. The best reviewers and editorial columnists of the day thrived under a condition of unrestrained freedom, which Emerson modeled in his own writing and encouraged in his letters. That radical sensibility inspired Fuller's intensity through a willingness "to forget ourselves, to be surprised out of our propriety . . . by abandonment." His model of authorship was never so sedate and staid as Greeley may have imagined, for he believed that "the way you write is to throw your body at the mark when your arrows are spent" (*JMN*, 8:400). He knew that "oracular genius" always asked "the aid of wild passions, as in gaming and war, to ape in some manner these flames and generosities of the heart" (*CW*, 2:190). It is telling that the works of Charles Fourier, which envisioned social cohesion arising from the free expression of the passions, were instrumental in Emerson's development of Fuller.

The key to the expression of those passions, according to a dominant trope in the culture at the time, was to be in the presence of a stimulating mind that might expand one's intellectual limits. As a way of describing influence and inspiration, the process of dilating to the size of a large intellect in one's presence is visible in the Fuller-Emerson correspondence, an epistolary space "like being set in a large place" such as the Concord woods, as Emerson described it in a letter to his brother William. Communion with "a very intelligent person," Emerson explained, enriches the soul much in the way having "the book of Nature" close at hand "on the table" stimulates "you [to] stretch your limbs & dilate to your utmost size" (*L*, 2:32). The timing of Fuller's immersion into Emerson's world enhanced the prospects of such growth. Emerson's break from the Unitarian Church coincided with Fuller's own departure from her family's farm and its domestic burdens; their lives intersected precisely when both were exulting in newfound liberation. This accounts for Emerson's early tone of release and euphoria in their correspondence, reflecting a kind of guilty pleasure at plunging "with eagerness into this pleasant element of affection"; he relished the escape from his "honorable prison" where his visitors brought him "never an earnest word." In his exchange with her, he willingly paid "the price of frankness" for its benefits of placing him in the role not so much of a true mentor, but of a confidante and companion in which "raptures of fire and frost cleanse pedantry out of conversation" (*L*, 2:239–40). Some of Emerson's greatest lines are addressed to Fuller, precisely because he had lost all sense of self-consciousness over his mentoring role. He is effusive, if not downright manic, as he invites her to "obey all beautiful motions. We could enjoy *and* abstain, *and* read *and* burn our books *and* labor *and* dream. But fie on this Half this Untried, this take-it-or-leave-it, this flash-of-lightning life. In my next migration, O Indra! I bespeak an ampler circle . . . an orb, a whole! Come, o my friend, with your earliest convenience, I pray you, & let us seize the void betwixt two atoms of air the vacation between two moments of time to decide how we will steer on the torrent which is called Today." He sings out in a kind of delirious serenade, then signs off "instantaneously yours," humorously deflating the expansive rhetoric with a dry recitation of the stagecoach schedule from Boston to Concord, as if to say flatly: poetry over, book your trip (*L*, 2:399).

It was in the context of this buoyant "hilarity and elegancy" of their letters that Fuller came to understand the power of transgressing cultural boundaries prohibiting a woman from entering the professions (*L*, 2:25). The liberal spirit of the correspondence enabled her to demolish the artificially imposed wall segregating belles lettres and philosophy from social and political reality.[43] Her writings for the *Tribune* embody Emerson's conviction that "true romance which the world exists to realize, will be the transformation of genius into practical power" (*CW*, 3:49). Greeley, Fuller's rumpled and harried editor, rapidly became aware of this special skill, calling her "the 'star' of the *New-York Tribune*," a reference not only to how she signed her contributions with an asterisk to differentiate them from Greeley's, but also to her status as one of his most admired authors.[44] As the foremost of Emerson's heroes of Eloquence, Fuller noted in *Papers on Literature and Art* (1846) that "newspaper-writing is next door to conversation," a category she elevated to an art form in the discussion forums she held at Peabody's Boston bookstore.[45] So if the Emerson-Fuller correspondence embodies one example of the mutual benefits that can accrue to vigorous epistolary conversation, then journalism, according to Fuller, "should be conducted on the same principles," namely a dedication to openness and democratic toleration embodied by a vital and level playing field of interaction for the growth of its participants.[46]

Such freedom allowed participants to alter their positions toward issues in the course of discussion. Emerson encouraged Fuller to regard an individual's shifting rhetorical ground, rather than a sign of weakness, as a natural (and even healthy) sign of an open mind authentically engaged in the process of intellectual exploration. Emerson regarded preaching as the antithesis of this; he saw it as a pledge to defend a static, entrenched position, based on a partisan political model of exchange. Emerson felt the same way about traditional pedagogical practice as well, noting that "I hate preaching, whether in pulpits or in teachers' meetings. Preaching is a pledge, and I wish to say what I feel and think to-day, with the proviso that to-morrow perhaps I shall contradict it all. Freedom boundless I wish" (*JMN*, 7:239).

Fuller taught schoolchildren and led her adult conversations at the Peabody bookstore accordingly, noting that she had changed her mind on a central issue with the latter group on one occasion, which she described in a letter to William H. Channing. "I told them the great changes in my mind, and that I could not be sure they would be satisfied with me now, as they were when I was in deliberate possession of myself," she wrote, validated by their tolerance of her Emersonian commitment to "freedom boundless," as "they with glistening eyes seemed melted into one love.— Our relation is now perfectly true."[47] Newspaper editorial writing was an ongoing endeavor, like her conversations and teachings, which fostered the evolution of ideas and tolerated developing shifts in perspective.

Fuller took up the authority Emerson had always hoped to instill in his protégés. She could comment on the development of her fellow disciples, for example, with precision and aplomb. She wisely passed judgment on Jones Very, for example, refusing to be mystified by his madness, which bewitched and gulled Emerson into believing him a genius. "Talk with him a few hours and you will think all insane but he," Emerson gushed, insisting that "though his mind is not in a natural . . . state . . . he is a very remarkable person" (*L*, 2:173). Fuller could see the flaws in Very, whom she found "*infinitely* inferior in accuracy of perception to Mr. Dana" on the subject of Shakespeare. Here she was asserting her prowess in literary criticism, which modern readers would come to admire for her brave rejection of Henry Wadsworth Longfellow and early support of Herman Melville. She only grudgingly reviewed Longfellow at the insistence of Greeley because she knew her true feelings toward the popular poet were deeply unsympathetic and thus potentially threatening to the *Tribune*. Equally bold was her endorsement of Frederick Douglass, whom she lauded for his aesthetic power, an uncommon perspective in an era that viewed African-American literature in exclusively political terms.

Beyond his influence on her reading, Emerson was instrumental in the cultivation of Fuller's discriminating taste as a literary critic, which served her as literary editor and reviewer for the *New-York Tribune*. She learned from him the importance of assessing the quality of her contemporaries' writings. A piece by John Park on music, for example, she found lacking "in any deep insight into the secrets of art" beneath an otherwise impressive show of "high cultivation [with] a very liberal and delicate taste and great descriptive power," attributes that would have won the unqualified praise of most educated readers at the time. Her standards were higher, however, bearing the stamp of Emersonian skepticism in comments like, "I have been reading Milnes; he is rich in fine thoughts, but not in fine poetry, and his Christianity is often forced in till it becomes what Mr Alcott calls noxious."[48] She could also turn a critical eye toward her own writings, especially with respect to an acute sense of audience. After nearly a year of refining those skills under Emerson's guidance, Fuller addressed him as a colleague, regretting that she had sent a moody and mystical letter that "might destroy relations, and I might not be able to be calm and chip marble with you any more." She assures him that she is righting herself by "reading Plato all week," hoping to be "tuned up thereby" to "make a good statement this morning on the subject of beauty."[49]

Her self-diagnosis and prescription reflect the steady stream of reading Emerson recommended to her, often prompted by his criticisms of others in the transcendentalist circle. In this manner, his guidance was usually couched in assessments of contemporary authors and mutual colleagues. Emerson's declaration that Fuller was incapable of writing a bad book was a statement that truly seems to have unleashed her powers more than any other in their correspondence. Emerson suggested that her skill as a conversationalist and maintenance of "a journal rich gay perceptive & never dull" could be directly translated into great writing. Such skill might also inoculate her from the current trend in which all "the fine wits [are] writing quite characterless & mechanical books—so that the vivacious books are now only the exceptions." Emerson sees Alcott providing the antidote to "the old hum-drum I have met a hundred times," a lethargy Fuller's vigorous prose also promises to reverse. Alcott takes flight "the instant he seizes a general question [and] treats it so greatly & godlike, himself so self poised," a phrase Fuller ironically would use against Emerson in *Summer on the Lakes.* Alcott is "eagle winged, & advancing, [and] he takes himself out of all competition or comparison & folds in his bosom far epochs and institutions." This praise for Alcott seems directed more toward Fuller, particularly as a hope or benediction for her professional success: "I must think ill of my age & country, if they cannot discover his extraordinary soul" (*L*, 2:198). It was to his great pleasure that the "age & country" did in fact discover Fuller's extraordinary soul, if not Alcott's or Thoreau's.

Such an investment and commitment to her future in literature filled the sails of Fuller's progress, encouraging her on one occasion to share her "poetical," though "sickly in its tone," journal entry on "winter clouds." Paying respect to the sage's limited time, she wrote, "I hesitated about sending you any papers now because you are busy writing." She then immediately shifted to an image of nourishment and refreshment that came to characterize the mutually enriching educational dynamic of their relationship. With a deep sense of sympathy for his own process of literary production, she offered her journals to Emerson as a balm for being "strained up to your subject all the day . . . like some grove of private life, into which you might step aside to refresh yourself from the broad highway of philosophy." She commended them to his "sacred safe keeping," a phrase consonant with her natural image of the grove as a source of revitalization. This was a trope Emerson no doubt found irresistible given the sacrosanct role of the natural world in his larger universe, from which his own subjects—like "Circles," "Manners," and "Wealth"—often ironically distanced him.⁵⁰

Fuller's "grove of private life," a creative space integral to her authorial development, had a liberating effect on her mentor. Such intimacy brought Emerson a new appreciation for both her private world and the social relevance of transcendentalism. The gender boundaries of his concept of heroism expanded accordingly. "Manners," Emerson's essay, clearly bears the influence of Fuller and testifies to the success of his mentorship. "It is a chief felicity of this country that it excels in women," he observed, with Fuller particularly in mind. The language implicates her even more directly when he asserts that women inspire men to "unloose our tongues and anoint our eyes . . . to say things we never thought to have said." Emerson is grateful that "for once, our walls of habitual reserve vanished and left us at large; we are children playing with children in a wide field of flowers." As in "Heroism," Emerson invoked her unmistakable image in "Manners" in "the wonderful generosity of her sentiments [that] raises her at times into heroical and godlike regions, and verifies the pictures of Minerva, Juno, or Polymnia" (*CW*, 3:88). In a more socially grounded vein, his praise for wisdom useful to the populace surfaced in *Memoirs* when he described the diversity of Fuller's audience. "Manners" similarly extolled the virtue of appealing to all classes, a point readily applicable to how effective writers can speak to the masses. This was exactly the skill Fuller perfected with the *Tribune*. "If the aristocrat is only valid in fashionable circles and not with truckmen, he will never be a leader," Emerson wrote (*CW*, 3:125). Such a democratic anti-elitist authorial persona drove effective mass-market writing, and proved one of the key difficulties that plagued the transcendentalist reception in New York. Fuller achieved such a democratic public profile while also appealing to the educated literati, a feat essential to commercial literary success that America's first professional author, Washington Irving, had mastered decades earlier with his critical diplomacy.

Emerson learned a great deal from mentoring Fuller. She helped to develop his appreciation for art, for example, as her own mastery of the subject was nurtured and inspired by Samuel Gray Ward. She so revered Ward as her artistic mentor that his marriage to Anna Hazard Barker remained one of the most devastating events of her life, a loss with emotional fallout second only to her father's early death. Fuller taught Emerson to appreciate George Sand, Goethe, the world of mythology, and an approach to friendship that was more socially open and inviting. Indeed, the pattern in Emerson that Caleb Crain has identified as "seduction, adoption, rebuff," which characterizes so many of his professional and personal relationships, particularly with Ellery Channing, mitigated his failed mentorship of Jones Very, Henry David Thoreau, Christopher Pearse Cranch, and Charles King Newcomb.[51] The early stages appear to be marked by Emerson's overexuberance, perhaps spurred on by the youthful vitality in each individual. Emerson interestingly also found infants irresistible for many of the same reasons, and was hopelessly drawn toward them. The most effusive daguerreotypes of Emerson reveal a kind of delirious half-smile as he leans his face toward a child. One image taken with his grandson is particularly revealing of a kind of joy that youth brought out in Emerson, a careening recklessness he gleefully indulged.[52] After that initial phase, adoption would ensue, and then judgment would take over.

Over the long term, however, he never decisively rejected any of his followers, but rather showed ongoing loyalty and support for their personal and professional endeavors. It was precisely at the judgment phase that all but Fuller among Emerson's promising youths faltered. Unlike her male counterparts, Fuller withstood his judgment by reinventing herself as a creature of the New York periodical press. Whereas Thoreau responded to Emerson's scrutiny and emotional distance by retreating into his journal throughout the 1850s and reinventing himself as a natural scientist out of his beginnings as a philosopher and social critic, Fuller thrived in the commercial literary marketplace. The fate of their own professional careers attests to their own attitudes toward the market, which had Fuller protesting the culture's systematic denial of women into the professions and Thoreau questioning the habitual collaring of men into a commercially driven existence. Fuller's assertion that women should be allowed to become ship captains if they chose serves as an apt predictor of her professional trajectory, just as Thoreau's questioning of why we labor the way we do anticipates his dedication to his journal and resistance to the urgent pressure to print. That deadline-driven climate Thoreau loathed was precisely the one in which Fuller would thrive.

Like Thoreau, Fuller discovered novel and practical applications of Emerson's Platonic ideal. Plato was at the heart of Fuller's relationship with Emerson, and served as a crucial turning point that shaped her into a more market-ready author than Emerson's other promising youths. Fuller rebelled against the way Plato was admirable to Emerson as "the broadest generalizer," defining him in such a way that would anticipate her socially responsive journalism in the *Tribune*. In her view, "Socrates is a man, not an angel," and not an abstracted idea. "The mere idealist vexes me more than the mere Realist, because he seems to me never to have lived. He might as well have been a butterfly; he does not know the human element." She immersed herself precisely in that human element, and adopted a mode of authorship grounded in social bonds and sympathy as the key conviction for driving moral reform. Her unique power as a transcendentalist in New York enabled her to "find the divine in the human" like "the wise chari-oteer" and "manage both his steeds" of principle and practice.[53] When addressing Emerson directly on the subject, she softened the blow consid-erably, but still made clear her misgivings, for example about the painter Washington Allston, whom she admired deeply when "he got engaged upon his art, and flamed up into a galaxy of Platonism" when she saw him speak. But her qualification is telling: "Yet what he said was not as beautiful as his smile of genius in saying it."[54]

Fuller not only carved out her conception of authorship by differentiating it from Emerson's Platonism, she also crucially revised his notion of friend-ship for a more socially cohesive model directly adaptable to the populous New York setting. Emerson's chilling line, "Friends, there is no friend," in her lexicon instead turned toward the possibility of human communica-tion with the hobbyhorses of her vast new urban audience. But she espoused the grounded and socially responsive mode of authorship that served her so well with the *Tribune* not in spite of Emerson, but precisely because of the way he conditioned her environment for intellectual growth.

Financial pragmatism also marked Fuller's development. She reproached her brother Richard, for example, for adopting Thoreau's contempt for monetary profit, noting that "the circulating medium" he so despised had supplied him with his beloved volumes of Horace and Virgil, a point she punctuated by enclosing five dollars with the letter to remind him of civi-lization's dependence on capital.[55] Fuller later became increasingly alert to how sales figures for her books could function as a measure of the reach of her social reform agenda. She triumphed, for example, with *Woman in the Nineteenth Century*, which "was sold off in a week to the booksellers and $85 handed to me as my share. Not that my object was any wise money, but I consider this the signet of success." "If one can be heard" by a mass audience, she concluded, "that is enough!"[56] She thus rapidly discovered how integral pragmatic economic concerns could be for the achievement of her moral and aesthetic goals.

One of the telling signs of her graduation from Emerson's mentorship into the commercial world of professional authorship rooted in the exigencies of the literary market is her *Tribune* review of Emerson's *Essays: Second Series*. Here, she has clearly ascended from the role of eager young apprentice and is now judging the master with particular attention to his merits and defects in the literary markets of England and America. Lauding him for winning the British market, Fuller dissects the sociology of his preference overseas as a factor of economy and labor. She notes that the British "have ears refined to appreciate these melodious accents" of Emerson's prose only because "a far larger number are at leisure to recognize that want of such a voice," a point tactfully respectful of her American readers. "Heated by a partisan spirit, necessarily occupied in these first stages by bringing out the material resources of the land," Americans, Fuller explains, lack the leisure and training necessary "for the enjoyment of books that require attention and reflection" in comparison to their British counterparts. Pointing to Emerson's prose itself to explain the discrepancy, her wily account is in the voice of a seasoned professional author attuned to the necessities of winning the popular audience with literary and intellectual subjects. His flashes of brilliance in a "house of medals" consisting of "single passages and sentences [that] engage our attention too much in proportion," she notes, come at the expense of thematic and conceptual coherence, missing the effects of "the free circulation of the heart's blood from the moment of birth." This organization of writing into a "string of mosaics," interestingly, was also her chief criticism of Thoreau's writing style that led to her rejection of "The Service."[57] Fuller's assessment is not just a killing off of the master in this case, but provides a measured recognition of the debts Emerson's readers, like his protégés, owe him "from benefitting by the great gifts that have been given," particularly an "instinct with life in its fullness and depth."[58]

What perhaps pays homage the most to Emerson's successful mentorship of Fuller was that she passed on precisely the kind of courage he taught her. The hero he recognized and cultivated in her, she in turn saw in others. As Emerson reflected, "the circle of friends she sat with were not allowed to remain spectators or players, but she converted them into heroes if she could."[59] Caroline Sturgis, who worked directly with Emerson to become one of the most prolific *Dial* poets, was among the more prominent women to benefit from Fuller's inspiration. Sturgis's career augments the gender implications of Emerson's fruitful mentorship of Fuller, suggesting a broad and deep set of intellectual relationships with young women writers, which included her sister, Ellen Sturgis Hooper. At one point, Emerson regarded Sturgis as "the Ideal friend," a powerful compliment given the considerable theoretical weight he attached to the concept of friendship (*L*, 2:334). Emerson's work with Sturgis, which resulted in some twenty-five poems in four volumes of the *Dial*—eleven in the October 1840 issue alone— burned brightly until her marriage and the loss of Fuller quelled her productivity and slackened her ties with Emerson and the Concord circle. At the height of their work together in 1840, Emerson said of Sturgis, "I write letters lately to Caroline, with whom I have agreed that we are brother & sister by divine invisible parentage, and she has sent me golden epistles" (*L*, 2:336–37). Sturgis would not have flourished if not for the combined influence of both Emerson and Fuller.

Before her departure for Europe, Fuller's circle of friends was never wider than in New York, to which she bid a fond adieu on August 1, 1846. New York was ideal for her authorial practice of principled transcendentalist journalism, for it embraced her Emersonian individuality as "a person who is independent, and knows what he wants, may lead his proper life here, unimpeded by others." New York also provided a powerful platform for Fuller to practice her brand of social activism for "the superlative importance of promoting National Education by heightening and deepening the cultivation of individual minds, and the part which is assigned to Woman in the next stage of human progress." This was a syllabus of monumental significance with an ambition uniquely pedagogical, as she envisioned herself by then as nothing less than America's mentor.[60]

2

Henry David Thoreau: A Poet's Apprenticeship

Two months before delivering his 1837 Harvard graduation address on "The Commercial Spirit of Modern Times"—a biting satire of the conventional New England work ethic—Henry Thoreau wrote a love poem. "Sic Vita," the lyric written for Lucy Jackson Brown, is one of many early signs that poetry for Thoreau was not merely a private pastime, but an intense professional ambition of greater importance to him than prose writing. The lyric addressed not just Brown, the sister-in-law of Emerson, but also courted Emerson with an eye toward initiating a poetic apprenticeship. In a professional sense, Thoreau was less concerned with Brown's reception of "Sic Vita" than with Emerson's. He had hoped his precise and intricate verse styled after metaphysical poet George Herbert would signal his dedication to the craft and discipline of poetry, and thus demonstrate his readiness for Emerson's mentorship. Certainly the painstaking effort and care he poured into the seven jagged stanzas shows that he labored strenuously over the poem. The composition of his commencement address was comparatively effortless. Mechanically constructed and clenched with the pressure of momentous vocational self-definition, "Sic Vita," among other poems he would struggle to perfect through the early 1840s, exhibits an almost debilitating self-consciousness. Despite his powers as a prose craftsman, Thoreau never dreamed in May 1837 that he was embarking on any vocation other than poetry, much less the sort of social criticism and philosophy that made him world famous.

Henry David Thoreau, 1854 crayon portrait by Samuel Worcester Rowse
(Courtesy Concord Free Public Library)

At odds with the defiant prose and its liberal repertoire of punning and
paradox, stylistically ranging from arabesque lyricism to incisive humor—
the quizzical sight of an ice block fallen from a delivery cart peppers an
otherwise sober passage on the ice trade in *Walden*—is the rather stiff and
stilted poetic voice of "Sic Vita."[1] Much has been written about Thoreau's
apprenticeship under Emerson, but comparatively little has been said about
the vocation of poetry he was immersed in during the first five years of
their relationship. His prose, of course, has taken the spotlight from his

verse, and for good reason. But Thoreau's conception of authorship, and Emerson's best intentions for him in that regard, began with poetry. Known primarily as a sharp-tongued prose craftsman adept at skewering the commercial world's impact on social behavior, the young Thoreau is hard to imagine wedding his authorial craft to poetry at the onset of his career, let alone making one of his earliest forays into verse with a love poem. Yet for those who knew him, the poem signified his baptism into the transcendentalist literary circle. It was a work so indelibly etched into Thoreau's local memory in Concord that Bronson Alcott chose it among hundreds to read at his funeral. "Sic Vita" became something of a legend more for Thoreau's romantic presentation of it to Brown than for the shape and content of the verse itself. In an ingenious calculated display of romantic chivalry, Thoreau used his poem written from the point of view of the fresh violets he had gathered from the Concord woods to wrap the flowers, loosely tying them with straw and tossing the bundle through Brown's open window on a sunny May day in 1837. More than just a pitch to Brown, whom he was clearly smitten with, this was an auspicious and dramatically choreographed entrance into the center stage of American literary culture.

While Thoreau was still in residence during the last months of his undergraduate career at Harvard, Brown and her two children had been briefly lodging at the home of Thoreau's parents in Concord. Thoreau had been adroitly assisting her with odd jobs, gradually working his way into her good graces. "He loved . . . Mrs. Brown and was a son to her," according to Emerson's governess, Elizabeth Weir, who likely underestimated the power of Thoreau's passion for the older woman.[2] Weir had little knowledge of Thoreau's capacity to adore older women with children. "Sic Vita," furthermore, cannot be underestimated as merely a boy's ode to a revered mother figure because Brown "was the focus of Thoreau's first noticeable interest in the opposite sex," as Carl Bode notes, making the poem the first written expression of love, anticipating his smitten longing for the elder Lidian Emerson recorded in his journal years later.[3] "She depended on him [and] would say, 'Run over to Mr. Emerson's and see if H[enry] is there. Get him to come over and see if anything can be done about my stove's smoking.'" From there the intimacy grew, for "while at work at these jobs, he would prolong the conversation. It seemed a favor to ask him to do something," since he was so eager to oblige Mrs. Brown.[4]

Without the companionship of her husband, who had squandered her fortune and fled several years earlier, Brown particularly enjoyed the company of Thoreau, who was uncharacteristically garrulous and affable in her presence.[5]

"Sic Vita" displays a striking glimpse into the fraught inner world of Thoreau's ambition. Simultaneously an expression of literary ambition and romantic love interest, the poem is an early sign of how, according to Emerson, Thoreau had "always looked forward to authorship as his work in life, and fitted himself for that." While pursuing poetry, Thoreau neglected his talent for prose. His longing for an unattainable woman in "Sic Vita" would prove a fit emblem of his longing for what would be an unattainable vocation. Not until the mid 1840s, after toiling at verse writing under Emerson for nearly a decade, did Thoreau realize that "he could write prose so well—and he talked equally well." Therefore, "he soon gave up much verse-writing, in which he was not patient enough to make his lines smooth and flowing." Emerson remembered, "my first intimacy with Henry began after his graduation in 1837," because Brown "would bring me the verses of Henry."[6] Brown orchestrated Thoreau's introduction to Emerson just one month before his dramatic pitch through her window and into his mentor's heart. Like Jones Very and Ellery Channing, Thoreau had been inspired by Emerson through his reading of *Nature*, and later remarked that it had inaugurated a "new era" in his life.[7]

Wide-eyed with anticipation, Thoreau was overjoyed that Brown agreed to walk with him amid the blooms of spring on a Sunday in early April from his family's residence on Main Street in Concord ten minutes across town to Bush, Emerson's stately mansion on Post Road. Brown turned out to be such an important intermediary facilitating their relationship that "if it hadn't been for [her], Emerson might have easily lost sight of his youthful neighbor," as Harmon Smith observed.[8] Despite the modest quality of Thoreau's poetry that everywhere bore the mark of an amateur, Emerson read the youth's verse both to appease his persistent sister-in-law, and to engage this alert mind brimming with vital energy. From their first meeting on the porch of Bush that April 1837, Emerson was acutely aware of Thoreau's verbal agility and singular thirst for the cultivation of the soul in nature that made him stand out among recent Harvard graduates. Despite this favorable impression, Emerson's heavy reliance on Brown's intermediary role in the early months of their relationship became particularly apparent when she departed in the middle of summer, effectively silencing communication between him and Thoreau. Brown thus provided the means through which Thoreau reached Emerson, the true object of the budding poet's desire, in a courtship literally and rhetorically wrapped around violets signifying modesty, the token of the twenty-year-old poet's humble introductory bow.

The humble author pose was a stock rhetorical gesture that made a show of neediness, however highly articulate, for literary tutelage. It had become a romantic sentimental convention expected of aspiring writers requesting guidance from established figures in the publishing world at the time. Writing a few decades after Thoreau, Emily Dickinson was particularly coy in her self-presentations, for example, as she donned the modesty requisite of new authors' solicitations of mentorships from notable literary figures. Her letters to Thomas Wentworth Higginson aptly illustrate her self-effacing, almost fawning queries: can you "say if my Verse is alive?" and "do you find my gait spasmodic?"[9] Just as Thoreau had responded to Emerson's lectures designed to inspire young literary minds like his, Dickinson replied to Higginson's "Letter to a Young Contributor" in the *Atlantic Monthly* offering practical advice for novice poets. Both would send their best work to establish a literary mentorship with each luminary. Pervasive in the culture at the time was the ritual code of modesty designed to avert the appearance of egotism through a sentimental scenario expressing the need for the vulnerable young author's rescue by a powerful patron. Both solicitations mark first attempts at moving essentially private writing into the public sphere of the literary market by presumably reclusive authors averse to the publishing world. The "white heat" of desire that characterized Dickinson's courtship of Higginson also found expression in Thoreau's efforts to capture Emerson's imagination.[10]

This chapter explores these tentative yet distinct steps toward professionalizing the poetic craft in Thoreau's career. Thoreau was deeply dedicated to this goal until his friendship with the poet Ellery Channing (the younger) led him astray from his mentor and toward a declaration of independence from poetry—at least of the stand-alone sort he had written under Emerson—to unleash a new and fully realized authorial voice. Channing's usurpation of Emerson's mentorship would thus explain the bold experimentation visible in the pastiche of prose and poetry found in *A Week on the Concord and Merrimack Rivers*, a work prompted by Channing's novel suggestion to write it while living deliberately in a hut on the shore of Walden Pond. Emerson may have financially underwritten the enterprise of Thoreau's life at Walden, but Channing was the creative impetus behind it, providing much as he did throughout their friendship a model for transcendental authorship Thoreau emulated. Channing appealed to a young man ripe with recalcitrance after enduring years of toil trying to reach Emerson's lofty ideals for poetry. The defiantly individualistic Concord saunterer and consummate conversationalist could not have entered Thoreau's life at a more opportune time to inspire Thoreau's liberation from the pursuit of Emersonian poetry. Once liberated, Thoreau approached authorship by plunging headlong into nature first, full bodied and naked into Walden Pond, and letting the writing emerge organically from the experience. As Channing grew increasingly significant in Thoreau's life, Emerson's influence waned. Little did Channing know, he was simultaneously transforming the lives of the two most powerful thinkers of the Concord circle precisely by becoming Thoreau's new mentor and Emerson's new pupil.

"Buds of Promise"

Thoreau's metaphorical self-presentation in the first line of "Sic Vita," "I am a parcel of vain strivings tied," could not be more appropriately suited to a promising youth aspiring to cultivate his verse under a luminary like Emerson. Humbly allowing that his aspirations are but "vain strivings," Thoreau cloaks his vocational objective in his romantic overture to Brown. What makes it feel so anti-Thoreauvian, so totally at odds with his rebellious prose, is its conventional formality, from the romantic address toward his love interest to the stilted rhyme scheme and forced meter. Yet the poem's strength lies in its ability to signal Thoreau's affinity for nature and mistrust of poetic convention, which would have appealed to Emerson. (Poetic convention arose as a major concern only later in their relationship when it became clear that Thoreau was not acquiring the polish, rhythm, and rhyme Emerson demanded.) In a professional sense, it was apparent by the end of Thoreau's career that he did not write his early poetry in vain, but the process instead offered a discipline that prepared him by the mid 1840s to "fulfill in the medium of prose the role that Emerson had described for the poet."[11] But that was never the intention at the beginning of Emerson's mentorship of Thoreau. The original objective was to take the "bunch of violets without their roots" signifying humility, "and sorrel intermixed," a token of ill-timed wit, and somehow make a poet "bloom," if only "for a short hour unseen" with "tender buds" and "branches green." Drawing from popular flower symbolism at the time as seen in Mrs. E. W. Wirt's *Flora's Dictionary* (1835) and *The Poetry of Flowers and the Flowers of Poetry* (1841) by F. S. Osgood, and speaking in the first person as the flowers, Thoreau highlighted his limitations as a neophyte poet. Ill-timed wit refers both to his quirky meter visible in the timing and cadence of his lines, as well as the compressed time of the shorn flowers' life. Made for the outdoors of "Those fair Elysian fields," he is taken indoors "But to stand/ In a bare cup."[12] The sentiment echoes the highland ballad Thoreau excerpted for his parting salutation upon graduation from Harvard: "My heart is in the Highlands, my heart is not here/ My heart's in the highlands a-chasing the deer." He prefaced the quote by confessing that "those hours that should have been devoted to study have been spent in scouring the woods, and exploring the lakes and streams."[13] The sentiment is a glorious quintessentially Thoreauvian snub of the bookish element of Harvard. It is consonant with his poem "My Books I'd Fain Cast Off, I Cannot Read," which posits that "What Plutarch read, that was not good nor true,/ Nor Shakespeare's books, unless his books were men."[14] In *Walden*, he would similarly voice his preference for visiting trees rather than scholars. Ironically, Thoreau had immersed himself at this early stage in intensive study of both minor and major English poets.[15]

Although Thoreau temporarily enjoyed isolated aspects of pencil making in his father's shop and school teaching with his brother John immediately after graduating from Harvard, such work was primarily driven by economic necessity and tended to thwart rather than inspire his creativity. Thoreau's introduction to Emerson thus liberated his surging intellect into the realm of ideas while also promising a means of making a living as a professional author. Emerson's patronage brought Thoreau's dream of a literary career within reach through substantial privileges coveted by most aspiring writers. Such advantages included full access to Emerson's well-stocked library, an outlet for publication in the *Dial*, employment as an unofficial assistant editor of the journal (after Margaret Fuller had stepped down), and recommendation for inclusion of his verse in the antebellum era's most authoritative and prestigious anthology of poetry, Rufus Griswold's *Poets and Poetry of America*. Emerson's September 1841 letter to Griswold touting Thoreau's poetry was convincing enough to elicit the editor's request of the youth's best work. In the first of a series of frustrating missed opportunities that plagued his career over the course of the next decade—the most notable being his refusal of offers from Horace Greeley to write for the *New-York Tribune*—Thoreau squandered this ideal opportunity Emerson had created, as the quality of his manuscript submission of four poems failed to meet Griswold's expectations. Winning a spot in this highly influential volume could well have cemented Thoreau's career in poetry for posterity, as the anthology had precisely this function of establishing a contemporary canon of American poets at the time. It is highly probable that had his verse been printed in *Poets and Poetry of America*, Thoreau would have invested his best efforts in poetry and thus might never have become the vigorous prose writer capable of such monumental achievements as *Walden* and *A Week on the Concord and Merrimack Rivers*.

Emerson recognized Thoreau's struggle to launch his poetry career, and made every possible effort to open alternative avenues for his professional development. One such avenue was editorial work in the periodical press. Emerson playfully anointed him the "private secretary to the President of the Dial," charging him with establishing a department of "Ethnical Scriptures" for the journal. Thoreau promptly immersed himself in Oriental philosophy, particularly the *Institutes of Hindu Law*, from which passages appear in his journal as well as the January 1843 *Dial*.[16] His duties for the *Dial* also required soliciting new subscriptions and proofreading manuscripts; each, however, became a comedy of errors. Of all his contacts made while canvassing, he could not account for a single new subscriber; his proofreading for the October 1842 issue raised the ire of Margaret Fuller, who unleashed a tirade at Emerson for the uncorrected errors that littered her review. Emerson's own attempt to placate her by jocosely defending Thoreau's decision to include the irregularities because they made for "good Dialese" she found less than compelling, since his incompetence for the position was all too apparent in the typographical mistakes riddling eight of his own poems printed in that very issue. Emerson's emphasis on process through his "Verses of the Portfolio" conception of authorship clearly did not impress Fuller, who was off to a glorious career with Greeley in New York, happily leaving Emerson to resolve this dilemma of quality control created by the reinvented literary standards he had called for in Concord.[17] His loosening of the parameters for acceptable verse in the *Dial* therefore met with the liability of so many promising youths submitting "slipshod sublimo" products, to borrow Thoreau's own phrase describing Ellery Channing's more regrettable offerings.[18]

Emerson's desire to accommodate his developing poets despite their ostensible formal shortcomings sprang from his capacity to comprehend the full scale of their genius. With rhetorical agility and guile, Thoreau revealed his genius to Emerson by simultaneously expressing his kinship with wild nature and discomfort in cloaking himself in poetic forms. Thoreau marked the occasion of his poetic debut by casting himself as a vulnerable creature of nature like the once wild flowers that find themselves shorn, wrapped and thus displaced and domesticated. "Sic Vita" makes a striking solicitation for a patron and mentor when, speaking as the freshly picked flowers, he allows that he "was not plucked for naught" since "I might survive,/ But by a kind hand brought/ Alive/ To a strange place."[19] Thoreau's alignment with nature certainly made him irresistible to Emerson. But his will to survive in a semi-domesticated state, like the shorn flowers from the field placed in a vase, makes him vulnerable and dependent on "a kind hand" to keep him alive in that "strange place." Emerson of course would be that "kind hand." Thoreau's image in the poem as self-styled child of nature impressed itself so deeply upon Emerson that his mentor habitually associated him with organic life, thus singing his praises in one letter to his brother William: "Thoreau is a scholar and a poet and as full of buds of promise as a young apple tree." The promise of youth for Emerson always resonated with springtime images. His letter from June 1, 1841, is no exception, rejoicing in the natural bounty promised after having "finished our planting" as well as the bounty of fresh faces including a new governess, "Mary Russell for the summer, of Margaret Fuller for the last fortnight; and of Henry Thoreau who may stay with me a year." Upon completing the planting "we may write a few verses" (*L*, 2:402). The harvesting of these promising young minds now needed tending.

Emerson now turned toward cultivating Thoreau's creative mind, which vibrated through these roots to the bottomlessness of the human soul, the infinitude of the sky and universe beyond, and the sheer power of immortality. Herein lay the genius of his vision, signs of which appeared in his journal in the thick of his poetic apprenticeship in 1840: "I cannot see the bottom of the sky, because I cannot see the bottom of myself. It is the symbol of my own infinity."[20]

If "Sic Vita" in effect functioned as Thoreau's creative prospectus for an apprenticeship under Emerson, his appeal could not have been more favorably acknowledged than with an invitation to attend a meeting with Emerson's trusted inner circle of transcendentalists on "the nature of poetry" at Bush. Thoreau's attendance there led to his first published poem, "Sympathy," which appeared in the *Dial*. It was heralded by Emerson as "the purest strain & the loftiest, I think, that has yet pealed from this unpoetic American forest" (*JMN*, 7:230–31). Emerson's praise here speaks of not just his own adoration of the poem, but an attempt at publicizing the youth beyond the scope of the immediate Concord circle. Emerson's aggressive circulation of Thoreau's poetry included his instruction to Samuel Ward to copy "Sympathy" and send it on to Margaret Fuller. He disseminated word of his new discovery in separate letters to his brother William hailing his "great poet," and to Thomas Carlyle, presenting Thoreau as the face of "the most resolute realism in the young" who might provide a tonic for the devolution of "our Church" into a toxic "universal timidity, conformity, and rage" (*L*, 2:225). "I pine to show you my treasures," he wrote, beckoning the Scotsman to glimpse his crown jewel of those treasures, "a young poet in this Village named Thoreau, who writes the truest verses" (*CEC*, 137–38). To Fuller, Emerson heralded Thoreau's "good poetry and better prose," and to Aunt Mary Moody, Emerson's own intellectual mentor and confidante, he announced that "genuine poetry" was springing from the youth (*L*, 2:182, 224). Thoreau's dedication to the poetic craft reached its zenith in 1844—during which "he wrote the most poetry [and] was writing the best poetry"—tapering to a trickle of private verses by 1850, when he was thirty-four.[21] Thoreau indeed followed the pattern of Jones Very with his gargantuan surge of productivity followed by an abandonment of the form altogether. The fact that his first publication, "Persius," was in prose has misled many critics into thinking that poetry was never an essential part of his professional self-definition. The close of his poetic apprenticeship under Emerson, most agree, occurred around 1844, precisely when Emerson had furnished him with a copy of "The Poet," which declaimed, "I look in vain for the poet whom I describe," a comment that no doubt devastated Thoreau (*CW*, 3:21). Much of "The Poet" described what Thoreau likely recognized as the very curriculum of the poetic education he had undergone with Emerson, and his own shortcomings in trying to achieve its grand vision.

Among the more subtle yet profoundly pivotal of those shortcomings was his inability to wed the forces of the market with his poetic craft. This was a failure to reattach "even artificial things, and violations of nature, to nature, by a deeper insight." Thoreau likely could see that his poetry had not adequately apprehended the full scale of "the factory-village, and the railway" beyond their obvious function for the romantic poet as unsightly blights on an otherwise beautiful landscape. His dialectic, to Emerson's disappointment, was not rich enough for him to see "them fall within the Great Order not less than the bee-hive, or the spider's geometrical web." During his first meeting as a non-apprentice to discuss the nature of poetry in January 1840, Thoreau not only enjoyed a kind of informal confirmation into the circle of transcendentalist thinkers, he also found an occasion to appreciate the significance of poetry in his own career. The meeting likely interested him because the topic, the nature of poetry, appealed to his new professional self-definition. Those at the meeting— Bronson Alcott, Henry Hedge, Margaret Fuller, and Jones Very—were at stages in their own careers in early 1840 when they likely were not concerned with the aesthetic challenge of wedding their romantic visions with the market, of understanding commerce "within the Great Order, as the beehive" (*CW*, 3:11). Indeed, this meeting appeared a pivotal shift for Thoreau toward transcendental thought of the most stridently anticommercial sort, a brand of American romanticism one could easily see in a poem neatly wrapped around a collection of violets. Antimaterialistic sentiments were in an energetic yet relatively inflexible and blunt first wave, particularly at this stage in the thinking of Alcott, Fuller, and Very. Trade was the enemy, and its accommodation would begin to be considered deeply only years later, especially in Emerson's *Essays: Second Series*, Fuller's editorial writings for the *New-York Tribune*, and Thoreau's *Walden*. These writings displayed dialectics far more highly evolved and complex than most transcendental views in 1840. Indeed, the move to reconcile with market forces was certainly not part of Thoreau's vocabulary when he was crafting his earliest poet persona. Only later, as prose took over his career, did non-aesthetic occupations such as surveying, house building, and farming begin to enter into his imaginative authorial repertoire and color his artistic palette. As a poet, however, the surveyor in Thoreau that later became an explicit shaping force in his signature mode of perceiving natural phenomena—measuring the dimensions and depth of Walden Pond better than any commercial ice tradesman and weighing both its symbolic and monetary value much as Melville did for the White Whale several years later—was nascent in Thoreau's original professional self-image of a romantic idealistic poet.[22]

What later evolved into a mature understanding of the more admirable features of the market's forces, and a harnessing of them for what became his most powerful aesthetic vision in *Walden*, was embryonic at best in Thoreau's early poetry. Thoreau's position toward the market never acquired such sophistication in verse as it did in prose, and Emerson was the first to register his disappointment in that fact in 1845 through "The Poet." But Thoreau's vision of nature—a raw reaching back to a primitive intimacy rooted in the ancients that is so readily identifiable in his prose—was born in his poetry. Emerson's greatest impact on Thoreau, indeed his deepest influence, came during the formative years of Thoreau's career, when their relationship was intensely focused on the project of transforming him into a consummate poet. Thoreau never strained so hard to achieve an Emersonian aesthetic in his writing as when he hammered out with steely determination hundreds of poems, most of which were written with an acute eagerness to please his mentor. This early and seldom discussed phase in Thoreau's career not only establishes that he had initially considered himself a poet above all other professional literary identities. His study under Emerson during this impressionable and formative phase also sparked a fascination, even obsession, with the social and cultural function of the poet and the question of poetry that would last a lifetime. His overwhelming dedication to the topic is visible in nearly three decades of journal entries despite composing relatively few poems of his own in a limited number of years. As Emerson remarked in his eulogy that though "he

thought the best of music was in single strains; and found poetic suggestion in the humming of a telegraph-wire," it was clear how important
poetry was to Thoreau's life. For "he had the source of poetry in his spiritual perception," and his "presence was poetic, always piqued the curiosity
to know more deeply the secrets of his mind." To know Thoreau's life,
finally, was to know his poetry, for his "biography is in his verses."[23]

"A Compensation for Quality"

Thoreau's earnest desire to satisfy his mentor is evident in the sheer
quantity of writing he produced, mainly in his journal, which crested after
the fourth year of their relationship. Since that relationship was originally
brokered on the power of the youth's poetry, it is telling that Thoreau
began his journal promptly upon Emerson's suggestion in early October
1837. His instant whiplash response to the directive is almost comical in
its eagerness to conform to Emerson's program for literary development.
" 'What are you doing now?' he asked," read the journal's first words,
which tellingly are not his own but Emerson's. The entry, dated October
22, 1837, was recorded just six months after their first meeting and five
months after the composition of "Sic Vita." " 'Do you keep a journal?' "
he continued in the first words of innumerable reflections and musings he
would inscribe almost daily for the rest of his life. "So I make my first entry
today." Significantly, Thoreau's first submissions to the *Dial* were poems,
and a considerable portion of his journal from 1837 to 1841 is written in
verse. George Herbert and Andrew Marvel, the punning metaphysicals
whose meter he draws on in "Sic Vita," along with a quatrain from Burton,
adorn the inside cover in transcribed excerpts connected by the theme of
solitude. "Salute thyself. See what thy soul doth wear," the second line of
the verse from Herbert's "The Church Porch" encourages in diction one
could easily mistake for Emerson's exhortations made in his "American
Scholar" lecture just one day after Thoreau's August graduation from
Harvard. "Friends and companions, get you gone!" the Burton passage
commands. Beneath it, Marvel's "Garden" asserts that "Two Paradises are
in one,/ To live in Paradise alone."[24] The journal abounds with details
suggesting an earnest young student of poetry embarking at the age of
twenty-one upon independent study outside the curricular and institutional

confines of Harvard, in every way glorifying solitude according to the romantic image of the poet's craft.

Lines from "The Poet" by Goethe accompany his musings on spring. By October, the creative embers of spring still glowed, carrying him deep into autumn with the thought of his own auspicious calling into the vocation of poetry. Without the promise of spring's return, "men will become poets for very grief," he mused. Perpetual spring fuses with the rising tide of his poetic inspiration, for "no sooner has winter left us time to regret her smiles, than we yield to the advances of poetic frenzy." The expectation and presentiment are palpable in his brimming quest to first "avoid—even flee from us,/ To seek something which we know not,—/ And perhaps he himself after all knows not."[25] The precondition of isolation and total social withdrawal were of course impossible to achieve given the ever present and discerning eye of his mentor. At this early stage, ample evidence reflects this tension in Thoreau's desire at once to please his instructor and engage in the isolated romantic creative process. Thoreau indeed wanted and actively sought out Emerson's tutelage, but once he won his audience, he clearly strained under the burden. "The degree to which Emerson orchestrated Thoreau's career, the forms of writing he undertook, the moves he made when he did, even his commemoration after his death," Lawrence Buell marvels, is astonishing considering Thoreau "survived such handling to become a classic author in his own right." The intense intimacy of the mentorship suggests "suffocation would have been far more likely."[26] Emerson would never have more control over Thoreau's creative process than at the very beginning of his career when he was desperately trying to become a poet.

But in Thoreau's early career, he was a willing captive to Emerson's genius. Regarding his discipleship as a rare privilege, Thoreau considered Emerson the prize audience and towering figure in the world of New England letters he was. Immersing himself in all things Emerson, Thoreau began to mimic his mentor's mannerism and voice, and even combed his hair like him. James Russell Lowell quipped that he could not tell the two apart with his eyes closed.[27] Ednah Dow Cheney observed that Thoreau "talks like him, puts out his arm like him, brushes his hair in the same way." She mused that Thoreau had been "getting up a caricature nose like Emerson's," uniquely illustrating a common charge that Emerson's disciples had become caricatures of him.[28] Christopher Cranch, for example, literally caricatured Emerson, if not by mimicking his manner, then certainly by drawing what became a famous whimsical portrait of him as the transparent eyeball of the forest. Thoreau's own mother could not help but notice the pattern, yet couched her observation in her son's defense, telling Elizabeth Oakes Smith, "How much Mr. Emerson does talk like my Henry."[29] Emerson himself was well aware of his influence over his pupil, worrying that he was thwarting his personal self-reliance and individual literary growth. "In reading [Thoreau], I find the same thought, the same spirit that is in me," he remarked long after their fallout in 1863, as much disappointed in his disciple's inability to develop an independent authorial voice, as flattered and impressed by how quickly his pupil had taken up his learning. Indeed, the skill and agility are manifest, so that "tis as if I went into a gymnasium and saw youths leap and climb and swing with a force unapproachable," if only building on his own signature moves and turns, "though their feats are only continuations of my initial grapplings and jumps" (*JMN*, 15:353).

It is impossible to overestimate Thoreau's thirst for Emerson's authorial aura—from his pet subjects to his style, technique, and manner—which coalesced into a persona Thoreau emulated and internalized. This may appear a typical, even trivial, case of the disciple's hero worship of the prophet until one realizes Thoreau's considerable powers of empathy, which he poured into key figures in his life. This capacity of conjoining and virtually exchanging identities was demonstrated when, just days after his brother John had fallen ill with a fatal case of lockjaw, the same affliction struck him. Following John's death, the disappearance of Thoreau's symptoms revealed that his own illness was psychosomatic and thus triggered by an emotional response for his dying brother. When placed beside this incident, Thoreau's emulation of Emerson suggests not so much the mimicry of a quavering acolyte but the profound, and even unconscious, depth of his powers of compassion. Once Thoreau had found someone worthy of his intimacy, such as Emerson, Channing, or Fuller, he fully invested his heart and mind in them as he did in his natural and botanical subjects, from which he penned some of his most moving literary efforts. "Sympathy," Thoreau's debut publication in the *Dial*, lauded by Emerson as a sign of his burgeoning literary career, showcases his nuanced understanding of the process of compassion, and quite likely was Emerson's favorite of his protégé's poems. His seldom-recognized capacity for sympathy and strong emotional attachment emerges in the poem, which has sparked a history of alarmist speculation about the "real" love interest of "Sympathy." The wild speculation began with the suggestion that it is not written for Ellen Sewell but for her brother Edmund.

Written in June 1839, the poem could not have been intended for Ellen because she did not arrive in Concord until the following month. Edmund, however, did enter Thoreau's life just before the composition of the poem. Based on his status as Thoreau's closest friend, Channing had authorized the original assumption that the poem was "written to one E. S." He was not nearly as intimate with Thoreau in 1839, however, as he would be several years later. His speculating appears rather baseless in light of his non sequitur assertion that the poem was intended for Ellen, since it was certainly "not to [Thoreau's] brother John," whom no one had considered a likely candidate.[30] Thoreau himself placed this quandary in the proper perspective, noting in his journal that friendship "is a glowing furnace in which all impurities are consumed," a molten process that also kindled some of his best writing, especially when Channing became his best friend.[31] As with "Sic Vita," "Sympathy" is more important for what it says about Thoreau's view of friendship and the consuming power of sympathy at this stage in his career than for whom he ostensibly wrote the poem. He was certainly developing a nuanced understanding of how "the loftiest utterance of love is perhaps sublimely satirical . . . Sympathy with what is sound makes sport of what is unsound."[32] The purity of the sympathy expressed in the poem does indeed make sport of our own folly in affixing it firmly to one intended reader.

Thoreau may have strained in a literary sense to reach the level of quality Emerson had wished for in his verse. But his love for Emerson made him almost reflexively produce as many poems as he did, filling an entire notebook beyond the extant verse contained in his journal and those published in the *Dial* and *A Week on the Concord and Merrimack Rivers*. Thoreau particularly yielded to the advances of poetic frenzy during late summer and early fall of 1841. His journal from this period contains many polished poems carefully copied in ink from a separate notebook where he had originally drafted them. These poems, "Friendship's Steadfastness,"

"Wachusett," and "Westward-ho!" among the most notable, Thoreau entered in the journal as finished products separated and set off from the surrounding text. He titled most of them, especially during the height of his poetic apprenticeship with Emerson, often placing them at the top of their own fresh page. His intention was to craft the journal, in which poetry held a prominent place, into a product worthy of posterity. This process demonstrates not only the importance of poetry in his early literary development, but that he likely kept a complete repository of drafted poems from which he selected his best for the journal. This collection of poems kept separately from the journal during those early years Thoreau later destroyed upon Emerson's suggestion.[33] One can only speculate about the nature and number of false starts and overlooked gems it contained. These were likely more than mere scraps on the cutting room floor, but rather a comprehensive clearinghouse of the poetic products of Thoreau's surging young imagination.

If Thoreau's biography was in his poetry, as Emerson observed, a signal shift and defining moment in both occurred during the youth's burst of poetic productivity. This phase Emerson regarded as a liability to his development. Ironically, the verse that was carefully transcribed into the journal from his now missing folio notebook reveals that Thoreau was not indiscriminately peeling off verses without revision. In fact, he had been painstaking and meticulous during the creative process. As Franklin Sanborn explains, Thoreau composed a couplet, quatrain, or other brief metrical expression, and proceeded to "copy it into his journal, and afterward when these verses had grown to a considerable number, to arrange them in the form of a single piece."[34] This explains how some of Thoreau's verse can resemble a patchwork of rhyming maxims or epigrams, a versified form of Bronson Alcott's "Orphic Sayings," published in the July 1840 *Dial*. This process, as practiced by Thoreau, exemplifies Roland Barthes's concept of a text as "not a line of words releasing a single 'theological' meaning (the 'message' of the Author-God) but a multi-dimensional space in which a variety of writings, none of them original" (although in Thoreau's case many were) "blend and clash." This mosaic method, as Fuller called it, embodies Barthes's formulation of how "the text is a tissue of quotations drawn from innumerable centres of culture." If the "writer can only imitate a gesture that is always anterior, never original," as Barthes argues, then

Thoreau's journal points to how saturated he was in his reading. This early phase in his career consisted of mainly the English metaphysical poets, ancient Greek and Roman poetry, and Goethe.[35]

Thoreau constructed smaller poetic units with ease. But in their slow accretion, which necessitated the alteration of lines to establish regular meter and a rhyme scheme, he struggled mightily. Emerson's composition of his essays and lectures followed precisely the process Thoreau found so difficult. He would trace back through entries and mark with a slash a passage he would then copy into the new manuscript. The slash mark reminded him not to use that passage again. In his poetry Emerson was even more mercenary and thus far more efficient than Thoreau, whose approach demanded that he tailor and significantly alter each verse. Emerson's "The Snow-Storm," for example, required no such laborious revision, but came to him in prose almost entirely without changes in a journal entry. He lifted the text and simply broke it into shorter lines, adding uppercase letters at the beginning of each.[36] Robert D. Richardson has commented that this example best represents how poetry to Emerson was an action, more verb than noun, rooted in the process, rather than a product of creation. Such an emphasis on process formed the core concept of the verses of the portfolio Emerson detailed under the heading of "New Poetry" in the October 1840 issue of the *Dial*. Indeed, Emerson found that creative process sacred, and willingly crossed the lines separating prose from poetry, private journal from published verse, gliding as deftly and smoothly over those barriers as "the snowstorm itself over definitions and fences, giving us a concrete performance, a sample of Coleridge's organic form," as Richardson explains.[37]

The poem beautifully articulates Emerson's sense of nature as a dynamic vital force embodying the ideal process of creativity. The storm's "tumultuous" "masonry" is not only an aesthetic performance representing a model of Coleridgean unity. It suggests a model of authorship Emerson wished to engender in his young protégé. The ideal transcendental poet, Emerson believed, should take his or her readers by storm, arriving like the snow, seeming "nowhere to alight" and touching all with "whited air," in an expansive vision coloring their entire world, from "hills and woods, the river, and the heaven/ And veils the farm-house and the garden's end." The poem's effect should be arresting like the snowstorm, and thus halt the flow of life, "The sled and traveler stopped, the courier's feet/ Delayed," separating "friends" and "housemates" from each other and captivating them in a "tumultuous privacy of storm." Like powerful poetry, the storm demands the attention of the private individual, disrupts routine, and directs thought toward the organic world. "The north wind's masonry," further, refuses to obey a formalized routine process. Instead it is a "fierce artificer," "speeding . . . his wild work/ So fanciful, so savage, nought cares he/ For number or proportion," evoking Emerson's distaste for regimented results-oriented labor and preference for unfettered liberal methods of poetic production. Here nature's aesthetic, as seen in a snow-storm's architecture, is more efficient than man's art. The character of this wild savage storm parallels the attributes he had hoped to cultivate in Thoreau's poetry, for in him he found a youthful "myriad-handed" sensibility promising a pastiche of sharp mismatching images—"On coop or kennel he hangs Parian wreaths," capable of "mad wind's nightwork" and "The frolic of architecture of the snow"—for a stunning finished product revealing an "astonished Art" when "the sun appears." Thoreau seemed to have the tools of this wild mason, but somehow the dawn did not illuminate the final result of "astonished Art."[38]

The difference between Emerson's and Thoreau's composition processes was that Emerson could more shamelessly raid his journals because they consisted of greater syntactical refinement to begin with. His pupil, on the other hand, dutifully employed the same method, but with dubious results given the rougher original drafts from which he drew. The difference, in part, can be attributed to the fact that Emerson, sixteen years Thoreau's senior, had learned to streamline his method, which he had slowly honed and perfected into supreme efficiency for more than a decade, and had acquired a sense of discipline for when to take up the pen and thus more effectively capture his moments of inspiration. By contrast, Thoreau's experience writing at the time was limited to the handful of essays he had written at Harvard. He drew from the essays for entries in his commonplace notebook containing passages excerpted from his readings rather than reflections and ruminations approaching anything like Emerson's journal.[39]

Emerson had apparently used two methods to compose his poetry. He alternated between prose transposed into verse with few changes, and deliberately crafted verse usually written in pencil in short segments separately and later altered and stitched together into a coherent whole. There is neither evidence of fully composed poems first written in prose in Thoreau's journal, and almost no instances, except for his shorter couplets that he either never developed or intended to stand alone, of longer poems written in one location. Emerson produced his poem "Shakespeare" precisely in this manner, as its original draft is titled and is isolated into two pages of an early poetry notebook. The marks of his labor indicate that this was likely his first, or at least a very early, draft of "Shakespeare," since the poems appear in manuscripts in only three other titled fair copies neatly inscribed in ink.[40] If this was his workshop, it is clear that Emerson did not follow one method of writing poems, but was wildly diverse in his approaches. His composition process ranges from this version of "Shakespeare," completed in one sustained effort in one location, as shown by his erasure of the penciled title, and the presence of both pencil and ink in several lines, to "St. Augustine," written more according to the accretion method he likely instructed Thoreau to employ. Four separate draft fragments of "St. Augustine" exist in one journal, for example, and three others are in separate locations. These fragments he shored against his ruin, as T. S. Eliot would have it, as he synthesized, revised, and expanded these disparate passages from diverse locations to create an ink fair copy of "St. Augustine."[41] Thoreau's process was so steeped in this method that it is difficult to tell which fragments he intended to conjoin and which ones he wished to separate, as in the "Old meeting-house bell," which Bode argues, "although usually not indexed as a separate poem, should be parted from 'The Old Marlborough Road,' which precedes them in the Journal."[42]

Perhaps the best example of Thoreau's distillation of scattered insights is "Inspiration," a pastiche of other poems drawn together for a unique and revealing glimpse inside his creative process. In a telling and fascinating turn, Thoreau was clearly violating his own idealized vision of poetic creativity voiced in "Inspiration." He had also actively used Brown as an intermediary to solicit the patronage and guidance of Emerson despite his glorification of independent creative inspiration recorded at the beginning of his journal. In a verse that evokes Jones Very's insistence that God was the true author of his sonnets, Thoreau posits that if inspiration derives from multiple and diverse sources figured in "all the Muses," rather than from "behind me for my wit," then "will the verse forever wear—/ Time cannot bend the line which God hath writ."[43] The poem ends with an anticommercial sentiment. It is not tinged with irony or with any playful undercutting as in the satire of Yankee business in the first chapter of *Walden*. Instead he renders a stock convention common to romantic poetry. The arduous cost of inspiration he imagines in his willingness to "fathom hell or climb to heaven," and thus "esteem that cheap which love has bought," concluding that "Fame cannot tempt the bard/ Who's famous with his God."[44] The isolated romantic creative writer idealized in the poem ironically was not created by a divinely inspired poet, so much as a resourceful pragmatist scouring his notebooks and weaving his insights from literally dozens of separate locations. Thoreau obviously found value in "Inspiration," a poem consisting of an assembly of odd parts lying about his poetic workshop, since he would later cull out the various ingredients of this potpourri and liberally spice the prose of *A Week* with its quatrains and couplets.

Emerson's worry was not in Thoreau's process, as the above examples describe the disciple appropriating his mentor's creative process. Without a clear sense of the cause for the dubious results, Emerson concluded that poetry "of the second degree" can be attributable to how "mass . . . is some compensation for superior quality." After hearing Thoreau read his verses to him the prior evening, Emerson recorded his impressions, straining to find some hope in an otherwise overabundance of what he deemed second-rate verse. Like "a cargo of sea-shells discharged on the wharf," the quantity and diversity of Thoreau's verse struck him as so many "whole boxes and crates of conchs, cyraes, cones, neritas, cardiums, murexes." The cargo's yield lacked in quality, however, since "there should be no single pearl oyster nor one shell of great rarity and value among them." This 1842 entry bears the tone of a final assessment, a statement with little hope for an ongoing future in poetry, or at least growth toward the production of a "single pearl oyster." Emerson drew directly from the entry a passage that appeared in "The Poet," which Thoreau took as his mentor's last judgment of his verse. Sometime thereafter, a conversation between the two concluded with Emerson commanding Thoreau to burn his poetry notebook, which had been a repository of more than five years of literary labor, a directive that all but erased and reversed the progress of their relationship. Although at the time he willingly complied with the grim suggestion, Thoreau later regretted destroying his poems. The incident coincided with his learning of Emerson's displeasure with his verse in several key passages of "The Poet," one of which came directly out of Emerson's journal entry that recorded his impressions of poetry Thoreau had read to him the previous evening. Thus Thoreau's verse provided the impetus for Emerson's jeremiad bewailing the creative shortcomings of America's young poets. The promising buds of the author of "Sic Vita" were now the foil for his signature exhortation to literary greatness.[45] Emerson put a slash through the segment of this journal passage describing the heights not reached in Thoreau's poetry, and prominently displayed the excerpt in "The Poet." What was first a direct critique of Thoreau's verse, Emerson had transposed into his definitive statement on the craft: "we hear the primal aboriginal warblings, & attempt to write them, but lose every now and then a word or syllable or whole verse, and substitute ignorantly something of our own, and so miswrite the poem, which becomes stupid and unaffecting by our blunders" (*JMN*, 8:257). It was precisely this excessive self-consciousness that Emerson condemned in Thoreau's verse, for which he had only himself to blame, given his excessive vigilance and intimacy—a presence that Thoreau himself ironically invited and coveted—that likely marred these first five years of his apprenticeship.

What Thoreau could not perfect in fine-tuning his lines he appears to have compensated for by writing as much poetry as he possibly could. Paradoxically, his best poetry emerged at this time, yet was mostly invisible to Emerson, who had become hardened to reading and critiquing his pupil's work for so many years without a sense of progress to satisfy him. Instead, Emerson met the tidal wave of poems from 1840 to 1841 with understandable fatigue that brought a blindness and insensitivity to the new level of quality Thoreau had actually reached. Emerson had also clearly been badgered by Fuller regarding the quality of his work, and was becoming worn down by her rejection of fifty-six of the sixty poems Thoreau had submitted for publication at the *Dial*. Fuller never expressed the unbridled enthusiasm Emerson did for his poetry; Emerson could not help but make concessions to Fuller's pointed, often unsympathetic, readings of his work. These forces conspired to bring Thoreau's wave of poetic productivity crashing to the shore.

Enter Channing

By 1843, Emerson became disillusioned with Thoreau, especially his trick of paradox, and began to favor Ellery Channing instead as his poet apprentice. Emerson and Thoreau simultaneously reached out to Channing to replace each other, with Thoreau looking to him as a new confidante and model for poetry, and Emerson seeking him as a new literary pupil. By 1844, the shift was complete, as Emerson confirmed his new alliance in "Experience" by grousing about Thoreau through general allegations against "young men who owe us a new world" followed by a description of the poet he seeks in a metonymic profile of Channing. Indeed, other signs point to Emerson's new favoritism of Channing, the foremost of which is his essay "Mr. Channing's Poems." Published in late summer 1843, the essay coincided with his disdain for Thoreau's "A Winter Walk." Further cementing the rearrangement of alliances was the "Verses of the Portfolio" department Emerson established for the *Dial* specifically as a means of accommodating the unfinished verse of Channing.[46] It was clear that Channing had gained favor with Emerson as early as 1840, when his call for in-progress verse appeared in the *Dial*, revealing that his fondness for Channing had already been cultivating for three years before his laudatory essay. So in the brief interval between 1837, marked by the composition of "Sic Vita," and 1840, Thoreau's poetic apprenticeship rose just as dramatically as it fell. By 1842, Emerson's frustration with Thoreau was palpable, as his July letter to Margaret Fuller shows. Ironically, his disappointment in Thoreau's "A Walk to Wachusett"—"I do not like his piece very well," he sniffed—was qualified by how "I admire this perennial threatening attitude, just as we like to go under an overhanging precipice." He saw this efficacious quality as unaffected and inherent in his temperament, as "it is wholly his natural relation and no assumption at all," which for Emerson was a virtue in an era of inauthentic highly conventional rhetorical posturing. That perennially threatening quality, however, by 1842 was undercut by its failure to deliver on its promise, since the talent that " 'delayed to strike' . . . never struck at all." Emerson then speculated pessimistically that "our American subsoil must be lead or chalk or whatever represents in geology the phlegmatic" (*L*, 3:75).

Three issues, however, must be considered when weighing the severity of his condemnation of Thoreau. Emerson's letter to Fuller is not uniformly negative, as his barbs are couched in his admiration for Thoreau's "perennially threatening attitude," which likely attracted him in the first place. Next, Emerson did not volunteer his dismay over Thoreau's unfulfilled promise because it had been a constant concern gnawing at him. Instead, he was clearly responding to Fuller's negative feedback on Thoreau's writing, and to a certain extent was trying to placate her by honoring her position. "I am sorry that you, and the world after you, do not like my brave Henry any better," he commented before forwarding his own misgivings toward his apprentice. This was a delicate situation in which he was speaking as publisher to her editor of the *Dial*, trying to assuage a potential conflict of interests over the publication of his favorite pupil. Finally, Emerson's criticisms of Thoreau fit his pattern of rotating patronage, in which he committed himself to a young writer's philosophical and aesthetic guidance, and engaged the full scale of his power in the literary market to launch their professional career, only to move to another when his interest in the former faded and when he felt content he had depleted all of his resources for the latter. With his interest in Thoreau waning, Emerson began again to play the role of magnanimous patron to Charles King Newcomb, his latest delight. In this same letter to Fuller, he lauded Newcomb's "Dolon," a work that was a struggle to publish even in Emerson's own *Dial*, and that eventually became a professional dead-end for the youth.

What finally signaled to Thoreau the end of his poetry career? Was it Margaret Fuller's serial rejections of his *Dial* submissions? Emerson's condemnation in "The Poet"? Thoreau's own self-judgment? All of these contributed, but none more than the entrance of the man who would become the closest and best friend of his life, Ellery Channing. In the summer of 1842, the garrulous and free-spirited Channing was introduced to Thoreau while lodging at Bush as Emerson's guest. Channing had a more sardonic wit and visceral relation to nature than Emerson, which resonated with an aspect of Thoreau's sensibility that Emerson found coarse. Thoreau's journal entries had been more spontaneous lately and began to treat nature with a playful improvisational attitude. His verse, however, was frequently compromised by the problem of utterance, shackled by the formal demands of meter and rhyme, and, above all, hindered by Emerson's judgmental gaze. One cannot imagine Thoreau's image of devouring a woodchuck raw in *Walden*, for example, emerging from the context of self-conscious rumination about the viability of his poetic expression and his capacity to transmute inspiration into words. His pronouncements about language's limitations in *Walden*, particularly in the chapter "Sounds," are not self-referentially rapt with anxiety about his own capacity to take wing in lyrical flight.

Conversely, a novice poet's voice narrates "Great God I Ask Thee," a prayer "that my weak hand may equal my firm faith." The poem is saturated in fear "that I may greatly disappoint my friends" by revealing weakness in his "relenting lines." His fantasy during these difficult early years of his poetic apprenticeship was to speak silently as nature does, an image that haunts the poem "Haze." To ascend "transparent-winged,/ Owlet of noon, soft-pinioned,/ From heath or stubble rising without song," was to engage in silent creation without verse. The weaving image of the poem's opening lines, "Woof of the sun, ethereal gauze,/ Woven of Nature's richest stuffs," evokes the processes of creative writing that yield this ethereal "sun-dust" from the "Toil of the day," a glow Thoreau wished his own literary labor might produce. The "weak hand" he feared would "disappoint my friends" in "Haze" disappears into the silence of misty "Aerial surf." The silent mist is a liberating realm in which the demands of willful utterance—much less the labor of collating and altering disparate verse paragraphs from his journal into measured rhyming stanzas—cease to tyrannize. "The Poet's Delay" portrays the romantic poet awaiting inspiration in a way that evokes his own anticipation of professional maturity, especially in the image of perpetual, and potentially hopeless waiting, since "The birds have sung their summer out,/ But still my spring does not begin." He resolves to "wait the autumn wind/ Compelled to seek a milder day."[47] Thoreau's hunger for freedom showcased in "My Love Must Be as Free" drives the image of Emerson as "the fowler's net/ Which stays my flight." The net is a foil to "the favoring gale/ That bears me on" with a freedom in nature modeled by Channing's attachment to the woods and his preference of the rustic expanse over the domestic duties of fatherhood that beckoned him homeward. "I cannot leave my sky," is in many ways not only Thoreau's declaration of his intended focus on the horizon "beneath the sun," but also a line that Channing might have uttered upon returning to his dismayed wife from one of his notorious disappearances into the thicket.[48]

More than anywhere else in his writing, a passage in *A Week* represents Thoreau's final decision to abandon his original dream of becoming a poet. In it, he casts himself as an "unskillful rhymer" to whom "the Muse thus spoke in prose," the creator of "a ripe fruit, which the reapers have not gathered." Though not harvested in highly visible and profitable publications of his poetry, his yield "bears for ever, annually watering and maturing it, and man never severs the stalk which bears this palatable fruit."[49] It is profoundly ironic that Thoreau would pronounce himself no longer a poet in *A Week*. The work itself was constructed from his commonplace books consisting primarily of poetry, which he kept during his poetic apprenticeship under Emerson. As an essential component of his early poetic practice, "the commonplace book is valuable both for the light it sheds on Emerson's poetic theory and for its powerful afterlife in" *A Week*, as Meredith McGill astutely observes. The book, which consists of poems by Thoreau, Channing, Emerson, and ancient and modern poets, largely incorporates Emerson's "stylistic diversity and temporal incoherence" of his commonplace method theory of poetic production, McGill explains, "both in textual terms and in terms of the life of the writer."[50] *A Week* distinctly bears the pastiche quality of not only a commonplace book. More specifically, it is the work of an Emersonian poet apprentice seasoned in collecting and sampling poetry from his mentor's and Harvard's libraries for the production of an anthology of British poetry that never came to fruition. *A Week* marks Thoreau's distinct turn toward a new sensibility and relation to nature. His utmost respect for poetry as the highest utterance of humans met with his equally powerful desire for the physical encounter of nature. If Thoreau were ever to break away from Emerson, it would be directly into nature, and usually with Channing by his side, notebooks in hand, thoughts flowing as freely as their steps through the woods. The two sauntered through a world both profane and sacred, regarding it alternatively with ironic distance and reverent awe. It is testament to Emerson's conscientious mentorship and patronage that he was constantly supplying his pupil with the tools of his own independence, from his initial funding of his study of British poetry, which required trips to Harvard's library from Concord, to providing him the real estate for his cabin at Walden Pond, which he occupied shortly after Channing presented him with the idea in March 1845.

Channing, more than any transcendentalist with perhaps the exception of Bronson Alcott, respected and admired Thoreau's poetry, which he cast in his biography, *Thoreau: The Poet-Naturalist*, as the product of a hard-working and complex individual. This portrayal was Channing's attempt to reverse his own reputation for haste and shallowness in his writings, which was frequently attached to Thoreau by association. Channing's book directly answered James Russell Lowell's attack on Thoreau in *A Fable for Critics* (1848). Lowell's images of Thoreau stretching his short legs to walk in Emerson's footsteps and of him picking over his discarded apples particularly stung Channing, since they so grossly caricatured Emersonian apprentices as so many Swiftian Lilliputians. The barb robbed Channing and Thoreau of the accomplishment of enduring the rigors of balancing individualism with received knowledge unique to transcendental training. Channing also took exception to Lowell's claim that Thoreau's relationship with Emerson had tainted his writing into a facile conflation of his mentor with nature. In a separate review published the year after the appearance of *A Fable for Critics*, Lowell condemned *A Week* as the product "of one who has so long commersed [*sic*] with Nature and with Emerson," implying that theirs was a commercial rather than a communal relationship. The two rivers of the title "run Thoreau or Emerson, or indeed, anything but their own transparent element," Lowell claimed, regarding the verse in *A Week* as digressions, so many snags impeding travel down the river. Similar allegations would be leveled against the mixed-genre digressions in *Moby-Dick*. Lowell found "fault with what we may be allowed to call worsification," although he conceded "the prose work is done conscientiously and neatly."[51]

Channing's liberal streaks of irreverence and humor—Hawthorne called him a "gnome" and others dubbed him the casual transcendentalist for his erratic, unpredictable habits that "made him more at home in the woods than Concord"—seem to have influenced Thoreau during the mid-1840s.[52] Indeed, he honored the Thoreau who during his early school-teaching days read to his students a mellifluent sentence, randomly shouting "Boot Jack!" to illustrate the effect of diction and, of course, elicit gales of laughter.[53] "My Boots" is Thoreau's mock-Miltonic verse only half-joking at the sacred status of his soles' walking companions. "An open sole— unknowing to exclude the cheerful day," he puns, "they quaff the dewy nectar with a natural thirst."[54] Channing recalled that "sometimes [Thoreau] twanged a tune of true prose on the strings of his theorbolo, as where, instead of Cowper's church-going bell, he flatly says, 'Dong sounds the brass in the east,' which will pass for impudence" with more pious readers.[55] Thoreau's irreverence toward the Transcendental Club, with whom he had been so honored to convene in 1839 to discuss the nature of poetry, yields by 1850 to his satirical "Among the Worst of Men that Ever Lived." In it, the group considers as food for thought history's worst men. "Let our thoughts ascend/ Experienced our religion and confessed" that their meeting, however idle, served the purpose of elevating them above such scoundrels. The smug self-congratulating thought sends them into silence. "Then to a heap of apples," which they devour, as "our Icarian thoughts returned to ground/ And we went to heaven the long way around."[56]

Not only did Channing appreciate Thoreau's impudence, he also understood his professional dilemma. Pinpointing Thoreau's understanding of the authorial role, Channing observed that "he did not court admiration, though he admired fame." Channing noted that Thoreau's more ambitious efforts revealed how "in his verse he attained to beauty, more often to quaintness." While singing his praises—"What subtlety and what greatness in those quatrains! Then how truly original, how vague!"—Channing discloses an understanding of authorship the two mutually shared, which was rooted in the principle that "it is the worst of lumber if the poet wants to float upon the breeze of popularity." They also shared the view that "he will be popular in spite of his faults and in spite of his beauties," since popularity is never the true poet's intention.[57] Channing answers directly to Lowell's allegations of flunkeyism to Emerson by asserting that Thoreau was "no servile copyist" to his mentor. In language reminiscent of Emerson's backhanded praise of Thoreau's poetry, "which pleased, if not by beauty of particular lines, yet by the honest truth, and by the length of flight and strength of wing," Channing made a similar observation (*JMN*, 6:304).[58] "He has no killing shots—*his* thoughts flowed" not elegantly, but with a raw strength, according to Channing. Thoreau was "no tender slip of fairy stock," Channing went on, "but the toughest son of earth and of heaven." Never vulnerable to facile mysticism, "the little Yankee squatting on Walden Pond was not deceived by an Egyptian stone post, or sand heap."[59] Fuller also found him wanting in elegance, noting that "Henry's verses read well, but meseems he has spoiled his 'Rumors' by substituting 'And simple truth on every tongue/ for all the poems are unsung,' or some such line [for] *the* one that gave most character to the original" (*L*, 2:90). Emerson believed "their fault is, that the gold does not yet flow pure, but is drossy and crude. The thyme and marjoram are not yet made into honey; the assimilation is imperfect." Greek poetry obviously influenced him, but it was too primitive and raw for Emerson, who found an archaic quality in it, for "it seems as if the poetry was written before time was" (*JMN*, 6:304).

Nature functioned as Thoreau's muse, as figured in the glowing moon and smell of ripening corn in a passage in which the subject moves from Nature to self and on to poetry: "A field of ripening corn, now at night, that has been topped, with the stalks stacked up," he wrote, observing his own soul in the process; "I feel as if I were an ear of ripening corn myself. Is not the whole air a compound of such odors indistinguishable?" Moving directly into the scene's poetic allure, he asks, "What if one moon has come and gone with its world of poetry, so divine a creature freighted with its hints for me, and I not use them."[60] Though written in prose, such instances reinforce the sense that Thoreau "mounts above prose," as Channing well knew.[61] The poet apprentice who had toiled under Emerson now with Channing had a like-minded soul with whom to share his daily walks, and humanize nature. Theirs was a friendship rooted in mutual passion for organic processes, mysticism, and a critical eye toward social convention, particularly those governed by free-market capitalism. Their three "professions," as they called them, included writing, observing, and lecturing; both authors had ventured into the New York market to advance their careers with Horace Greeley's *Tribune* but to no avail. They were most comfortable as Concord's inseparable saunterers, renegade outlaw nonconformists, and partners in crime, in the process reinventing the professional transcendental poet into a bohemian of nature rather than the city. Their trust established the foundation of a relationship in which Thoreau could be "simple and unconstrained" in sharp contrast to the pressure to be complex and formal in his writing and self-presentation to Emerson (*CW*, 2:189). Indeed, Channing appreciated and understood Thoreau's poetry in ways that Emerson had not, especially his coarse wit and contrarian irony. Channing knew Thoreau would never be a cuddly genius, and therefore advised Emerson to see past how "his effects can all be produced by cork and sand" and admire how "the substance that produces them is god like and divine" (*JMN*, 8:75).

The final tableau of the Thoreau-Emerson poetic apprenticeship is best captured in Emerson's initial exuberant acclaim for "Sympathy," and his shifting view of his disciple that would eventuate in his decision not to include the poem in his anthology *Parnassus*. "Smoke," "Mist," and "Haze" did find their way into the collection, however, as Emerson chose earthy elliptical meditations on natural phenomena, works distinctly Thoreauvian in a way that bore little of his own influence over his development as a poet, but instead harkened back to his love of the more stark ancient Greek and Roman verse that was uniquely his own. Emerson's selections imply that he wanted to immortalize the Thoreau who favored the pared-down and simple beauty of primitive, unadorned verse, which he regarded as a pure literary form. Transcending scholarly bookishness, this type of "poetry cannot breathe in the scholar's atmosphere," according to Thoreau.[62]

Thoreau's poetic apprenticeship landed him a place in a band of displaced drifters. His inner development was complexly interwoven with his struggle over vocational identity. Two problems this wayward generation faced were an unwillingness to accept positions expected of them, such as "a higher calling or an appropriate task that never seemed to materialize," as David Robinson explains.[63] Among others in the cohort such as Jones Very, Thoreau vacillated between will-less achievement as figured in the soundless poetry of "Haze," and a more militant, extraordinary ambition to develop his powers of aesthetic perception and self-culture. His industry, however differently oriented from the free market, was quite real and deeply driven specifically to transform himself into a larger-than-life Emersonian poet. Two journal entries dated June 25 and 26, 1840, particularly speak to the latter drive with its Emersonian exhortations, definitions, and resolutions designed to spur him on to success. One motivational maxim reminds him to eschew complacency in a particularly stellar anticipation of his celebrated vigorous morning work in *Walden:* "Let me see no other conflict but with prosperity—if my path run on before me level and smooth, it is all a mirage—in reality it is steep and arduous as a chamois pass." His commitment to nonconformist individualism rings out in commandments to strengthen his will to resist mainstream convention, "to stand outside the wall and no harm can reach you." Upon closer examination, however, a quietist or even Taoist strand emerges in his program for self-development that reflects a passivity in truisms such as "He will get to the goal first who stands the stillest," and "he who resists not at all will never surrender," both of which animate the core principle that would later define the world-famous theory of "Civil Disobedience."

On the issue of the production of poetry, Thoreau's program for self-development seems to delineate ways of attaining "the best poetry" in his writing, only to undercut them by ruling out willed authorship altogether, a position clearly undermining his professional ambition. "The best poetry," he asserts, "has never been written," which implies of course that it never will be written by him or anyone else for that matter. "For when it might have been, the poet forgot it, and when it was too late remembered it—or when it might have been, the poet remembered it, and when it was too late forgot it." Such a statement puts into perspective the humble pose of his first serious poem, "Sic Vita," which confesses he is out of nature as a poet, like the shorn flowers, and out of time as ill-timed wit. The poet's decentered placement with respect to experience that is displaced into either the past or the future but never immediate leads Thoreau to conclude that poetry writing is impossible, and that true poetry exists in nature and in living deliberately. In this sense, "the highest condition of art is artlessness," a truth that would have everywhere placed Thoreau's poetic aspiration into a mode of passive receptivity in the manner of Wordsworth and Shelley. But Thoreau seems to have gone further with his moral perfectionism. Authorship so idealized—utterance is not experience to him, but experience recollected or foretold and thus cannot be poetry per se—is unlike the English romantics or even fellow Emersonian disciple Jones Very who felt that poetry *was* possible, and that poets were thus necessary as conduits to channel the divine spirit in nature. Thoreau instead seems to have ruled out, or at least skeptically regarded, the possibility that poets could artificially create "the highest condition of art" in written verse.[64]

When Thoreau began an anthology of British poetry (mainly Scottish and English), instigated and paid for by Emerson, it involved trips to Cambridge to consult the Harvard library. Robert Sattelmeyer has found fault in both Thoreau, for his "misguided appraisal of his literary vocation," and his mentor, given "the deeply ambivalent effects of Emerson's patronage."[65] Emerson was instead genuinely interested in the project himself, and almost considered it a collaboration. He later compiled an even larger poetry anthology, *Parnassus*, that included the ancient Greek and Middle English poetry that Thoreau had gravitated toward. Ironically, it was Greek and Middle English poetry that led him astray from the original project, which restricted him to English and Scottish contemporary verse. The assignment was profoundly antithetical, if not downright blasphemous, in light of Emerson's intellectual declaration of independence from English models for aspiring American authors in "The American Scholar." Thoreau soured on the project, abandoning it by 1844 to begin in earnest composing *A Week*. His highly idealized conception of the vocation of poetry challenged him not merely to survive what appeared a limited success in the genre, but to carry with him the measurable gains accrued from that early training. In an 1843 lecture, he upheld poetry as represented in Homer, Ossian, and Chaucer. It is a study he valued enough to incorporate into not only a *Dial* article, but also *A Week*. For to Thoreau, "the loftiest written wisdom is rhymed or measured" as well as a "natural fruit" close to speech and action, "spoken or done."[66]

II

TRAFFICKING IN ART

3

CHRISTOPHER CRANCH: FINDING THE PAINTER
IN THE POET

Thoreau's ritual burning of his manuscript poems at the command of Emerson signified the end of his poetic apprenticeship, from which he would emerge like a phoenix from the ashes to resurrect his career as a prose writer. In an eerie echo of Thoreau's fiery vocational rite designed to liberate him from his former incarcerating professional identity, Christopher Pearse Cranch, transfixed by Emerson's charismatic influence in 1840, fed twenty-four sermons he delivered during his soul-killing stint as a substitute preacher, or "supply minister" as it was then termed, into the fire. He vowed to burn even more than these: "They are old clothes. I feel myself too large to get into them again. I do not stand where I stood a year ago."[1] The private ritual held profound public implications. Like Thoreau, Cranch reached a point in his life when Emerson's formulation of the ideal transcendental poet grew from an abstract concept he admired at a vicarious distance into the ideal core principle driving his life's ambition. This new vocation promising soaring spiritual and aesthetic ecstasy heightened Cranch's awareness of his own hollow soul, highlighting in horrifying detail the man he had become: a diffident conciliatory neophyte, straining to please congregations through safe and conformist preaching.

Whereas Thoreau had little to lose in abandoning what he had always considered the temporary occupations of schoolteacher and manufacturer of pencils in his father's shop, Cranch had considerably more at stake when he heard his transcendental calling. Like Thoreau, Cranch had been struck with the revelation upon reading Emerson's *Nature* during the summer

Christopher Pearse Cranch (Photography Collection, Miriam and Ira D. Wallach Division of Art, Prints, and Photographs, New York Public Library, Astor, Lenox, and Tilden Foundations)

of 1836 that his life's work must change. Demonstrations of transcendental self-knowledge and self-reliance functioned to prove one's fitness for an Emersonian apprenticeship. Cranch was no exception to how each disciple's commitment to the Newness could be measured, at least initially, by the manner with which they made their professional declarations of independence from careers and identities ruled by economic and political interest. Once liberated into the literary and artistic life of self-culture, most struggled to reconcile Emerson's pressure to professionalize their craft with the antimaterialistic transcendental ethos. But none struggled more mightily than Cranch to break from his former occupation, carrying with him the remnants of the conflict well into his various professional reincarnations as a poet, journalist, art critic, children's writer, musician, cartoonist, and landscape painter.

Unlike Thoreau, Cranch had been more deeply invested in his prior occupation, thus making for a more volatile spiritual climate, which intensified and threatened to rupture his attempts to remake himself into Emerson's American scholar and poet. At the time, he had been struggling to launch his career in the Unitarian ministry by preaching in Portland, Maine, after graduating from Harvard the year before, in 1835. Saddled with the unenviable task of winning the favor of a church that might adopt him on a permanent basis, Cranch became wary of other preachers' congregations, who initially received him politely but typically yearned for their regular minister's return to service. While in Portland, Cranch had been exposed to the radical transcendental influence of William Ellery Channing, who encouraged his liberal inclinations. Emerson had penetrated his consciousness, as the young minister began keeping a commonplace book of quotes from *Nature* and the essays. But unlike most collections of memorable lines readers saved from their favorite authors, Cranch illustrated his excerpts, at first haphazardly, and later with self-conscious care and precision. Soon, the drawings were no longer idle and jocose captions caricaturing Emerson's wisdom. They rapidly developed beyond visual shorthand for the author's otherwise unwieldy mixed metaphors and outlandish imagery into rudimentary works of art in themselves. This workshop of paper and ink caricature—simultaneously satirizing his master and struggling to assimilate his philosophy like a riveted yet incurably whimsical schoolboy—would eventuate in his transcendental search for the divine in nature, particularly through canvas and oil in his work as a professional painter.

With few pastoral duties and relatively little connection to the community or the personal affairs of their congregations, itinerant supply ministers like Cranch faced many idle hours. As Cranch found himself ruminating upon Emerson's richest lines during such vast stretches of unstructured time, the images they conjured took shape beneath his hand. What had begun in 1837 as a pastime of "making comic illustrations of some of Emerson's quaint sentences" soon transformed into an absorbing, elaborate project under the encouragement and collaboration of James Freeman Clarke, editor of the *Western Literary Messenger*.[2] This was the birth not only of the now iconic visual representation of Emerson's "transparent eyeball" readers of *Nature* have come to recognize, but of a vocational awakening leading to transcendental poetry and landscape painting that would forever change Cranch's life. Cranch's immersion into transcendentalism was neither as flip nor as carefree as his drawings may suggest. Instead, it was rapt with the spiritual turmoil of a once dedicated and unwavering young minister turning his back on the pulpit for a new kind of faith.

Cranch's sense of wasted effort in supplying pulpits from the far North in Bangor to Richmond in the South, with assignments in between at Portland, Providence, Andover, Boston, and Washington, convinced him that the West would do him some good. In the process of traversing the eastern seaboard, desperate to settle his professional future, the neglect of his own spiritual vitality weighed heavily on his conscience. Cranch's transcendental urges—Henry Hedge in Bangor was already referring to him as a transcendentalist at this time—led him to believe that relocation to St. Louis to supply Clarke's pulpit and edit his *Western Messenger* would provide the tonic for the chill he felt in the East. The *Messenger* was most sympathetic to transcendental thought, after the *Dial* and Horace Greeley's *New-York Tribune*. In that more open and tolerant atmosphere of the West he might discover the spontaneity and society he felt were sorely lacking in his character. "I am not free enough," he concluded. "I am not bold enough for a minister of the Word of Life," the essential feature of which was "a habitual independence and disregard for the opinion of men." In Louisville his mentor was Clarke, who showed him a model for such boldness that "must converse freely and about everything." Such independence,

Cranch realized by observing Clarke, was marked not by withdrawal from society, for "in the West it is especially necessary that no member of society should forget his relations and isolate himself." This environment promised to reverse the effects of his preaching in the East, which he believed had transformed him into a cautious conformist begging for his congregations' approval. This left Cranch bitter in his failure to become the confident prophet he had longed to be, heroically brandishing his singular message throughout each parish. Clarke preceded Emerson in alerting Cranch to his own shortcomings through the bold, fearless manner with which he wore his professional identity, leaving the youth "Over and again" to "chide my timidity, my reserve, my sensitiveness." His Emersonian leanings in 1837 were clear: "I want what might be called *spontaneousness*" combined with a dynamic public presence unafraid of his audience, but actively coursing through it like a "quick, deep . . . strong-moving stream, winding about among men, purifying and gladdening and fertilizing the world."[3]

Cranch viewed Clarke as the ideal Unitarian preacher to emulate, particularly admiring how his ministry accommodated his distinct transcendental leanings and literary life as editor of the *Western Messenger*. Before his arrival in Louisville, it became apparent that his difficulty in securing a permanent position in the ministry was linked to his blacklisting as an affiliate of radical transcendental Unitarians Hedge and Channing. By 1840, his association with the movement ran much deeper. The conservative clergy, whom Cranch described in a letter that year to his former Harvard roommate John Sullivan Dwight as "the sapient owls of the A.U.A. [American Unitarian Association]," spread word and "quite ignored me. My name is expunged from the list of *safe* men. I am of the goats and not the evangelical sheep. It is your quiet non-committal man who receives the sweet plaudits and puddings of ecclesiastical patronage. I have had the misfortune to have associated with Emerson, Ripley & c those corruptors of youth, and have written for the Dial, and these are unpardonable offenses."[4] Though hardly considered the dangerous heathen and militant rebel he posed as here—his tone mocks the sensationalistic language of transcendentalism's dissenters in a way his college chum would have appreciated—Cranch rightly ascribed the cause of his professional frustration. His alliance with transcendentalism became explicit and public in 1837 and 1838, with his defenses of Emerson in "Mr. Emerson's Oration" and

"R. W. Emerson and the New School." Both pieces appeared in the *Western Messenger* to counteract the conservative Unitarian assault on Emerson's Harvard Divinity School Address led by Norton Andrews. Clarke had encouraged these submissions from Cranch, and in the process confirmed how politically engaged transcendental activism could be fitted to the position of Unitarian minister. Backing the New School did not, therefore, necessitate the abandonment of his original vocation. But it did demand that he reform himself according to the new "western" paradigm—really only New England in a western locale—of Clarke's Louisville model.

With regional, ecclesiastical, and aesthetic paradigms in flux at this stage in Cranch's career, a vocational crisis loomed. Like Cranch's early illustrations of Emersonian wisdom, Clarke proved to be a stepping-stone to greater and grander ambitions. The answer to Cranch's vocational quest lay not in the West, because his tiny and "scattered flock" of parishes in the remote rural outposts of Peoria and Freemont, though he cared for them, threatened to severely limit his long-term personal and professional growth.[5] Indeed, Cranch's conclusions about Clarke and the West, and his dismissal of all things eastern, especially New England, would prove drastically shortsighted. Louisville and Clarke were indeed only setting the stage for his real career launch, which would take place in New England under the tutelage of Emerson. Louisville only prepared him as a kind of finishing school for his apprenticeship to the transcendental trade that brought a much more radical future wholly outside the reach of the Unitarian Church. Cranch could plainly see that the ministry ultimately controlled and conditioned every aspect of Clarke's position, from his orations, which were limited to the pulpit, to his literary work for the *Messenger*, which operated under its auspices. But the promising new vistas of that transcendental life of the heroically independent Emersonian poet came with the extraordinarily demanding cost of abandoning the financial, institutional, and spiritual security of the Unitarian faith. Although the Unitarian Church offered predictability and safety, Cranch could not resist the careening energy of his artistic ambition spurring him to flee the establishment.

The three years after reading Emerson's *Nature* saw Cranch accelerate in a feverish rush toward the world of art and poetry, impelled by such events as Emerson's lecture series "The Present Age" in December 1839. This period, which is the central focus of this chapter, witnessed the transformation of a multitalented young minister into a promising Emersonian protégé. Cranch's apprenticeship began with his correspondence with Emerson that led to the publication of his verse in the May 1840 *Dial* and extended through his volume of *Poems* in 1844. The literary mentorship commenced precisely when Cranch had first discovered his passion for painting; he would turn transcendental philosophy into verse and landscape art in celebration of and gratitude toward Emerson, his new patron and mentor whose insights he had immortalized in his myriad caricatures. Cranch first visited Emerson in August 1840, one month after beginning an apprenticeship in landscape painting in Washington. With careers in painting and poetry rising simultaneously, it is ironic that visual art would lead him astray from the Concord circle, since caricature, a rudimentary visual art, originally served as his means of accessing, understanding, and even humanizing Emerson.

The lively spirit of those caricatures exuded the playful character for which Cranch and his work became known. Many critics, from Edgar Allan Poe on, have commented, usually with reference to his caricatures and his musical prowess, that Cranch was the most charming and humorous of the transcendentalists.[6] The caricatures represent not only Cranch's wit, but also the wit that was always already inherent in Emerson's mad phrasings, sparkling lyricism, and acerbic criticism. It was not simply that Cranch had a sense of humor—a seeming rarity in light of other more austere protégés such as Jones Very and Charles Newcomb—but more precisely, that he was capable of apprehending and literally drawing out Emerson's own. The caricatures attest to the youth's dreams of training under Emerson for a literary career; if he could find the playfulness in Emerson, he might also be capable of versifying his transcendental metaphysics in an equally exuberant and fresh way. By 1842, Cranch's induction into the world of professional poetry was confirmed with the appearance of his verse in Rufus Griswold's *Poets and Poetry of America*. As he began to take strides toward a successful career in poetry, he became the best pupil of William McLeod, his painting instructor. McLeod, however, was not Emerson, and landscapes were not poems, despite how Cranch reached for the transcendental divine through images of nature in both forms. This dual interest mounted pressure on Cranch to choose between these two mentors and career paths in the increasingly specialized commercial markets for literature and art.

Compounding this tension between these professional paths was Cranch's early spiritual crisis. His multiple talents, instead of making Cranch a mere dilettante, speak to a more profound spiritual crisis that belies the superficiality associated with aesthetic dabbling for amusement.[7] Emerson would have dismissed Cranch outright had he sensed such pretension. Having approached transcendentalism from the perspective of a struggling young minister—freshly graduated from the Harvard Divinity School, licensed to preach and traversing the new nation in search of a church that would finally ordain him—Cranch grappled with his desire to replace his faith in the Unitarian God. Emerson's "New School," as he described it to his father, "preaches the spirit rather than the letter."[8] At this early stage, his considerable painting skills had not yet matured enough to convince him that he could access the divine through oil and canvas, leaving him with a fresh hunger for the Newness and an attendant dedication to the vocation of transcendental poetry.

Illustrating the New Philosophy

After logging thousands of miles during several years of preaching in a dizzying array of towns, Cranch underwent what David Robinson describes as a "serious emotional crisis."[9] Exhaustion from travel and the galling realization that the meanings of his sermons had been lost or misconstrued conspired to rob him of his spirit. While he seemed blacklisted from service in some areas, his attempts at veiled radicalism in others were received curiously. His convictions emerged meek and muffled in subterfuge: "I have not attacked Calvinistic doctrines by name, but indirectly; and this I could not avoid, if I wished to preach what I believe to be truth." Much to his chagrin, he was far too cautious: "Many good orthodox people thought I preached sound doctrine, and even a good old ultra-Universalist lady was pleased" with his gospel. This was not the reception he had anticipated, and it led to a sense of profound isolation, "the feeling of desertion and of standing alone which one experiences in the Unitarian pulpit here." That sense of desertion, Cranch believed, could be remedied through "larger earnestness, directness, voice, gesture, and unction." He searched for a tonic for this "reserved *secretive*" masking of his inner longing for an Emersonian outburst on the scale of the Harvard Divinity School

Address. His goal was liberation from "this besetting diffidence [that] lies at the root of all my reserve that keeps me again and again silent and cold, when *no one* could tell how deep and strong the stream which ran hidden within."[10]

Many of Cranch's letters and journals from this time reveal such self-criticism and disappointment in his own compromised principles. Art and literature promised him total freedom to express his transcendental conviction. But he did not construe the aesthetic life as a simple substitute for organized religion and the ministerial profession.[11] Cranch himself was quite candid in pointing out that transcendentalism was not necessarily a unified movement, let alone a strict quasi-denomination of secular worshipers.[12] "Strangely enough," Cranch wrote in a piece entitled "Transcendentalism" for the *Western Messenger* in 1841, the year he officially abandoned the Unitarian ministry, "all the 'New Lights' of Philosophy and Theology, in foreign countries as well as in our own, however independent in thought, are, by a singular mode of generalizing, lumped together into a 'Sect,' honored with the cognomen of 'New School,' and 'Transcendentalists.'" He could not resist the humor in the situation, reflecting that "It might amuse almost, to see how this love of wholesale classification melts down obvious differences persuading us that this new movement . . . is not a many headed monster . . . but is *one*-headed, and may and must die, as only 'the latest form of infidelity.'"[13] Theological rebellion indeed characterized the movement, but as Emerson also emphasized, not to replace old-guard Unitarianism with a new clearly defined standard. Like Cranch, Emerson would also make a concerted effort to point out the very real diversity among transcendentalist ranks, in keeping with the core principle of radical tolerance of individualized spirituality. "There is no such thing as a Transcendental *party;* that there is no pure Transcendentalist; that we know of none but prophets and heralds of such philosophy," he argued, distancing even himself from the role of prophet to the many disciples he mentored at the time (*CW*, 1:205). Emerson preached no uniform "gospel" to his followers, but instead sought what he might learn from them first, and then proceeded to guide them aesthetically and professionally according to their own strengths. Cranch had held firm even as late as 1882 that Emerson "dared to ope the windows to the breeze/ Of Nature, when sectarians shuddering frowned,/ While through the close air of their cloistered ease/ The leaves of creeds fell fluttering to the ground."[14]

Cranch's letter to his father, sounding a more gently persuasive tone than the mocking belligerent one in "Transcendentalism," underscored how untenable it is to ascribe theological coherence to the movement. In the letter Cranch reassured his father that he had not fled to some bizarre heathen sect, but instead joined a philosophical movement with unique spiritual dimensions. In the loosest sense they might share a faith "grounded in what is deepest in the soul. And his philosophy is spiritual; is religious in the highest degree, for it effectually removes all possibility of skepticism by proving man to be created a religious being, a being who has an inner light . . . whereby he acquires a knowledge of God and duty and spiritual things." In the next paragraph, he affirmed that "my faith is as strong as it ever was, in the truth and the divine origin of Christianity," and that "there is nothing in anything [Emerson] says, which is inconsistent with Christianity."[15] Even in those areas, he would be forced to reconcile his liberal leanings to the doctrinaire, not the least important of which was his own father.

Cranch would maintain his faith in Christianity even after abandoning his aspiration to become an ordained Unitarian minister. His faith had already been deeply shaken by his unsuccessful attempt at a career, and thus his capacity to find God increasingly depended on the development of his poetic skill and artistic palette. Cranch's vocational crisis was not that of a dilettante trading religious duty for aestheticism, vocation for inclination.[16] Instead he was pitted between professions and faiths, all of which he took equally seriously. Cranch would only choose an occupation in which he could locate the divine through his creativity. His caricatures, oddly enough, showed signs that he would find his professional and spiritual future in the visual arts.

It may appear that Cranch's caricatures of Emersonian wisdom, the metaphorical icons of his thought, are more interested in apprehending how the "earthy diction" of his mentor's insights "teeter on the verge of the ridiculous," as one critic has observed, than in locating any divine source in them.[17] On one level the drawings indeed highlight the humorous results of literalizing Emerson's figurative language. They render absurd mismatched images and amalgamations of human figures and natural phenomena, from dogs and cats to melons and trees. Cranch pokes fun at a jejune reader's apprehension of Emerson's claims in cartoon depictions of his outlandish metaphors. He takes delight in alternative anti-institutional notions of accepting God by way of individual ecstatic encounters with nature. In these scenes, nature is not an externalized aesthetic object to be admired from a distance, but instead becomes an extension of the self. The famous transparent eyeball strides barefoot with clouds canopying his head, for example, a garish icon of heightened sensitivity distilled into the power of vision to filter and mingle with nature. Other drawings more emphatically capture ecstatic Emersonian moments, much like Thoreau's exaltation in "Ktaadn" for "coming into contact with it—rocks, trees, wind on our cheeks! The solid earth! The *actual* world! The *common sense! Contact! Contact!*" Thoreau's immersion is so deep that it sends conventional knowledge of identity and geography into blissful oblivion. "*Who* are we? *Where* are we?" he asks, exulting in the lack of substantial answers in light of nature's deeper claims on categories that otherwise pretend to neatly define our lives.[18]

Such an ecstatic encounter with nature that abandons reason, to the brink of madness, is the subject of Cranch's illustration of Emerson's "I fear to think how glad I am." There is silliness indeed in finding a joy in nature that abandons reason and control over commonly held notions of conventional identity to effectively scare the wits out of the philosopher. He depicts Emerson wildly running through a rainstorm, his house and field tiny in the background, his exuberant body in the foreground splashing in a puddle, with his right knee and arm raised high as his foot is about to come splashing into another puddle. To the right in the corner a small onlooker, proportionally tiny, since his head reaches only to Emerson's knee, looks on aghast with mouth gaping and arms outstretched, seeming to call out for him to control this reckless and wild abandon. Can the soul unleashed in nature really be capable of this? he seems to ask. His affirmation lies in the all too ridiculous and human bursts of exuberance, especially in the context of antebellum propriety, as seen in the formally attired figures of both the trekking eyeball and Emerson dancing in the rain, a rustic forerunner of Gene Kelly's delightful puddle-splashing, umbrella-spinning urban frolic in *Singin' in the Rain*, a thirsting for nature's shower amid so many lampposts and concrete sidewalks.[19]

Such "Emersoniana," as Cranch called these drawings, are the only known illustrations of Emerson's writing. Clarke sensed the novelty and quality in the drawings of the Phi Beta Kappa Address, and thus mailed them immediately to Emerson. In an effort to show solidarity with Emerson, whose oration had incited the ire of conservative Unitarians led by Andrews Norton, Clarke hoped the drawings would cheer Emerson during the darkness of the siege he was enduring. Indeed, the caricatures functioned to remind Emerson of the inherent optimism at the core of his ideals, even in an address so clearly bewailing the shortcomings of their contemporary intellectual culture. "The gravest things have also a comic side," Clarke assured Emerson, as evidenced in the "talent in drawing diablerie & such like" of one "C. P. Cranch." In addition to restoring Emerson's characteristic optimism, Clarke was also introducing him to Cranch, an admiring youth with a unique appreciation for his philosophy: "If you should ever meet him I would ask him to make some sketches with his pen" (*L*, 2:190).

Among Cranch's "Emersoniana," human figures often conjoin with either nature or machinery to illustrate the two contrary states of exalted inspiration and exploited reified labor. "The mechanic a machine" captions a human figure whose limbs are flat boards attached by hinges, his body angled at work with a hammer and saw. Cranch illustrates "The sailor the rope of a ship" with a man whose torso and arms are coiled rope (*L*, 2:190). Emerson's attack on the reifying effects of the specialized professions that transform workers into their tools meets with the counter example of figures unified with nature. Interestingly, they are neither seriously nor heroically rendered, and appear just as ridiculous as the men ossified by their trades. That is, Emerson's superlative, outlandish metaphorical language designed to stun the reader out of his complacency often makes the communion with nature he touts in opposition to the commercial world appear ridiculous. Cranch has neither misinterpreted nor trivialized Emerson in this sense, for it was Emerson who acknowledged how "we seek with insatiable desire to forget ourselves, to be surprised out of our propriety, to lose our sempiternal memory and to do something without knowing how or why." Cranch's drawings capture that reckless abandon that surrenders to intuition in all of its hilarity and incongruity with the sober world of top hats and sallow coats, confirming that "the way of life is wonderful; it is by abandonment" (*CW*, 2:190).

Once immersed in nature, the Emersonian figures find themselves not in romantic isolation, but busily moving, connecting, and interacting with elements of nature that are themselves surprised by the figure's gleeful embrace. Cranch's landscapes also convey a busy and kinetic genial nature, with sharp curving lines and interconnected clusters of activity drawing the eye from rivers to streams, from roots to branches. This technique is visible in Emerson's naturalist "tying things together—discovering roots running under ground [and] remote things cohere [and] flower out from one stem," a figure Cranch depicts as a tree whose underground roots are visible, as heads, human figures, a pumpkin, and a potted plant grow out of the branches.[20] The focal point is a man holding a branch of the tree with one hand and the tail of a rather surprised and unwilling hog with the other. This is a brilliant satirical rendering of the cohesion of man and nature, both beasts and vegetation, so crucial to Emerson's thinking. Not only is the physical link between humans and animals tenuous—especially in grabbing a resistant hog by the tail—constructed artifice also awkwardly asserts itself into the blend in the form of a potted plant and a house on a hill that appears also to be growing from a branch. Cranch's own skepticism toward the applicability of refined philosophy to raw nature presents itself in his images of civilized humanity's artificial constructs clashing with the organic world. This attitude is absent from his more believing renditions of the divine in the organic world in his later landscape paintings.

Though irreverent, none of Cranch's satirical drawings convey a mean spirit, but instead seem to delight in the exaggerated images and metaphors Emerson favored in his prose. Indeed, they acknowledge the visual quality of his prose, featuring mismatches and transpositions of elements in conventional scenes to render them otherwise apparently daft and nonsensical visually, if not metaphorically and philosophically profound. "The good man angles with himself; he needs no other bait" is Emerson's claim that one's best resource for attaining sustenance is his own skill and ingenuity.[21] Cranch captures the literal image of a man dangling by a fishing pole, with his toe dipping into a pond and a wide-eyed school of fish closing in on him, one springing from the surface with teeth bared. The fish seem joyous, the man terrified, in this humorous rendering of Emerson's metaphor, again depicting figures of nature shocked at the sudden commingling and interaction of a human in the natural world. The images function for the budding Emersonian as a way of imagining his own immersion in nature and the folly it might entail.

Elsewhere, Cranch pokes fun at the silliness of conventional behavior (people as bugs, women lashing with whiplike tongues) condemned by Emerson. "Men in the world of today are bugs," reads the caption on an image of a Franklinesque "great man," rendered like Swift's Gulliver to so many Lilliputians, sweeping away human figures as he barges along: "They are content to be brushed like flies from the path of a great man." An image of men with eyes up and down their limbs says: "We are lined with eyes; we see with our feet." The drawing also corresponds with the emphasis on eyes and feet in the famous transparent eyeball image. One piece, titled "Moral Influence of the Dial," depicts a man reclining on a bed with a glass of wine and a copy of the *Dial* on the floor, his maid polishing his boots. The caption asks, "Why for work art thou striving, . . . To the soul that is living all things shall be brought," as the figure justifies his self-indulgent leisurely repose through the *Dial*'s aversion to acquisitive market-driven behavior. The image cleverly exposes the privileged socio-economic status of *Dial* readers, which enabled most of them to renounce specialization and excessive labor based on transcendental principle. The presence of the maid and the wine offer an alternative view to the now prevalent emblem of self-culture as taking place primarily at Walden Pond and the surrounding woods. In addition to lampooning the labor implications of the transcendental philosophy, Cranch also parodies the intellectual culture of transcendentalism. Like his illustration of Emerson fearing "to think how glad I am" as he romps in the rain is a drawing of Theodore Parker lunging at a bookshelf while the bookstore owner raises his hands in fear nearby; a dog and cat race after him, teeth bared. "TP's supposed delight on visiting a book store or library in Germany," the caption reads, highlighting the transcendental reliance on European models, particularly its overexuberance for German romanticism, as seen in the innumerable volumes of Schiller and Goethe that lined the shelves of Elizabeth Peabody's bookshop on West Street in Boston.[22]

Cranch's concern for the formation of a unique American literary tradition stemming from "The American Scholar" surfaces in an image of a man stepping from a watercraft made of Shakespeare and Virgil volumes onto one with "July 4" on its spine. The caption reads, "They pin me down." This private collection of *Illustrations of the New Philosophy* suggests Swift's Gulliver and many of the political cartoons appearing in the periodical press at the time. The "great man" drawing particularly anticipates Cranch's Swiftian children's books, *The Last of the Huggermuggers: A Giant Story*, and *Kobboltozo: A Sequel to the Last of the Huggermuggers*, which he illustrated himself in similar fashion. By the time of their publication in 1856 and 1857, Cranch had already moved beyond his transcendental apprenticeship, as had all the Emerson protégés to varying degrees by the 1850s.[23] It is noteworthy that these two children's volumes were the most commercially successful books of his entire career, eclipsing the narrow circulation of *Poems* (1844) he dedicated to Emerson.

The Poetic Apprenticeship

Whereas James Freeman Clarke gave Cranch hope during his work with him in Louisville in 1836 that a Unitarian minister could also espouse core transcendental principles, the professional fate of John Sullivan Dwight all but dashed it by 1841. When Cranch was preaching at the church of Frederic Henry Hedge, who was one of the original members of the Transcendental Club, he was overcome with a profound depression caused by the news that Dwight, his best friend and former Harvard roommate, had been forced to resign from his pulpit for his Emersonian sympathies. The "trouble in my head and brain" he complained of arose from this conflict Clarke had originally resolved for him.[24] The buoyant and charismatic Clarke had encouraged, guided, and even collaborated on Cranch's caricatures. This early tutelage of Cranch not only provided an outlet for his artistic expression, but also reflects his brimming optimism and playful assimilation of Emerson's views. Dwight's coerced resignation subsequently cast a severe shadow of doubt over Cranch's hope for his own career.

Cranch responded by going to the source of his inspiration and soliciting Emerson himself to assist in placing his poems in a literary journal and, ideally, to adopt him into the exclusive circle of his protégés. There he might enjoy the liberation "As in days of old when Plato freed/ The Athenian youths into a heavenlier sphere," as he described in "Emerson," the poetic tribute he later wrote on the occasion of his friend and mentor's passing. Emerson's round desk at Bush was the hub of a network Cranch later recalled as "a bond of brotherhood."[25]

Sensing this liberation and acceptance into a literary circle he had admired and wished to join for years, Cranch's return to the East from Louisville was one of the most euphoric moments of his life. During that winter of 1839–40, his attendance at the first three of Emerson's ten lectures on "The Present Age" dawned a new horizon of his career. Theodore Parker, whose exuberance and almost gymnastic enthusiasm Cranch found infectious, became for him the "learned Theban" and "the very athlete of scholars." Writing to his sister Margaret, Cranch reported, "We have transcendental and aesthetic gatherings at a great rate—and they make me sing at them all . . . in fact I am quite a singing lion." He passed his evenings immersed in stimulating literary culture like no other in the West: "I go into Ripleys about 9 . . . and drink ale" or "go to the oratorios—sometimes to lectures—sometimes to parties." With the caricatures preceding him via Clarke, word had spread of his talent, so that he was showered with praise and warmly received at each of his stops throughout Boston. The time was ripe to submit his first poems, "Enosis" and "To the Aurora Borealis," to Emerson for publication in the *Dial*. The poems were accepted with great praise from Emerson. Their appearance in that first issue of the *Dial*, which appeared in late June 1840, paradoxically precipitated the nervous depression that the news of Dwight's dismissal the following summer would exacerbate. His father's alarm at his apparent shift in alliances was met with Cranch's defensive letter of July 1840 discussed earlier. The following month, he met with Emerson, a full year before Dwight's crucifixion by transcendentalist dissenters.

The confluence of all these events, and not just the singular effect of Dwight's professional demise, conspired to descend on Cranch with tremendous force, creating a vocational crisis that thundered suddenly into his life. Indeed, the evidence points to a crisis in affiliation between the Unitarian ministry and Emersonian transcendentalism, which likely plagued him during his last preaching stint in Maine. The confluence of Cranch's submission of his poems to Emerson immediately before leaving for this journey dramatizes the closeness of the two vocations that he was hoping to reconcile as Clarke had. But in Emerson, Cranch found a different, more radical model. The depth and intensity of transcendental conviction ruled out the possibility of also preaching for the Unitarian Church. It is precisely at this volatile crossroads in Cranch's life that he began in earnest to cultivate a career as a professional poet, and to retract, question, and sour on old alliances. Intensifying this phase of fraught negotiation between desired and forbidden commitment in Cranch's life was his mutual declaration of love to a married woman he met through Dwight. The event was particularly telling of his more general desire at the time to act on his aesthetic intuition in life-changing ways that would violate conventional social behavior while riding the stimulating wave of ongoing conversation, singing, playing the flute, and reading German. Prior to the event, which ended amicably, Cranch had also made another impulsive declaration of love, this time to Emersonian transcendentalism against the vocational mores of the Unitarian Church and those of his father. The collision between these forces was indeed traumatizing, making for a rough transition from the pulpit to the artistic life.

The onset of Cranch's three-year nervous disorder coincided precisely with that of his poetic apprenticeship under Emerson. The immense pressure of launching a mentorship for a career as a professional poet appears to have triggered the plaguing anxiety that began around the time of Emerson's invitation in August 1840 and ended with the publication of *Poems* in 1844. His volume of verse marked the end of his poetic apprenticeship under Emerson, and the beginning of his concerted effort to establish a career in painting. The prospect of finding the divine in an anti-creed like transcendentalism predicated on the independent discovery of the Universal Being in nature mounted unique and acute spiritual pressure on Cranch. Despite his overt misgivings toward the ministerial vocation, he responded to this pressure by maintaining his Unitarian faith, if at a distance from church politics, the rest of his life. This commitment to the faith is evident in his defensive letter to his father, which nonetheless touts the spirituality of the New School.

The derivative nature of the early poems Cranch sent to Emerson speaks to his spiritual vulnerability and attendant dependence on Emerson's philosophy during this time of vocational crisis in his life. Many have noted how "Enosis" and "Correspondences" particularly read like versified summaries of Emerson's philosophy.[26] Cranch had not found the independence of vision yet to discover sublime ethereal energy through his poetry. Instead, he replicated Emerson's views, pantomiming his mentor reading God in the book of nature that corresponds with the soul, in such lines as "Nature is but a scroll; God's handwriting thereon." Cranch's title and keynote for his poem come directly from chapter 4 of *Nature*, titled "Language," in which Emerson celebrates the "radical correspondence between visible things and human thoughts." In the first line of "Correspondences," which posits in a philosophical tone that "all things in Nature are beautiful types to the soul that can read them," Cranch draws from Emerson's observation in "Language" that "this immediate dependence of language upon nature, this conversion of outward phenomenon into a type . . . in human life, never loses its power to affect us." Cranch's first verse ends with the assertion that "man unconsciously uses figures of speech every moment," which "through our commonest speech illumine the path of our thoughts." These lines do not so much invoke, as desperately cling to, Emerson's original claim that "man is an analogist" whose "power to connect his thought with its proper symbol, and so utter it, depends on the simplicity of his character" as a measure of "his desire to communicate [truth] without loss."[27]

But to paint Cranch as a meek mimic of his master here does an injustice to the broader sources he drew upon for his poetry. "Correspondences" does indeed render Emersonian thought, especially from *Nature* as discussed above. But Cranch also appears to have been influenced perhaps even more by Emanuel Swedenborg's doctrine of correspondence between inner and outer worlds. Dwight, Cranch's Harvard roommate and closest friend, was deeply immersed in the Swedish philosopher's thought, as evidenced by his publication, along with Charles A. Dana, of more than thirty articles conjoining Swedenborg's principle of harmonialism with Charles Fourier's theory of attractive industry in Brook Farm's journal *The Harbinger*. The versified philosophy of "Correspondences" and "Inworld" and "Outworld" derives from an influence in Cranch's life that predates his meeting with Emerson and thus draws directly from Dwight. Cranch's passion for Swedenborg came initially from Dwight and was distilled in his reading of *Nature*.[28]

The core principle of self-reliant radical individualism faced the socially vivacious and sunny Cranch with the prospect of austere isolation. But he knew from observing Emerson that solitude could also bring an august dignity and poise. In "Enosis," which means union, Cranch struggles with the isolation attendant to the transcendental renunciation of the superficiality and fragmentation of perfunctory social interaction. His stark image of an abandoned place of worship, "We are columns left alone,/ Of a temple once complete," points to his own fears of the consequences of renouncing the ministry for an Emersonian poetic apprenticeship. But his hope ultimately wins out in the belief that all souls will eventually blend when they are fed by nature, "like parted drops of rain/ Swelling till they meet and run,/ Shall be absorbed again, /Melting, flowing into one."[29] The promise of nature mending his soul, significantly, still exists in the poem as a deferred dream, rather than a fully realized union with a community of like-minded companions and supporters. August 1840 was indeed a time when Cranch seriously questioned whether a subversive and controversial literary movement could fully replace the automatic and institutionally safeguarded fraternity of the Unitarian ministry.

Cranch's self-doubt arose from his status as a neophyte poet not yet capable of harnessing the sublime in his verse. His spiritual crisis rose and fell in direct proportion to his competence as a poet, and later, an artist. Until he could amass enough expertise in his verse and paintings, he would struggle with misplaced spirituality. The vocational crisis manifested itself first in what would otherwise appear to be an unproblematic, and even typical, letter of introduction to Emerson accompanying "Enosis" and "To the Aurora Borealis." The letter reveals three father figures contesting for control of his professional and spiritual life. Not only was he potentially parting with his own biological father, Cranch was also making strides toward supplanting Clarke, his colleague and confidante, with Emerson. Clarke advised Cranch on an early draft of "Correspondences," the ultimate proclamation of his faith in Emerson's philosophy. Cranch's letter opens with him asking, "if the enclosed pieces are worthy of a place in the New Magazine . . . will you stand as their godfather?" His projection of Emerson into a surrogate for his increasingly skeptical biological father combines with his tenuous hold on God the Father in the wake of his ministerial struggle. Cranch credits Emerson with providing him a new anti-institutional non-denominational spiritual lease on life, since "I have owed to you more quickening influences and more elevating views in shaping my faith, than I can ever possibly express to you." Two days later, Emerson's response satisfied Cranch's request threefold by accepting his poems for publication in the *Dial*, admitting him into "our Cambridge circle . . . because it is not confined to Boston, though it does not extend far," and most important, inviting him to visit alone "to see how well our experiences tally."[30] Cranch was overwhelmed. He was no exception to the frequently stultifying effects of the over-exuberant welcoming embrace Emerson applied to every one of his disciples, a response that drove Charles Newcomb to refuse replying to his correspondence for a protracted period, and falsely led Ellery Channing to believe that his poetry needed no further development despite its unfinished appearance.

The prospect of meeting with Emerson in August 1840 obviously imposed undue pressure on Cranch. The situation placed him in a position of making what he knew was an all-determining personal impression on the individual who had meant the world to him for inspiring the revitalizing core values shaping his very sense of self. Cranch could not bear making the visit alone, as Emerson suggested he should, so he recruited George Ripley and Theodore Parker to make the trip with him by foot from Boston to Concord. On their way, the trio gathered Bronson Alcott before arriving at Emerson's doorstep. Safely folded into the familiar company of Emerson's established friends and associates, Cranch happily receded into the background. Had he made the visit alone and been fully himself, free of the nervous depression plaguing him, he might have unleashed the full range of his charm, humor, and multiple talents, perhaps establishing the relationship on firmer, more intimate grounds. As it was, Cranch was the subdued opposite of his extroverted self who dazzled the associates of Brook Farm with his multiple talents. Emerson could see the youth was exceedingly nervous in his presence, and took it upon himself to do most of the talking and entertaining. He "read poetry—of his own— of his anonymous young lady correspondents, and of old Ben Jonson's."[31] They filled the hours trekking through the woods behind Walden Pond and picked huckleberries, as Cranch did his best to contain his anxiety.

In the context of declaring love to a married woman, leaving the ministry, and successfully courting Emerson much to the chagrin of his offended father, Cranch faced chronic bouts of depression. "Painting seemed to relax him during the spells of depression when he could not write or think," DeWolfe observes.[32] Painting not only served as a tonic for his emotional strife. More specifically it also functioned to return him to the pastime that had originally drawn him to Emerson, and with it the original principles on which he had first encountered transcendentalism. Painting had pointed him toward the divine in ways that poetry had not, since most of his efforts were directed toward replicating Emersonian doctrine in verse. In painting, he could harness a more original medium through which to access the transcendental divine in nature in ways that would develop into a more unique and less derivative vocational identity. Accessing the divine was predicated on finding an aesthetic medium conducive to it, and painting provided that outlet. It is telling indeed that the activity that would calm his nerves from his depressive bouts triggered by his vocational anxiety would position him toward the career to which he was best suited.

This darker, conflicted Cranch is corroborated by Lawrence Buell's biographical portrait of him, which importantly recasts old images of him as a carefree pleasure seeker, entertaining guests at Brook Farm and amusing the children with animal noises. Buell notes that the ideal concept of communion with nature, "though designed to inspire, could ironically leave one feeling isolated from others and despondent."[33] Julie M. Norko has cast this malaise as a conflict with vocational duty, to which I would add that the spiritual conflict became in essence a professional one. David Robinson has also looked at the somber side of Cranch's later poetry written specifically to process the emotional pain of his break with Robert Browning, with whom he had become extremely close while living in Europe.[34] There is no question that Cranch's professional ascendancy in poetry was imminent, particularly among the *Dial* group. No other poet contributed more to the first two issues, as two poems appeared in the October 1840 *Dial* and eight more in January 1841. Clarke had also praised his verse, and Greeley reprinted "To the Aurora Borealis" in his *Tribune*. Cranch had established himself as the preeminent transcendental poet; his visit to Emerson therefore functioned more as a coronation than a social call. On the surface, the publication history of his poetry would make it appear as though "the summer of 1840 was a happy one for Cranch," as Joel Myerson has claimed.[35] But his successes in amassing notoriety as the most widely published transcendental poet only redoubled his vocational crisis.

Further testifying to his searching spirituality at this time is that he seriously considered joining Brook Farm by July 1841. Emerson's protégés showed skepticism toward the experiment in communal living at Roxbury,

Massachusetts, with the notable exception of Charles Newcomb, who had become a fixture there since its inception. Newcomb, perhaps the least employable and professionally inclined of the disciples, found refuge from the literary market and Emerson's pressure to publish at the transcendental commune. Brook Farm functioned similarly for Cranch, who at his most wayward, with "no plans; no prospects, save of the vaguest sort," toyed with the idea of joining, despite misgivings toward its pretensions of providing a "panacea" or "pitch plaster for the healing of the nations."[36] Once there, Cranch hardly could be described as spearheading the ideological and political dimensions of the experiment into a significant future. The ebullient Cranch never engaged politics as he had earlier in his defenses of Emerson and the New School, but instead turned Brook Farm into something of a party, bringing his multiple and entertaining talents to charm and woo its denizens.[37] Escapist pleasure best describes his stay there, as he did little to forward his poetry or painting careers. Marianne Dwight witnessed the group transfixed by his "sweetest and most delightful music" carrying them away with his "sweet, rich voice." The effect was so arresting and "strange," because it "seemed like a dream, from which I had just awakened." Dwight and company had received him as a charming musician with a dreamy voice. He had all but seduced her with his painting lessons, as her description casts her as a smitten pupil to his handsome and captivating art instructor. "I have come nearer to him than ever before," she confessed to her friend Anna Parsons, delighting in how "he has sat at the table and painted with me every day that he has been here," and even produced a work specifically for "my own unworthy, grateful and happy self." Not only was his music and painting welcome entertainment for the Brook Farm associates, his humor was on colorful display, since he "mimicked for us all manners of insects and animals."[38] If ever there were a time when Cranch perfectly fit the description of the dabbling dilettante, it was during his stay at Brook Farm. But in the greater context of his professional predicament, his visits appear as attempts at easing the pressure of choosing among his competing vocations, and thus a temporary release from his more intense training to develop his skills and command recognition in the markets for art and literature.

The years from 1840 to 1844, bracketed by Cranch's visit with Emerson and the publication of his *Poems*, marked the young poet's concerted effort to expand into the magazine market with his poetry. But a long silence passed between Emerson and Cranch since that magical summer of 1840 before the correspondence resumed. Cranch had sent his next packet of poems to Emerson with the excuse that he had been struggling for months to produce anything new. "They were written last winter, since which time an affection of the head has indisposed me almost entirely to any inspiration of mental labor," he wrote, alluding to the nervous disorder that had set in upon their first meeting. Emerson could read the signs of vocational crisis in Cranch's immediate transition in his comment that he had "lately taken very vigorously to landscape painting, which I am strongly tempted to follow in future instead of sermon writing." Oddly, he never mentioned poetry as a vocational option, instead pitting the ministry at odds with painting. "Whether I turn artist or not," presumably leaving poetry in the category of an avocation, "I become more and more inclined to sink the minister in the man, and abandon my present calling *in toto* as a profession." He blamed the institutionally coercive Unitarian Church for his facing such a troubling decision in the first place. "Verily our churches will force us to it whether we will or not," he declared, ending the paragraph in dangling unresolved paralysis, a rhetorical maneuver obviously soliciting Emerson's advice on the matter.[39] He then lavished Emerson with praise for his work, clearly signaling his own inclination for a liberating career dedicated to the production of Emerson-inspired poetry.

As Channing had done in the last lines of his introductory poem to Emerson, Cranch intimated the answer he preferred to hear from his mentor. Sinking "the minister in the man" was Cranch's preference, as he proclaimed his lifelong commitment to Emerson in terms of his newly formed faith. Writing to a former Unitarian minister radically at odds with the church, one can hardly image Cranch longing for the pulpit when he confided, "Your thoughts have had a deep influence on my faith and opinions." Right on cue, Emerson replied as Cranch had hoped, advising in no uncertain terms "you must quit the pulpit as a profession" and instead "serve and celebrate [the nation] with your pencil." Oddly, Emerson made this statement after his opening lauding the youth for his excellent poetry, and his reliance upon it to fill the pages of the *Dial*, extending a lengthy apology and explanation for not including "Outworld" with the poem "Inworld," which did appear in the issue. He promised that "the piece shall appear whole in the next number, with apology for the divorce in the last," a gesture revealing sensitivity to Cranch's craft and an earnest attempt at advancing his career in poetry. Strikingly, Emerson mentioned the prospect of poetry only in passing at the end of the letter and did not emphasize it as a promising alternative to the ministry. This is likely because Emerson presumed that Cranch would go on writing poems only as a secondary occupation, given his pupil's reference to his nervous condition and failure to write since the previous winter. Alert to this sign of disinclination toward authorship as his primary source of income, Emerson adroitly followed Cranch's own leads and reinforced, in true transcendental fashion, his disciple's intuition implied in the previous letter.

Writer's block for various reasons, usually involving compromised health, would crop up among his protégés, particularly the taciturn and laconic Charles Newcomb, from whom Emerson could not inspire sustained production despite repeated efforts. Since Cranch had posed his vocational choice as strictly between the two options of the pulpit and the easel, and alluded to "an affection of the head" that prevented him from profitable literary production, Emerson was happy to endorse the career in art that Cranch so obviously longed for. In keeping with his care for his protégé's financial well-being, Emerson gave his blessing to such a career, which would demand immediate financial sacrifices, but "great compensation will overpay their integrity, and fidelity to their own heart." On the basis that his art will place him in the good graces of "the most polished societies," Emerson exhorted his pupil on to winning "the multitude"—now including poetry in his formulation—who "when they hear the song or see the picture do not suspect its profound origin." His wish for "the richest success [to] attend your pencil or pen" again hints at the possibility of poetry, if only as a secondary interest to art in adding to his riches, which is ostensibly spiritual according to his rhetoric, yet implying everywhere financial concern in the diction of wealth achieved from favorable audience reception in both "polished societies" and "the multitude."[40]

Ungraceful Daubing

The month before Emerson's encouraging reply to Cranch, he had mentioned receipt of his poems in a letter to Margaret Fuller, who was then editing the *Dial*. He reported that the verse "will fill two or three pages" of the journal "if you are in want of more matter for this number." He said he would have immediately sent the poems along to her were it not "for [their] most ungraceful daubing of our poor merits in the letter prefixed" (*L*, 2:450). This alluded to Cranch's unabashed and even excessive praise, reaching the point of hero worship, which Emerson humorously called "daubing" to describe his pupil's awkward ingratiating concluding paragraph (in which Cranch even begged "pardon for such blunt praise") as the crude blotches of an unskillful painter.[41] Since Cranch's verse had appeared in the previous number of the *Dial*, Emerson was confident that these new poems would also be suitable, and thus selected eight of them for publication, among which "The Riddle" won the favor of Horace Greeley, who reprinted it in his *Tribune*. Bearing the distinction of publishing the greatest number of poems in the *Dial* shortly after achieving that honor with the *Western Messenger*, Cranch appeared poised to enter a long and fruitful relationship with Emerson. But Emerson's polite reply to Cranch in October masked his playful yet cutting remark about him to Fuller the month before. "Ungraceful daubings," of course, would never suit the *Dial;* Emerson found Cranch's work competent but sorely lacking in originality. Further, he knew that Cranch was bound for a career in painting, so he did not continue to actively nurture and promote his pupil's verse. He had encouraged others like him, yet without such poetic gifts, to enter the painting profession. To Emerson, Cranch was a competent supplier of verse, polished but lacking original inspiration. Signs of Cranch's adoration for Emerson appear in his poem "The Prophet Unveiled," from 1839. Although the Emerson figure of the poems warns him "Not to be dazzled mothlike, by his flame/ But to go as independent as I came," Cranch cannot resist being utterly overwhelmed by Emerson's charismatic brilliance in "the lighted hall" with "Meteors of truth through beauty's sky still brightening." His imagery evokes stars, jewels, and soaring birds in an ecstatic tear of exultation. "Pearls prodigally rained, too large and fast," transfixing the young listener.[42] Cranch never recovered from Emerson fever, the intensity of which may have prevented a more human understanding of him and thus a more coequal and intimate working relationship.

Perhaps embarrassed by Cranch's adulation, Emerson never felt comfortable enough with him to nurture his poetry into a more unique vision. If his "ungraceful daubings" remark was an early foreshadowing of that issue, then by 1843 it would become fully voiced in his skeptical response to Cranch's proposal to publish a volume of his poetry. In the letter, Emerson finally talked business in a concrete sense to Cranch, and most of it was not encouraging. He was skeptical of the book's profitability in the New York and Boston markets, noting that many young writers were being forced to pay for the production of their own books. Whereas Cranch's poetry dominated the transcendental periodical press in terms of numbers of pieces accepted, his name was not widely enough known throughout the broader literary markets to make his poetry sell in book form. Periodical presses would continue to favor Cranch for his smooth, pleasing, and eminently readable style; his engaging personality shone through most of his submissions. But to enter the book trade with such fare put him at a disadvantage, because most readers could find his seemingly ubiquitous caliber of verse throughout cheaper periodicals. Emerson was well aware that the packet of poems included many that he himself had solicited, lauded, and published in the *Dial.* He was not abusing Cranch through an elaborate bait and switch so much as he was proffering wily advice as a seasoned veteran. Emerson was quite accurate in foretelling the fate that would befall Cranch's volume. Cranch resolved to publish it himself with Carey and Hart of Philadelphia, a press not listed among those Emerson reluctantly recommended he consult because there was so "little hope for success of the venture."[43]

Signing with Carey and Hart was a bold stroke of independence, made with the intention of breaking into the publishing world to begin amassing profits for a secure financial future not available in magazine writing. His hope was to gain enough profit from the 1844 *Poems* to secure his financial future in a way that magazine writing, at least in the esoteric venues in which he was appearing at the time, could not. His economic outlook was uncertain until he married Elizabeth De Windt, a wealthy descendant of John Adams. Their family home at Fishkill-on-the-Hudson would provide an ideal setting for his painting career. Elizabeth's father patronized Cranch's art by funding his first voyage to Europe. While abroad, Cranch enjoyed further fiscal backing from New England expatriates like William Wetmore Story, who went so far as to share his fortune with Cranch while abroad. Like Cranch, Story traveled overseas to develop his artistic skill and access the richer continental art market after abandoning a more conventional occupation, which for him was the law. His bond with Cranch spared no expense, as he granted his friend full access to his reserves as if he were close kin. "You ought to never need when I can help you. My purse, my dear friend, is ever at your service," he vowed to the man whose profile he had sketched while training in Boston. "Let us spend together and make life as happy as we can."[44]

Cranch's paintings never brought him the income he had hoped. From 1846 to 1849, sales of paintings returned only two thousand dollars in profit, barely a living wage. In 1850, he earned a meager eight hundred dollars. His income vigorously rebounded with the sale of his children's books published in 1856–57. After the smashing success of *The Last of the Huggermuggers*, publishers offered Cranch five hundred dollars for the sequel, *Kobboltozo*. The lavish production for these two volumes, with ornately decorated binding, met the rising demand for children's Christmas gifts. Both works were widely advertised and featured illustrations in the signature playful style Cranch had mastered in his whimsical caricatures of Emerson's writings. Publishers solicited a third work, which Cranch wrote, but it did not appear due to an international economic depression.[45] Decades later, Cranch returned to poetry after leaving it behind with his 1844 *Poems*.

Emerson had understood that Cranch wanted to be a painter and heartily endorsed that choice in 1841. But by 1844, he was highly skeptical of Cranch's sudden desire to collect his poetry into a salable volume, especially given his three-year bout with nervous depression that blocked his creative powers. It is telling of Cranch's desperation that he dedicated *Poems* to Emerson without first consulting him, a gesture that anticipated Whitman's exploitation of Emerson's letter in praise of *Leaves of Grass*. One can understand Emerson's rather perfunctory and conciliatory letter acknowledging receipt of "the beautiful little volume of poems," politely, yet with surprise, noting "the deeper obligation you had put me under, by the inscription." His graciousness intends to convey humbly that he is not worthy of such an honor, but it can hardly conceal his annoyance at the surprise inscription that may have struck him as self-serving. The letter is peppered with qualifiers like, "had you asked me beforehand," and "as you have thrust me into place." Further, Emerson's worry that his poor name will damage the reception of the book extends his humble gratitude, yet clearly underscores his original sense of the book's dubious chances in the market. "I must only hope that your fair and friendly book shall not suffer," he wrote, echoing his earlier prediction of its demise. Just as the 1843 letter shied away from a full acceptance of mentoring Cranch's poetic development, the 1844 letter noted rather disingenuously that "I should like to talk over with you very frankly this whole mystery and craft of poesy." Rather than specifying when and how that consultation might occur, Emerson instead referred Cranch to his published writing on the subject, specifically "my chapter on 'The Poet.'" Referring him to his writing, though kind, is of course not extending a concrete invitation to build "sweetness and elegance of versification" into the powerhouse he demands in "The Poet." Emerson does not come off as a warm and inviting potential mentor here, so much as a self-described "vigorous, cruel critic [who] demand[s] in the poet a devotion that seems hardly possible in our hasty, facile America." Hasty and facile, indeed, would also describe the manner with which Cranch assembled and published *Poems* against Emerson's cautionary advice. Further, his reference to recycled *Dial* poems that appeared in the volume as "old friends" placed Cranch's significance in the past tense, diminishing his priority as an active poet worthy of Emerson's close attention and care.[46]

Credit is due to Emerson for releasing Cranch from his debts to his mentor. Emerson could see that Cranch's career was shackled by his ideal definition of the poet's vocation. Cranch had initially felt he could repay Emerson only by becoming a poet, the most exalted occupation of all Emerson's writings on vocation. Compelled to "give all to have this," as he wrote in the poem "Soul Flower," Cranch the painter struggled, mainly out of gratitude to Emerson, to become a poet. *Poems* reads like the rhetoric of his first letter to Emerson, in which he almost begged his mentor to endorse his painting career, but followed through with poetry out of a sense of gratitude to the man who freed him from the ministry to pursue arts. Cranch of course knew poetry was the epitome of human expression to Emerson. He also knew Emerson was more muse than mentor when it came to art, because Emerson described himself as "necessarily a dull critic in art."[47]

Under Emerson's influence, Cranch would refine his concept of poetic inspiration according to his mentor's poem "Bacchus." In it, the poet metaphorically drinks of nature's pure wine for a "chaste" intoxication, which allows "seeming-solid walls of use/ [to] Open and flow." Wine is not a figure of reckless careening mysticism, but a channel into antiquity and "pleasure through all natures."[48] The influence of "Bacchus" on *Poems* is unmistakable. Cranch's "The Poet" attempts to signal his fulfillment of its definition of the ideal poet. He details his process of learning deeper, more serious truths than those of the carefree Harvard days described in the volume's opening poem, "College Lyfe," a nostalgic self-portrait of his life as a pupil prior to Emerson's influence. The insinuation is that Cranch began with a jejune and rambunctious spirit like that of his drawings of Emerson's quotes. But the charming drollery of his genial rhymes gives way to a darker, more mature vision in the succeeding pieces. "Strange harmony" resonates through his next poem in the volume, "Ode to the Wind," as the looming presence of nature brings a "melancholy winter wind . . . while the sleeping snow/ Lies like a death-trance, underneath the moon!" effectively sobering the frolicsome "College Lyfe."[49]

"I cannot paint that glorious dream," Cranch proclaims bitterly in "Music of Nature," intoning precisely his vocational crisis between poetry and painting. He regrets that "words are such cold things" that constrict his creative expression. "I can but give a gleam," he admits in the poem, allegorizing how his desire to become a painter has been stalled by his poetic efforts. "Music of Nature" ironically describes his painter's dream of light and vision, which is finally animated through a third medium of music. Artistic vision is unmistakably rendered in painterly terms of light throughout *Poems*, from the stars at the end of "College Lyfe" and at the heart of "To the Aurora Borealis" to the "ruby's gleam," "primal beam," and "color and light" shimmering throughout other verses.[50] In "Soul Flower" Cranch enters into the costs exacted by his vocational choice through the image of the sanctum of the "inner shrine" and "primal beam" that shines from the human heart despite storms of death and sin. He exhorts himself and readers to guard and watch that "inner shrine" figured in the soul flower beneath the sea that blooms despite "storms," "wrecks," and "bodies of men . . . drifting far overhead." In the final verse, the speaker asks a frantic series of four questions. The language sets up the requirements and demands for attaining the lofty mantle of Emersonian poet with the authority of one who has already acquired it. He must "write for future as for present ages," a point Emerson emphasized throughout his essays. Antimaterialism is essential for the aspiring writer, who "must learn to scorn the wreath of vulgar fame." He dutifully and earnestly demonstrates his own grasp of the basic tenets of transcendentalism, including a self-reliant firmness in the face of conformist critical dissent: "o'er the pages/ His burning brain hath wrought, wreak wantonly/ Their dull and crabbed spite, or trifling mockery." Despite such mockery, he seeks not the glamour of adoring popular reception. Emerson would have likely smiled at this attempt to appease him, but would have been sorely disappointed at the forced and mechanical images of creativity Cranch employed. The bee is his natural metaphor for the poet, "Stealing a sweetness from the poison blossom,/ He garners up the honey of his thought," to demonstrate his own capacity to forge a path "through all nature like the sun" in the manner of the true poet.[51] This likely struck Emerson as a pupil's fulfillment of duty, a kind of gratuitous recitation of Emerson's teachings.

Cranch even made a nod to Emerson's habit of setting the poet's art in social opposition to those who scorn it, a theme particularly visible in "Self-Reliance." Writing in October 1838, Cranch was likely referencing the controversy sparked by Andrews Norton following the Harvard Divinity School Address that summer in the lines, "Who scorns the Poet's art, deserves the scorn/ Which he would heap on others' heads; that man/ [likely Norton] Knows not the sacred gift and calling born/ Within the Poet's soul when life began." Here, Cranch speaks the language of spiritual vocation's "sacred gift" and "calling born" with the conviction of a man, like Emerson, who had fled his position as Unitarian minister for a literary career. His poetic calling, however, is entrenched in duty and requirement as well, in a kind of self-imposed incarceration in a profession close to, but missing completely, the rich mine of talent he would discover in landscape art. His tone evokes something more like a prison sentence than blessed gift. From birth, the poet "Knows that he *must* speak, and not for fame,/ But that his heart would wither else within its flame."[52] Utterance is not a choice, but an imposition; Emerson's intervention would rid Cranch of his passive theological calling, encouraging him instead to consider vocation a conscious choice to be mediated by and implemented in a real market with a discerning and paying audience. The flame need not die; he "*must* speak" his passion, but not necessarily as a poet, Emerson suggested, liberating him to become the artist he always was.

As in Thoreau's poetry, Cranch appears to have placed a value on silence that extends beyond its requisite function as Emersonian symbol of inward contemplation. In "Silence and Speech," Cranch laments the inadequacy of language as he does throughout *Poems*, this time targeting "thoughtless clamour." With the notable exception of "The Prophet Unveiled," which likens Emerson's words spoken from the lectern to meteors, Cranch generally condemns language as a pale reflection of the spirit whose corresponding essence can be read in the scroll of nature's types. Cranch's ear for music is divine in the poem. His Donne-like metaphysical brashness, "Godlike Silence! I would woo thee—," with its long stentorian emphasis, functions as a slow gallant prelude to the quick cadences of the poem's middle stanza that introduces a new ABAB rhyme scheme. In a poem purportedly extolling the virtue of silence in opposition to speech, Cranch's playful melodies disclose his unmistakable love for sound. But it is the sound of music he adores, and the sound of chatter, "Babbling and muttering," he abhors. His trochaic metrical shift begins with "Masses without form or make,/ Sleeping gnomes that never wake;/ Genii bound by magic spells;/ Fairies and all miracles," all tokens of the silent yet vibrant magical inner world of the imagination. Significantly, that inner world also includes "Thoughts whose faces are averted,/ Guesses dwelling in the dark;/ Instincts not to be diverted/ From thy ever present mark," all ostensibly defining the romantic sublime that is both "Terrible and beautiful!" The lines also bear out his vocational crisis, highlighting the tension between his conscience and his "instincts," his nascent artistic talent figured in the "thoughts whose faces are averted."[53] Writing poetry, indeed, functioned to defer his dream of manifesting those untapped thoughts of that colorful imaginative world. The prosody of this verse, furthermore, reveals that the musician in him belies the poet, much in the way his use of light makes his aptitude for painting outshine that of verse.

Cranch's forced sense of belonging to the sacred class of poets revealed that he believed more in the beauty and truth of Emerson's ideal, and loved it even, than he did in his own powers as an artist. This is glaringly ironic given the primacy of self-reliance and nonconformity in Emerson's paradigm. That he could make the shift toward self-love and nurturance of his own gift for visual art testifies to the benefits of Emerson's honesty in his critical reaction to his tepid and derivative poetry. Commonly portrayed as rejecting Cranch coldly, Emerson instead drew out the best in Cranch, as his cruelty functioned as a kindness. Critics have pointed out that Emerson wanted to have little to do with Cranch after he made the professional transition from poetry to art. Emerson could hardly be blamed, however, since he had no expertise to teach Cranch in the finer points of artistic production. Samuel Ward, dubbed "Raphael" for his extensive critical knowledge of the art world, would have been a better mentor for Cranch at that stage than Emerson.

In the same *Poems* of 1844 are even more direct tributes to Emerson, such as the previously discussed "Correspondences." In this context, four years after its original publication in the *Dial*, it appears less a poem than a series of maxims closely related in form to Bronson Alcott's "Orphic Sayings," with content that parrots Emerson in a way that not only reflects *Nature* of 1836, but also his 1841 essays "Compensation" and "Circles." Cranch's insight that "Everything here has its own correspondence,/ Folded within its form, as in the body and soul," is pure Emerson, lines that could be mistaken for his mentor's assertions in those essays.[54] Yet Cranch is engaged here less in literary larceny than in humble tribute. Setting Emerson's theories to verse is Cranch's way of showing both how deeply he internalized their meaning under his tutelage, and just how beautiful those ideas can be in an aesthetic form like poetry. Yet in Cranch's hand, Emersonian transcendentalism would never be more aesthetically pleasing than on canvas.

Transcendentalist ideals in Cranch's landscape art exhibit far more mastery and thus more control over its major themes than his imitative poetry. This is likely due to the fact that Asher B. Durand and Thomas Cole, the foremost painters of the Hudson River School, had instructed him to do "no copying during his apprenticeship," which he preferred, and thus learned "directly from nature."[55] On canvas, he no longer struggled to appease his master with demonstrations of concepts learned, of thoughts replicated. For the first time Cranch was capable of both emotionally processing his independent aesthetic growth away from Emerson while still honoring his debt to him by locating a divine source in nature through a quintessentially transcendental lens. God could not be found "beneath the drowsy preacher's drone," or in the marketplace of the "Grumbling little merchant man,/ Deft Utilitarian," but rather in "The inborn sweetness of the rose," and "The meaning of the utmost star." Emerson indeed sympathized with Cranch's rejection of his ministerial vocation that confirmed the divine was not in church, but in nature, and was accessible to those "Whose inward sense hath not grown dim;/ Whose soul is steeped in Nature's tinct,/ And to the Universal linked."[56] Cranch grew more resolute over the years that "the priest . . . With waste of words, half truth, half error mixed" occluded human contact with the divine. Written in 1875, "In a Church," from *The Bird and the Bell and Other Poems*, anachronistically evokes the rebellious energies of the late 1830s and early 1840s, unleashing a torrid condemnation of the spiritually darkening effect of the preacher, who becomes metaphorically "spread betwixt/ Nature and God a cloud that dimmed the sun,/ and made the inspiring church a vaulted tomb."[57] Although Cranch maintained his faith, he increasingly found the mitigation of his access to the divine through the authority figure of a preacher intolerable in the decades following the Civil War.

As the Unitarian Church and its ministers failed to reveal the divine to Cranch, he more fervently dedicated himself to the quest for it in his landscape art. As his primary conduit between his soul and nature, art for him finally was "neither wholly material nor wholly spiritual [but] the beautiful child of the wedlock between Nature and Soul; and she is the more beautiful, the more she bears a resemblance to both parents," as he wrote in Brook Farm's journal, *The Harbinger*.[58] More than the luminist painters—with their washed-out, blurred brush-strokes that erase the painter's presence in an ethereal haze—Cranch appears to have arrived at the epitome of transcendental expression through landscape art. Indeed, his work even more than Washington Allston's embodies a self-reliant presence while also celebrating nature's energy, variety, sound, and dynamism.[59] Cranch's clear lines assert himself as the creator of the scene, avoiding the limitation Emerson saw in Allston's "merit [which is] merely outlinear, strictly emptied of all obtrusive individuality, but a vase to receive and not a fountain to impart character" (*JMN*, 5:195). Indeed, the fountain that imparted char-acter in Cranch frequently took the form of a waterfall.

These cataracts were not unproblematically self-contained and inde-pendent, however. Cranch's *Landscape with Boy Fishing*, from 1845, *Landscape* (1849), and *Landscape with Waterfall* (1851) all depict waterfalls splitting around large boulders and reintegrating to allegorize Cranch's relationship with Emerson, and transcendental friendship by extension. It is indeed significant that this motif was produced at the time Cranch wrote of "parted drops of rain . . . flowing into one" in "Enosis." Cranch recog-nized the need to abandon his dream of becoming an Emersonian poet, but also maintained the influence of his mentor's sacred vision that enabled him to locate the divine in nature, even through oil and canvas.[60] A prepon-derance of waterfalls dramatizing this split/union appear in the late 1840s and early 1850s, exactly coinciding with the end of his *Dial* contributions and correspondence with Emerson. Interestingly, Cranch valued Emerson his whole career despite losing touch with him upon embracing painting. He wished to commemorate his self-reliance *and* his shared unified vision with Emerson late in his career, and thus presented *Landscape* to him in 1874. "The split waterfall, which Cranch abandoned for almost two decades, returns as the dominant motif in the painting he created for Emerson as a testament to his lasting influence," Stula notes.[61] The touching tribute won Emerson's unqualified praise, as it did that of "Mrs. J. M. Forbes . . . an incessant painter [who] praised it warmly." The book of verse titled *Satan: A Libretto* that Cranch had sent along with the painting, as one might expect, received far less attention from Emerson. "The book with its dangerous title lies on my table, and waits a prosperous hour." But more than a slight of Cranch's literary efforts, Emerson was once again backing Cranch the painter as he had in 1841. In 1874, he could look back on his promising youth's vocational crisis, and its attendant nervous disorder, and clearly see how "you are the victim of your own various gifts; that all the muses, jealous of each other, haunt your brain."[62] The state-ment is an uncanny recapitulation of Cranch's 1840 letter to Emerson soliciting his support to leave the ministry for a career in art. Emerson could see his promising youth decades later still wrestling with his muses. One brilliant landscape hung before him and another dubious volume of poetry sat on the table by his side.

Ironically, the two bifurcated streams of their lives reunited naturally in the end. A manuscript letter dated October 13, 1874, indicates that their relationship finally grew intimate, and above all, authentic. In it, Cranch accepts an invitation to dine with the Emersons, promising that he and his wife will "gladly meet you at the train you mention."[63]

4

SAMUEL GRAY WARD: A FINANCIER'S AESTHETIC

Seated beside Jones Very at Harvard's commencement exercises in 1836, Samuel Gray Ward seemed yet another young aesthetic rebel poised for his turn with Concord's leading light. The tableau would prove misleading, however, as their proximity during the ceremony was by accident of alphabetical order only. In fact, the two were virtual strangers at Harvard, which is not surprising given their disparate temperaments and career trajectories. Very, the zealot infamous for proclaiming he was the second coming of Christ, would occupy transcendentalism's radical fringe at the farthest imaginable distance from Ward, who was to become a worldly aristocratic Boston banker and art critic. Both, however, shared the distinction of donning professional identities that tested the tolerance of a transcendental movement well known for accommodating eccentricity. Very extended Emersonian radicalism to unheard-of levels, while Ward sent shock waves throughout the transcendental community with an entirely different, yet perhaps more violent breach of the circle's collective ethos. With great expectations to marry Margaret Fuller and embrace an aesthetic life of art and literature—a royal wedding of sorts in Emerson's Concord kingdom—Ward sinned unpardonably by instead marrying wealthy socialite Anna Barker and accepting employment in her father's banking firm.

Although Ward may have never considered Fuller in a romantic light despite their intense intimacy and companionship, and courted Barker from the first day he met her, different levels of understanding of Ward's wedding plans ranged from Fuller herself to the Concord circle (led by

Samuel Gray Ward (Houghton Library, Harvard University)

Ellery Channing, the younger) who expected them to marry and were stunned when they did not. Fuller's own painful response to the news of their engagement illustrates this discrepancy of expectation, especially the nature of their relationship as Ward imagined it. Indeed, the proposal to some violated the sacrosanct anti-trade ethos of the Concord circle, and the aggrieved, the foremost of whom were Fuller and Channing, duly registered their shrill protests. By contrast, T. S. Eliot's bank work in London in the next century was understood by his literary circle to be a regrettable, but finally unavoidable, concession to economic necessity rather than an endorsement of the capitalist culture. Indeed, Ezra Pound even established an organized fund-raising drive on his behalf to relieve him of what he believed was mindless drudgery. Although Eliot's banking position effectively answered his financial needs, his predicament was deemed an alarming aberration by the Bloomsbury circle, which collectively resolved to rescue his talent from the presumably destructive forces of the market. They proceeded from the assumption that his poetry could never come to fruition in an environment located at the crucible of the capitalist world and thus in hostile opposition to the nurturance of literary genius. Unlike Eliot, Ward faced no immediate threat of poverty or acute economic necessity, making his marriage and banking position appear nothing less than a Faustian oath of unfettered avarice to some in the Concord circle.

Compounding Ward's sin was his failure to reap the aesthetic dividends of marrying Fuller, whose own literary pursuits promised to complement and enrich his future career as professional author. Together, they would have made the most powerful couple of the transcendental movement, a force to reckon with on the art and literary scene well beyond the Concord clique. Writing to a friend in 1882, thirty-two years after Fuller's death, Ward acknowledged her considerable talent, noting that "her literary insight and powers of assimilation were something astonishing." After being married to Barker for nearly half a century, he could confirm with a hint of regret that "I have never known a woman of [Fuller's] equal in these respects and as so much of it lay in the direction of my interests, it was a great stimulus to me."[1]

Ward had indeed set up the expectation himself by cultivating an intimate relationship with Fuller, and proclaiming that he was ill suited to business. In what eventually proved a deeply ironic self-description, he insisted at one point that he possessed an intellectual and poetic disposition more like that of his close friend and Harvard classmate, Ellery Channing.[2] Ward had tutored Fuller in art history, and she had expanded and deepened his appreciation of literature. She was appalled not only by the personal affront his engagement to Barker represented, but also by his apparent betrayal of the transcendental ethos. His voice had originally gone up with the rest in condemning the materialism behind the surging wave in the development of capitalism that threatened to overwhelm them. By the ranks of bankers at the heart of the rival financial world opposite their own, he had committed treason against the Newness. Ward's defection carried all the significance of a Parisian Left Bank Bohemian joining the rival industrialists of the Right Bank. Had he abandoned his aesthetic ideals in hot pursuit of mammon?

The wide gulf separating these two worlds was insurmountable to Fuller at the time. Only later, after moving to New York City and circulating more vigorously amid the world of trade, did she begin to accommodate certain features of the free market into her outlook. But prior to her salaried position for the *Tribune* and book contracts through which she gained a better appreciation for the business world, trade remained the enemy, and thus she could only see Ward's decision as a sacrifice of his artistic ambition. "This man needs be the painter of our country," she mused when gazing on him. "The very mould of this man's face was built for the life of statues, buildings and splendid landscapes. He will set the century on fire, with the beauty of his conceptions," a messianic warrior triumphing over coarse materialism by "burn[ing] up the stubble of our degeneracy in a flame which shall lick away the stars." Fuller further clarified that his vocational betrayal had cast out such celestial vitality and vibrancy for the dead wood of business. "I will confess, once and for all, I had longed to see you a painter," she wrote to Ward after learning of his engagement, "and not a merchant . . . when I learned you were to become a merchant, to sit at the dead wood of the desk, and calculate figures, I was betrayed into unbelief." Opposite Barker's demand for a higher income as a condition of her acceptance of his proposal, Fuller would have rather received him as a battered aesthetic warrior tattered and torn from crusading in the name of artistic truth, and even on the brink of poverty, than installed in a brokerage. "I would you had starved yourself lean," she insisted, coloring her ideal portrait of him in the romantic hues of the starving artist. Now shattered was her ideal image of him living despite his material condition "for two-score years, over a few shavings in some garret, and therein fixed an iron spear in the hard breast of Art, and forced it to yield its elixir." This was the hero she yearned for, one who would struggle mightily with "great despair" as "over five hundred failures of your pencil stung your palm" in his noble quest for "the beauty of his conceptions." This, she urged in ironically employed economic rhetoric, was her hope, since her own commitment to professional authorship "has failed to pay its dividends, yet my capital stock" in creativity "is not overdrawn." She then distinguished her economic principles from his, declaring herself an heiress of another sort, an anti-Barker "born to a fortune, though not of pence, for which last, truly, I cannot bow."[3]

The personal affront of Barker and Ward's marriage on October 3, 1840, scarred Fuller deeply. Robert Hudspeth observes that it was a date she "noted each succeeding year."[4] But conjecture regarding her status as jilted love interest needs to be balanced against her other concern to maintain the unity of the Concord circle, the core of which the Ward-Barker marriage threatened to destroy. She intensely cherished what Emerson described in his essay "Friendship" as a "circle of godlike men and women variously related to each other, and between whom subsists a lofty intelligence." Ward's centrality to that circle is evident in the fact that Emerson wrote the essay with Ward in mind as his ideal friend, according to a virtual critical consensus that includes Lawrence Buell, David Robinson, and Caleb Crain (*L*, 7:391).[5] Thus his removal from it might prove devastating. As Robinson points out, Fuller's despair was directed not only at the loss of a potential husband, but also at the potential dissolution of the Concord circle, urging that she "had hoped that the circle would remain as it was: a unified community of souls attempting to define friendship and experimenting in a new form of dialogue and intimacy."[6] That unified bond specifically was forged not only on an experiment in dialogue and intimacy, but also on the group's romantic and unconventional sense of vocation.

Like Fuller, Channing's dedication to the romantic ideal stood in equally hostile opposition to conventional professions. He thus severed Ward from his affections with a dramatic flourish, if only to warm to him again in the succeeding months when he needed financial assistance from his friend. Channing, one of the least professionally inclined of Emerson's protégés, vented his protest to Fuller, whose own career ironically struck a balance between the commercial and the literary more successfully than any disciple in her work as a journalist in New York City: "Why did he marry a fashionable woman, older than himself. And to marry a woman that had rejected him, what nonsense! There could have been no offering or rejecting, if the thing had been right."[7] Not unlike Zelda Fitzgerald, who almost a century later had only accepted F. Scott Fitzgerald's marriage proposal upon his attainment of a socioeconomic status suitable to her own, Barker, a New Orleans heiress, informed Ward that "very little probability" of marriage existed, unless his "scholar's life gave place to some lucrative profession."[8] Channing was outraged not only by the marriage, but also by the conditional quality of her acceptance according to an economic standard, which he felt transformed the transcendental ideal of spiritual intimacy into so much barter.

Noticeably absent from this chorus of dissent were Emerson and Elizabeth Peabody. Interestingly, the only individuals in the Concord circle to endorse the marriage were also the most professionally inclined at the time. Showing her accommodation of the world of trade in her own pursuits, Peabody readily acknowledged the contradiction between her transcendentalist affiliation and her own entrepreneurial efforts, and was capable of thriving on the paradox.[9] Also harnessing the power of commerce, Emerson's aggressive self-promotion on the lecture circuit generated a demand extending west as far as California and overseas to Europe. Their own respect for business success in their transcendental value system inclined them to support the marriage. In Emerson's floral diction wishing his "beautiful, pure, and happy friends,—peace and beauty" is a distinct reference to their new economic "power and the perpetuity" of their combined wealth, promising "the sure unfolding of all the buds of joy that so thickly stud your branches" (*JMN*, 7:404). Regarding Barker as a treasure and a godsend, Peabody also could hardly contain her enthusiasm. She "was most happy for Mr. Ward . . . for any body must be so *blest* at having won Miss Anna Barker!" The event was significant enough to have penetrated her subconscious. Peabody admitted to her friend John Dwight Sullivan that she had dreamed Barker married him instead, which made her "almost die of joy by way of sympathy" for Sullivan.[10] Clearly, Barker's money and her father's banking position for Ward were assets rather than liabilities to Emerson and Peabody. Neither took the engagement as a defection from the Concord circle and renunciation of its values.

Reactions to Ward's engagement were also articulations of transcendentalism's, and more generally literary romanticism's, relation to the free market. Views toward the Barker-Ward marriage and the jilting of Fuller had the interesting side effect of drawing out the spectrum of economic values in Emerson's circle. Opponents tended to want to keep the world of business separate from aesthetic pursuits, whereas supporters found they could fruitfully coalesce. Emerson regarded the wedding not as a sacrifice of Ward's interests in art and literature, but as an opportunity to enrich them. Ward's marriage provided him privileged access to elite culture, which Emerson regarded as a fortuitous expansion of transcendentalism.

But the wedding of business and transcendental philosophy represented in the Ward-Emerson relationship did not emerge seamlessly. Ward initially appeared to have rejected his Emersonian apprenticeship for one arranged by his father-in-law in the banking industry. After completing his training in banking, Ward replaced his own father, who had retired from his powerful position as agent to the English brokerage of Baring Brothers. By Fuller and Channing's accounts, he was a disgrace to the transcendental coterie because he had sold his soul along with his aesthetic sensibility and considerable talent as an art critic to the world of trade. But Emerson and Peabody knew better. Through Ward, Concord's writers now had access to Boston high society. Ward, however, was not merely a conduit to Emerson in this regard. Emerson genuinely admired and respected his wealth and commercial success, holding him up as a model to emulate in the management of his own finances.

Not only was Ward's financial and occupational profile anomalous among Emerson's protégés. His approach toward authorship also went against the grain of the disciples. Opposite the stubborn resistance to revision Very and Channing would exhibit, much to the chagrin of Emerson, an annoying and often critical impediment to his attempts to professionalize these precocious youths, Ward was obsessive about presenting only flawless manuscripts for publication. By contrast, Newcomb refused to correct his original draft of "Dolon" after Emerson had persistently begged him. Very insisted that the Holy Spirit had authored his sonnets, which thus emerged onto the page in a state of sacred perfection, rendering moot any question of revision. Channing held fast to Emerson's own precept set forth in "Verses of the Portfolio" stipulating that polished prosody was a superficial grace that diverted poets from authentic utterance of the soul. Ward's concern for the sanctity of his name in the literary market coincided precisely with his emergence into independent wealth. The professionalization of the Emersonian protégé had indeed been a constant and ongoing struggle until the commercially inclined Ward entered the scene. In fact, Ward's vocational crisis, if there was one, worked in the reverse, pitting him with the challenge of finding a way to accommodate literary labor in his life of business and finance. Indeed, Ward only picked up his pen when he had the financial independence to do so.

When Ward did take up his pen, he naturally gravitated toward art history and criticism. Among Emerson's disciples, Cranch and Ward were the most deeply connected to the world of art. Whereas Cranch's marriage freed him from his conventional vocation to become an artist, Ward's marriage to Barker denied him the career in painting that Fuller and Channing envisioned. Instead, Ward became the wealthiest of Emerson's promising youths, and the most thoroughly independent, both financially and philosophically. Since Cranch, the other Emersonian art expert, had occupied more than his share of the *Dial*'s columns by supplying the journal with the vast majority of its verse, it was inappropriate for him to also contribute art criticism and history. Thus, the *Dial*'s need for an art critic was filled by Ward, whose connection to art and aristocratic Boston provided it with a unique voice and perspective, while personally offering Emerson a muse that helped materialize his otherwise disembodied Platonism. As a link to an alternative universe apart from Concord, Ward enabled Emerson to explore in greater depth the urbane world of commerce, fashion, and manners, in which he found much to admire as well as criticize. For Ward was a creature of that world, a true Boston Brahmin of aristocratic ancestry tracing back to the Puritans.

"A Master in Life"

"Art is the Creation of Beauty," Emerson wrote in his journal, in as near a definitive articulation of his aesthetic as he would ever make. "But nothing is arbitrary nothing is insulated in beauty," he observed. "It depends forever on the necessary & the useful. It is the sign of health & of virtue. The plumage of the bird" is one of many outward signs of vitality in nature that are inherently beautiful. As in any triumphant work of art, "Fitness is so essential to Beauty that it has been taken for it" (*JMN*, 5:206). Such health and vigor were everywhere evident in Ward, according to Emerson. "Solid, graceful, well-formed, and elevated by just sentiment," he embodied his ideal self-reliant individualist. Emerson was struck by "how easily he rejects things he does not want, and never has a weak look or word." Emerson was "impressed by the finished beauty of that person" as much as his meticulously prepared *Dial* submissions. Interestingly, Emerson borrowed the rhetoric of art criticism to describe Ward as a "picture to look at as he sat," a work of art and master artist, exclaiming, "What sincere refinement! What a master in life!" If his other protégés had been performing for him in some capacity in conversation and writing, Ward's performance made a singular impression on him. "I compare this man, who is a performance, with others who seem to me only the prayers," for finally he could behold a disciple who had eagerly taken it upon himself to become his own patron, to forge ahead successfully into his career without excessive dependence on his aid. Ward's "performance" stood for a complete, well-orchestrated life, established and active rather than passing through an awkward developmental phase filled with flaws and thus offering only "prayers" brokered on potential (and in some cases desperate hope) for personal, professional, and literary success. Such self-sufficiency brings a gliding "fluency in the existing world" that Emerson appreciated. He ended the letter noting how "Alcott and Fourier['s]" associationist tendencies "will find it the harder to batter it down" compared with such poised individualism (L, 2:279).

While Emerson could admire the culture of Ward's social graces and aesthetic knowledge, the aspect that moved him most was economic. This is not surprising, since Ward became the only Emerson protégé to patronize him with significant financial assistance. When part of Emerson's Concord residence was destroyed by fire, Ward matched the highest contribution of all donors with five hundred dollars to pay for reconstruction. In addition to such generosity, Ward's financial skill prompted Emerson to put him in charge of an investment fund he had established with Henry Wadsworth Longfellow to aid the chronically needy Bronson Alcott. Ellery Channing owed nothing less than the establishment of his career to Ward, who introduced him to Emerson and generously financed and promoted his poetry. As he amassed greater wealth in his role as American agent to Baring Brothers, the English brokerage firm, Ward became increasingly active in patronizing the arts and intellectual culture. After he established himself at the forefront of the cultural elite upon acquiring a home on Fifth Avenue in New York after the Civil War, Ward's financial advice and capital contributions made a profound impact. The three most significant areas of influence were his donation of twelve hundred dollars to Louis Agassiz's museum at Harvard, his invaluable consultation with E. L. Godkin, editor of the *Nation*, that saved the struggling journal from failure, and his part in founding the Metropolitan Museum of Art, the most important and lasting of his many acts of patronage.[11]

Behind such philanthropy was a pursuit of capital, guided by Adam Smith's laissez-faire principles, as opposed to the collectivist approach soon to be espoused by Karl Marx. Emerson's letter to Caroline Sturgis extolling the virtues of his young apprentice sets Ward against Charles Fourier and Bronson Alcott precisely to illustrate his preference for economic self-sufficiency, in contrast to their reform-driven associationism. Emerson quipped, "I found myself much warped from my own perpendicular and grown avarice overnight." He felt a guilty pleasure that his stimulated interest in the management of capital should become so embarrassingly visible. This was the seductive effect of "hearing this fine seigneur discourse so captivatingly of chateaux, gardens and collections of art" in a delicious overnight indulgence in the conversational subjects of "money and lands and buildings." The frigid opposite of Ward's outlook was Fourier, the champion of self-described socialist Albert Brisbane. Along with Swedenborg, Brisbane established the philosophical foundation for the collectivist experiment in communal living at Brook Farm. Emerson mentioned Alcott in this context as a dry collectivist and ineffectual reformer, forever struggling against market forces rather than joyfully flourishing with them. In this manner, Fourier and Alcott represent the opposite of Ward, who appears "so felicitously adapted to this world that it seems as if they must lose by being transferred to any other" (*L*, 2:279).

The associationist movement irked Emerson because it did not thrive in "the existing world and society." Written four years before his adoring description of Ward's "talk . . . of his new purchased farm [and] of the house and buildings he is to raise," Emerson's rejection of George Ripley's invitation to join Brook Farm exhibits how his economic theory was already firmly established by the time he met Ward. Emerson's laissez-faire beliefs, displayed in his principled objections to the collectivization of capital and labor featured at Brook Farm, explain why he would have received Ward's entrepreneurial acumen so warmly. The letter ends with a series of numbered claims verified by the successful commercial agrarian Edmund Hosmer, "a very intelligent farmer and a very upright man in my neighborhood." Hosmer advocated the core values that separated Emerson from Brook Farm and distinguished Ward from his fellow disciples like Newcomb and Cranch, who heartily endorsed the commune. Chief among those were private property and the worker's right to command a wage based on the quality of his labor, a maxim at the heart of the competitive ethos driving the literary market. To Emerson, Ward became the champion of the free market and the living example of how "the equal payment of ten cents per hour to every laborer," as Hosmer argued, "is unjust." If a worker "comes who has no capital but can do twice as much . . . in a day [then] his skill is his capital," and therefore "it would be unjust to pay him no interest on that" (*L*, 7:435–37). Like his Scottish friend Thomas Carlyle, otherwise known for his vicious attacks on industry and its morally corrosive effects, Emerson attacked the cold utilitarian ideology of "the Age of Machinery" but concluded with surprising optimism in harnessing industrial power. "Mechanism is not always to be our hard taskmaster," Carlyle argued in support of an enlightened laissez-faire system, "but one day to be our pliant, all-ministering servant; that a new and brighter spiritual era is slowly evolving itself for all men."[12]

Ward's capitalist bent and commitment to ascending to professional expertise in all of his pursuits gave Emerson the rare pleasure of mentoring and marketing a "master in life." For this reason he immediately wrote to Fuller on hearing of his engagement to Barker that "Ward I shall not lose" after the "invitation to Elysian tables." His unwavering support is overwhelming in his declaration that "I have never had occasion to congratulate any person so truly. What an event to him!" He welcomes the "ebb" and wonders about "the consequences to the history of his genius," not to suggest that it will be necessarily deleterious, as Charles Capper has argued, but that it might lead "tomorrow to fresh fields and pastures new," as he quoted Milton (*L*, 2:327). Without the constraints of tending to his immediate economic needs, a burden that encumbered his early relationships with Channing and Thoreau, Emerson felt at liberty to discuss a wider range of topics more frequently in the role of a coequal in his correspondence with Ward. His letters to Ward, for example, are not hampered with the impossibly high standard for poetic accomplishment he habitually held over Thoreau during his poetic apprenticeship. Nor does he shift tones and roles from friend to martinet to goad his pupil into a more professional orientation toward the authorial craft. Instead, Emerson indulges in the luxury of guiding a disciple in his writing and thinking, and of arranging for the publication of articles, poetry, and books for an accomplished gentleman, an author like those who surrounded Emerson during his Harvard days and earlier. Such writers were lawyers or preachers not under pressure to make literature the primary, if not sole, means of living. Unlike Thoreau and Channing, Ward never lodged with Emerson out of necessity, nor was he relegated to chopping wood to remain financially solvent. Emerson particularly relished Ward's stability mainly because his moment of instability during his requisite vocational crisis was relatively brief and needed no intervention on Emerson's part to be resolved.

Ward's status as one of his most finished protégés entitled him to consult with Emerson over a difficult case like Channing. In the process, Emerson enlisted Ward among "the more fortunate [who] must wait for the less," like Channing, "with a sure trust in the remedial force of nature." Emerson praised Ward's support of Channing, because "if we outgrow our early friendships there is no help, and undoubtedly where there is inequality in the intellect." An authentic spirit like Channing is worth saving, he suggests, despite the uneven quality of his writing. "True society is so rare," according to Emerson, "that I think I could not spare from my circle a poet as long as he could offer so indisputable a token as a good verse of his relation to what is highest in being." He promised therefore to "be useful to your friend" based on this rationale, which is notable for how it addresses Ward as an intellectual equal and peer.[13] Here Emerson freely speaks of how he can justify his patronage of Channing, who is the lesser talent in such a way that makes Ward not only a close confidante, but a pupil of the highest rank in terms of aesthetic and professional counsel second only to Margaret Fuller. If Channing was a recalcitrant freshman skirting the edge of acceptability in his performance, then Ward was his trusted and seasoned senior graduate student, wily beyond his years.

But before he was a "master at living," Ward was an apprentice desiring to become Emerson's "American Scholar." In fact, he had not resolved the tension between his literary and commercial ambitions in 1838. While working in the New York office of Jonathan Goodhue, Ward felt a peculiar "vexation" linked to his misgivings about making himself a businessman. "My *prospects* as they call them are bright," he wrote one friend, indicating this early unease between economic and creative standards of success that he would later resolve into a harmony that impressed Emerson. "As to my life," he continued, "that is rather my death—and I do not care to speak of it."[14] In a move little different from Channing's departure for Illinois to cultivate the land and his soul according to Emerson's admonitions, Ward took up a Berkshire farm from 1843 to 1848, announcing to his father that his temperament was ill-suited for the banking life after plodding through a dreary apprenticeship in the trade furnished by his father-in-law. Ward's wanderlust appeared to set him on the same trajectory as Channing. Impressed on his soul was the temperament of a poet, he insisted in no uncertain terms to his father. "Long before I entered into trade, I had a disinclination for its pursuits. From a very early period, I looked upon myself as a student and literary man, and so far as I had planned at all my views of life were of this complexion."[15] Rather than abruptly reversing ground and utterly abandoning this conviction, Ward's later embrace of trade, though a sea change in his life, certainly did not signal the end of his love affair with art and literature. If anything, banking only placed him closer to those worlds, in which he could participate variously as a producer, consumer, critic, and patron. Indeed, Ward's economic privilege released him from the narrowness of specialization, and thus he was capable of ranging freely throughout the myriad intermediary roles then becoming increasingly prominent, and pivotal, in the literary market. Whereas Channing would return to Boston from farming with an even firmer commitment to defining himself a poet at all costs, Ward returned from the Berkshires with an immersion into the world of trade that was neither reluctant nor forced, but triumphant. He may have retreated from the market with Emerson's idealism guiding the way, particularly compelled by the power of nature as a universal force that is uncontainable by the "liliput interference that strives to barricade it out; as if it did not force itself into pits of theatres and cellars of markets . . . wild, untamable, all-containing Nature."[16] But he returned to the respectable and prestigious position vacated by his own father with Baring Brothers. By all accounts, he outdid his own father, exhibiting a unique capacity to perform and negotiate under immense pressure.

Ward's strong standing with Emerson was partly due to his having emerged from the Berkshires not out of desperation, and not leaving a failed enterprise in his wake. The move instead was that of a gentleman farmer experimenting in a more spare subsistence-driven household economy now ready to raise his growing children amid the society of an urban dwelling. Anna, his wife, was also unaccustomed to being away from the social engagements and gatherings among the fashionable elite, and thus favored the move. Emerson was pleased with the transition to greater stability, not least because Ward had touched him with the hand of God. Upon his return from Europe in October 1839, Ward stunned Emerson with a portfolio of art containing large engravings of the ceiling of the Sistine Chapel. "I have your portfolio in my study and am learning to read in that book too," Emerson said, playfully assuming the role of pupil studying a foreign, yet powerful form. Beholding the engraving of Michelangelo's "miracle by forms," Emerson observed that "much genius finds its way to light in design as in song," only with a celerity he himself no doubt felt upon perusing the portfolio. "But the eye is a speedier student than the ear; by a grand or a lovely form," such as the hand of God that seemed to touch him as well as mankind in Michelangelo, "it is astonished or delighted once for all and quickly appeased." He asked "to keep your prints a little while, if you can spare them," so he could savor the details he may have neglected "until I have got my lessons by heart."[17]

If Ward had brought Emerson in touch with the divine through a world of art previously foreign and incomprehensible to him, his protégé would also give him a privileged glimpse into the urban world Emerson condemned in so many of his writings, yet longed to know at a deeper level than his travels on the lecture circuit through New York and Boston had revealed. Feeling rudderless in the seaside town of Natasket Bay in July 1841, Emerson entreated his friend to buoy him from his malaise. Nature was not providing him the signs and tokens of reassurance he had hoped, so Emerson admonished his friend to "save me, dip me into ice water, find me a girding belt" for "I find no emblems here that speak any other language than the sleep and abandonment of my woods and blueberry pastures back home." He had "had enough of seeing the obedient sea wave forever lashing the obedient shore." The panacea he located in Ward's executive and administrative temperament was a capacity for decisive action and sense of direction that could give him "some man, work, aim, or fact, under the *angle of practice*" to save him from the amorphous dissipating abstraction that threatened to make him glide away into a "stream or a gas and decease into an infinite diffusion." He was specifically calling on the Ward he admired in the commercial setting, not a dreamy aesthete, but "an elector and rejector, an agent, an antagonist, and a commander." Emerson made clear that he wanted to hear not of Ward's "garden, or gardenette, but I wish to know how the street and the work that is done in it look to you."[18] The urban world of executive action was what Emerson thirsted for, not only as a symptom of his boredom while moored awaiting appointments at this seaside village, but also as a tonic for his broader sense of isolation. Such detachment inhered in Emerson's authorial role predicated on abstracting philosophical ideals from nature in solitude.

When he first met him, Ward had just returned from Europe. Emerson was drawn to his practical qualities and knowledge of the European art world. Like his portfolio of European art, "Beautiful to me among so many mediocre youths as I see, was Sam Ward when I first fairly encountered him, and in this way just named." His "innate genius," to say nothing of his social class, wooed Emerson (*JMN*, 7:432). Not only did he respect his knowledge of art history, Emerson also found him to be a fellow Platonist sharing "the same material system of stars, in the same immaterial system of influences, to the same untold ineffable goal" for a similar radically optimistic hold on the universe.[19] Among the sketches in the portfolio Ward gave to Emerson when they first met was Raphael's *Endymion*. Emerson expressed deep gratitude for the work and hung it in a prominent place in his study, where it would remain permanently. The sketch functioned as a metonym for Ward, who later became affectionately known as "Raphael" to the Concord circle.

Ward became Emerson's future vision of what America might become, a combination of the worldly and the ideal, that could successfully bring Boston's equivalent of Paris's Left Bank, at least in this one relationship, together with the Right. As David Baldwin succinctly states it, "Emerson's interests in Ward depended on Ward's combining the two polarities of dream and hope, and worldly effectiveness."[20] Whereas Baldwin finds that Emerson deemed Ward ultimately unsuccessful in this enterprise, their lasting friendship embodied precisely how effectively the Boston world of art and intellect could meet the Boston world of business and society.

"Epiphany and Eclipse in Book Shops"

After Fuller introduced Ward to Emerson in 1838, two years after Ward's graduation from Harvard, their relationship built strength through the 1840s and then faded, not because Ward joined the business ranks in 1850. In fact, he had already been steeped in commercial banking well before that. Instead, the dissolution of the *Dial* in 1844 appears to have cut off a key connection between the two, since Ward had been such a steady contributor to the journal, and Emerson had taken great delight in seeing his expertise in art criticism grace its pages. Emerson's vision of the ideal and Ward's worldly and social attributes did not weaken, but rather sustained their relationship. Ward learned much from Emerson, who inspired him to retreat to the Berkshires to undertake an agricultural life akin to that touted in "The American Scholar." Ward did what Thoreau would do years later: remove himself from industry and the market to undertake a life of deliberate living closer to the land and the forces of nature, further from the charlatanism of the urban center Emerson had frequently derided. Ellery Channing's first impulse upon being inspired by Emerson's writings was also to retreat from the urban to the agrarian life. In his case, he fled New England to begin an ill-conceived stint as a farmer in Illinois.

It is important to emphasize Ward's learning from Emerson, because he is often regarded as his equal, given his superior knowledge of art and art criticism. Certainly, Ward "did not fall into the position of a disciple seeking from Emerson a solution of the problems of life; but he brought to Emerson the highest appreciation of the things which Emerson valued," about which he cared a great deal but knew little.[21] Although Ward may not have been desperately looking for solutions from Emerson, he certainly changed his own life as other disciples had based on his initial reading of *Nature*, remaking himself into a gentleman farmer in the Berkshires. Emerson's correspondence with him indicates a mentor-pupil relationship that aided Ward on issues from how to hone the art of balancing business and letters in his life to how he should approach reading to serve his authorial practice. Because Ward was so self-sufficient financially compared with the other Emerson protégés, he appears more materially autonomous than his rather needy counterparts. Such aesthetic and economic self-sufficiency signals precisely the type of successful protégé Emerson had always longed for: one who could extol the ideal in art and nature while also seeing to his own professional development. Indeed, it was this issue that so irritated Emerson about Channing, prompting him to say, "No man deserves a patron until first he has been his own."[22] Ward embodied this principle by establishing himself in a profitable professional situation before launching his writing career, effectively becoming his own patron in support of his ongoing literary endeavors. His consistent contributions to all four volumes of the *Dial* have led Joel Myerson to conclude that his publications there would have continued had the journal not ceased operation.[23]

Among the Emersonian disciples, Ward stands out for his unique approach toward professional authorship in at least two ways. He took great pride in his finished, polished work, and embraced a professional approach to authorship despite regarding it as his secondary occupation. Both characteristics Emerson found quite refreshing, especially given his fruitless ongoing struggle to encourage Jones Very and others to revise their work. "What do you bring us slipshod verses for?" Emerson asked Ellery Channing in utter exasperation at one point. "No occasional delicacy of expression or music of rhythm can atone for stupidities."[24] Ward needed no encouragement to produce clean print-ready manuscripts because he held himself to his own high standard. Indeed, there is not the slightest hint in the voluminous Emerson-Ward correspondence of any of the bitter disappointment or exasperated frustration Emerson showed toward his other pupils' resistance to professionalizing their craft.

Yet even with such financial and literary autonomy that would make Ward more of an equal in the eyes of Emerson than his other disciples, Ward nonetheless began his relationship with Emerson firmly cast in the role of the eager young apprentice. When he first met the thirty-year-old Emerson, the twenty-one-year-old Ward had just been inspired by "The American Scholar" and the Harvard Divinity School Address, the magnetic works that attracted all of Emerson's followers. Emerson exposed Ward to *Antigone*, at one point sending him his own critique of the play along with commentary on Augustine's *Confessions*, driving him toward higher aims than "the general mediocrity of thought produced by the arts of gain." This was hardly "a sort of Transcendental Professor Higgins snootily refashioning Ward after the Emersonian ideal," according to Caleb Crain.[25]

Instead, Emerson appears to have been playing to Ward's strengths by encouraging him to apply to his literary methods his already firm independence and inclination toward action in business.

As discussed in Chapter 1, Emerson exhorted Fuller not to read in any conventional sense in which she passively followed an author's words from beginning to end straining to assimilate every nuance of their meaning. Instead, he told her to be more mercenary about books, and shamelessly extract them for her own individual needs rather than abasing herself to the author to support his. Emerson taught Ward the same lesson, warning him that reading can become a bland form of consumerism, "a foolish conformity that does well for dead people."[26] His advice is to be a producer and not an admirer. "Our admiration accuses us," he boldly stated. "Instead of admiring the Apollo or the picture, or the victory at Marengo, we ought to be producing what is admirable, and these things should glitter to us as hints and stints merely."[27] Emerson also cautioned against worshiping texts as though they were permanent and sacred, a process that subordinates the individual to a higher power, effectively silencing the otherwise powerful authorial voice. The impermanence of texts, he argued, is evident in the way the novelty of certain passages that may have stimulated once can wane over time, as others previously neglected suddenly attract and inspire. This process of reading is thus a symptom of the larger "cycles of epiphany and eclipse in book shops" that can elevate one work to the pinnacle of esteem, only to have another in due time topple it from its helm in the literary market. With brutal honesty, Emerson observes that however permanent it may seem, even the most brilliant writing is ephemeral, and finally compromised.

As he did for his other protégés, Emerson encouraged Ward's independence and confidence by exposing the ultimately limited power of "any book" that we like "so little while." He warned him not to be enamored of works whose pages "seem cut out of the sky and its letters were stars" because "in a short time we cannot find there, with any turning of the leaves, the celestial sentences." The emphasis as always in Emerson's tutorials is on reading serving the individual, rather than the individual lowering himself to any text. He allows that with the growth of the individual, once brilliant passages may fade in significance. "Relatively to individual needs," which are paramount in the transcendental schema, "the fiery scriptures in each book" either "disappear once for all" or else "have a certain inter-mittency and periodical obscuration like 'revolving lights.' "[28]

Emerson's emphasis on the importance of resourcefulness in reading appealed to his protégé's business acumen, which pledged to unite "the character of a literary man and a man of business."[29] Indeed, the dedication to literary production at once engaged with, yet not beholden to other authors' works is a direct echo of "The American Scholar" and its condemnation of literary flunkeyism to English and European models. Upon the dissolution of his relationship with Fuller, Ward's development toward such an ethic is on display in the fragments of his letters she copied in her journal. They describe an author actively integrating his inclinations toward business into an overarching aesthetic to define his developing professional identity. The type of thinker and writer he fashions for himself is one who is not withdrawn or contemplative, but fully engaged in the exigencies of the market, as he would be in both finance and art: "I do not love to reason over, think over, or write over past sensations. . . . The principle of action is strong within me, and I cannot endure that the beautiful in feeling should not be manifested in high action, rather than in that inward life which to many of the highest seems to suffice." By insisting that the "beautiful in feeling" be manifested by the "high in action," Ward effectively activated and animated aestheticism, rescuing it from its otherwise detached, languid, and passive moorings in the popular antebellum romantic mind.[30] The union of the two uncommonly linked spheres promised to unleash a new untapped power in Ward's life that could not only enrich him personally, but bring permanent wealth to the public domain of art criticism through his *Dial* writings, and appreciation through his instrumental museum patronage in the growing nation. By Emerson's account, he had never met one so steeped in the arts and literature, in Raphael and Goethe, yet so "felicitously adapted to this world," with the elements of his life "perpetually blending themselves" into vital harmony (*L*, 3:279).

Such radical individualism that courses so close to the blasphemous renunciation of sacred canonical literature in the letter finishes with an equally rebellious wish confided in his friend with a conspiratorial whisper. After telling of his recent invitations to lecture in England and edit Theodore Parker's new quarterly journal, which would later become the *Massachusetts Quarterly*, he confessed that "if I could really do as I liked," signaling he would never really act upon this fantasy, "I should probably turn towards Canada," for herein the mechanism of fame and "literary power would be consulted by that course and not by the public road." This is not a rejection of public self-promotion in the literary market so much as the voice of an overexposed and road-weary public lecturer idealizing wild nature through a longing for Canada, a country seemingly immune to the rampant industrial development of the United States. (More than a century later in the United States, escape to Canada from the Establishment was to become a cliché among the counterculture.) The wild rebel in Emerson thus refused to be silenced by his acquisition of the formidable "literary power" he had established precisely through "the public road."[31] These are the words of one of our most significant authors surging at the height of his powers and stopping to assure his pupil that the mechanism of literary fame will not quell his thirst for nature. But the public road beckons, and it is not without pride that Emerson shared his recent conquests in the literary market with his commercially inclined friend, who ironically saw literature as an extra-commercial activity. Despite Ward's dedication to a professional finished product in his writing, he never courted the mass market with the zeal of Emerson primarily because authorship was always his secondary source of income. His attention to detail in his writing paradoxically employed the method not of a sloppy amateur, but of a meticulous professional.

Emerson's emergence into the limelight of London literary society, among what he called "some good specimens, chiefly of the literary-fashionable, and not of the fashionable sort" associated with superficial cosmopolites, was perhaps the most overwhelming induction into authorial celebrity of his entire career. It is significant, therefore, that the urbane Ward was the muse he sang the praises of this "Babylon" to, accounting for its lions—Macaulay, Thackeray, and Wordsworth—and mocking its lambs who fail "to appeal in any manner to the imagination." Interestingly, these impressions of English society and culture, which he placed virtually unaltered into "Traits of English Society," were originally for Ward's eyes only, and indeed grew out of his respect for his pupil's well-connected status among the elite circles of Boston. Ward was fascinating and valuable for Emerson precisely because of his ties to Boston's established cultural and literary figures, who were inevitably patronized by wealthy financiers like Ward. Emerson's attraction to the fashionable literary set of London, as with his admiration of Boston, was tempered with his usual cutting acknowledgments of its shortcomings. As for the London set, though they "know everything" and are "rich, plain, polite, proud, and admirable . . . it ends in the using," a comment Ward could appreciate for its Machiavellian self-interest and cunning in exploiting them for higher ground in the literary market. "I shall or soon have enough of this play for my occasion," he wrote, appealing simultaneously to Ward's understanding of the superficial theater of this social game and of the necessity of winning at it.[32]

One letter in the Emerson-Ward correspondence particularly reveals their depth of commitment to achievement and production. In it, Emerson bashed Philadelphia for being a "very large granny" in which he "found no Atrides," no murderously ambitious young men, no youthful vitality and aspiration, no "strenuous men or man of public opinion; a deference to the opinion of New York; a fear of Boston; and in this great want of thought, a very dull timidity and routine among the citizens themselves." A captain of industry like Ward could only appreciate Emerson's verdict. One can imagine Thoreau or even Channing, with their hostility to trade and dedication to leisure, blanching at his criticism of how "the absence of the usual excitements of trade" in Philadelphia had given the place a catatonic "lymphatic appearance." Emerson worried, "If the world was all Philadelphia, though the poultry and dairy market would be admirable, I fear suicide would exceedingly prevail." Predictably, in this toxic atmosphere there were no stars in either the literary market or the sky: "I look eagerly for the stars at night, for fear they would disappear in the dull air."[33]

Emerson's judgments of Philadelphia and London strike a curious and seldom-heard chord in his thinking, measuring the vitality of a community according to the innovation and vigor of its market. His use of an economic standard for measuring cultural worth appears out of character for Emerson, until we recognize his signature emphasis on energy and innovation driving these critiques. Vitality, whether in the forest or the city, drew Emerson and Ward alike. Ward's early renunciation of trade and escape from the market voiced in his letter to his father proclaiming himself a transcendentalist aligns perfectly with Emerson's romantic embrace of nature. Like Ward, Emerson also sought out the stimulation of the urban center as much as he yearned for the escape of Canada's boundless forests. "It is because I am so idle a member of society," Emerson confided in his pupil, "because I do not get the lesson of the world as it is set before me, I need more than others to run out into new places and multiply my chances for observation and communion." This nonconformist wayward persona, hungry for fresh observation and new experience, appealed to Ward; it did not strike him as a sin to avoid at all costs, so much as a model worth emulating. Ward functioned as a muse inspiring Emerson to reimagine his own occasional foray into the city "whenever I get into debt" as a "plunge into this great odious river of travelers, into these cold eddies of hotels and boarding houses—farther, into these dangerous precincts of charlatanism." Emerson succinctly defined the purpose of his own free-market enterprise in "namely, lectures, that out of all the evil I may draw a little good in the correction which every journey makes to my exaggerations." He added, "I hate the details, but the whole foray into a city teaches me much," revealing that the agora regularly profits him creatively as much as it does monetarily.[34]

By 1844, four years later, Emerson was freely indulging his practical and commercial inclinations with Ward. He specifically emphasized how compatible authorship could be with the world of business. "I prize every book of facts, I believe, much more than practical men, so called, do," he wrote to Ward. Emerson was not only supporting Ward's practical occupation in trade, but also establishing himself in the fellowship of the nonliterary professions. "Much of the best society I have ever known in Concord," he assured his protégé, was not attached to aesthetics or the *Dial*. Instead, the "Social Club" he enjoyed the most "consists always of twenty-five of our citizens—doctor, lawyer, farmer, trader, miller, mechanic," who are "the solidest of men," who make Harvard University "a wafer in comparison with the solid land which my friends represent." Emerson was not only flattering Ward's commercial side. He was also idealizing the practical trades rooted in facts, the way Thoreau would in his championing of the farmer's direct unartful language as heard in his calls to his teams, not unlike Wordsworth's idealization of peasant speech in his preface to *Lyrical Ballads*. Further, Emerson appears to have reconciled this practical side of Ward to his aesthetic expertise in art history. Refusing to see the man of letters as alien to the man of business, Emerson deftly fuses the two together in his praise of both books of nonfictional reportage and the conversation of the "Social Club," this prototype of today's Rotary Clubs of professionals. He implies that the poetry in such books and discussions that otherwise contain no verse per se is more deeply appreciated by those with poetic dispositions like himself and Ward. But rather than being permanently blind to such lyricism in the world of facts, "practical men" possess an untapped capacity for such vision, according to Emerson's formulation.[35]

In a letter penned during the spring of 1844, Emerson's language turns on the pleasures of leisure in a way that a businessman and transcendentalist like Ward would find especially delightful. "I do not know an idleness so delicious as dilettantism in fruit trees to promise the happy operator a dateless longevity," he effused.[36] The release from trade into the business of growing and picking fruit bears a delicious result, like the sort Ward enjoyed in his art criticism and poetry. Yet that "dilettantism" of trafficking in fruit trees, by all accounts, was just as precise and meticulous in Ward's literary work as it was in the way he traded stock. His contributions to the *Dial* included four poems in the first and third issues of July 1840 and January 1841, but nothing appeared by him in the next volume. This is likely because he had adroitly suspended his writing to tend to his wedding plans and pursue employment of the sort his bride had demanded. He then made a single contribution in the third volume and reaffirmed his presence with three more in the fourth.

"Father, Aid Thou Thy Son"

The fascinating aspect of Ward's *Dial* writings is that as he drew closer to financial independence, he became more particular about the finished quality of his writing. Ward's distinctly professional care for the craft coincided precisely with the years following his marriage, when he built the fortune that made him independently wealthy. More than coincidence, Ward's financial independence directly fueled his increasingly self-assured writings. Financial attainment augmented the authority he had already established in art history and criticism. His increasingly autonomous sense of authorship had far-reaching implications for his understanding of the politics of vocational ambition, especially in the context of his relationship with Emerson. In sharp contrast to a disciple like Charles Newcomb, who passively surrendered control of all revisions of "Dolon" to his mentor, Ward exacted rigid control over his writings, piloting them into print according to his own, rather than Emerson's, agenda. His publications in the third volume of the *Dial* were restricted to a single piece called "The Gallery," for example, a dialogue discussing the true principles of art. This was the only submission he allowed to be printed of the four that Emerson had hoped to run in the second October number. What he did not anticipate was Ward's alarm at his name being associated with his work, which he had originally submitted unsigned. When it came to his attention that Emerson had told Sarah Clarke and Ellen Hooper that he was the author of the pieces, Ward immediately withdrew them for further revision, leaving for publication only "The Gallery," which he felt was up to standards he could associate with his identity. Emerson then swore his *Dial* staff to secrecy, putting an "editorial muzzle" on himself as well, sarcastically musing that "as many as six or seven subscribers to the Dial shall be kept in profound ignorance of our secret, and who knows but that the next Number may record the death of subscribers whom curiosity has burst."[37] The close-knit character of the Concord circle meant most *Dial* readers were well aware of the authorship of the unsigned pieces in the journal. Emerson had no pretensions of Ward becoming a literary celebrity of such magnitude that those outside the circle would be desperate to know the young author's identity.

Emerson nonetheless held Ward's writing in high esteem, as evidenced by the location of his pieces in the *Dial*. Ward's early poetry was so prominently displayed and strategically placed as to suggest his importance to Emerson. Two of Ward's typically polished poems, the prosody of which would never be mistaken for the ragged slant rhyme of a lesser poet like Channing, had won the coveted honor of immediately preceding and following Emerson's "The Problem" in the *Dial*'s first volume. A declaration of vocational independence and arguably Emerson's most important poem, "The Problem" functioned as nothing less than the verse equivalent of the Harvard Divinity School Address. "The Shield," a sonnet on Washington Allston, the American painter most beloved by the Concord circle, precedes "The Problem" and "Come Morir?" follows it. Horace Greeley admired "The Shield" enough to reprint it in the *New-York Tribune*, and James Freeman Clarke also inquired about it for inclusion in the *Western Messenger*. The poem, written by Ward but signed only "J.," depicts a father preparing his son for his first battle. The old man advises him to "'take thou this shield my son,/ Long tried in battle and long tried by age/ Guarding by this, thy fathers did engage,/ Trusting to this, the victory they have won.'" Once in battle, however, the youth is overcome with the desire to shed the shield and thus his dependence on tradition and hereditary past. He throws it "on the ground," for "those fatal arms oppress me," and "suddenly/ Comes back my strength—returns my spirit bold." Liberated from the yoke of paternal guidance and influence, the youth appears to face battle autonomously. But Ward deftly weaves a rich parable of mentorship by confirming the necessity of both self-reliance, as the son "heeds no law but what within he finds,/ Trusts his own vision not to other minds," and reliance on the father's encouraging spirit. Thus the son is "alone, unarmed—yet not alone" because "He fights with thee—Father." Pivoting on the word "Father," Ward's final exhortation concludes the poem: "Father, aid thou thy son." True aid in this sense is not the patriarchal protection represented by the shield displacing the power of the son's "own vision."[38] Liberating the pupil to realize his own powers aids him more effectively than oppressing him with the shield's weight of inheritance and tradition. Indeed, he is a swifter, better warrior without the encumbrance, armed instead with autonomy and intuition.

The key to "The Shield" lies in the father's spiritual, rather than material, support of his son in battle. As an allegory of ideal mentorship, the poem pays homage to Emerson's tutelage of Ward. This is especially evident in how the father does not vanish in his absence, but maintains his influence, instilling a presence and self-possession in his son as a figure who forever "fights with thee." Emerson never encumbered Ward with the literary equivalent of an unwieldy inherited shield, but instead accompanied him in spirit through his lasting influence. Certainly Emerson nurtured Ward's "own vision" and never administered any coercive or directive pedagogy, nor did he burden him with any received talismanic advice. Ward recognizes the subtle challenge of proper guidance, as his admonition to "aid thou thy son" emerges as something of a riddle.[39] How, exactly, can aid be given if not materially? The answer lies in the subtle art of mentorship, the vapory mist of a father's presence in a son's life without actually being there, of an immortal stamp of encouragement without external impositions.

It is thus fitting that "The Shield" preceded, and in effect prefaced, Emerson's "The Problem." If "The Shield" disparages traditional forms of tutelage as seen in the image of the father imposing his relic upon his son, it then calls for a romantic transcendental, and thus more effective, form of guidance. Crucially, that alternative aid is rendered from the youth's perspective of shedding the weight of inheritance to find his own inner shield in the form of self-reliance. This perfectly sets the keynote for Emerson's poem that follows "The Shield" in its original publication in the *Dial*.

"The Problem" looks to shed equally encumbering inheritances for a lighter and more self-sufficient spiritual outlook with wide-reaching professional implications. As in George Herbert's "The Collar," Emerson rejects the shackles of the "cowled churchman['s]" professional identity. Although he appreciates the artistry of theologians in the language of the divines, "like the volcano's tongue of flame" their "words are music in my ear," he concludes that "for all his faith could see,/ I would not the good bishop be." He in effect throws off the cowl, a hooded garment worn by monks representing an oppressive professional fate—"I see his cowled portrait"— threatening to conceal and dominate his spirit that should otherwise be liberated. Like Ward's shield, the cowl is precisely the problem of the poem's title. Both poems define professional identities by rejecting oppressive mantles of inherited dogma. Dropping the shield in Ward's poem is a gesture perfectly matched to Emerson's refusal of the enshrouding cowl of organized religion. Emerson can appreciate the linguistic passion of the theologians "by groves of oak or fanes of gold" but not in "monastic aisles." He realizes that the source of the clergy's passion is in nature rather than an anthropomorphic domineering God. Emerson finds a pantheistic foundation in the writings of the divines through the discovery that their muse is less ecclesiastical than it is natural, a voice that "Still floats upon the morning wind,/ Still whispers to the willing mind."[40] As such, their writings are accessible to secular thinkers with literary, rather than ministerial, vocational aspirations. His own literary inspiration paradoxically uses the sources of transcendent canonical writings of theologians for his secular sense of authorship bent on creativity outside the confines of organized religion. One could imagine the youth of the "The Shield" admiring the speaker of Emerson's poem for assertively selecting, rather than passively accepting, what he finds spiritually valuable in religious writings. Like Emerson's speaker, Ward's youth in his poem actively extracts from a traditional credo figured in the shield only his father's love and support, while shedding himself of its material and conventional substance. The self-reliant resolutions that close each poem capture Ward's understanding of how Emerson had influenced him.

Even more explicitly than "The Shield," "The Consolers" pays tribute to Emerson's mentorship. Appearing in the April 1844 issue, "The Consolers" was the last poem Ward published in the *Dial*. It identifies the forces of nature, rather than Emerson per se, as the "consolers" of an otherwise "solitary . . . pilgrim, on a lonely shore." In the poem, Emerson does not appear as the messianic savior figure of Christopher Cranch's "The Prophet Unveiled," for example. Cranch locates the source of his inspiration in the charismatic oratorical performance of his mentor, from his voice, "this deep-toned wisdom borne to me," to his physical stage presence, "the spell his *visible* presence o'er me threw," to his published writings, "the page his inspiration wrought." Ward, by contrast, never stands in such mystical awe. Cranch worships, but is not activated or even empowered to achieve any spiritual insight of his own. Ward avoids Cranch's attitude altogether, which shows no independent thought, but remains stammering in his master's presence, for "if I spoke," he confesses, "it seemed to me my thought/ Was but a pale and broken reflex caught/ From his own orb." Awestruck, Cranch becomes a passive consumer of Emerson's wisdom, "silently . . . / Drinking in truth and beauty" and his "serene and sympathizing smile." Interestingly, Cranch perceives his own powerless fanaticism here, suggesting that the way to individual empower-ment was to become more intimate with Emerson. This conclusion was similarly reached by the legions of promising youth at the time who sought a literary apprenticeship under his guidance. Thus Cranch understands that his autonomous empowerment can be gained only by coming nearer to Emerson's source of genius, "That nearer intercourse might give me right/ To come within the region of his light." Only through rigorous discipleship might Cranch overcome the "dazzled, moth-like" effect of "his flame" and "go as independent as I came."[41]

Cranch's tone of adoring disciple in "The Prophet Unveiled" never surfaces in Ward's "The Consolers." Emerson does not constitute the source of spiritual growth through a larger-than-life persona for Ward, but instead is instrumental in alerting him that the key to individual development lies in nature. Through his orphic pronouncement that the wind emanating from "heaven free" will lead him to salvation, Emerson liberates Ward from lonely barrenness not by an attachment or a gift for which he was indebted, but by pointing him to the source of inspiration for spiritual growth that had always surrounded him but remained untapped. With his new power, Ward grows, but with no fawning devotion in the process as Cranch does. Ward credits Emerson for a subtle yet profoundly influential shift in his relation to nature. Casting himself as a "bare and branchless tree," the speaker of "The Consolers" at first seeks solace from "the solitary hours" in nature, but it is vast and unresponsive as "the ocean silent at my feet," and its message is repetitive and ineffective: "The universe did its old tale repeat." But alerting him to the necessity of his solitude as a precondition for the reception of nature's divine energy is an Emerson figure "with healing wings" bearing the message, " 'Thus bare and branchless must thou be,/ Ere thou couldst feel the wind from heaven that springs.' " Needy loneliness reverts to necessary and even sacred individualism, opening the soul to wind springing from the heavens. That divine source is larger and more powerful than Emerson himself. Its gusts also stimulate growth, as "now again fresh leaves do bud for me." Fascinatingly, Ward's speaker still appreciates that state of solitude not as cold isolation, but as stately independence, in which being bare and branchless yields a greater sensitivity to the soul's "quiet song, coming from heaven free." Emerson emerges as a timely voice guiding Ward toward the true source of nature's power, which he can access himself. Solitude is no longer despairing loneliness, but through the arboreal metaphor of winter's dormancy it becomes a psychic state of mind. He even begins to long for such solitude after his metaphorical leaves have grown in. Within the bare and branchless state lies that "quiet song" always available to those still and reverent enough to hear it "coming from heaven free," an infinitely renewable resource of energy refreshingly free of obligation and repayment like that which began to crowd into Ward's increasingly complex web of social and professional contacts in Boston.[42]

Ward regarded his poetic craft as seriously as that of his art and literary criticism. He had planned on contributing poetry criticism to the January 1844 issue of the *Dial*, and eventually submitted "Translation of Dante," one of many translations he had written with Emerson's encouragement. Translating Goethe while living as an American scholar and farmer in the Berkshires was perhaps the most typically transcendental tableau of Ward. The project brought him into close contact with Emerson, who assumed the role of marketer and editor of his pupil in carrying out the arrangements for the publication of what would be Ward's only published volume. Emerson had wanted his protégé to take more interpretive liberties in his translation, but Ward insisted on adhering strictly to a more classical rendering of Goethe's work. *Essays on Art by Goethe; Translated by Samuel Gray Ward* (1845) spurred Emerson to action. Publicizing the work, he believed, would also serve the greater good by democratizing Goethe. He energetically bounded into the possibilities for a book "not cabalistic," but one that "can lie in the college libraries & public reading rooms, & go to remove that local *prestige* against Goethe, by vindicating his claim to the largest sense possessed by his contemporaries." Emerson's desire to endorse Ward as a way of making Goethe accessible to a wider audience is consonant with his promotion of Ellery Channing's verse to serve the broader aim of democratizing poetry through unfinished yet authentic portfolio poetry. Emerson praised Ward's inclusion of Goethe's interior of the ancient Vatican based on Philostratus's imagined description in "a few paragraphs of modern rhetoric [that] is daringly German." Requesting more of this sort of contemporary appeal, which worked against Ward's classical inclinations, Emerson proposed "two chapters more, I think, which I hope you will prepare for the second edition." The project instilled in Ward the value of furnishing great works for the enjoyment of the wider public (*L*, 3:286).

Ward's expertise that Emerson enjoyed the most, however, was his art criticism. His poem "To W. Allston, on Seeing His 'Bride,'" which pays tribute to Allston's masterpiece painting, appears as a lyrical addendum to Fuller's energetic, if technically compromised, "Record of Impressions Produced by Mr. Allston's Pictures in the Summer of 1839," both published in the *Dial* of July 1840. Ward captures how the heavy-lidded bride burns with a love she herself cannot quite comprehend, paradoxically making the viewers' "tired spirits mount at such dim visioned company." Though his subject appears weary, the effect of the painting is like that of a fountain oasis, "flowing water in that plane of care," and leaves Ward proclaiming he does "not count/ Weary the way in which thou hast gone by."

Perhaps the most telling display of Emerson's influence on Ward's aesthetic is in his article from July 1843 in the *Dial*, "Notes on Art and Architecture." In it, Ward shows a strong grasp of the process of artistic production as the result of well-conceived thought derived from a deep connection to nature. He found it "childish to lament the absence of good painters. We should lament the absence of great thoughts, for it is the thought that makes the painters." The trope of seasonal dormancy and bloom that drives the controlling images of "The Consolers" emerges in the essay as part of Ward's demonstration of the necessity for artists to have a close kinship with nature, which provides "consolation when all around us looks so cheerless." As in "The Consolers," his prose explication locates the true consolers not in a messianic mentor figure like Emerson, but in "the noble plant we would so fain see" whose cycles of "cold and retarding spring, its green growth of the stalk, that it may in summer bring forth its flowers" speak to how "by our destinies we may be one of these." His principle of beauty derives from the example of the flower, whose isolated parts combine so that the "sum of their united force and beauty [becomes] transfigured, glorified." Artistic labor, if it is to be successful, must be grounded in this principle and proceed "silently and faithfully" with an eye toward "perfecting as he may his talent" and "inward satisfaction."

Because Ward earned his wealth in trade, he could more easily idealize artistic labor and insist that it remain untainted by commercial interest. Art, according to this principle, should never be produced for "outward . . . gorgeous successes apparent," and the artist should never succumb to the temptation "of some devil to work out effects instead of painting from his heart." This takes uncommon reverence—to paint on one's knees, as it were—to witness "the hand of God even in the mixing of colors." According to Ward, art should never be so much a means of acquiring wealth as a means of accessing divine energy through nature. Interestingly, it was not through inward, quiet, consistent labor that Ward finally won his affluent bride and his high-profile position as a Boston financier. Those were instead calculated moves to make outward "gorgeous successes apparent," which he could wholly rationalize because he executed them one remove from the aesthetic world.[43]

Ward's commentary on architecture has deep implications for his understanding of Emerson's influence on his life, and on the literary careers of his fellow disciples. Ward observes that the history of art regrettably reveals seemingly endless variations of apprentices alternately imitating and rebelling against their masters. He therefore calls for creators without direct masters, as in "The Shield"—artists not beholden to immediate debts of inheritance, but instead reaching back further to more stable, permanent, timeless, and universal sources, as in nature's wind song that Emerson alluded to in "The Problem." For Ward, that timeless source in architecture lies in the simplicity and unity of ancient Greek structures. Greek architectural style can be replicated endlessly without any loss of vitality in the finished products, he claims, unlike whole genealogies of masters and apprentices that become merely a series of contradictions and rebellions. At their worst, disciples produce weak imitations of their masters' visions. Their models should instead be the beauty inherent in timeless Greek structures. "What one man designed, his successor changed," Ward explained, "so that to the most unpracticed eye, the grossest inconsistencies are constantly apparent," making the viewer conclude that "there is no good architecture, but in the mind of the artist." It is not that neoclassicism should be used as so much decoration, as in the ornamentation of modern buildings with Greek facades ("how unmeaning is the pretense of a Grecian front?" he asks), but that its forms can function as the source or blueprint for infinite creative rearrangement and innovation.[44] This speaks volumes to Ward's understanding of his relationship with Emerson. He never rebelled, nor did he strain in imitation of his mentor, but instead took his advice to consult timeless universal sources (rather than Emerson's own works or lectures) and derive his standard for creating, and criticizing, art. The result was a long and satisfying relation not only to the art world, but also with Emerson.

Ward was a friend and consultant to Emerson, a shrewd and incisive arbiter of taste in art and architecture, and a forbidden confidante in the power of trade. Ward had a professionalizing presence in the cohort of Emersonian disciples, with a range of expertise he took great pride in, extending from the nuances of business to the function of the lowest detail in the design of a cathedral or landscape painting. He affected his fellow apprentices by raising Emerson's expectations for financial and philosophical autonomy. Ward proved to Emerson that his young followers could be their own patrons—and even accomplished professionals and masters in life—before indulging his own and others' generosity. It is telling that among the generation of Emerson's promising youths, he would be closest to Fuller, rather than gravitating toward his old friend Ellery Channing, as Thoreau had. Certainly he remained friendly with Channing, and rescued him from his innumerable dubious ventures with timely cash donations. For Fuller—with all of her imaginative and literary power, and her immense classical training—to have been so deeply in love with Ward tells us much about his sophisticated background and intelligence. Other than Fuller and Thoreau, Ward was the closest to Emerson of the apprentices. Newcomb, Cranch, Very, and Channing could all blame Ward for pressure they felt from Emerson to professionalize their craft. Yet as with the other protégés, Emerson saw to it that his friend's best manuscripts were published and promoted in both book and periodical presses to make a difference in the development of the nation's culture. His patronage, in Ward's case, never felt patronizing; his mentorship never felt pedantic; his marketing never strained for profit. Ward presented him with no undue obligations, either aesthetic or financial. He was a pupil from whom he could expand his critical and factual knowledge of art, yet not struggle with or question his own established beliefs, for he was in Emerson's eyes a master at life and a finished man.

PART

III

RECKLESS ROMANTICS

5

ELLERY CHANNING: SATURDAY AFTERNOON PROFESSOR; OR, CONCORD'S MAD POET

Whereas Christopher Cranch and Samuel Ward tapped into Ralph Waldo Emerson's endless fascination with the world of visual art, Ellery Channing the younger entered his life as his next poet apprentice following Henry David Thoreau. Emerson had initially invested his faith in the genius of Channing on the recommendation of Ward, whom he trusted as the most professionally stable and financially solvent of all his protégés. Aesthetically, Ward had also established himself as an authority on classical art history and criticism in Emerson's eyes, assuming at several key phases in their relationship the role of mentor to Emerson's wide-eyed apprentice. So in October 1839, when Ward forwarded a packet of fifty poems to Emerson on behalf of Channing, Emerson was naturally inclined to respond favorably to Ward's former Round Hill School class-mate. The transaction placed Ward in the role of intermediary to Channing, whose poems were a final desperate attempt to escape the shackles of a more conventional occupation. If the poems themselves had the air of economic speculation about them—the first of them bearing the appearance and function of a versified self-promotional advertisement and cover letter—it was because Channing had just reluctantly invested his money, if not his heart, in a farm in McHenry County, Illinois. Standing at this vocational crossroads, he yearned for an apprenticeship with Emerson as much as he dreaded a life of farming in Illinois. Playing out the first in a series of conflicts between fiscal responsibility and romantic whim that would shape the rest of his life, Channing imbued that bundle of poems

Ellery Channing (Courtesy Concord Free Public Library)

he had forwarded to Emerson in the care of Ward with his dream of becoming a professional poet.

An undated and critically unexamined poem in Channing's youthful hand suggests how serious he was about making a favorable first impression on Emerson, especially in comparison to his haphazard farming venture. In a vocational self-fulfilling prophecy of sorts, Channing had almost willed his failure at farming. While his industrious neighbors rose before dawn to tend their fields, Channing, who lacked the essentials of the trade ("He had no fence, no oxen, no plough, no barn, no wife, and no breakfast, besides having no floor to his house"), blissfully slept.[1] His floorless cabin signified how baseless and insubstantial his foray into agriculture was, especially compared with the energy and imagination he poured into winning an apprenticeship with Emerson. Fascinatingly, the free-spirited man who would later be listed as a "do nothing" on Concord's town register, and who was inseparable from his alter-ego canine companion ironically named Professor (since the dog was the more professionally inclined of the two), and who playfully (and self-reflexively) anointed Bronson Alcott a "Don Quixote of the soul," assured Emerson of the seriousness of his vocational ambition.[2] "Here mildly thanks thee— Emerson! A youth," read Channing's first line of his introductory poem, his crucial and calculated first impression on Emerson that would bear the same function as Thoreau's "Sic Vita."[3]

Channing was anything but mild in his recent raucous antics—ranging "from rhapsody to clowning, as bewildering as if a deacon had turned a cartwheel in his Sunday suit"—under the pseudonym of Hal Menge in the *Mercantile Journal.*[4] In case Emerson had been aware of these satirical and undisciplined writings, or even if he had not made the connection, Channing was careful to cast himself as a youth whose wild days were past, "Whose life was shuttering like a gusty day,/ But now he well perceives a morn of truth." The new beginning thus figured is Channing's genuflection before Emerson, his vow of sober obedience that takes the form of a prayer, "Thou tranquil active man think thee I pray," couched in grateful tones and formal diction, "How grateful is this heart of mine to thee." Little did Emerson know that behind this mask of dutiful obedience and commitment was a Don Quixote of the soul, whose entrance on the Concord stage was hardly so sedate and reverent, but instead blew in "like a gusty day."[5] Such refreshing irreverence had a magnetic effect on Emerson, as he would make Channing and his dog Professor his preferred walking companions for the next decade, joining them on the trails at least twice daily by the late 1840s. "I have very pleasant Saturdays with Ellery quite punctually now for a long time," Emerson recorded, observing that "he is, and remains, the best company, always superior and inexplicable" (*L*, 3:396). Along with Thoreau, they dubbed themselves "Saturday afternoon professors," a moniker prompted not only by Channing's appropriately named hound (*JMN*, 11:36–38). The title also captured their gleefully spontaneous yet philosophically authentic ruminations on concepts as expansive as the terrain they roamed, from Channing's secret garden laced with wild lupine stretching more than a quarter acre to the sylvan woods spanning Walden, Flint's, and White Ponds, far from the silent lecture stalls of Harvard awaiting their Monday morning professors and students. For as much as Emerson took sweet pleasure in communing with Channing in free nature, as a project to develop into a professional poet suitable for the literary market Channing proved alternately exasperating and challenging. In mentoring Channing, Emerson felt pressure to professionalize the recreation they shared and thus worked to reverse ingrained dichotomies in the broader culture between leisure and work, private and public writing. With delicate aggression, he would bring his Saturday afternoon professor into the market by making transcendentalism more compatible with the publishing world.

Before he had ever considered himself a transcendental poet, Channing showed a predilection for commercial authorship. His earliest publications as Hal Menge reveal his Addisonian leanings, echoing Washington Irving's mad satire in *Salmagundi* and *The History of New York*. Such writings do not just speak of an undisciplined wildly discursive temperament colliding with Emerson's poised reserve. They also reveal Channing's desire to tap into popular forms of writing, drawing from the humor of Dr. Johnson and the English wits, and the caricature made famous by Charles Dickens. Comic innuendo surfaces in his review of John Greenleaf Whittier's poems in one issue of the *Mercantile Journal*. His style is pure Addison and Steele, as seen in the all-caps outlandish name of his imagined interlocutor, and their quibble over the relative importance of American writing: "Intemperate praise is folly—but after FRIZZLE said to me, 'Whittier hath an indifferent poem in the last Magazine,' I resolved feebly to desire the Americans to read him and contradict my worthy friend FRIZZLE."[6] Channing was not only dabbling in British satire at the time, he was also trying his hand at other popular forms such as gothic narrative in "Diavolo" and a series of six literary essays titled "Shakespeare."

Channing's affinity for popular forms from humor to gothic indicate that from the beginning he had been interested in making a living from his writing, in appealing to and winning a readership that might provide him a sustainable income and even renown in the literary market. In this light, it is peculiar that Hal Menge would decide rather suddenly to reinvent himself as a transcendental poet and Emersonian disciple. Irving and the British wits were worlds apart from the transcendentalists in subject, style, temperament, and core ideological values. Given Channing's desire for fame in the popular press, and his willingness to exploit established and fashionable forms, one might have more easily imagined him angling for a mentorship under Irving or one of his Lads of Kilkenny. Indeed, had he been a New Yorker rather than a New Englander, his high birth as a descendant and namesake of William Ellery Channing, a signer of the Declaration of Independence, and his defection from a legal apprenticeship in 1835, would have matched him perfectly with the well-born youths who fled their legal and medical training to join Irving's circle. It was Emerson, however, who had touched Channing through his lectures and *Nature*—the work that also transfixed Jones Very, Henry Thoreau, and Charles Newcomb—prompting him to find the ideal natural setting in which to cultivate his poetry. Channing thus went directly to Emerson for his literary rebirth to nurture his talent a short distance from Boston rather than exiling himself in a far-flung midwestern locale. The stimulation, attention, and sheer theater of Concord's literary stage beckoned.

Channing mythologized his own vocationally rudderless life as the essence of the romantic artist in "Paul, A Sketch," a profile of John Paul Richter he wrote for the *Mercantile Ledger*. Employing the genre of the literary sketch, again borrowing from an Irvingesque light nonfiction discursive popular form, Channing renders the portrait of a romantic dreamer akin to Geoffrey Crayon, Irving's own narrative persona for *The Sketch Book* (1819), a wayward bachelor "ever conceiving, never performing," "a thought waster" prone to "unexampled absurdity" yet "so far from selfishness, so worthy of love."[7] These features also defined Channing most of his life, as this "do-nothing" of Concord and his dog, Professor, cut an image also like that of Irving's Rip Van Winkle and Wolf. Neighbors could not help but see the parallels between Channing and Professor, who was forever burrowing into nature, impulsive yet good natured and affable, a "born companion" happiest on walks and out in the open air, and a soul that loved his freedom.[8] Just as Rip the agrarian socialist is averse to the frenetic acquisitive behavior of his wife, yet whose community supports him into perpetuity as its resident "historian," Channing helped his neighbors consistently and also benefited from their patronage. Echoing Rip's historian role, Channing became locally known as the unofficial poet laureate of Concord, yet one that seemed to be in a perpetual state of development, never fully arriving at accomplished expertise.

In a gesture that affirmed their dedication to Channing's poetic training, an ample portion of the Concord community in 1846 generously donated more than three hundred dollars to support his trip to Europe, which he rather arbitrarily decided was essential, "nay, that it is a matter of life and death," as Emerson explained the plan to Ward. All concurred "that he should set out for Havre and Italy" for his poetic development. Emerson's endorsement—which came only after careful scrutiny into his pupil's seriousness ("serious as he is capable of being") through a "challenge . . . to talk it through with him"—was essential to raising the funds (*L*, 3:327). Despite leaving behind his sick wife, Ellen, Channing departed for Rome after collecting contributions from Horace Greeley, Caleb Cushing (the politician), Caroline Sturgis, and Emerson, all of whom found the trip justifiable for the cultivation of their youthful poet neighbor.[9] "Where are you going?" an onlooker called out to Channing while he was trundling his trunk in a wheelbarrow down a bumpy dirt road the morning of his departure. "I'm going to Rome!" Channing shouted back, his reply taken as the type of sally for which he had become notorious. Yet Channing had literally just begun the first steps of a long transatlantic journey on that day in March 1846. And with his characteristic whimsicality, he not only neglected to say good-bye to his wife and children, he returned for home unexpectedly after sixteen days, declaring that Salem's shore glittered as brilliantly as any in Europe.[10]

Channing's realization that, "As for beauty, I need not look beyond an oar's length for my fill of it," as he said on one boating excursion with Emerson, aptly represents what made him an ideal walking companion for Emerson (*JMN*, 8:230–31). Emerson delighted in Channing's instinct for the miraculous in nature, and therefore dedicated himself to supporting his career through aggressive editorial, financial, and creative assistance. One of Channing's chief weaknesses could be discerned from his great gift as a conversationalist, for he was a man whose best insights, Emerson feared, might be lost in the ripples of the pond at the end of his oar. Emerson thus suggested he transcribe the gems of his spoken comments in a book titled *Concord Walking*. The offer was neither perfunctory nor insincere; Emerson was ready to back the project with his full arsenal of creativity and profound power in the literary market to attract influential publishers and vast numbers of readers. Yet Channing balked, and the project never came to fruition.

As with his other protégés, Emerson patronized and encouraged Channing's literary interests—a trip to Europe to cultivate his poetry, a volume dedicated to recreating the stimulating conversation of innumerable Concord walks—which he himself would have adored pursuing. The specialization of his own career toward lecturing prevented such indulgences, but certainly authorized him to support endeavors of this sort by his protégés. He admired Channing's commitment to becoming the professional, and even popular, poet he himself had always wanted to be. Part of the appeal of mentoring promising youths for Emerson was that it afforded him the opportunity to live out career ambitions he thought were no longer available to him. Emerson earnestly drove his apprentices toward a vision of professional success best suited to their individual talents while minimizing the liability of their weaknesses, and not in a spirit of self-sacrificing philanthropy, but to enhance his own personal and professional development in the process. Since Emerson's own critics had condemned the versification of his poetry, but lauded him for the soul beneath the imperfect lines, he embraced Channing as a means of developing his theory of democratic verse. The theory simultaneously functioned as an implicit defense of Emerson's own "husky . . . singing" while more explicitly touting the unorthodox approach of his latest apprentice (*L*, 1:435). Channing thus became a pioneering and radical project who put both mentor and pupil in the position of revolutionizing the transcendental authorial role, a challenge they faced with innovations otherwise obscured by overwhelming critical emphasis on Emerson's frustration with this erratic youth. By forwarding an expanded and liberalized definition of the poet's role, Emerson could challenge the hegemonic privileging of metrically pleasing verse that might have prevented both his and Channing's rise to success as poets. Emerson's most radical understanding of the poet's role indeed would emerge from his mentorship of Channing, but not without shattering old paradigms prevalent in the literary market and, paradoxically, held dear by Emerson himself.

"Here Mildly Thanks Thee—Emerson! A Youth"

Soon after Thoreau's poetic apprenticeship under Emerson had waned, Emerson reported to his English friend John Sterling that the twenty-five-year old Channing was now "the best poet we have" (*L*, 3:181). Thoreau's departure for New York in pursuit of a professional career in the periodical press as a nature writer left Emerson without a youth to mentor for the first time in years. Replacing the often morose and hard demeanor of Thoreau was the amiable, even Irvingesque, "affectionate playfulness" of Channing, whose verse made Emerson "very happy to meet this kindness." Emerson found "a highly poetical temperament and a sunny sweetness of thought and feeling which are high gifts" in the packet of poems Ward had forwarded to him. His reply to Ward in October 1839 includes what appears to be a general description of Channing's poetry. But the endearing tone of the previously mentioned undated and unsigned manuscript folio of nine Spenserian stanzas in Channing's unmistakable handwriting perfectly matches what Emerson describes. No other lines by Channing in the packet other than what was likely the top poem correspond with the "voluminous eloquence of his Spenserian stanza," Emerson observed. The poem addresses Emerson directly and in flattering terms designed to endear himself to the famous luminary. Critical emphasis has been placed on Emerson's harsh qualifications of his praise, especially his claim that Channing "goes to the very end of the poetic license, and defies a little too disdainfully his dictionary and logic" (*L*, 2:227).[11] More telling than these misgivings, however, is his praise for the Spenserian stanza, which "is itself an indication of great skill and cunning." Indeed, without evidence of Channing's capacity to produce competent fixed-verse stanzas, which the poem accomplishes nine times as proof of his skill, the sunny and playful treatment of subject would not have sufficed to impress Emerson. The logic of Emerson's comment asserts that although Channing's demeanor is amiable, more of his real poetic prowess can be found in his versification.

The untitled poem, whose first line reads, "Here mildly thanks thee, Emerson!—a youth," functions simultaneously as a letter of introduction and a self-promotional advertisement of Channing's poetic skills. As indicated by Emerson's praise for Channing's metrical "skill and cunning," the poem impressed him with its ambitious if not flawless Spenserian stanzas of eight lines of iambic pentameter and a ninth in Alexandrine hexameter following consistently an ababbcbcc rhyme scheme. This impressive feat appears all the more astonishing given Channing's notorious reputation for irregular prosody, tin ear for rhyme, and abuse of all manner of grammar and spelling that would plague his verse throughout his career. The poem provides evidence, therefore, that far from lacking aptitude, Channing had little patience for the composition of such carefully choreographed performances like this one, designed on this one occasion for Emerson's eyes only to exude the genius of a precocious prodigy. In an effort to prove himself worthy of an Emersonian apprenticeship, Channing selected meter for his introductory poem that was exceedingly fashionable at the time. Spenserian stanza was the preferred form of the wildly popular and critically revered *Vision of Don Roderick* by Sir Walter Scott, *Childe Harold's Pilgrimage* by Lord Byron, *Adonais* by Percy Bysshe Shelley, and *Lyrical Ballads* by William Wordsworth. Emerson and Channing were not only familiar with all of these works, they regarded the latter in particular as a seminal text of profound influence on American transcendentalism.[12]

To avoid appearing too egotistical, Channing knew better than to attempt to exhibit any original transcendental thought in his introductory poem. Instead, the main subject of his poem—Emerson's character and his own apprehension of it through his reading of *Nature*—is better suited to the occasion of a young author vying for an apprenticeship. His technique of extrapolating from the philosophical tenets of *Nature* to sketch out the character of Emerson, however, often seems smarmy and perhaps too openly worshipful. "And thy mild work of *Nature* have I read/ Though tracks high critical ideology/ Into my mind/ It is a tune instead/ showing to all of us where we should be fed" is certainly not an intellectually ambitious response to what was then Emerson's signature literary achievement. Channing may have underestimated Emerson's capacity to see through ingratiating hero worship; he never encouraged it and rarely warmed to such adulation from his pupils. Channing portrays Emerson as "living everywhere/ In spiritual insight, all away from strife" in an Edenic natural world, "under the canopy of fragrant air" away from "social hum." In the next stanza, Channing self-consciously qualifies his presumptions about Emerson's personal character, indicating his awareness that he might have trivialized and thus offended his reader. "And said I, for thee not, a social hum,—/ For this, that though, I am not acquainted with thee" Channing admits, quickly defending his impression of Emerson by asserting a literary kinship with him: "My inference to such concludes will come/ Of a fair, intellectual family."[13]

Indeed, one of the main objectives of the poem is Channing's desire to be adopted into the "intellectual family" of the transcendental circle. The poem is saturated with self-effacing humility and deference, as Channing strikes the humble pose of the neophyte approaching the master, much in the way Thoreau did in his early poems delivered to Bush by Lucy Brown. Such a deferential stance of course places him in a position of desiring an education. But a curious twist foreshadows the Channing that would later defy Emerson. Do "not laugh at me," he demands, anticipating derision for casting the concept of an "intellectual family" in an extended metaphor of nature as a maid "with a rich load of golden lovelings." His portrayal of Emerson and the broader Concord circle "at whom I feebly guess" employs a second-person direct address Emerson found off-putting for its calculated desire to please. "I know the lines would have pleased me if addressed to a third person: and I think bad *praise* much more annoying than *criticism*," Emerson confessed to Ward. Channing anticipated that Emerson might wince at "This small youthful move/ But I do think of thee as one host from above." After anointing him a heavenly host of sorts, Channing later changes ground, vowing to return his disapproval, should it come to that, for "I'll frown back as well/ For shock of conflict, I do surely own."[14] At this late stage in the poem, Channing insinuates himself into the code of the transcendental circle's social conduct predicated on self-reliance and authenticity that sanctioned opposition and disagreement, which at times could be downright hostile. Emerson recorded in his journal, for example, one evening to his delight that "Jones Very charmed us all by telling us he hated us all." Authenticity ruled the day: "Sincerity is more excellent than flattery," Emerson wrote, affirming "it is the highest compliment you can pay" (*JMN*, 7:124). Channing shows strength of fortitude by breaking through the mask of the fawning follower and instead offering Emerson a glimpse at his own self-reliance. Indeed, the irascible side of Channing surfaced: "There's something in a frown incredible,/ Tis the high comical."[15]

Most important, the poem ends by intimating the very means by which it should be consumed in furnishing Emerson with an assessment of Channing—who is part job applicant and solicitor of patronage craftily presenting his qualifications—and his literary strengths and weaknesses. Emerson duly responded directly to Channing after receiving another packet of poems from Ward. "I have seen no verses written in America that have such inward music, or that seem to me such authentic inspiration. Certainly I prize finished verses," he wrote, declaring that "yours are not." The virtue, however, "I prize at such a dear rate [is] the poetic soul, where that is present, I can easily forgive the license and negligence" (*L*, 2:252–53). Without reference to Channing's introductory poem written in Spenserian stanzas, one might take Emerson's criticism as occurring without a prompt or precedent, when in fact, Channing himself had provided it for him in the conclusion of his introductory poem. Alluding to his own rhythm-deaf verse, Channing's concluding couplet acknowledges "I almost fail to these poor lines I've sung/ To put my timing name, yet I will not forsake/ The true thought of these lines, no other will partake." To leave a lasting impression, Channing uncharacteristically reworded the last line, which he originally phrased, "prithee let other not forsake."[16] Any errors at this early stage, as Channing had prescribed in his poem, Emerson gladly overlooked to find the "true thought" in Channing's words, which became "authentic inspiration" in Emerson's. From this moment, Emerson discovered in Channing's verse "a steady autumnal light . . . a certain wild beauty immeasurable; a happiness lightsome and delicious fills my heart and brain" (*JMN*, 7:276). Channing returned the love, yearning for Concord years later after attempting to forge a career with the *New-York Tribune*, confessing, "I have one reason for setting in one place in America; it is because you are there . . . I come to Concord as a place attracted by you."[17]

The "True Madmen of this Nineteenth Century"

Channing came to transcendental poetry when Emerson himself was surging at the height of his powers as a poet between 1836 and 1846, yet enduring a profound crisis that would forever change his theory of poetry. Approaching publication of his first volume of poetry, which included "Merlin," "Bacchus," and "Hamatreya," all prosodically unconventional for the time, Emerson was facing the crucible of his own career as a poet. The seldom-questioned judgment of antebellum critics would condemn Emerson for lacking technical competence and a poetic ear, though they allowed that he exuded the soul of a poet. Only later, particularly by 1857 and 1858 with "Brahma," and "Adirondacs," did Emerson revert back to the fixed meter of the neoclassical dipodic line of his youth. Indeed, there is evidence that Emerson even excised irregular lines from "Adirondacs," a sure sign of his late return to metrically even, consistent verse.[18] But when he undertook the poetic mentorship of Channing in 1839, he saw poetry in an entirely different light.

In the late 1830s, when Emerson's alternative understanding of the function of poetry was simmering, Channing's introductory packet of poems brought it to a boil, prompting his full commitment to a radical new aesthetic. Whereas Emerson loved rhythmic rhyme as a child, especially the folk forms of ballads, hymns, and nursery rhymes, at the age of thirty-six and in his prime years as an author he loathed it. At this time he chided Poe's sing-song meter, dismissing him as a mere "jingle-man," and downplayed prosody as secondary to a poem's movement of thought in his famous formulation in "The Poet" that "it is not meters, but a meter-making argument that makes a poem" (*CW*, 3:6). The philosophy, he believed, makes the meter, and not vice versa. According to Emerson, excessive attention to meter reveals a commercial aesthetic too eager to please the burgeoning mass readership of the antebellum literary market. Critic Terence Whalen observes that "Poe's writing was not only regulated by the market, per se," as Emerson could plainly see in Poe's versification and aggressive methods of self-promotion in *Blackwood's* magazine, "but also by the instability of the publishing industry [and] the national investment in a capitalist future," especially given the recent Panic of 1837. Emerson was acutely aware of the changing tide that saw "the rise of information of an economic good," and wanted to protect both himself and his protégés from such forces that "tended to undermine traditional standards of literary value by stressing the growing complicity between capitalism and signification," as Whalen explains.[19] Emerson's resistance to meter, and consequent sanctioning of Channing's disregard for it, can be read as his resistance to the market. Paradoxically, the market's influence on the means of production and consumption of literature demanded that professionally ambitious poets make concessions to commercialization and thus bow to conventional versification, especially in the era before Whitman's *Leaves of Grass* (1855), the work that shattered Longfellowesque form. Thus Emerson's promotion of poetry as meter-making argumentation distances the poem's value from its musical affectations, but interestingly, does not dismiss it altogether. Instead he organicizes the pleasing measure as a natural outgrowth of the poem's "argument," which he describes as "a thought so passionate and alive, that, like the spirit of a plant or an animal, it has an architecture" or formal structure "of its own," not superimposed, but already intrinsic to its very essence (*CW*, 3:6).

Such a romantic paradigm effectively, even heroically, defies Lockean rationality along with the industrialist ethos of artificial manufacturing to situate the process of poetic production closer to nature. He thus locates power in "Rhyme; not tinkling rhyme but grand Pinaric strokes as firm as the tread of a horse." This sort of bold musical cadence "vindicates itself as an art," like "the stroke of the great bell of a cathedral" that "knocks at prose and dullness with the stroke of a cannon ball." Emerson calls for a "Rhyme which builds out into Chaos and Old night a splendid architecture to bridge the impassible, and call aloud on all the children of morning that the Creation is recommencing. I wish to write such rhymes as shall not suggest a restraint but contrariwise the wildest freedom." Unlike affected tinkling or jingles, as with "the very first note of the flute or horn or the first strain of a song," a poem's rhyme should make us "leave the world of common sense and launch at once into the eternal sea of ideas and emotions." Lockean rationality be damned—for while "You shall not speak truth in Prose, you may in Verse," Emerson mused in his journal on a sweet late June day in 1839 (*JMN*, 7:218–19). This paradigm, however, obviously does not lend itself well to an accessible pedagogy, and instead tends to subvert the notion that versification could be taught at all. Channing understood and fully abided by the romantic principle of intuitive poetic composition opposed to the rationality associated with artificially constructed prosody more deeply and consistently than Emerson himself, whose poetics would eventually shift toward a more formal approach. Indeed, Channing's unwavering belief in literary production as an organic process provides the key to understanding his otherwise mystifying reluctance to revise his verse.

Emerson's mystification of the process of composing uniform meter springs from his emphasis on the construction first of an argument whose meter would naturally follow. This is precisely the pattern of his essays, which show distilled philosophy whose lyricism tends to attach itself to already shapely ideas. But the theory was ultimately exposed as unteachable to poets-in-training like Channing. Openly admitting to being rhythm deaf, Channing regarded his poetry primarily as thoughts or "arguments" with an "architecture of its own," thus rendering the onerous task of imposing a pleasing rhyme scheme contrary to both his own natural temperament (which he understood as epitomizing transcendental nonconformist individualism) and Emersonian poetic theory. The Channing-Emerson relationship appears to have been brokered on a mutual disdain for the superficiality of metrical precision as aesthetic window dressing hiding the core of the poet's spirit. At the beginning of the mentorship they would embrace this belief since Emerson trusted that the "skill and cunning" of the Spenserian stanza in his pupil's introductory poem promised future development in this area. Emerson was therefore willing to promote the youth based on his current strengths, but in doing so, gave the false appearance that he never expected him to develop a more mature metrical form.

The unrestrained vigor of Channing's poetic composition process appealed to Emerson because it so readily associated itself with wild nature. To be a transcendental poet, both believed, meant to live close to the organic world. In this way, the disciple's understanding of the poet's role resonated with the mentor's professional self-definition rooted in remote

nature. Channing knew that if McHenry County, Illinois, was too remote
and isolating to forge his poetic craft, Concord was just rustic enough, yet
densely populated with stimulating like-minded literati for him to flourish.
Emerson regarded Concord's wilderness as integral to his professional
identity, a point he emphasized since it tested his new wife's tolerance for
rural living. Since "I am born a poet, of a low class without a doubt yet a
poet," Emerson reasoned with Lidian, she must leave her intimate and
familiar Plymouth and make their home in rural Concord. Channing and
Emerson sought out the essence of nature in rural homes to break through
the artifice of city life, much in the way the aesthetic lens of their shared
theory of poetry sought something deeper than form as a measure of its
aesthetic quality. When Emerson was most fond of Channing's verse and
strenuously defending it in his "New Poetry" piece for the *Dial* in October
1840 he argued that polished melodic verse was a mask hiding inner empti-
ness. Later, in his preface to Channing's *The Wanderer* (1871), he tempered
his claim to suggest that rhythmic verse was the lesser gift of the poet.
Given these two arguments, it is ironic that one of Emerson's greatest
efforts in promoting Channing to the broader popular market for poetry
was his solicitation of Henry Wadsworth Longfellow's endorsement, the
very embodiment of the Fireside Poets and unnamed target of their spite
for urbane, formally dressed verse. (James Russell Lowell, a prominent
New England Fireside Poet, was an outspoken critic of transcendentalism
whose acerbic dismissal of Channing and Thoreau as Emerson's flunkies
rallied Channing to their defense in *Thoreau, the Poet-Naturalist; With
Memorial Verses.*) In a letter dated December 27, 1846, Longfellow praised
Emerson's volume of poetry, but regarded the second series of Channing's
verse with serious misgivings, since "it does not command the spontaneous
admiration which I like so much to feel," with the conciliatory allowance
that "still I see in it much to awaken sympathy; and much that you told
me I should find there" (*L*, 3:364).

Channing inspired Emerson to develop his democratic theory of poetry
precisely to justify the private unfinished journal writing he defined as
"Verses of the Portfolio." The theory functioned as a mechanism of
publicity while distancing such poetry from polished commercial verse
designed to attract an audience in the literary market. But rather than
hypocritically marketing Channing through an antimarket aesthetic,

Emerson worked with the exigencies of the literary market to carve out a new space for his protégé and others like him. In an echo of Wordsworth's argument for the democratization of poetry in the preface to *Lyrical Ballads*, Emerson's preface to Channing's eleven poems he published in the *Dial* defended "private and household poetry" over and against that which flourished in the publishing world. Wordsworth posited that the speech of peasants represented an unaffected language closer to nature. Although Percy Bysshe Shelley argued that Wordsworth's focus on nature did not bring with it an authentic embrace of the masses, "many of New England's intellectuals," especially Emerson in "New Poetry," "felt that the turn to nature they made with the help of Wordsworth *was* a turn to the people," as Lance Newman observes.[20] That turn was fueled in part by the larger cultural climate of ideological experimentation attendant to the political friction of Jacksonian democracy and the economic strife of the Panic of 1837. Arguing against "the straitest restrictions on the admission of candidates to the Parnassian fraternity," he advocated for those "denied the name of poetry." In the roles of advocate, mentor, and publicist, Emerson crafted what in effect became his best letter of recommendation for Channing by making him the representative of "a new style of poetry."[21]

Grown from American soil, this "new style of poetry" embodies the democratizing effects of the young nation's skyrocketing literacy "that has brought the works of great poets into every house, and made all ears familiar with poetic forms," inspiring "the very talent of the masses of society."[22] Lawrence Buell usefully describes Emerson's prospectus as "a revolutionary extension of the realm of authorship beyond mainstream print culture" for a "counterestablishment aesthetic," featuring Channing as the "poster-boy example."[23] Buell links this subversive current to the experiment in communal living at Brook Farm. But in the context of Emerson's marketing of Channing's career, "New Poetry" appears more nationalistic in its call for a proto-Whitmanian American poetics everywhere defying excessive ornamentation and old world refinements. "Crude" like the young nation itself, the youth's verses "have never been filed or decorated for the eye that studies surface" for an exclusive fraternity concerned with superficial appearances. Thus, "the writer was not afraid to write ill; he had a great meaning too much at heart to stand for trifles, and wrote lordly for his peers alone." "This is the poetry of hope" signified by this youth's future, the talent inherent in the masses, and the future of the nation itself in its revolutionary defiance of European models, Emerson wrote, since here is "no French correctness."[24] Emerson had similarly defied European models three years earlier in his Phi Beta Kappa address delivered at Harvard in 1837. In it, he also argued that the American scholar should not be a delicate creature sheltered in a "protected class," trifling with "turning rhymes" as "a boy whistles to keep his courage up" or as a means of "seeking a temporary peace by the diversion of his thoughts from politics or vexed questions" (*CW*, 1:64). Instead, he should be placed at the epicenter of culture, and not allowed to escape into dilettantish irrelevance. In the context of Channing's Emersonian education, this meant pressure to professionalize his craft, to live up to the hope promised in the *Dial* preface. Bringing forth private verse into the spotlight for public consumption was not without its ironies and paradoxes, of which Emerson was fully aware. He could account for the seeming contradiction in publicizing his pupil's work because his formula posited that such unfinished verse "should not be shut up in the portfolios of a few friends but should be set free to fly abroad to the ear and heart of all to whom they rightfully belong" (*L*, 2:253). Emerson made clear to Channing in his January 1840 letter that his poems had outgrown the insular enclave of "a few friends" in Concord, and were thus ready for wider circulation and exposure to figures like Longfellow.

What troubled this formulation was that the local enclave of a "few friends" Emerson wanted Channing to escape to reach a broader market was precisely what was fueling the youth's best poetry. His two prose books and later biography of Thoreau speak to Channing's favorite subject and mode: people and conversation. Examples abound throughout his poetry. Thoreau is the "Hermit" of *The Wanderer* and "Rudolpho" of *Near Home;* Emerson appears in multiple poems, including "The Sage," "Emerson," and "Ode" from *Poems: Second Series* (1849). "Sleeping Child" commemorates Emerson's son, Waldo; his own son, Edward, is the subject of "Too—, Three Years Old." He casts Elizabeth Hoar as the "Lady" of "Believe, that thus a humble worshipper." "Hillside" of *The Wanderer* depicts the Concord denizens Marston and Mary Russell Watson. The Concord community, particularly the inner circle of Emerson's promising youths, was of vital significance to Channing and his sense of authorship. He wanted to cultivate not only the art, but also the lifestyle of transcendental authorship, through the walks, conversations, sharing of journals, and epistolary correspondence with his friends. The countercultural aesthetic Buell identified in Emerson's "New Poetry" preface to Channing's verse is readily apparent in the character of the cohort with whom Channing so clearly identified.

Channing was a shaping force if not the face of the collective identity of the young transcendentalists he valorized in "The Youth of the Poet and the Painter," his autobiographical serial story written for the *Dial*. Published in May 1843, just months after the release of his first volume, *Poems*, which was financed by Ward and edited by Emerson, the narrative functions in many of the same ways "New Poetry" had in supporting, defining, and ultimately defending Channing and his work. The tale justifies both the newness of poetry and his radical vocational positioning toward the authorial role utilizing Emerson's key arguments from "New Poetry." Whereas Emerson transforms his support for Channing into a theory of democratic poetry, Channing dramatized his authorial coming of age in a four-way fictional correspondence in which one deep sympathizer, Mathews Gray, functions as his chief advocate and Emersonian apologist for Edward Ashford, the free-spirited idealistic poet and Channing figure. In the epistolary narrative, he portrays himself and his peers as reckless romantics "who have lately sprung into existence, as distinct from the youth of the last generation, as Italians from Icelanders—the children of the new birth of the century." He appeals to the circle's generational distinction that bears an identity as unique as a nation's character, employing a filial/tribal metaphor to describe this group whose main distinction is their disaffiliation from established "sects or associations, for the centre of their creed consists in the disavowal of congregations, and they wander solitary and alone, the true madmen of the nineteenth century."[25] Such renunciation of conventional social networks among these solitary wanderers ironically brought them together. Channing was nostalgically looking back on the community of writers in which he thrived during the early 1840s and valorizing this radical breed of aesthetic rebels.

The fictional letters of "The Youth of the Poet and the Painter" function as a collective autobiography of the "young men [who] were born with

knives in their brain," as Emerson recalled them.[26] Letters, like the innumerable conversations in Channing's life, were ephemeral, especially in the
way Channing treated them; he admitted at one point that they served as
a handy way to light his stove. The tale thus functions as Channing's version
of *Concord Walking*, an intimate prose portrait, however fictionalized,
capturing the otherwise fleeting local literary communication. Margaret
Fuller's conversations at Elizabeth Peabody's bookstore in Boston would
also be published to immortalize the brilliant insights of those exchanges.
But where "The Youth of the Poet and the Painter" differs from transcrip-
tions of Margaret's Conversations or the plan for *Concord Walking* is that
in its fictional form, the correspondence is primarily self-referential in its
focus on the social and aesthetic ramifications of his vocational crisis and
rebirth as a romantic poet. Thus the scope is considerably narrower,
however locally focused on Concord, than a work like *Concord Walking*,
designed to give voice to a diverse array of perspectives from the town's
literary lights.

In the tenth letter of the story, Ashford proclaims, "I have no conception of anything which has a right to be called poetry, unless it come living
out of the poet's nature like the stream gushing from the rock, free and
clear."[27] Beneath the valorization of Ashford's distinctly transcendental
poetic idealism—especially in his preference for forest and field over society
despite how he "crave[s] the hearth on these chill evenings though my
roof must be open to the sky"—lurks Channing's profound vocational
crisis. Ashford is acutely aware of the financial costs of his idealism, which
places him outside conventional vocational pursuits, linking him to others
by "golden bracelets of love" rather than the interest "made of bank-bills."[28]
Like Channing himself, Ashford vows to retain his childlike wonder
and imagination. "Childhood is a painting set in health and artlessness,"
not unlike Hawthorne's Pearl of *The Scarlet Letter*, an essence Ashford
observes in "a gipsy figure moving among the woods . . . gracefully
from tree to rock, a silent motionless mirth . . . passing before me like a
sunbeam with its shadow."[29] Her artlessness and mirth represent Channing's
own poetry, freely moving and infinitely self-satisfied in an intuitive
connection with nature.

But Ashford's poetry (and Channing's by extension) must face an adult
world of responsibility and artifice, and with it comes his bittersweet

acknowledgment of his mentor's theory, a direct allusion to the "Verses of the Portfolio." Ashford's friend, Mathews Gray, is equal parts Emerson and Ward, given the aesthetics of his sage Emersonian transcendental advice and his surname alluding to Channing's confidante Samuel Gray Ward, combining for an ideally sympathetic advocate and promoter. Gray commiserates with James Hope over the vocational crisis awaiting Ashford were he to embrace the life of a professional poet. Gray feels that Ashford may weary of the process of preparing "a good many dull verses, print them on the whitest paper, with notes of introduction" like the sort Emerson had supplied Channing on two occasions, "and engage a favorable critic to make them a pretty review," as in Emerson's "Mr. Channing's Poems" that appeared September 1843, just one month prior to this installment of Channing's story. Emerson's sense of Channing's literary weaknesses in both "New Poetry" and the review surfaces unmistakably in Gray's description of how "the production of verse is natural to him, and that by abundant encouragement from his friends, he may be led to write with more attention to critical rules." Channing's own reaction to such advice appeared a stubborn commitment to that previously mentioned childlike freedom from constraint, which often expressed itself as a thorny recalcitrance captured by Fuller's observation that he was "a great genius with a wretched little boy trotting beside him."[30] To the protests of Ashford's peers and chief patron, "he for some years will pay the least possible respect to measured and formal art," as Gray predicts (*L*, 2:331). Was it that transcendental poetry need not be spelled correctly or versified uniformly?

Gray's language then replicates Emerson's sense of Channing's resistance to formal poetic convention as a phase to be outgrown, which for the time being renders an artless verse that has won his heart. Such favorable qualities are apparent in "this portfolio literature [which] has long had a charm for me, which I cannot value too greatly," as Gray confesses. Emerson's approach toward preparing Channing for a career as a professional poet was perhaps never better expressed than in Gray's resolve to "do my best to inspire him in a belief in his powers, though I should make a very gradual approach to any formal criticism of what he may send" (*L*, 2:181). However, the final letter of the narrative exposes Channing's unwillingness to alter his own poetic practice. In it, Gray, functioning as the voice that truly understands Ashford, an otherwise misunderstood poet, suggests something permanent in the youth's neoplatonism. Ashford justifiably resists his mother's rigid disapproval of his craft that springs from her utilitarian economics, according to Gray, since "any disposal of his means, unless devoted to some formal business in a city, she considered a misfortune." After dismissing Mrs. Ashford's unreasonable intolerance, Gray's words rapidly become Channing's defense of his own vocational choice, and a justification of precisely the type of poet he shall remain: "Were he not so delicately constituted, [and] were it not necessary for him to surrender himself to many more impressions than the mass of men, I should not insist so positively upon him placing himself among the woods and fields." Such delicate constitution and nonconformity, interestingly, are not without their "discordant tones," which nonetheless should remain unchanged. Those imperfections inhere in the artlessness of the sketch artist whose impressions strive not for verisimilitude but a spiritual impression that, however flawed, must be expressed, for it is an "inevitable necessity to unburden their hearts and confess their imperfections before the stern beauty of the perfect." He goes on to lament the prevailing standard for poetry that is "too full of conventional existence" and "tameness," echoing Emerson's call for original literary creation emphasized throughout his addresses and essays, and especially in the Divinity School Address and "The Poet." If a principle indeed existed supporting Channing's resistance to measuring his lines with better care, it derived from his belief in the sacredness of confessing the limitations of human thought, language, and art to capture and fully convey "the stern beauty of the perfect" in nature (*L*, 2:283).[31] Indeed, Channing never assumed or pretended his or anyone else's poetry could contain such perfection. He took solace nonetheless in the shadowy imperfections of poetry precisely because of its power to witness, if not embody, that sacred essence of perfection in nature.

"Fifty Thousand Subscribers, Power and Fame"

Channing wished to achieve the magnitude of popular success enjoyed by Longfellow, only through an artless style of a manuscript poet. He promoted this label, a unique brand in the literary market, in earnest as his public poetic identity more than a decade before *Leaves of Grass* heralded the lyric power of radically unaffected spontaneous utterance or "song."

Channing took seriously the letter Emerson had sent registering his preference for "the first draught and to be present at the secret of creation before the vamping and rhetoric are used which are but 'the brushers of noblemen's clothes'" (L, 2:253). It thus made little sense for Channing to succumb to ornamentation at the expense of transcendental romantic mysticism's emphasis on intuition. This aesthetic resonated with Whitman's sentiment that "great poets are also to be known by the absence in them of tricks," particularly in self-consciously cadenced and metrically affected verse.[32] Emerson himself, in his kindness and encouragement of this early letter, had perhaps misleadingly implied this construct as a mutually exclusive binary. His rhetoric privileges intuition and spirit as the forces of good to combat decorative verse and its malignant association with what transcendentalists found corrupt in antebellum society at large: a misplaced faith in excessive Lockean reason (of dry conventional Unitarianism) and entertainment-driven materialism (of popular literature designed primarily to appeal to the senses). In verse, the former ironically appeared in the worst of Emerson's own logic-driven philosophical poems, while the latter surfaced in Emerson's critique of Poe as a huckster of superficially pleasing jingles.

Kathryn B. McKee has observed that Channing's "privileging of perception over mode of expression" indicated that "he remained true to his own poetic philosophy," which "essentially paralleled Emerson's views."[33] She usefully underscores the mutual misunderstanding at the heart of this, a general point made more powerful when that misunderstanding is construed as an expression of the ironic tension inherent in a professional mentorship in transcendental poetry like the one Channing had undertaken. Emerson of course lamented that "our wonderful Manuscript Poet" had found that label quite comfortable, and thus proceeded without the expectation that he grow beyond it into verse that an editor might favor (L, 2:331). Far from unreasonably demanding respect from Emerson as McKee asserts, Channing sincerely felt he had built something unique both on the grounds of Emersonian self-reliant individualism and in the spirit of Emerson's ardent support of his method. Such considerations revise Francis Dedmond's relentlessly negative portrait of him.[34] To Emerson, he seemed "prolific of good verses," however problematically he "showed me many which would content and delight every soul that was not an Editor." In a telling comment, Emerson began to regard Channing as a perpetual child, yet paradoxically inhering the transcendental idealization of childhood's poetry: "A true poet that child is, and nothing proves it so much as his worst verses: sink or swim—hit or miss, he writes on and is never responsible" (*L*, 3:102–3).

Channing's poetic soul of a child, however, was not without professional ambition. From the beginning of his mentorship, Emerson had envisioned Channing as the savior of his fledgling *Dial*, a role he hoped would make him a literary celebrity. "He ought to write every month for the Dial," Emerson mused, "which ought to have fifty thousand subscribers and ought to yield him house, diet, clothes, power and fame" (*JMN*, 8:276). Looking back on his career, Channing reaffirmed his belief in the goal Emerson had set for him, expressing deep disappointment that his writing sold poorly since "there is no other test of the value of the poetry but its popularity."[35] Channing's early trouble in reaching a market not ready for formal poetic experimentation was legendary. Thoreau deemed it all but miraculous in a letter to Emerson, for example, that a bookseller's patron actually purchased *one* copy of Channing's *Poems*. Much of Channing's professional demise, however, was beyond his control. In one emblematic turn of fate, *The Wanderer* had just begun to build momentum in sales in a market that finally had embraced him when a fire destroyed all of the publishers' unsold stock of the title. Although such misfortune plagued his career, Channing was among the most widely published of Emerson's protégés. From his first publication of the poem "The Spider," in 1835, until his death sixty-five years later, Channing aggressively circulated his work in seven volumes of poetry, biographies, church Christmas annuals, gift books, and in innumerable periodicals. Among his greatest achievements was his inclusion in the pantheon of Rufus Griswold's *The Poets and Poetry of America* (in both the 1842 and 1847 editions), if only as an addendum at the back of the volume under the category of "Various Authors" for his sing-song "The Arched Stream."

Reprising Channing's favorite literary subject—the moment of his own poetic calling—"The Arched Stream" dramatizes how "Nature said" that "Thy verse shall gush thus freely on" like the stream before him. Nature promises that "Some Poet" who is Channing "yet may sit thereby,/ And cheer himself within the sun,/ My Life has kindled in thine eye." In

Griswold's introduction to the volume, Channing is mentioned for his innovative aesthetics in conjunction with Emerson and "others, whose names are in this volume, for Poetry . . . written for the coming ages," however unrepresentative "The Arched Stream" was of such innovation.[36] Emersonian protégés Christopher Cranch and Jones Very have entire sections dedicated to them in *Poets and Poetry in America* featuring multiple poems, but neither is mentioned in the introduction. It was clear by their inclusion in Griswold's anthology that Emerson's protégés enjoyed a certain measure of cultural prestige. Much of that prestige Channing consciously manufactured in "The Youth of the Poet and the Painter," a stylized self-portrait of an angst-ridden Emersonian apprentice torn between conventional and transcendental vocational choices. Channing's self-promotion through the exposition of his quintessentially rebellious and romantic artist's crisis and defense of his professional nonconformity even in the already nonconformist world of professional poetry relied heavily on refuting conventional occupations rooted in the ethos of free-market capitalism. In this way, Channing rebuffed the commercial world precisely as a means of entering it as a professional author.

"The Youth of the Poet and the Painter" offers a lively and vigorous satire of the professions, assaulting middle-class New England morality, especially the conventional economic wisdom of one Mr. Penny, who like the debt-ridden farmers Thoreau skewers in "Economy" of *Walden* dutifully invests his capital savings in land that gradually runs him into deeper debt. Channing urged Thoreau on to great exaggeration, and was the source of his more acerbic burlesques of bourgeois New England. Channing's influence "tempts me to certain licenses of speech," Thoreau admitted, "i.e., to reckless and sweeping expressions which I am wont to regret that I have used. That is, I find that I have used more harsh, extravagant, and cynical expressions concerning mankind and individuals than I intended." Thoreau found "it difficult to make to him a sufficiently moderate statement," for which one must finally credit rather than fault Channing. Should bland moderation cool the rhetorical fire of *Walden*, "Civil Disobedience," or "Walking"?[37] Although Thoreau regretted on some level the indiscretion and lack of restraint Channing inspired in him, he likely relished the total release from propriety and constraint that Emerson had bred in him during his poetic tutelage. Channing unleashed the wild Thoreau from the clutches of Emerson, who had made him his docile and perennially frustrated poet acolyte.

Drawing Forth Virgin Gold

The wit Channing and Thoreau shared was their own unique creation, separate from their mentor. Although Emerson certainly could appreciate their humor, Channing's signature quips—he once described farming as "an attempt to outwit God with a hoe"—could never be ascribed to Emerson (*JMN*, 14:157). Noticing the lack of original invention in Nature on one walk, he mused, "They had frozen water last year; why should they do it again?" (*JMN*, 11:185). Channing had an uncanny capacity to spot pretension, a habit of mind Thoreau would have found especially appealing. "E. laughed at Nuttal's description of birds," Emerson recorded in his journal. " 'On top of a high tree the bird pours all day the lays of affection,' etc. 'Affection!' " roared Channing, " 'Why, what is it? A few feathers, with a hole at one end, and a point at the other, and a pair of wings; Affection! Why, just as much affection as there is in a lump of peat.' "[38] Sophia Ripley found observations of this sort jejune, especially as they appeared in "The Youth of the Poet and the Painter." Conversely, Thoreau adored "their wit highly," found them "full of life," and anxiously awaited each sequel.[39]

Given the closeness of their friendship—made so by Thoreau's introduction to Channing shortly after the death of his dear brother John, and by Channing's novel suggestion that Thoreau write his next book in a cabin he helped build at the shores of Walden Pond—it is not surprising that Channing would make several cameo appearances as "the Poet" in *Walden*.[40] In a segment written like a dramatic script in the chapter "Brute Neighbors," Thoreau hears Channing approaching his hut and initially takes him for an "ill fed village hound," an inside joke of course alluding to Professor, Channing's dog and alter ego. "As I have my living to get, and have not eaten today," Channing announced, "I might go afishing. That's the true industry of poets," especially those among the Saturday afternoon professors of Concord. The Hermit, who is Thoreau, says he is deep in thought and thus instructs the Poet to fetch the bait so he might finish his own intellectual fishing, or philosophical angling of "how the world lay about at this angle." Thoreau throws out the bait of a "few sentences of Con-fut-see to reel in his thoughts" before the Poet's return, "that they may fetch that state about again." Fishing for his ever elusive thought that brought him "as near being resolved into the essence of things as I ever was in my life," he begins a pursuit that anticipates the chapter's conclusion depicting his folly of chasing but failing to catch the loon who seems to outwit and mock him. So when the Poet returns with bait, he effectively rescues the Hermit from the frustration of his impossibly abstract metaphysical hunt, thus reminding him that satisfaction in finding bait can make for satisfying hunting in and of itself. Channing's companionship does not lower Thoreau's standards so much as it pulls Thoreau out of himself, alerting him to the satisfaction near at hand and the transcendence that awaits in the immediate natural world, thus releasing him from his fruitless pursuit of "the essence of things" remote and exceedingly abstract.

Of all Thoreau's "Winter Visitors" of *Walden*, Channing is his most beloved. "A farmer, a hunter, a soldier, a reporter, even a philosopher, may be daunted" by "deepest snows and most dismal tempests; but nothing can deter a poet, for he is actuated by pure love." With his characteristically unpredictable "comings and goings," Channing "made that small house ring with boisterous mirth and resound with the murmur of much sober talk," bringing a carnival atmosphere ("Broadway was still and deserted in comparison") to the otherwise silent Walden woods. Never was the hut more festive than with Channing under its roof. Inspiring "regular salutes of laughter," Channing's visits combined "the advantages of conviviality with the clear-headedness which philosophy requires." Thus Thoreau made Channing his longest guest in residence, hosting the "poet to board for a fortnight about those times." Besides Channing's own biography of Thoreau, nothing speaks to their friendship more than the pages of *Walden* in which the Hermit pays tribute to the company of the Poet.[41]

Like his friendship with Thoreau, Channing's relationship with Hawthorne also kept him grounded, and provided a healthy skeptical distance from which he could regard the more eccentric elements of literary Concord. He once made a comment lauding Hawthorne and chiding Alcott in good nature for his abstruse and convoluted principles behind his ascetic banning of eggs, milk, butter, or meat from his diet. Expanding his criticism toward the *Dial* in general, Channing praised Hawthorne, his fishing companion of some twenty years since 1846. Channing delighted in the way Hawthorne ate meat heartily and imbibed freely in libations, unlike Alcott and his English friends. Intent on protecting Hawthorne from the *Dial*'s vegetarianism and mysticism associated with Alcott's Fruitlands, Channing wrote, "Alas, for the unleavened bread! Alas for the unleavened wit! I relish the Yankee theorem—'Eat your victuals and go about your business!'" calling for "A magazine written by professed drunkards—gentlemen who eat nothing but beefsteaks and believe in Original Sin." In demanding Hawthorne's loyalty to "strong drinks and strong meats . . . the gentle art of angling," Channing warns of the corrupting influence of the more eccentric transcendental trends, fearing "the day of horrors come [when] the Twice Told tales of love and malice shall be fused in the grim Behemic melting-pot!" Channing hoped Hawthorne would never surrender to such whims of culture Alcott had been gorging on and that threatened to divert Hawthorne from the essence of his art—original sin, love, and malice—and lead him "to sell himself body and soul . . . for twelve volumes of the Greaves MSS, or some book of metaphysical stuff" and thus leave himself on the margins of the literary marketplace, "fit only to be sold at the shops of second hand booksellers, or enjoy their existence as wrapping literature!"[42]

Hawthorne also saw the liabilities threatening Channing's career. Hawthorne never feared Channing would foolishly invest in trends like vegetarianism and Fruitlands at the unprofitable margins of the literary world. Hawthorne instead expressed concerns, also voiced by Emerson, that under the stimulating conversation enjoyed on excursions with Channing lurked the dark reality that perhaps his verbal wit on these occasions had gone unrecorded and thus was never transformed into potent literary credit. "Up gushed our talk like the babble of a fountain," Hawthorne recalled, "the evanescent spray was Ellery's" as well as "the lumps of golden thought, that lay glimmering in the fountain's bed, and brightened both our faces by the reflection." He could taste the riches Channing might have minted from his spoken wit into the currency of profit and fame to make him both intellectually and materially richer: "Could he have drawn out that virgin gold," Hawthorne suggested as though he were speculating in California gold, "and stamped it with the mint mark which alone gives its currency, the world might have had the profit and him the fame. My mind was richer merely by the knowledge that it was there."[43]

At the age of forty, Hawthorne was seasoned enough to know as Emerson had that the twenty-five-year-old Channing was brimming with untapped talent. The ephemeral nature of Channing's poet lifestyle, from its conversation to its burned letters and journals, were all too apparent to Emerson, who noted that "in able conversation we have glimpses of the Universe, perceptions of the soul's omnipotence but not much to record" (*JMN*, 5:363). He thus made note of Channing's finer comments to build into his own writing, since his younger friend had no interest in using such "conversation with a friend" as "the magazine out of which all good writing is drawn." Emerson could take an observation of Channing's, transform it into lyric beauty in his journal, and excerpt it directly into a lecture or essay. Emerson understood Channing's verse much in the way he saw Channing's conversation: both contained a "storehouse of chaotic treasure which others might sometime fit into acceptable patterns."[44] His disciple's offhand remark that all the beauty he needed was at the end of his oar, for example, sent Emerson to his journal, marveling at the comment and seeing the beauty through Channing's angle of vision. He "did not know whether he used the expression with design," but knew its rich value. Through his pupil's eyes, Emerson could see the overflowing treasure of insight, "such color, such transparency, such eddies; it was the hue of Rhine wines, it was jasper and verd antique, topaz and chalcedony; it was gold," he wrote, unfurling the kaleidoscope Channing had alerted him to but had not bothered to unearth himself, one resplendent with "green and chestnut and hazel in bewitching succession and relief without cloud or confusion"—indeed, the perfect vision only Channing could make visible (*JMN*, 7:230–31).

By 1857, more than ten years after the halcyon days of their early relationship, Channing wrote Elizabeth Hoar expressing his anguish at Emerson's increasing distance and coldness. He mentioned his "living within a stone's throw of your house, when a word from you might have made the days seem at least a little inhabitable—a word you could not speak." Rather than venting anger at Emerson for abandoning his decade-long mentorship, he is observing, quite realistically, how they had grown apart, and how Emerson's public stature and intensely private demeanor meant that "you can never be where I am and I can never be where you are" (*JMN*, 2:238). Vilifying Emerson as one who exacted the sacrifice of the "one good half" of his life "to be near his remorseless hand" leaves him devastated after being forced, according to his maudlin sentimentalization of the relationship, to pay "a fearful price I have had to pay for loving him." Indeed, his payment of that price was a necessity for which he had only himself to blame, rather than Emerson and his trail of "all the hearts he has frozen" in his personal relationships. Channing would come to a more accurate and mature understanding of their relationship when he dropped the pitched histrionics and took account of his own deficiencies. By 1859, he was beginning to achieve such an understanding, confessing that "I have failed utterly and entirely in my own estimate and that of all others to justify myself in their or my own light as a writer at all, more especially as a poet."[45]

It seems to have been something of a ritual of graduation from an Emersonian mentorship for his protégés to turn on the master in defiance in an ironic confirmation of self-reliant individualism. Thoreau's look back in anger at Emerson, for example, has been well documented; Whitman vents anger at him in *Specimen Days*, railing on his "dandified theory of manners" published in his essay, "Manners." Whitman's most damning allegation is that "in [Emerson's] inmost heart the grandest attributes of God and Poets is always subordinate to the octaves, conceits, polite kinks, and verbs," a sentiment that points to the crux of the controversy over poetic meter plaguing Emerson's mentorship and publicity of Channing. Distancing himself from his former advocate, Whitman ascribes his youthful intoxication in Emerson to an intellectual fever, a "touch . . . of Emerson on-the-brain," an affliction that presented itself with symptoms that even the most stalwart independents like Margaret Fuller displayed. At the end of one visit she confessed, "I ought to go away now; these last days I have been fairly intoxicated with [Emerson's] mind," while Whitman recalled "read[ing] his writings reverently" and regarding him "as 'Master.'"[46] Whitman was not blind to the delicious irony inherent in most transcendentalist mentorships of how "the best part of Emersonianism is, it breeds the giant that destroys itself."[47] Channing's pessimism clearly is not unique, or unusual, as it comes mainly during the mid 1860s when he was bitterly looking back on his career. Indeed, he was acutely aware that his books were not popular, and to a certain extent felt cheated by his investment in Emerson's patronage. But he was not alone, as Thoreau similarly critiqued Emerson's praise as "always discriminating" and containing "some alloy of patronage and hence of flattery about it," opposite of how "praise should be spoken as simply and naturally as a flower emits its fragrance."[48] If praise seemed judgmental to Thoreau, it was only because it often had to be if it was to advance the youth's best professional interests, for which he or she was primarily responsible. "No man deserves a patron until first he has been his own," Emerson insisted.[49] Thoreau registered his above complaint in 1852, precisely when his falling-out with Emerson had begun, a time of turmoil and discord that prefigured precisely the pattern of Channing's struggle with his mentor throughout the next ten years.[50]

Emerson's insistence that authors be their own patrons first before seeking support from others likely referenced Ward's and Emerson's respective financing and editing of Channing's first volume, *Poems*.[51] Unlike Thoreau, Channing was from a family of means with a long history of educational attainment and aristocratic breeding, forming one of the most notable lineages in New England at the time. The claim that Emerson was in the business of inspiring his promising youths to sacrifice the better parts of their lives for his attention, and in the process freezing their hearts and dashing their hopes, would appear to be corroborated by his seemingly cold and flip dismissal of these disappointing poets in an 1857 letter to Caroline Sturgis Tappan. In it, he laments how "Newcomb proves the rich possibilities of the soil, tho' his result is zero. So does Ellery. But who cares? As soon as we walk out of doors Nature transcends all poets so far, that a little more or less skill in whistling is of no account" (*L*, 5:87). Indeed, Emerson's economic language in discussing the unfulfilled career potential of his protégés shows a concern for profit and results. Emerson's "who cares?" out of context appears a blithe abandonment of his responsibility; but the larger context suggests that he indeed cared not only to edit and secure publication of Channing's *Poems*, but also its *Second Series* that appeared in 1846.

Emerson arranged for Channing the same terms as his own with his publisher Munroe. Emerson's deal—the author bore all expenses of production and of copies to the editors at 30 percent discount from retail price and 20 percent for trade—worked to his advantage, "for my books uniformly pay for themselves, and this book of poems is much more sure of an easy sale than its foregoers." By 1846, Emerson's international renown had risen to unprecedented levels, so his books more than paid for themselves. He mistakenly assumed Channing's *Second Series* would also sell better than his first, and was convinced he was protecting his pupil from the typical half profits contract in which publishers owned the property of the book, the variations of which Emerson roundly distrusted, "for the best offers of the booksellers are not good" (*L*, 3:350–51). Although Munroe printed far fewer copies of Channing's volume than the fifteen hundred he did of Emerson's, the terms of the contract were identical, and thus worked to Channing's distinct disadvantage given his lack of visibility in the literary market at the time.[52] This oversight reveals not so much neglect, but a misplaced care for the professional development of his protégé. Among other odd jobs like the sort Thoreau performed in and around Bush, it would take Channing a considerable amount of wood cutting for Emerson at fifty cents a cord to make up for his losses on the book.[53] Significantly, Channing joined Thoreau as the only authors Emerson compensated for their contributions to the *Dial*. In his "Account Book 1840–44," Emerson recorded paying "to WEC for a poem 10.00" and elsewhere, "Cash to WEC for *Dial* papers 10.00."[54]

Thus his seemingly flip "who cares?" does not accurately represent Emerson's attitude toward his disciples' careers, but rather suggests something of the frustration with Channing, who he believed had "more poetic genius than anyone" but confessed he had "some defects that prevented him from writing a single good poem."[55] In the broader context of his transcendental paradigm, Emerson pointed to the hard truth that nature's music finally is better than our own: that fine whistling, like impressive gymnastics, according to Emerson's broader transcendental perspective, is always secondary to the artistry visible in nature, from its snowstorms to the play of light dancing in the splashing water at the end of an oar.

Channing's poems point to his undeniable talent as well as his carelessness. His approach toward authorship troubles the dichotomy that privileges slow meticulous writing over sudden bursts of inspiration. Channing's best and most memorable line of his entire career appeared in "A Poet's Hope," a poem he improvised when Mrs. Samuel Ward, in a playful dare, challenged him to the task. The subject of poetic composition had arisen in casual conversation and led to his frenzied tear into the poem that ends with him laughing and smiling in his belief in the eternal with the affirmation, "If my bark sinks, 'tis to another sea."[56] Under the circumstances of its serendipitous composition, the poem is original and virtually error free, bearing nothing of the derivative mimicry and adulating praise of the "Snow Storm," a clunky jingle that does not even approach Emerson's treatment of the same subject; or "Ode" from *Poems: Second Series* that sings praises to Emerson ("Some weary footed mortals . . . pursues [*sic*, verb agreement problem] thy grand imperial flight"); or his references to Emerson's "Circles" in the line "The circles of thy Thought, shine vast as stars"; or the places where he marvels at how his mentor's "Intellect divine serenely towers." Although "The age is vain and thin,/ A pageant of gay sin," Emerson stands impervious and proud, "The pins of custom have not pierced through . . . / Thy shining armor," in an image that evokes the heroic narrative persona of "Self-Reliance." "Ode" suffers the limitations Emerson fretted over: verb agreement, botched and slant rhymes, or the mangling of words to produce unnatural rhyme, such as the transformation of dutiful into "duteous" in order to rhyme with "courteous."[57] "A Poet's Hope," unlike these examples, glories in his own powers, "My empire is myself," harnessing the force of nature for his muse. But the poem does not fall prey to the solipsism of the isolated romantic author, and instead points outward in a series of social and relational gestures whose sympathy averts infallible, self-aggrandizing egotism. The "soft glaze of a loving eye" and "the pure shapes of the human form" transform time and death's "infinite cold sorrow" into "icy charms," like John Donne's "Death Be Not Proud," outwitting death itself and thus discovering a new source of life.[58]

The first of Emerson's final two acts of literary patronage for his protégé came in his 1871 preface to *The Wanderer*, which argued that Channing's verse constituted "new matter" and "new art." The pioneering first wave, he argued, must be understood as containing imperfect techniques, "as the first daguerres were grim things enough, yet showed that a great engine had been invented." His poems, furthermore, eschew "all the prose of artificial transitions." In an organic aesthetic analogy, Emerson compares the verse to "a series of sketches of natural objects, such as abound in New

England, unwreathed by the thoughts they suggest to the contemplative pilgrim." Now Channing "is a naturalist" capable of "strokes of skill that recall the great masters" and whose "interest in nature is not pedantic but insatiably curious of the hint it gives of its cause, and its relation to man." Indeed, he is not one to "count the stamens in the aster, nor the feathers in the wood-thrush, but rests in the surprise and affection they awaken." Unpredictability and surprise, he argues, drive the "one essential talent of his art." His verses are unique, "novel and sincere," and do not suffer from the malady of conventional popular poetry in which "reading a line or a stanza" means "that we can guess the rest." Emerson directly challenges the reader not only to abandon conventional expectations, but to see beyond the superficial imperfections and not look down on "this rude pamphlet" as so much "charcoal-sketching." Instead, Channing "requires a good reader," a "lover of woods and hillsides" who will find himself rewarded by the author's "wide reading in a wide variety of studies," which informs but does not tame "his invincible personality."[59]

A "colloquial poem" by one who "does not regard the public" but has "written to himself," *The Wanderer* is the epitome of romantic disavowal of the literary market "for which we may even thank the poet," according to Emerson. Without the rhetoric of hope befitting a younger poet's promise, Emerson instead casts Channing's defective meter as a disability, comparing him to an unnamed "highly-esteemed painter who was colorblind." The "rhythm-deaf poet" is like the "famed orators," who might include Emerson himself, who stammer and pause before "warming to their subject." Emerson confesses that he too is annoyed with "a needless or even willful neglect of rhythm," not just as a matter of principle, but also because it has blocked his potential "to outdo his rivals" who instead have drawn the public's accolades. That "facility of grace in his art," Emerson laments, is often neglected by Channing, who therefore "risks offense by harshness."[60] This sentiment is of course ironic in light of Emerson's suggestion one paragraph later that Channing should be thanked for refusing to write for a commercial audience (figured as "the public"). Such tension—a desire to see him "outdo his rivals" competes with a desire to thank him for disregarding "the public"—is emblematic of Emerson's overall experience with Channing, his frustration in mentoring and marketing him meeting precisely his delight in his rebellion against the pressure to conform to the literary market for commercial poetry. Both mentor and pupil finally concurred that such an antimaterialistic stance might provide a tonic for the increasingly industrial landscape of the Gilded Age while simultaneously proffering a salable but unique literary product.

Emerson made his final and most lasting tribute to his protégé by including two of Channing's poems in *Parnassus,* his edited anthology from 1874. In a letter dated December 20 of that year, Channing thanked Emerson for the honor of being appointed to such a group. "Even to select a single piece is a wonder," he wrote, signing off, "Thanking you for your constant kindness."[61] Emerson selected two of Channing's finest poems for the anthology. "The Hillside Cot" features dialogue and quoted lines, one of Channing's strong suits, of a hermit who shares his "tale of moon, and sun, and stars," ending with the somber declaration, "If I note my powers" to cohere with "the essence of the whole, and of/ Ourselves" nature "hustles" us "to the grave" with "its malarial trick." At the close of the hermit's prayer, the poet persona finds redemption in nature nonetheless in the most moving and affirmative segment of the piece. Sounds of "night hawks" ripping "the air above/ my head" combine with the sight of "the blazing dog-star" and "the low comet trailing to the south" to release the narrator from the shackles of decay, disease, and death, as he notices the hermit "bend his reverent gaze, and leave/ us free."[62] "Flight of the Wild Geese," the other poem anthologized in *Parnassus,* also effectively uses quotation, but in this case its strength is in the vigor of detail. Note the precision of "feathers glossy, quills in order," and the leader's call to "start this train, yet rings no bell;/ Steam is raised without recorder." The meditation satisfyingly places the birds on their journey utterly liberated from maps, "sweetmeats in odd jars," and with "the horizon of To-morrow" as their destination, which depends not on nations, geographies, "opinion, nor hiving sops of wit." That sense of liberation—transcending both geographical and rhetorical boundaries—aptly captures Channing's charisma, his utter belief in "the horizon of To-morrow" toward which Emerson wished also to take flight.[63]

Although his talents coalesced in poems such as these, Channing's natural skills were better suited for a career as a memoirist of the local Concord scene—which prompted Emerson to suggest coauthoring *Concord*

Walking—than as a poet for a mass audience. He was more a writer on the order of Boswell, as his "Youth of the Poet and the Painter" and biography of Thoreau suggest. Or, he might have fared better with free verse than to have forced his Emersonian insights into Longfellowesque meter. His self-proclamation that "*I* am universal; I have nothing to do with the particular and definite," for example, bears an uncanny resemblance to Whitman's famous lines toward the end of "Song of Myself," "Do I contradict myself?/ Very well then I contradict myself,/ (I am large, I contain multitudes)."[64] The rebellious liberal streak running through the writings and deliberate living of Thoreau, and the bold democratic poetic theory of Emerson, began with Channing. Though Channing never approached drawing fifty thousand subscribers to the *Dial* for power and fame, he reinvented and revitalized the transcendental poetic role by expanding its aesthetic and professional liberties with his signature irreverent wit and eye for virgin gold in the natural world. All too aware of Thoreau's "brave apprenticeship" at which "the worldling/ Laugh in his sleeve at thy compelled devotion," Channing's great strength in providing the poetic muse and model for Emerson's "Verses of the Portfolio" would become his own compelled devotion, a brave apprenticeship whose ending was inscribed in its own beginning.[65]

6

Jones Very: A Poet's Zeal

Often rebelling despite himself, Ellery Channing made earnest attempts at conventional enterprises such as landowning, farming, and raising a family with the best intentions, only to allow his poetic self-concept to lead him into a pattern of indigence. However neglectful of business and domestic responsibilities, he remained an inspiration to Emerson and Thoreau, who revered him for his creativity and nonconformity that pushed the boundaries of the ever widening modes of authorship practiced in antebellum Concord. But no transcendentalist embodied a more wildly radical sense of the poet's social role than Jones Very, whose ungodly zeal rocked the very foundations of New England's literary and religious communities.

Channing's transgressions of the social role of the poet were derelictions and indiscretions compared with Very's brazen violation of the authorial role by proselytizing his own personal gospel of obedience to divine will featured in his poetry. Whereas Channing frequently appeared rudderless, Very was riveted to a purpose he had clearly defined. To him, he had no choice in the matter. He understood vocation quite literally as a divine calling from an external voice demanding his obedience. At one point he told Emerson, who considered autonomous intuition sacrosanct, that human free will could only be measured in proportion to one's obedience to God's will. "You do not disobey because you do the wrong act," Very reasoned, "but you do the wrong act, because you disobey. And you do not obey because you do the

Jones Very (Photography Collection, Miriam and Ira D. Wallach Division of Art, Prints, and Photographs, New York Public Library, Astor, Lenox, and Tilden Foundations)

good action, but you do the good action because you first obey" (*JMN*, 7:123).

Obedience to divine will was paramount in Very's peculiar theological fusion of antinomian Christian quietism—especially its passive yet direct and unmitigated relation to God—and transcendentalism's ecstatic fusion of the self and the Universal Being.[1] This religious orientation rendered authorship will-less through a complete erasure of the self and subordination of the creative conscience to the channeling of the

Holy Spirit's words. Very never understood himself as a poet so much as a man chosen to speak God's will and record it in rhyming verse. Emerson's role in shaping Very's response to that voice forms the subject of this chapter, specifically as seen in the effects of his patronage that began as friendship and eventuated in editing and negotiating a publishing contract for *Essays and Poems* (1839). Emerson's editorial practice reveals his fluctuating levels of aesthetic and economic investment in Very. Specifically, his editorial work for Very replicated "the pattern of Emerson's career," described by Joel Myerson as moving "from taking risks in order to make large profits, to balancing smaller profits against fewer risks."[2] The financial investment pattern of Emerson's own negotiations for book contracts indeed matched that of his investment in his promising youths. In Very's case, Emerson's liberal gamble on this eccentric genius gave way to careful career management and responsible mediation of the most pivotal publication of the poet's career.

Tension mounted, however, when Very's attempts to convert Emerson to his spiritual vision met Emerson's pressure to establish a professional literary career. Very's missionary work by no means was designed to promote his poetry, but ironically, it had precisely that effect, at least in the short term. Emerson's fascination with Very the man was inseparable from his enthusiasm for his poems, contrary to critical attempts to pry them apart.[3] Very's public profile forged through his essay writing and proselytizing formed a dialectical relationship with his poetry. Indeed, Very's antics—including proclaiming his status as the second coming of Christ and forcibly baptizing an array of prominent New England figures, from Unitarian minister Henry Ware to Nathaniel Hawthorne—inadvertently created a theatrical public spectacle of him as messianic mad poet, thus attracting Emerson's patronage. Certain dimensions of Very's public profile were by no means new to the world of antebellum American romantic poetry, but gained considerable currency in the self-aggrandizing verse of Walt Whitman, America's poet of democracy, and the self-indulgent eccentricity of figures like McDonald Clarke, the Mad Poet of Broadway. But anything fashionable about Very's madness was entirely unintentional, for there was nothing affected about his obsession, which for all who encountered him was jarringly real.

Emerson's "Brave Saint" Is Born

Each of the promising youths Emerson inducted into his "personal pantheon of discovered geniuses" possessed a singular extraordinary power of character that captured his imagination.[4] Very's eyes, more than any other attribute, expressed his genius to Emerson. A survey of Very's portraits consistently reveals piercing dark eyes and a narrow arresting gaze in an otherwise pale, almost wooden visage. Emerson responded to that penetrating stare in part because of its potential for counteracting the offensive fueled by the "longaninity"—Bacon's term describing a potent cocktail of "information and tenacity of purpose"—of Andrews Norton, who gathered in opposition to the radical Divinity School Address "the power and culture of his community so much as to think it holds a hundred writers" (*JMN*, 7:63).[5] Very, raised in Salem by unwed parents in a notoriously intolerant social and religious climate, teetered on the brink of madness throughout his life. "The eyes of an insane person seem to diminish the distance betwixt you & him," a transfixed Emerson noted in his journal. Such intimacy led Emerson to confide his darkest secret in "J[ones] V[ery] that I could scarce bring myself to feel a concern for the safety and life of my nearest friends that would satisfy them" (*JMN*, 7:132). Very's magnetizing "power of eyes to charm down . . . ferocity in beasts is a power behind the eye," and commanded Emerson's utmost respect, for "it must be a victory first achieved in the will before it can be signified in the eye" (*JMN*, 7:52).

Barzillai Frost was one of the first such beasts whom Very subdued in a confrontation that impressed Emerson beyond measure, winning his total commitment to the young mystic. Frost, whose corpse-cold sermonizing typified what Emerson assailed in the Divinity School Address, "began to tower and dogmatize with many words" at a teachers' meeting hosted at Bush in October 1838. Then "astonishment . . . seized all the company when our brave saint . . . fronted the presiding preacher," much to Emerson's delight. "Instantly I foresaw that his doom was fixed; and as quick as he ceased speaking the Saint," who resembled to Emerson the supernal angel of a Raphael painting who dashes the royal Syrian Heliodorus to the ground while attempting to raid the Temple at Jerusalem, "set him right and blew away all his words in an instant" (*JMN*, 7:127). Relishing the application of Raphael's religious allegory of swift and righteous justice, Emerson immediately cast Very as his metaphysical warrior, not unlike the "fair girl" heroine he had imagined Fuller to be, as discussed in Chapter 1. In "Heroism," Emerson described Fuller valiantly "repel[ing] interference by a decided and proud choice of influences," one who is "so careless of pleasing, so willful and lofty" that she "inspires every beholder with some what of her own nobleness." As with Very, Emerson located Fuller's heroism in "the power and the charm" to tame ferocious opponents, attributes as fresh as they were potent in "her new born being" (*CW*, 2:153).

In one swift stroke Very had "unhorsed" the chilly Frost in the name of passionate Emersonian spirituality "and tumbled him along the ground in utter dismay like my Angel of Heliodorus." In a gesture typical of his method of accosting other Unitarian clergymen, Very indicted Frost for "a departure from the truth" with "every word he spoke" such that he virtually stripped "the book from his hands and thrust him out of the room" (*JMN*, 7:128). This triumph of authenticity over dogmatism invigorated and inspired Emerson's faith in "plain dealing" and "true relations" to overcome society's tendency to show "not its face and eye, but its side and its back." Very had achieved what others too rational and sane could not: "To stand in true relations with men in a false age." Fate seemed to cast Very as Emerson's warrior and brave saint, appointing him to battle with the conservative Unitarian faction whom Emerson had designated as the enemy in the Divinity School Address. This was the Very who took Emerson by storm, the Very self-styled in his poem as "The Warrior," a soldier "conquering the world" in a show of power to those who might have doubted or mocked him. "I triumph now your hour of mirth has past," the voice of the poem proclaims, because "I am of Him who gives the quickening spirit born/ And wield forever the conquering word/ Its power shall beat in atoms mountain high/ And through the parting sea shall lead me dry."[6]

Emerson believed that such a bold poetic achievement was "worth a fit of insanity, is it not?" Such a bargain highlights the uncertain effects of Emerson's patronage and raises questions about his ethics. How reckless, for example, was Emerson's endorsement of Very's "true relations with men," especially those attending the poet's public proclamations of his own true relation to God? Was it appropriate and did it support Very's best interest for Emerson to promote and patronize his disciple despite costs—which would prove dear in the end—inherent in Very's mystical state that projected a public figure "all men agreed was mad"? How could Emerson be sure this was only a temporary "fit," an emotional imbalance sure to regain its poise? (*CW*, 2:119–20). And if it was, how could he be certain this passing episode would not indelibly mar Very's reputation and exclude him from the privileges of a healthy career and the support of his community? Emerson knew Very's life and career were on a collision course with the theological and literary conventions that governed Protestant antebellum letters, and was fully aware that it might do permanent damage to his disciple. More than any other of his mentorships, Emerson's tutelage of Very calls into question the ethics of Emerson's sometimes cold utilitarian resolve "to do with friends as I do with my books. I would have them where I can find them" but not "lose my own vision" in theirs (*CW*, 2:126). Despite its very real costs to the poet's safety and mental health, Emerson could not resist Very's power, the victory won behind his eyes that enabled him to defeat Frost so decidedly. In the wake of this initial infatuation, Emerson later worked to stabilize Very's career and thus insure his well-being, as he had for his other apprentices. Despite this support, Very did not achieve success in his subsequent career as a preacher, rising no higher than supply minister.

Emerson's trivialization of the issue of Very's mental health as it appeared in the appallingly flip line from "Friendship" mentioned above did not mean that he blithely drove Very into the fray like a lamb to the slaughter. In some ways, the bargain he accepted of a "fit of madness" for "true relations with men" is a figure of speech intended to end his paragraph on Very (who is its unnamed subject) with rhetorical effect (*CW*, 2:126). Elsewhere Emerson deployed similar economic tropes that set up an outrageous bargain, a tempting offer with the devil, and stuns his reader by saying that he would gladly accept it in order to illustrate the primacy of principle over material comfort or personal safety.[7] In this case, he did not exploit Very's madness to support his war against Andrews Norton and the historical Christianity of the conservative Unitarians, though he certainly relished sending Very back to Cambridge after his asylum stint as if he were shooting "an arrow in the heart of society" (*JMN*, 7:123).

Emerson cared too much about Very to sacrifice his fledgling career and mental well-being to win this controversy and advance his own mounting fame. The most convincing evidence that Emerson's flip tone was merely rhetorical is visible in his instrumental role in publishing Very's poetry and essays, which appeared in 1839.[8] This editorial and promotional work represented Emerson's best efforts to safeguard his protégé from professional oblivion in the wake of his dismissal from Harvard.

Emerson's editorial work for Very was in some ways payment of a debt he felt he owed his apprentice not only for the inspirational war he waged partially on his behalf, but for the wisdom he learned from him.[9] Emerson gained considerable insight from "convert[ing] him instantly into an invaluable teacher of *his Science*" since, as he confessed in his journal, "I think we learn as much from the insane as the sane." Dealing plainly with mad mystics such as Very promised to transform an otherwise insane individual into nothing less than a "messenger of God to you," for "Insane men have a great deal to teach you" (*JMN*, 7:115). Much of what Emerson learned from Very expanded his interest in the spiritual and social role of the poetic vocation. By contrast, Whitman, Clarke, and Channing's revolutionary reinventions of the romantic poet figure at the time spoke nothing of the profound zeal driving Very's poetic practice, an interpretation and application of the poet's work coextensive with his bizarre missionary campaign that escalated the stakes of the Divinity School Address debacle.

Very began his career conventionally enough, progressing expeditiously through his undergraduate studies at Harvard from 1834 to 1836. Entering as a sophomore, he quickly achieved high status by winning the coveted Bowdoin Prize for his essays on classical literature in consecutive years. In the two years following graduation, he served as a Greek tutor while enrolled part time as an unofficial student of the Divinity School. Regarded as "the ideal instructor," Very won high praise from his freshman students. One said he "owed more to Jones Very, who was Greek Tutor, than to almost any or all others in the faculty" at Harvard.[10] His promise was indeed great and his trajectory of ascent well established. Yet his curious poetry—all tidy, metrically uniform Shakespearean sonnets steeped in biblical allusion dramatizing his self-abnegation in service of the Holy Spirit—began piling up at a furious rate. The poems were integral to what Emerson later called a "certain religious frenzy," a profound emotional and spiritual crisis that reached its nadir when Very was committed to McLean's Asylum from September to October 1838 (*CW*, 2:119). The onset of the episode Very dated from the beginning of the "two years succeeding my senior year" when he struggled to banish his own will and independent thought in order to fully obey the divine voice. As 1838 approached, coinciding with his meeting of Emerson and "towards the end of the second year," Very explained, "I felt I was going about all my engagements without any interest in them of my own and yet I felt very happy for I had so long persevered in this course that it had wrought out for me much peace and content."[11]

Life changed for Very not when he met Emerson in early 1838, as one might expect. The watershed event instead occurred two years earlier, at the end of his undergraduate career, when he first encountered Emerson's *Nature*. Very purchased his copy almost immediately after its release on September 9, 1836. His well-thumbed and manically annotated volume bore the sort of underlinings, marginal comments, and bookmarks of his tattered personal copy of the Bible, to which he obsessively clung two years later. His bible before his Bible, Very's copy of *Nature* exhibits overwhelming evidence of his acute awareness of the culture's tendency to mitigate and sully language through materialistic and political self-interest. He particularly warmed to the contention that the poet's language must remain untainted by "duplicity and falsehood" of the sort that dominated the reifying discourse of the commercial world to which so many writers objected from both sides of the Atlantic, especially Emerson and Orestes Brownson in America, and Karl Marx and Thomas Carlyle in Europe. Very noted in the "Language" chapter of *Nature* that "the lip is the parcel of the mind" and elsewhere underscored lines asserting the primacy of the invisible over the material world, all affirmations of Emerson's signature neoplatonism that stood in direct opposition to the surge of mechanized mass production and its attendant debasing wage labor and avaricious consumerism overwhelming the market.[12] Very first laid eyes on *Nature* in September 1836, during the turbulent months leading up to the Panic of 1837, highlighting the instability of a concept such as aesthetic vocation in the context of a nation "poised on the verge of the most accelerated capitalist development in modern history," as Carolyn Porter powerfully describes.[13]

One of the ironies of Very's annotations of *Nature* was how literally he took Emerson's directives, and how predisposed he was to implement them so dutifully into his life. For all his cheering underscores of Emerson's neoplatonism and his support for the authenticity of intuition, it is indeed odd that Very would read this highly abstract text so literally. From it, Very gleaned his sense of the ideal relation between God and man, affirming his deep distrust of faculty like Andrews Norton, who had been exhorting him to place his faith in the visible evidence of God's miracles reported in the Bible by Jesus's disciples. For such distrust of the senses, Very nonetheless read *Nature* "as if it were a conduct-book filled with supernal imperatives," as Edwin Gittleman aptly observes, receiving it "as a literal rather than a figurative testament about the nature of God."[14] Very resolved the paradoxical tension of literalizing a text that emphatically privileged the spiritual over the material world by devoting his career to this higher calling. Very was particularly responsive to Emerson's lament in "The American Scholar" that "there is no work for any but the decorous and the complaisant," and thus leapt at his call to break from "the thousands of young men as hopeful now crowding to the barriers for a career" and become instead the "single man [to] plant himself indomitably on his instincts and there abide." The promise that "the huge world will come round to him" was the wind in his sails (*CW*, 1:69).

Very became so struck by Emerson's formulation of accessing the divine spirit that he adapted his mentor's model of self-immersion in nature—famously figured in the brilliantly bizarre mixed metaphor of the transparent eyeball in the forest—to his own model for the production of poetry.[15] Very's sense of the Holy Spirit as the true author of his poems was predicated on a hollowing out of the self to enable the Universal Being to flow into its vacant space. In precisely this way, "all mean egotism vanishes," as Emerson wrote, "I am nothing; I see all; the currents of the Universal Being circulate through me; I am part or parcel of God" (*CW*, 1:10). Elsewhere in a journal entry, Emerson was similarly possessed "whilst I behold the holy lights of the June sunset," so that "sometimes I am the organ of the Holy Ghost." This sentiment perfectly matched Very's connection to God, except for the qualifying phrase, "and sometimes of a vixen petulance." Whereas Emerson recognized such "vixen petulance" as a counter to ecstatic exaltation (like those detailed in the pragmatic

"Experience" essay that follows the lofty idealism of "The Poet"), Very refused to acknowledge such moments during his mystical episode (*JMN*, 7:9). More attuned to his own capacity for rancor and spite, and more willing to reside with it peacefully or eradicate it physically, Emerson had a deeper belief than Very in the restorative quality of a physical relation with nature. He marveled, for example, at how "my good hoe as it bites the ground revenges my wrongs and I have less lust to bite my enemies" (*JMN*, 7:x). Very instead fixated on the ecstasy figured in the transparent eyeball, which became the functional model for the mechanism through which he would become a conduit for the Holy Spirit, a conception of authorship that enabled him to produce more than three hundred poems over the course of eighteen months.

In "The Song," Very's sonnet Emerson was sure to include in *Essays and Poems*, the powers of the divine are poetically figured through a deific nature like that pouring through the transparent eyeball. "Nature's lore" is so intensely electrifying that "my fingers drop the strangely scrawling pen" in the process of full surrender and immersion into its enchantment. Authorship and religious dogma become irrelevant as "I plunge me in the river's cooling wave,/ Or on the embroidered bank admiring lean." This gesture of Emersonian abandonment and liberation adheres to the signature transcendental close scrutiny of the minutia of nature. Thus "insect life" and "pictured flowers and grasses green" appear through a child's idealized perspective, which in this case is that of the poet in his youth.[16] Even in such Emersonian verses in which the divine is located in nature without heavy-handed biblical references, Very's fingers paradoxically "drop the strangely scrawling pen" to tap into higher energies that take over the creative process. Other romantic poets, from Wordsworth to Whitman, employed a similar conceit, yet never with the pronounced full-bodied immersion of Very, whose poems show an almost ascetic abstinence from metrical or technical affectation. His sonnet form fits like a uniform of sorts, a kind of standard ledger or container he regards as irrelevant or incidental to the utterance emerging directly from his palpitating soul.

In the throes of unmitigated inspiration, Very relegates the human community to a lesser priority like metrical ornamentation. This accords with the Emersonian effect of losing oneself so deeply in the divinity of nature that society "is then a trifle and a disturbance." For in God, one finds as Very had "something more dear and connate than in streets or villages" (*CW*, 1:10). The alignment of the transparent eyeball passage with Very's mystical episode is uncanny not only in the removal of the self to channel the divine, but also in the primacy of one's service to that open channel to God over all other social relations, figured in Emerson's "streets or villages." Society was not only subordinate to Very's mystical vision, it became a troubling obstacle when he attempted to spread the word of his spiritual achievement.

The Proselytizing Poet

Anything but a genial missionary, Very's company could be abrasive, however unintentionally so. At his most badgering and coercive, his radicalism turned hegemonic, inadvertently undercutting the liberalism in Emerson's dialectic that had created and conditioned his individualistic theology in the first place. His missionary rounds involved alternately cornering individuals and forcing them to confess their spiritual inadequacy to him or coercing them into being "baptized" by him. The most glaring and infamous of these episodes horrified Elizabeth Peabody and infuriated Henry Ware, as he forced himself on separate occasions into their chambers with the intent of purifying their sullied souls. Once fully immersed in his mystical frenzy, Very even turned the tables on Emerson, accusing him of a false relation to the divine. Unlike with Ware and Peabody, he did not press the issue with the man who had served as his mentor, inspiration, and literary model. Very eventually found his way out of this hegemonic trap by way of the literary market. But until he arrived at that peaceful resolution, he had left a trail of tears, many of which were his own.

Like Emerson, Very sought to convert Harvard undergraduates to his spiritual vision. A letter to Harvard divinity student Rufus Ellis sent two months after Very had been discharged from McLean's Asylum is the Rosetta stone of his proselytizing rhetoric and unique mystical theology. Sent on Christmas Eve in 1838, the letter is clearly intended to convert not only Ellis but the entire "Junior Class and such others as you may think it will approve," such as, "Lippit, Renouf, Washbourne, Allen." Seeking a broad audience, he pointedly instructed Ellis, "as I cannot write many if you would copy or permit to be copied anything said in them it would promote the design for which they are written." That design of attaining grace he described as "narrow and strait for it requires but one thing. To cut down the corrupt tree." According to his own will-less vision, he exhorted them to "live without interest in anything," such as material or political self-interest associated with corruption, and to "find your reward in peace." Yet Very's life since his September incarceration was anything but peaceful, as he had become a lightning rod of controversy. The letter then swings into the rhetoric of labor in an attempt to convince the students that they can work hard without moving hand or foot, a truism Very later used repeatedly to rebuff Emerson's pleas for revisions during their editorial consultations. Bridging as close as he ever would to his mentor's Divinity School Address, Very heavily emphasized vocation, warning with Emersonian aplomb, "until you have reached him you can not be called a laborer in the vineyard for the works before are dead works. You toil all night and catch nothing." Countering conventional occupational wisdom rooted in the mounting industrial revolution, the payoff of a right relation to God rings out in his crescendo: "Yet there shall come a morning in Christ and the net shall be filled." The ecstasy here is transcendental in its inner movement toward the divine, as "it is a treasure hid in your own field; seek diligently and you shall find where it is to be found." The images of full nets, buried treasure underfoot, and a release from useless toil all invoke productivity and wealth of the spiritual sort. "Obey God," and it "will make you rich . . . and you will be made a priest in Christ." In the same tone Emerson used when asking rhetorically whether Very's authenticity was worth a fit of madness, Very quips to the youths, "what other interest have you in the world than this?"[17]

But unlike Emerson, Very's view of a toil-less life of riches originates not in the infinitude of the inner self, but in the ever-present and abiding divine spirit. God "needst not rest, the shining spheres are thine," for "to Thee the world's long years are but as brief," according to Very's sonnet "Labor and Rest." His depiction of God's paradoxical labor-free work requiring no rest also puts the work of the prophet outside the boundaries of conventional acquisitive striving in the market. The prophets are vocationally correct, for "in thy calling heed no other call/ . . . And in thy glorious self the eternal Sabbath share."[18] By rebuking dutiful conformity to the ever expanding demand for labor attendant to antebellum America's market revolution, Very's appeal to Ellis and the divinity students not only echoes Emerson's rebellion against conventional careers, but also Thoreau's Harvard graduation address that proposed a reversal of the conventional work week to six days of leisure for each day of work.

The letter to Rufus Ellis is an extension of Very's charismatic self-image, made all the more ironic for its will-lessness, articulated in poems like "The Preacher." Speaking with the voice of an omnipotent preacher, he makes evident the influence of the pulpit charisma of such celebrity clerics as Channing (the elder) and Edward Everett. In the role of clerical father figure, Very addressed the Harvard students in his letter to Ellis in the same tone and persona he would don in "The Preacher." Their sustenance depends on their partaking of "the word I give you," for "in my name the crown of life have won/ Come hasten on thou shalt not want for I/ Will be your guide your rest and your defense." This persona of a spiritual mentor and guide gravitates toward the messianic ("my word it speaks will they but hear its voice/ I will uphold thee banish every fear . . . Thou hast been by my Holy Spirit led"), yet without the stridency and bombast of poems such as "The Prophet," in which the title figure addresses not acolytes but stunned and adoring masses.[19] "The Prophet speaks, the world attentive stands," Very writes, rehearsing his role as messiah with ecstatic blasts of powerful, arresting prophecy. The idolatrous frauds stop in their tracks at his holy presence and "at his rebuke behold a thousand flee," for "Deep on their souls the mighty accents fall,/ Like lead that pierces through the walls of clay," leaving them no choice but to "bow; for he can loose, and he can bind;/ And in his path the promised blessing find."[20]

Beyond Harvard divinity students, Very stalked those he felt were extreme religious hypocrites and spiritual frauds like the Unitarian minister Henry Ware. A witness at the scene of perhaps the most telling of these incidents reported Very forcing his way into Ware's study at Harvard while the professor was counseling a student on the finer points of sermonic eloquence. Very announced that he had come into privileged understanding of the twenty-fourth gospel of Matthew through his direct connection to God, which had established that the second coming of Christ was now "in him." It is important to note that while proselytizing in person, Very never championed himself as a hero (however much he did so with gusto in his poetry), but instead presented himself as a model for spiritual fulfillment.

He maintained that such fulfillment was lacking in even the most respected of theologians like Ware. He had found God through an eradication of the self and exhorted Ware to recognize and validate his accomplishment. Such an expectation was stunningly naive, of course, as Ware met him with considerable resistance. George Moore, the divinity student at the scene, reported that Very was willing to yield to Ware's objections, "but the spirit would not let him—that this revelation had been made to him, and that what he said was eternal truth—that he had fully given up his own will, and now only did the will of the Father—that it was the father who was speaking through him."[21] Julius Ward's recollection of the incident is that Very's frustration was so acute it drove him to tears.[22] As Gittleman observes, "tears may also have been shed at the failure of the inspired testimony, with the confirmation of the Bible, to convince Ware of the essential rightness of Emerson's view *when properly interpreted.*"[23]

Multiple offenses and breaches of decorum prevented Ware from even beginning to sympathize with Very's perspective. Not only was Very attempting as a student to trump his professor's reading of the Bible, he was also asking a Harvard Divinity School theologian to acquiesce in the authority of Emerson, who had been assaulted in print recently. The authors of those attacks on Emerson were Ware's faculty colleague Andrews Norton and his own father, Henry Ware, Sr., who had originally served as Emerson's mentor when he was preparing for his short-lived career in the pulpit. Once it had become overwhelmingly clear that his appeal to Ware had failed, Very uttered words that undoubtedly stunned his superior, yet when taken from his socially narrow and myopic perspective, his motive appears anything but sinister. He was not so much trying to "unhorse" Ware as if he were Barzillai Frost at the teachers' meeting, but instead was seeking genuine succor from Ware, a young enthusiastic minister who preached the virtues of an intimate relation to God, yet with a decidedly anti-Emersonian literalist textual approach to the Bible. "I had thought you did the will of the Father," Very said with utter sincerity, "and that I should receive some sympathy from you—but I now find that you are doing your own will and the will of your father."[24] Though he meant no offense, plenty was taken, as Harvard moved to have Very removed from his tutorial duties.

His next attempt at finding a sympathetic ear would be Emerson, to whom he immediately sent a packet of his essays on Shakespeare. In the interval, he paid a visit to Elizabeth Peabody, who had originally discovered his genius while attending his lecture on Shakespeare. With her, he took on an even more authoritative role, placing his hand on her head and demanding total submission to his newfound power to baptize through his direct channel to the Holy Spirit. She recalled his menacing presence and how there was "something unnatural—and dangerous in his air." As he declaimed, "I am the Second Coming—Give me a Bible," she "trembled to the center" since "I felt he was beside himself and I was alone in the lower story of a house." Peabody was equally unsettled when she learned that he had made his rounds to several Baptist clergymen, two of whom physically resisted his efforts to baptize them and "had actually bodily put him out of the house." Charles Wentworth Upham reacted to Very as Andrews Norton might have, venting his anger not at the young man but at his mentor, railing "against the transcendentalists, calling Mr. Emerson an Atheist," and demanding Very be committed. Upon hearing this news, Peabody went straight to Very's mother's house and asked for an explanation. She immediately vouched for her son's sanity and urged that he "should *not* be carried to the Insane Hospital," arguing that he was the one who had been treated brutally. Very later defended himself by asserting that those about him suffer an "insanity [that] is profound" while "his is only superficial."[25]

Remarkably, there was no self-aggrandizing or posturing evident in his demeanor according to Peabody and Very's confidante, Harvard professor of rhetoric Edward Channing, who noted "his union of gentleness and modesty." Though frightened by him at key moments, Peabody was in fact drawn to Very as when she first saw him deliver a speech on Shakespeare and spirituality without resorting to "sanctimony" and "in the most devout tone—yet so free from cant as to command their reverence." She went on to note how "he had nothing of self-exaggeration" and that "to hear him talk was like looking into the purely spiritual world—into truth itself," since he was so utterly convinced that he had "obtained self-annihilation and become an oracle of God." After Very's death in 1880, Peabody regretted not keeping open "discourse with a Spirit so rare," musing that "we might have more of heaven upon earth than we do were we only faithful to [such] opportunities—and took counsel of our *hearts*."[26]

Interestingly, Very's attempts at winning his transcendentalist friends and supporters to the full submission of God's will he had achieved often bore inadvertent consequences, leaving him misunderstood and thus unbearably frustrated. On one visit to Concord, for example, Very announced quite seriously to his hosts, "I hate you all." They misread his frustration as attempted humor, and only drove him deeper into defeat. This messianic persecution complex also surfaced in "Worship," Very's poem depicting nature and God's deep resonance with him in stark contrast to his alienation from the human community, which he took as a requisite social burden all prophets must bear. "The prophet walks unhonored mid the crowd/ That to the idol's temple daily throng," braving both indifference, "His voice unheard above their voices loud," and opposition, "His strength too feeble 'gainst the torrent strong."[27] Although Emerson likely laughed along with the others at Very's bizarre antisocial announcement, he deviated from the "voices loud" in this case in his appreciation of the poet's authenticity, noting in his journal that when "J. Very charmed us all by telling us he hated us all" that evening, it struck him that "sincerity is more excellent than flattery" (*JMN*, 7:124).

Upon his second visit to Peabody the same evening he had attempted to baptize her, Very unfurled a "monstrous folio sheet of paper on which were four double columns of sonnets." He then left these "utterances of the Holy Ghost" with her to read.[28] A crucial watershed moment in Very's coming of age as a professional author, this visit was precipitated by his fruitless proselytizing that reddened his normally pallid face with frustration, his cheeks streaked with tears on at least one occasion. His missionary work had inadvertently elicited a backlash of spite and violence. The Holy Ghost, he insisted, opposed violence, although Emerson certainly championed his brave saint at the teachers' meeting for violating the sanctimonious Frost. Such hostile confrontations were clearly just as unsettling to Very as they were to his interlocutors. Yet his physical presence had demanded their submission to his sense of truth. "He seemed to expect from me a full acknowledgement of his mission and a participation of the same," Emerson observed of Very. Even the most sympathetic of his auditors, such as Peabody, Emerson, Channing, and Hawthorne, were made to feel some combination of discomfort, irritation, and fear in his presence. Only Emerson respectfully differed with him and established a common ground of peaceful disagreement, especially on the issue of self-annihilation and complete obedience to a higher authority, which did not sit well with his faith in self-reliance. "I asked him if he did not see that my thoughts and my position were constitutional, that it would be false and impossible for me to say his things or try to occupy his ground as for him to usurp mine. After some frank and full explanation, he conceded this," Emerson wrote of a pivotal moment that encouraged Very to give up proselytizing and instead concentrate his efforts on writing (*JMN*, 7:123). Print media enabled Very to channel the divine voice he incessantly heard without such dubious results. Publication and the literary market, as Peabody observed, necessarily accompanied his repudiation of "the role of proselytizer," so that "his whole duty was to utter the words given him by the Holy Spirit" on the page, leaving him "not responsible for their effect or non-effect upon others."[29] Once in print and free from direct interpersonal confrontations, Very felt a deep sense of accomplishment in facilitating his vision to those interested, and in finding material remuneration in serving the needs of the Holy Spirit.

Editing God's Poet

Very's defiance of conventional vocations common to antebellum life was highly visible until 1845, when he retreated into an obscure and marginalized career as a "supply minister" to various churches in the vicinity of Salem, where he resided with his sister. During both the highly visible ecstatic phase following his expulsion from Harvard and his retreat into anonymity after 1845, Very persistently stood at the margins of his culture. He was averse to raising a family as Channing had, for example, and to plying various trades as Thoreau had, such as school teaching, pencil manufacturing, and surveying. Such interests were anathema to his constitution. Yet for one interval in his career in the late 1830s, he did approach authorship as a commercial enterprise rather than because he considered himself a joint-stock company in partnership with the Holy Spirit. Instead, he came to the realization that the literary marketplace could actually serve his religious aims. Very had applied his ambition toward a higher plane in his proselytizing, but he would find the market an appealing alternative to forcing himself on others going about their business.

Emerson proved instrumental in Very's move into the literary market. His mentor's arrangement for the publication of his slim volume *Essays and Poems* (1839), however, was anything but easy, as an author convinced he is only transcribing words from a higher source poses a particularly difficult dilemma for editing. Authors who participate in the rigorous revision of their work indeed imply their agency in its creation. Very thus felt it presumptuous and indeed blasphemous to revise the words of the Holy Spirit. Obedience to the voice that originally called him meant that Very would follow God first and Emerson second. "The Disciple" poetically illustrates Very's exclusive recognition of divine authority. In the poem, he condemns the atheistic self-reliance of those who "find no work for Thee [i.e., God] to do,/ And blindly on themselves alone rely," a charge detractors of transcendentalism frequently aimed at Emerson.[30] Elizabeth Peabody remembered that "Mr. Emerson said Mr. Very was very averse to correction—declaring that it was the utterance of the Holy Ghost."[31] In addition to Channing, here was another Emersonian poet protégé resisting revision, yet for an entirely different reason—one that proved even more intractable, given the higher authority he obeyed. Upon Very's death in 1880, Bronson Alcott recalled that Very "professes to be taught by the Spirit and to write under its inspiration. When his papers were submitted to Emerson for criticism the spelling was found faulty and on Emerson's pointing out the defect, he was told that this was by dictation of the Spirit also." Emerson then retorted that " 'the Spirit should be a better speller,' " which Alcott dismissed as a meaningless barb since in his estimation "the printed volume shows no traces of illiteracy in the text."[32] Part of that flawless look of the volume was owing to Emerson's editorial alterations, rather than any polishing done by Very.

Despite some misgivings about Emerson's selections for the volume, which suppressed the more mystical poems in favor of his more conventional fare, Very was eager to see it reach a paying audience. Very expressed a deep interest in his audience by seeking to capitalize on his fond following among the legions of undergraduates he had taught at Harvard, and among his supporters such as "Professor E. T. Channing of Cambridge," to whom he dedicated *Essays and Poems* "as a mark of gratitude." Indicating his preferred bookseller and manner of receiving royalties, he insisted it "would be best to leave a subscription paper at the Cambridge bookstore," and to have Emerson "send whatever money may accrue from it to" his brother Washington.[33] When the book was released, Very took deep pleasure in knowing that his trafficking with the human community was best executed through the exigencies of the literary marketplace rather than through personal encounters. When he arrived in Concord to obtain a written order from Emerson entitling him to his author's copies of *Essays and Poems* from publishers Little and Brown, which he then collected on his way back to Salem, Very was finally in his element. While Very was glorying in the support, love, and patronage at Bush, Lidian could not help but notice that the cake she served him seemed to have an especially fortifying and revitalizing effect on his demeanor. "Your cake was well supplied," he later wrote, thanking Lidian for her hospitality, which affected him like Emerson's management of his book's publication, since it "went to my heart to take it."[34] Book in hand, commanding new tangible professional direction, and basking in Lidian's sunshine, this was one of the most satisfying moments of Very's tumultuous eighteen-month odyssey. "How he sat there with a piece of gingerbread in each hand, so innocent and unconscious! And how beautifully he was talking!" This was Emerson's Golden Boy, now fit for a beautiful future, yet "innocent and unconscious" of the flaws he had already built into the foundation of his professional career.[35]

Were it not for the patronage of Emerson, despite its "ambivalent effects" on so many of his promising youths, along with the friendly support of Professor Channing, Very might have spent the rest of his days either in prison or permanently detained at McLean's Asylum for the Insane in Charlestown.[36] His brand of romanticism was far more self-destructive than Ellery Channing's or Thoreau's, but it began much as theirs had with an initial titanic surge of poetic production. Like Thoreau's prolific early years under Emerson, Very scrolled out in eighteen months almost a third of the nine hundred poems he would write over the course of forty-seven years from 1833 to 1880. The stint reached its zenith in the fall of 1838, fueled by Emerson's Divinity School Address delivered that July. As one might expect, evidence of Emerson's influence on Very abounds, from his distinctly transcendentalist polemics inserted into Greek tutoring sessions at Harvard to his poems themselves. It is seldom noted, however, that Very himself had encouraged Emerson's outrageous pronouncements that made the Divinity School Address famous. Emerson felt validated by Very's desire to discover redemption and the presence of God within himself rather than in the miracles described in the gospel according to the prophets and disciples of Jesus. This was the heresy Emerson found so compelling, the move toward inner divinity that motivated and shaped his Divinity School Address. Just as Emerson wrote "The Poet" with Ellery Channing in mind, he composed the address with Very in mind, especially the impression left by his two visits made just three months before the oration. Very had "the air and effect of genius" such that Emerson could "conceive hopes" for America (*JMN*, 5:475–80). From their earliest meeting they had a mutually inspirational effect that escalated and magnified the subversive bent of both Emerson's address and Very's *Essays and Poems*.

In his best poetry, Very audaciously and stunningly speaks with the voice of God. His cunning transcendental union with godhead begins with his widely anthologized poem "The New Birth," the first of a series of ecstatic visionary verse in *Essays and Poems*, setting the keynote for the last fifty pages of the volume. In it Very dons the familiar role of the romantic poet undergoing an awakening of the senses in an image at once quickening like a passionate beating heart and opening to a new heightened awareness. "In thronging haste fast pressing on they bid/ The portals open to the viewless wind," he writes in the fashion of Percy Shelley's escalating aesthetic-erotic climaxes in romantic lyrics like "To a Skylark." Yet in Very's hand, the trope abruptly pivots toward the devotional, as he imagines being called upon as God's medium.[37] The barriers between "the heaven and earth—their walls are falling now" open the floodgates of the divine calling which Very figures in the roar of "storm lifted waves." Here Very taps into the essence of vocation, as God's voice is unremitting, insistent, and powerful. "On from the sea they send their shouts along," the heavens overwhelming him like so many waves rushing onto shore; "Back through the cave-worn rocks their thunders roar;/ And I a child of God by Christ made free/ Start from death's slumbers to Eternity."[38] His more mundane biblical verse is flat by comparison, repeating the mantras of what David Robinson has called Very's "exemplary self," which in his interpersonal relations amounted to him pointing out spiritual insufficiencies in his auditors with the verbal affectation of antiquated Hebraic diction.[39] Very operated with only the best intentions based on principles Emerson, his mentor and muse, proudly smiled upon at several key stages of Very's radical religious activism.

The monstrous folio Very brandished before Elizabeth Peabody contained twelve columns of metrically well-mannered Shakespearean sonnets asserting his status as the second coming of Jesus Christ. In "The Cross," perhaps the most simultaneously devout and heretical of them, Very explicitly imagines himself carrying on Christ's mission, down to the crucifixion. With its deeply pious rendering of the meanings of Christ's sacrifice, the sonnet veers toward the blasphemous in conflating the poet with the savior, who prays, "With all his faith still aid me in the strife,/ Till I through blood like him the prize have bought;/ And I shall hang upon the accursed tree/ Pierced through with many spears that all may see."[40] Emerson knew that Very's enemies like Norton would see this only as heresy and evidence of the corrupting effects of Emerson's "antic tricks" that deceived with "an over-excited *convulsionary* style" the impressionable youths of Harvard. Such verse directly implicated Emerson. Conservative Unitarians saw Emerson's address as the corrupting "last instruction which those were about to receive, who were going forth from it, bearing the name of Christian preachers."[41]

The *Boston Morning Post* came to the defense of Emerson's assault on the "tyranny which custom and conventionalism have exercised over [Harvard Divinity School students]," confining them in soul-killing vocational identities. The editors argued that Emerson met resistance from the Harvard faculty's "own insensibility to the free spirit of the age and country [that] is the cause which leads the young men, committed to their care, to seek inspiration and instruction elsewhere."[42] Emerson's liberal philosophy was precisely where the collegians sought their inspiration and instruction. The strongest challenge to clerical authority since the Puritan witch trials, Emersonian transcendentalism was a force Norton believed would lead Harvard students to perdition. "Not since Anne Hutchinson had the Boston clergy been so harshly rebuked by one of the supposed elect, and Emerson's doctrine indeed savored of Antinomianism," Anne C. Rose observes.[43] Very's insistence that the Holy Spirit resided in him derived directly from Emerson's view that "the safety of God, the immortality of God, the majesty of God do enter into that man with justice" (*CW*, 1:78). Such an antinomian disposition meant Very was fundamentally incompatible with the doctrine and authority not only of Harvard's faculty and curriculum, but also of intermediary guidance (clerical or otherwise) between God and humans. If he could not be molded institutionally, and if he distrusted even personalized mediation, could he follow anyone's teachings, or even editorial advice, including Emerson's? With the exception of the Thoreau of the late 1840s and after, Very was the least compliant of the protégés, openly telling Emerson on one occasion "that you saw the truth better than others, yet I felt that your Spirit was not quite right. It was as if a vein of colder air blew across me" (*JMN*, 8:148).

Very had imprisoned himself in a role akin to that of Reverend Hooper, the semi-fictional figure of Hawthorne's "The Minister's Black Veil," whose ever-present crepe hiding his visage accuses all—from his own flock to the religious officials above him—of unimaginable secret sin. Although Very was "always vain in his eye," according to Hawthorne, "it was an innocent vanity" free from posturing or calculated attempts at deception. Hawthorne felt, as most would, that Very was "sanctified by his real piety and goodness." Had it not been for Very's "want of the sense of the ludicrous" which he found so abundant and compelling in Melville, Hawthorne might have even taken to him. Although Hawthorne expressed irritation with his tendency to address him as his spiritual "brother" and be "somewhat unconscionable as to the length of his calls,"[44] he still felt Very was best suited to his role as "one organ in the world of the impersonal Spirit" if only because it helped produce "such good sonnets."[45] But the price he would pay for these subversive poems was profound isolation. In his 1843 meditation on authorship, "The Hall of Fantasy," Hawthorne located Very "within a circle which no other moral race could enter, nor himself escape from."[46] He had done precisely what Whitman assured his readers he would refrain from being—a "stander above men or women or apart from them"—in his poetic self-definition at the opening of *Leaves of Grass*.[47] Very thus breached the democratic ethos of egalitarianism and tolerance by donning the reformer's righteousness that Emerson would eventually frown upon.

Very's social alienation can be traced to Emerson's ideal poet who regards the human community as "secondaries and servants" to his genius, "as sitters and models in the studio of a painter, or as assistants who bring building materials to an architect" (*CW*, 3:5). Only for Very, he transformed himself into precisely such a secondary and servant to God, who he insisted was the real genius behind his work. Hence he defied occupations, such as the Unitarian ministry, that cultivated authority in intermediary roles regulating and codifying the individual's access to God. Very's poetic self-definition resonates with Emerson's sense that every trade defines itself in opposition to others, even competitively so: "Every occupation, trade, art, transaction, is . . . a correlative of every other. Each one is an entire emblem of human life; of . . . its enemies" (*CW*, 2:59). According to this formulation of occupational identity, Very felt immense pressure to maintain his mystical role, for it represented nothing less than "an entire emblem of human life." According to this vocational formulation, a natural enemy to such a divinely inspired poet is thus an editor, or any other literary intermediary attempting to reshape the voice of God.

Very's rise depended heavily upon the intervention of precisely such literary intermediaries. Launching him into the professional world of letters, Elizabeth Peabody was the conduit between Very and his editorial work with Emerson. Like Hawthorne, Peabody was also drawn to Very's poetry. She admitted that she had puzzled over "and read them with wonder" and thus "wrote at once to Mr. Emerson and told him all these phenomena," just as she had promptly alerted him of Very's genius upon first hearing him lecture on Shakespeare.[48] Peabody's word spurred Emerson to action in both cases, revealing how vital her influence was—the literary equivalent of a stock tip—in encouraging Emerson's investment in young talent. Indeed, without Peabody's signal on both occasions of his lecture and the presentation of his manuscript of original verse, Emerson might never have fully deployed his powers to promote Very for publication in such a timely way.

Once placed in the position of editing his own work for publication, Very's professional identity rooted in his channeling of the Holy Spirit faltered noticeably, leading Emerson to change his views of Very permanently. Their editorial sessions started well enough upon Emerson's initial arrangements for the publication of the book. Very had abruptly transformed, however, and began responding to Emerson with cold, stock replies of the sort that he wielded against his most skeptical conversion subjects. Very insisted that he was under the command of a higher power and thus was incapable of assisting in selecting or altering poems for the book. He became irritatingly laconic in Emerson's presence. "I work hard without moving hand or foot," he repeatedly responded to Emerson's requests, anticipating Melville's intractable office clerk, Bartleby the scrivener, immortalized in *Putnam's Monthly Magazine* over a decade later in 1853.[49] Unlike at a prior meeting of theirs when Emerson found a way into Very's sensibility once he apprehended his vocabulary, his lexicon on this occasion left him baffled. On this visit Very was oddly despondent to all but Emerson's wife, Lidian, to whom he was particularly attracted. In fact, during their extended intimate conversations he felt as much passion for her as for any woman he had known.[50] During the early 1850s, Thoreau also produced enormous amounts of poetry inspired by Emerson and developed a crush on his wife.

Editing God's poet proved difficult indeed for Emerson. But did he respond, more than with any other protégé, with an editorial iron fist and seize control of the project in "the most high handed" manner, as Robert D. Richardson argues? Was his editorial process indicative of his resolve to shape the work unilaterally? Peabody reported that Emerson "selects and combines with sovereign will, 'and shall,' he says, 'make out quite a little gem of a volume.' "[51] But the editorial consultation that covered a three-day period in June of 1839 reveals that any dispute over parsing and spelling was of little consequence. The Historical Collation indicates that Emerson had actually made very few alterations of Very's versions of the poems. Apart from what can easily be dismissed as harmless and noninvasive copyediting, Emerson's other key editorial function of selecting which poems to include in the volume shows a more aggressive approach that scholars have denounced as patronizing and condescending. Helen Deese contends that Emerson's editorship was "conservative," yet she underestimates the utility of such an approach in light of the audience Very was facing, and the sheer power of the lynch mobs stirring in Salem in the 1830s.[52]

After a protracted four-year trial that allowed ample opportunities to land a progressive verdict, for example, the Commonwealth of Massachusetts instead convicted Abner Kneeland of blasphemy for publishing atheistic sentiments in his paper, the *Boston Investigator*. The Kneeland trial was well known at the time of Very's entry into the literary market, as the court determined that "an intended design to calumniate and disparage the

Supreme Being, and to destroy the veneration due to him" was indeed a punishable crime.[53] Kneeland would be the last person jailed for blasphemy in Massachusetts history, reaffirming the Puritan theocracy lurking beneath sham democracy. This posed an imminent threat to Very's heretical missionary campaign. The Kneeland verdict created a threatening climate for a controversial figure like Very, who had already suffered Salem's disapproving scrutiny as a child of unwed atheist parents. It is no coincidence that Hawthorne, also a Salemite acutely aware of the oppressive Puritanical glare, sympathized with Very as well, and made scapegoating a major subject of inquiry in his fiction. So in this context, any "high handedness" in Emerson's editing should instead be regarded as his recognition of Very's vulnerability.[54] At this stage, he was no longer "our brave saint" unhorsing self-righteous clergy, but a damaged and publicly branded victim of the controversy Emerson himself had sparked.

Given this threatening context, Emerson's editing of Very's book was more conscientious and sympathetic than "curiously detached," as Deese contends.[55] To fault Emerson for incompetence in handling the matter demands a more liberal editorial policy than the exigencies of the literary market—in this case driven by an angry Puritanical lynch mob who had already stigmatized and ostracized Very—would allow. Indeed, we might expect the author of the Divinity School Address to eschew conformity, but in this case it may have placed Very in the same predicament as Kneeland. It is well known that asylums were used as institutions to remove an individual from society, often with a medical diagnosis that had been bought off. *Put Out of the Way*, by Rebecca Harding Davis, testifies to the abuses of asylum commitments made to access relatives' (especially in-laws') money. Very was no exception, and we need to credit Emerson for understanding the full extent of the threat Very was facing rather than blame him for "curious" or "high handed" editorial moves. Very's continuation of his proselytizing upon release from McLean's prompted Emerson to act quickly on Very's behalf to put out his non-messianic poems, not only as a token of his admiration of his genius (epitomized in his tribute to Very in his essay "Friendship"), but to mollify his enemies because he could see a worse and more protracted reaction from the Salem community brewing.

Very's poem "I Was Sick and in Prison" particularly justifies Emerson's desire to defend his protégé from the lynch mob. It functions as a character defense in sonnet form. In it, Very's proselytizing is pitched in its most deserving and wholesome manner, coming off as the operation of completely sincere and altruistic good will, however poorly received and scandal ridden those good intentions were. "The bird must sing to one who sings again" and spread the holy word, "Else would her note less welcome be to hear," and meet resistance as Very himself had. With more community support of his mission, "then shall the brotherhood of peace begin." The language of mass religious revolution through incremental conversions is unmistakable in his promise to "burst the prison where the captive lies," a reference to Very acting as savior if only to liberate, "And one by one new-born shall join the strain."[56] Further, Emerson felt responsible in part for Very's predicament, because of the furor he had raised in the community with the Divinity School Address, which also set the stage for Very's mystical episode.

Two years after its publication, Emerson acknowledged the "genius" and "extraordinary depth of sentiment" in *Essays and Poems*. He spoke more pointedly about Very the poet than his poetry, emphasizing his strengths and unique attributes as a transcendentalist. Although Emerson's reference to Very's "little book" may appear patronizing, his *Dial* review paints an overall admirable portrait. Very's excessive "obedience," which Emerson complained of privately in his journal, paradoxically appears here as a unique expression of self-reliance. Emerson obscures Very's will-less deference to the external command of the Holy Spirit in order to cast him as a particularly zealous and idealistic voice of the Concord coterie, lauding him for achieving a state of "high and transcendental obedience to the inward Spirit." Emerson casts Very's muse in the more secular humanistic guise of "the inward Spirit" rather than the thoroughly biblical Christian one to which the young poet subscribed. There is more praise than disdain for his extraordinary dedication to that muse, which bears resemblance to Emerson's self-reliant scholar whose nonconformity risks "absurdity or even . . . insanity" for the sake of "entranced devotion" to his pure vision of "great sweetness" and "sublime unity." What may appear to be defects—a lack of "playfulness," variety of tone, and "extent of observation"— Emerson portrays as conventions Very boldly refuses in a way that purifies his poetry of superficial and corrupting strains of "pretension to literary merit." (That support of the unpretentious unfinished verse and rejection of affected ornamentation also appears in Emerson's "Verses of the Portfolio").

Clearly Emerson is praising the mystical poems that round out the latter portion of the volume, rather than the earlier ones he himself had insisted on including during their editorial process. His position in the review is clear: "With the exception of the first few poems, which appear to be of an earlier date," and which were written before his will-less phase, "all these verses bear the unquestionable stamp of grandeur," particularly those which "flow through him rather than from him."[57] This was a clear reversal of his inclusion of such bland verse as "The Hummingbird" and "The Canary Bird" that made up more than a fourth of the already small sampling of sixty-five poems selected from a pool of more than two hundred. Emerson could easily have chosen instead to include the poems of "grandeur" speaking with the voice of God. Why, then, would he originally publish Very's relatively pallid nature poems at the expense of those written during his ecstatic episode, only to deride the former and praise the latter? Why the odd reversal in his attitude toward Very's verse? What had possessed him to suppress from publication what he would later consider Very's best poetry in his review? Or, put the opposite way, why would he force Very's early poems into the volume only to condemn them in his *Dial* review?

Emerson's seemingly capricious treatment of Very—at first censoring and then celebrating his poetic fusions with God—was really his attempt at managing what he knew would be a highly sensitive reception into the literary market. His decision to censor so many of Very's mystical poems, however esteemed they are now by contemporary critics, should be understood as a conservative marketing strategy aimed at recovering a deeply stained and scandalized public image, which was punctuated by a string of confrontations with highly influential public figures and a protracted stay in an insane asylum. Very was, in some ways, Emerson's most delicate and vulnerable project from both a professional and personal standpoint. He knew that showcasing the mad mystical poems featuring God as the speaker, such as "The Promise," "The Creation," "The Message," "I Am the Bread of Life," and "Terror," carried the liability of alienating him even further from the literary community. Emerson was not somehow convinced that the bland nature poems were superior to such daring transcendental unions with godhead that spoke with quintessential Emersonian authority. He made sure, however, to mollify their effect, at once unholy and blasphemous in ways none of his other disciples' published writings had been, in the literary market, by placing them behind his more scholarly works, as the volume begins with his essays on epic poetry, Shakespeare, and Hamlet and then moves into his nature poems.

Emerson's acute awareness of the importance of a favorable first impression of the sort he arranged for Very upon entrance into the literary market surfaced in his journal observation that "it will take an imaginative and philosophical writer nearly as long to write the preface to his book—a preface of a page—as the book itself; and an advertisement will pain him for a week and then cost half a day to execute it" (*JMN*, 7:26). Emerson knew the essays and poems at the beginning of Very's book would make a pivotal first impression on readers—is he a worthy poet or a blasphemous madman?—and thus demanded careful assembly for the same reason an author pores over the prefaces and advertisements that constitute the face of his work. In this way, Emerson craftily framed more radical dimensions of Very's work. Astute readers of the volume would have noticed Very's echo of Emerson's rejection of historical Christianity from his Divinity School Address when he explains the link between pagan theology and epic poetry. The "popular belief in visible appearance of the gods" gave "occasion to noble description and tend[ed] to excite that admiration which is the leading aim of the epic."[58] Further, Emerson wanted to present Very's total literary corpus, spanning from his earliest scholarship and poetry, rather than rendering a book dedicated only to his eighteen-month mystical phase. Once the book was released, Emerson avoided the appearance of nepotism associated with dashing into print with a review. Instead he waited two years and sang the praises of Very's true strong suit.

Official histories of Emerson's editing of *Essays and Poems* tend to support Richardson's condemnation of Emerson for overriding Very's three desires for the book: to include "Letters to the Unborn," to present poems thematically, and to contain no previously published verse. But Richardson even admits that "Emerson thought he was putting Very's work in the best light, and perhaps the book Very wanted would not have gained as many readers." The caveat is not the provisional exception here, but indeed Emerson's guiding rule and responsible, caring editorial principle. Emerson should be lauded for preventing Very from throwing his quirky and reckless version of the book into the precarious market for transcendental writing. Instead of opening with "Letters to the Unborn"—a preface demanding that readers accomplish what he had by becoming indistinguishable from Jesus, which would have turned away most of them before they could glimpse his best poems—Emerson decided to lead off the volume with his Shakespeare essays. This was an ingenious tactic designed to revive Very's earlier reputation as a Harvard scholar by reconnecting readers with his days on the lyceum lecture circuit. This was a time when Very had won awards for his literary criticism as an undergraduate. The association with this earlier phase in Very's career was in fact the one that initially attracted not only Peabody but Emerson as well.

Emerson was interested in presenting a volume not so much to bring out a self-indulgent and eccentric volume of poetry—though he would certainly do just that decades later in *Parnassus*, his penultimate poetry anthology of the world's greatest verse in his view—totally heedless of expectations of audience and author. Emerson was hardly such an autocratic editor in this case, but instead proved just the opposite of this misleading master narrative, which casts Very as the victim, his book all but stolen by Emerson, leaving him with one "that appeared [which] was not really what poor Very wanted it to be." Emerson was instead acting with wise professional discretion in this case, preventing Very from becoming truly poor. What is even more misleading is the charge that Emerson lacked the authority to direct the shape of the book since his "own published work amounted to less than Very's in quantity."[59] Very was barely communicating with the outside world at the time, having gone into seclusion after his religious frenzy, corresponding with Emerson and others mainly through the agency of his brother, Washington Very.

Even more important than Very's obvious need for an intermediary to shepherd his work into the market was that Emerson hardly lacked credentials by 1839, but in fact enjoyed far greater exposure even at that early date through the periodical press and mass audiences of the lyceum circuit than Very would ever achieve in his lifetime. Quantifying Emerson's print publications is a misleading measure of his fitness for editing, furthermore, especially when one considers the breadth and depth of his international literary contacts and editorial assistance to figures that would include

Thomas Carlyle. Richard F. Teichgraeber estimates that "Emerson mania" began with Harriet Martineau's widely noticed and reviewed *Retrospect of Western Travel* (1838), which praised "The American Scholar," setting off a reaction in the media that hit a fever pitch with the Divinity School Address. His mounting fame was already transatlantic at the time, as British reviewers coined the phrase "Emerson mania," which aptly characterized a market well versed in the Newness. Emerson's first publication that produced a substantial royalty check was not *Representative Men*, but a volume of his essays arranged and edited with the assistance of Thomas Carlyle for the English market in 1841, as Teichgraeber has observed. The British market was indeed saturated with more than twenty editions of Emerson's works in the late 1830s, most of which sold thousands of copies.[60]

Emerson's scant quantity of verse published has little relevance to the depth of his connections in the literary market, established not only through his lectures, but also his early writings, "with the editors, readers, and reviewers of several of the most important Northern religious periodicals that shaped (and attempted to police) American literary opinion when his career began," as Teichgraeber explains.[61] The financial success of his early writings also supports his credentials as a professional author skilled at marketing his work. Sales of print runs of the Phi Beta Kappa address of 500 copies in September and 515 the following February earned him a royalty rate of 15 cents per copy, roughly half of what twelve lectures netted him the previous winter.[62] Emerson's output from 1838 to 1842 was impressive. It included the Divinity School Address, "Literary Ethics," "The Method of Nature," "Man the Reformer," three lecture courses on "Human Life," "The Present Age," and "The Times" (a total of twenty-eight lectures), and his next book, *Essays: First Series*. Despite his obvious authorial successes, it is perhaps spurious to measure Emerson's editorial competence in the first place by his writing. Editors were string pullers, intermediaries, log rollers, and prognosticators, without any expectation that they would also be prolific writers themselves. Emerson needs to be taken as seriously as Ticknor and Fields, George Palmer Putnam, or Evert Duyckinck in his role as editor. His editorial work should be assessed in light of the considerable influence over the literary market he had achieved by 1839 when he edited Very's *Essays and Poems*.

Emerson's advocacy of Very in his *Dial* review speaks to a deeper sense of responsibility for his disciple's career when we realize that his praise for his mystical poems actually ran counter to his own aesthetic principle. In "The Poet," Emerson's disaffection with Swedenborg emerges when he makes clear the distinction "betwixt the poet and the mystic, that the last nails a symbol to one sense, which was a true sense for a moment, but soon becomes old and false" (*CW*, 3:20). This was precisely the effect not only of Very's poetry, but of his poetic persona, which after a year of playing the role of divinely inspired seer, began to wear thin. Bronson Alcott, a close confidante at the close of the mystical phase, worried for Very's life at one point, saying he was convinced this shell of a man would soon die. Emerson's misgivings of his "earlier" poems in the volume tellingly speak to weaknesses he likely saw in Very's mystical works as well. The *Dial* review seems more an honest appraisal than a "patronizing" one: as transcendental poetry went, Thoreau's included, Very's *was* exceedingly narrow in scope, and ancient in its dogmatic devotional pitch. There is nothing Elizabethan about his Shakespearean sonnets, as they feature no wordplay or conceits. An audacious power is indeed heard in the more radical poems, in which Very assumed the voice of the godhead, but the craft still bore the stamp of blunt artistry, of language wrenched of connotative aesthetic power and instead funneled into testimony of doctrine. Nonetheless, Emerson remained faithful to his protégé when many other editors would have dismissed outright Very's last-minute request to include four new sonnets. He wrote back, amiably agreeing to print three or four of the new verses despite his efforts to keep the volume to a slim 175 pages at the 75 cent price he brokered with Little and Brown. Most important, Emerson accepted his request only because it did not threaten the royalties he had arranged for Very that promised him up to $150, a sum he sorely needed at the time.

The Kneeland trial made Very as much a moral as a psychiatric case. In addition to these powerful and determining dynamics is the professional one, especially the challenge Emerson faced of what to do with Very once he was discharged from McLean's Asylum. Emerson's editorial treatment of Very was not autocratic, insulting, or abusive. Instead, Emerson operated in Very's best interest to professionalize and thus make presentable before the public an otherwise scandal-ridden and broken madman. It was not so much an act of charity as one of profound respect, a kind of tribute to the genius he had so deeply admired as his "brave saint." The unenviable position of bringing Very before the public in print with a highly reputable publisher like Little, Brown demands a more sympathetic understanding of the difficult ethical and professional situation Emerson faced.

7

CHARLES KING NEWCOMB: EMERSON'S DARK APPRENTICE

After becoming an anecdote illustrating the extremes to which transcendentalists could go in their eccentricities, Charles King Newcomb is now remembered for the bizarre blend of portraits that adorned his walls—popular dancing girl Fanny Elssler was flanked by Jesus and the Catholic saint Loyola—his homemade shrine complete with crosses and fetishes, his loud chanting echoing into the wee hours of the evening, and his insistence on sleeping in long white gloves beneath a veiled canopy. As one of the original and longest standing residents of the experimental commune of Brook Farm in West Roxbury, Newcomb was notorious for keeping fellow boarders awake reciting his own variations of the more dramatic and mystical litanies he learned during his aborted training for the Episcopal priesthood. Submerged out of view from Newcomb's usual biographical sketches is the seer who captivated Emerson.[1] At the time, Newcomb was vigorously engaged in unifying nature's transcendental power with its dark forces through the inspiration of the works of Coleridge and Hawthorne as well as the scholarship of his own mother, Rhoda Newcomb.[2] During one of Emerson's darkest hours just after the death of his five-year-old son Waldo, Newcomb entered his life. In him Emerson found the ideal author of a short story he envisioned allegorizing the loss of his son, a project through which he might reconcile his guilt and anguish, while also advancing his philosophical paradigm into unfamiliar, and indeed darker, territory. To this end, he and his wife, Lidian, furnished Newcomb with letters describing his deceased son's ethereal character, thus fostering

Charles King Newcomb (Houghton Library, Harvard University)

the creation of the protagonist of his story "The Two Dolons." Paradoxically, and much to Emerson's delight, the tale would become the darkest, most violent and overtly gothic prose fiction penned in the history of transcendentalism.

Emerson was so taken by Newcomb's insight into nature's malevolence that he dedicated himself not only to arranging for its publication, but also to help establish a lasting and satisfying career for his protégé. The standard critical view is that, "For Emerson, the personal tragedy of Waldo's death was inextricably bound up with the failure of his literary sons, whose very lives were a reproach to the memory of that most promising boy."[3] Newcomb, however, was more a balm than a reproach to his mentor. The deeper Emerson probed into Newcomb's Coleridgean aesthetics and mysticism, the more ardent he became about publishing his writing and fostering his career. Mentoring and marketing Newcomb brought Emerson into the presence of forces as violent and stunning as Waldo's death itself, yet promised beneath the tangled vines of Newcomb's byzantine prose nothing less than reconciliation and redemption.

Theological Origins of Transcendental Hell

As the only figure close to Emerson from a non-Protestant background, Newcomb (though unattached to any church) brought with him the trappings of the Catholic and Episcopal Churches steeped in ritual, the power of sin, and the palpable presence of hell. Upon graduation from Brown University in 1837, Newcomb joined the Episcopal Seminary at Alexandria in what was then the District of Columbia. But Newcomb's preference for Roman Catholicism surfaces in passages he transcribed in his commonplace book dating from this period taken from the Latin Hymns of St. Francis Xavier, the Roman Catholic breviary, and the works of Saints Gregory, Basil, and Athanasius. This evidence suggests, as Judith Kennedy Johnson has observed, that if Newcomb's mother and Margaret Fuller had not strenuously resisted him, he would have joined a Roman Catholic rather than an Episcopal seminary.[4] Newcomb's sister, Sarah, in early 1838 had mentioned to him how remarkable his spiritual change had been in his one brief year before his exit from the seminary. She marveled "at the change that had come so blightingly over your once evangelical views," a tragic reversal of how an Episcopalian proselyte like him "was so *easily* made." She blames "the relapse of my brother into cold, heartless Unitarianism" on "the scheme formed by Miss F. [Fuller] to allure you from the Superstition of Romanism."[5] But the fact remained that just as vestiges of Unitarianism clung to Emerson after he defected from the ministry, strains of Catholicism were apparent in Newcomb. Elements of Catholic ritual indeed were essential to the self-styled philosophy he brought to Brook Farm in May of 1841, just one month after the experiment in communal living had begun.

The year before he joined Brook Farm, Newcomb's commonplace book tellingly contained passages by Emerson he had copied from Fuller. He never fully abandoned his passion for Catholic ritual and ceremony. Clinging to what Fuller would call Catholicism's more superstitious manifestations, he added to this base the German gothic mysticism, including Faust, as well as Goethe, and Schiller, figures Fuller had undoubtedly impressed upon him. Fuller's immersion in German language and literature was so intense that she had briefly considered writing Goethe's biography. But along with these predictable sources, one finds entries in the 1839 commonplace book by the English romantic poets Percy Bysshe Shelley and Samuel Taylor Coleridge. Coleridge's "Rime of the Ancient Mariner" was particularly compelling to Newcomb, who deeply apprehended the paradox of the Ancient Mariner's fate as too complex to be either sanctified or damned and instead explained it as "a union of opposites, a giving and receiving mutually of the permanent in either, a completion of each in the other."[6] The paradox of the Coleridgean One Life also rang true to Newcomb's mother, who observed the commingling of opposites in nature in "a sea of liquid fire embosomed in a wall of icebergs" in the poet's imagery.[7]

Newcomb's sense of hell and sin, to which Emerson had been drawn when reading passages by Coleridge in his commonplace books, hinged on the mutual dependency of these forces. Coleridge scholars have made the stunning insight that "Newcomb bridges the divide between Emerson's light and Hawthorne's darkness through Coleridge's *Biographia Literaria*."[8] Newcomb seized upon *Biographia Literaria*'s chapter 14, which opens and closes with emphasis on unity. The creativity in human nature, especially as practiced by poets, "diffuses a tone, and spirit of unity, that blends, and (as it were), *fuses* each into each, by that synthetic and magical power, to which we have exclusively appropriated the name of the imagination," according to Coleridge.[9] (It should be noted here that "synthetic" alludes to a bringing together of disparate forces rather than "artificial.") Indeed, it was in precisely that "magical power" Coleridge identified as a unifying force present in the imagination and in nature that Newcomb forged his vision, making him more willing and better equipped than any other transcendentalist to probe the darkest depths of human vice and sin.

Throughout Newcomb's journal one finds a view of sin and vice steeped in Coleridgean unification. It is not so much a bland relativism he espouses, but rather a fiery Catholic belief in accountability for reprehensible human behavior. He paradoxically traces the origins of sin to virtue. Licentiousness, or "sensualism," he observed, "is a vice founded in the virtue of sexuality." Thievery, though he refuses to tolerate it, sees "the same end in view [as] the owner [who] bought" the goods in the first place. The egregious underlying sin connecting all sins, indeed the most unpardonable in a Hawthornian sense, was the fulfillment of self-interest seen in one who aggressively takes from others to feed "his own life, but ignores the life of his victim." Hawthorne, an acquaintance of Newcomb, details the depravity of precisely such a "onesidedness" as Newcomb called it in his short story "Ethan Brand," which he dramatizes as "monstrosity in soul as in body." Hawthorne's protagonist dies with a marbleized heart hardened into limestone by his own reification of human souls during his quest to discover the unpardonable sin. Brand "ignores the life of the victim" in his pursuit, and in the process sins unpardonably, thus revealing what Newcomb describes as "the enormity and culpability of sin."[10]

Emerson recognized Newcomb's acute sense of vice and his intrepid forays into the darkness of the human soul that saturate his journal. This emphasis on the human capacity for sin combined with Newcomb's Catholic background in a way that cast Emerson's young apprentice as something of a Catholic priest, however unattached and transcendental. Emerson jocosely wrote to Fuller that he was glad to hear of the positive reception of the *Dial* in Providence and hoped that its latest issue might "cure our young Catholic Fra Carlo" from an illness he had been suffering (*L*, 2:319). A more telling line appears when Emerson alludes to Newcomb as "that San Giovanne" with whom he had hoped to share a "walk which was to be our confessional" (*L*, 2:270). The latter reference, also in jest, nonetheless is revealing of the role Emerson would take in his relationship with Newcomb following the death of Waldo during the frigid winter of 1842. Not only was Emerson's wife Lidian at a loss for how to handle the sudden death of the child whose fever seemed harmless on a Monday only to send the boy into delirium by Thursday, the day their physician informed them that he would not recover. Emerson also was utterly devastated and ill equipped to handle the loss given the current development of his transcendentalist thinking toward increasingly radical individualism and soaring optimism. For the first time in his life, Emerson needed a Catholic priest, and found him in Fuller's friend.

Emerson did not seek out Newcomb for consolation so much as a means of reconciling his philosophical brightness with his dark sense of guilt within. He was interested in the caustic medicine he associated with the Catholic confessional, yet wedded with an aesthetic sensibility that might enhance and complement, rather than destroy, his own philosophical foundation. Emerson made an ominous confession to Jones Very four years before Waldo's death that not only anticipated the nature of the pain he felt at his son's loss, but shows clearly how he processed his grief into self-blame and finally overwhelming guilt. He was concerned that his self-reliance and radical individualism had hardened him to the point of preventing mourning should his loved ones predecease him. "I had never suffered," he admitted, "and I could scarcely bring myself to feel a concern for the safety and life of my nearest friends that would satisfy them: . . . if my wife, my child, my mother, should be taken from me, I should still remain whole with the same capacity of cheap enjoyment of all things. I should not grieve enough, although I love them." This articulated precisely the reaction he would have to Waldo's passing. The dilemma, interestingly, hinged on a factor of teaching and mentorship, the capacity to "make them feel what I feel—the boundless resources of the soul—remaining entire when particular threads of relation are snapped—I should then dismiss forever the little remains of uneasiness I have in regard to them." Ironically, if he were to predecease them, so his logic goes, he hoped they would also "still remain whole" in his absence, a gift not of indifference or callousness, but of strength in independence. But when both parties are not equally outfitted with such stalwart self-reliance, Emerson knew the imbalance could be damaging. Little did he suspect that such "uneasiness" and guilt pangs would overwhelm him and challenge him to reassess his transcendental paradigm in order to "still remain whole" (*JMN*, 7:132).

Emersonian transcendentalism, insofar as it had evolved through 1842, also left Lidian Emerson at sea in her spiritual response to Waldo's death.

When she needed the consolation of religion most, the "foundation of her life" was missing, since her husband's philosophy had "unconsciously warped" the original principles of her faith so that "its fullness was gone." In her satirical "Transcendental Bible," Lidian exposes her discontent with her husband's credo's failure to provide a basis for sympathy from which an emotion like mourning might effectively be expressed. "It is mean and weak to seek for sympathy," she wrote with hyperbolic sarcasm. "And it is mean and weak to give it." This principle obviously has devastating implications when applied to the mourning Emersons, who of course needed sympathy. Further, any greater meaning ascribed to suffering, according to the gospel of "Self-Reliance," was asinine: "If any seek to believe that their sorrows are sent or sent in love, do your best to dispel the silly egotistical delusion."[11]

Lidian's tone of course is playful, but its import is earnest, considering that she became more religiously orthodox after Waldo's death. Emerson himself would react similarly by reaching for a clearer sense of spiritual direction than self-reliance afforded him. The loss of Waldo to scarlet fever, then known as scarletina, left Emerson guilt-ridden because he was convinced he had not suffered enough while mourning his passing. He felt pain indeed, as "Threnody," the elegiac poetic tribute to Waldo, testifies.[12] But he deemed it insufficient, especially in light of his own transcendentalist credo of self-sustaining independence that clashed horribly with the ethic of sympathy and self-sacrifice as aptly satirized by Lidian, whose "Transcendental Bible" endorses the governing codes of bereavement at the time.

When placed in the context of the culture's standards for bereavement, it is not at all surprising that Emerson would feel guilty for failing to suffer adequately for Waldo's death. Historian Ann Schofield explains that "the nineteenth-century cult of death," which Emerson had deliberately alienated himself from for philosophical and aesthetic reasons, "on both sides of the Atlantic, found expression in literary romanticism" of the sort he detested, as well as "in the garden or rural cemetery movement and in the development of the etiquette and material culture of mourning." More important, the material trappings of bereavement spoke to a deeper ethical code dictating that "if one did not display grief in every acceptable mode, this demonstrated a lack of respect for the deceased."[13] In addition, inadequate mourning also threatened to disintegrate social cohesion, since it sprang from a failure to sympathize, an aspect of Emerson's concept of self-culture that plagued him with guilt. "Our social ties are golden links to our uncertain tenure," as one antebellum commentator explained. The culture widely understood that acute despair at the loss of a loved one should eventually be rechanneled into compassion for the community. Such compassion promised to dispel "suspicion and distrust, those cankerworms that sap the life and purity of communities where they exist, while it restores and strengthens confidence between men." Emerson's work had instead been driven toward restoring and strengthening confidence within the individual, leaving him feeling as though he had violated this promise of social harmony, characterized by a "universal love [that] expels all selfish passions and prompts every heart to seek the general good." Considered "the most sacred of our social emotions," exemplary mourning was embodied in the image of Jesus weeping over the tomb of Lazarus.[14]

Emerson's aversion to sentimentality and self-sacrifice for social cohesion placed him outside the socially sanctioned method of emotionally processing death. He did not have an alternative readily available. "There could be no more harrowing testimony to the terror of idealism," as Sharon Cameron explains, "than this example of a self forced prospectively to imagine the loss it retrospectively refuses to feel."[15] This idealism signaled in "Experience" is ironically, even chillingly, the counterpoise to the idealized figure described in "The Poet," for whom "every touch should thrill" (CW, 3:4). In the face of experience, the poet is not lachrymose and damaged in the face of death, but is stalwart and autonomous. After merging identities with his son so that he "was a part of me, which could not be torn away without tearing me nor enlarged without enriching me," he now confesses that he "falls off from me and leaves no scar." Like a tree dropping its leaves early, the effect of his loss "was caducous" to Emerson. This sort of autonomy does not however lack affect, but instead acknowledges how "in the death of my son, now more than two years ago I seem to have lost a beautiful estate—no more." His controlling metaphor of a lost estate to describe his son's death, which he extends into further economic terms, is galling in its coldness. Yet beneath the self-reliant rhetoric even the image of a monumental loss of capital is not without its affective impact. A lost estate leaves a feeling of value irrevocably disappearing; "I cannot get it nearer to me," he laments (*CW*, 3:29).

The guilt Emerson feels in this formulation lies in the way Waldo's death "does not touch me," leaving him with a "grief [that] can teach me nothing, nor carry me one step into real nature." At the time Emerson first recorded these thoughts in his journal just after Waldo's death, he was ideally positioned for Newcomb's entrance into his life. The entry in his 1842 journal is most telling in this regard. The progression of three consecutive paragraphs indicates precisely this predisposition for Newcomb's priestly aid, caustic medicine, mythical formulation of the boy's passing, and assignation of Emerson's own role in it. "What opium is instilled into all that is called pain in the world!" begins the first paragraph, a meditation rendering his numbness in the lines that would become famous in their slightly altered form in "Experience." The frantic agony of loss for some, and its drama of wailing and gnashing teeth, he portrayed "as not half so bad with them as they say." Death be not proud, Emerson declaimed, not unlike metaphysical English poet John Donne, since we "court suffering" but find it a mere "scene painting, a counterfeit, a goblin." Beyond the trappings of cultural understandings of death, with their dramatization and hyperbolic "sharp angular peaks & edges of truth," we might encounter the deeper essence of Death. "That will not dodge me" in counterfeit hues or anguished wailing; "if aught can act & react with energy on the Soul, this will," he affirmed (*JMN*, 8:201).

Immediately following this brave affirmation is an entry dated February 21 that Emerson penned upon his return from a lecture he delivered in Providence less than two weeks after Waldo's passing. The trip came dangerously soon after his farewell to Waldo, which left him feeling unable to "ever dare to love" again (*L*, 3:8). He had confided in Caroline Sturgis the realization that "Alas! I chiefly grieve that I cannot grieve; that this fact takes no more deep hold than other facts, is as dreamlike as they," a sentiment echoed in both his journal and "Experience" (*L*, 3:9). The return "home again from Providence to the deserted house" sounded a different tone than the bold vow to confront and meet death with his own energy of the Soul. The trip had temporarily distracted him from the stark absence of Waldo's comforting presence, of the boy quietly playing while he worked at his desk. Indeed, for all of Emerson's insistence on letting nature's lessons, rather than scene paintings of it, guide him through his grief, now he was struck with a violently unnatural void. "As his walking into the room where we are would not surprise Ellen," he observed, "so it would seem to me the most natural of all things." In the absence of nature providing a moral compass in this case as it always had in the Emersonian paradigm, now he uncharacteristically yearned for divine intervention. "What a looking for miracles have I!" he exclaimed, wishing he could make his son materialize particularly when receiving callers. "Dear friends find I, but the wonderful Boy is gone" (*JMN*, 8:201).

The language of this journal entry then shifts in the next paragraph to answer the overwhelming sense of loss with a reach toward mysticism, reflecting an unusually desperate Emerson hungering for spiritual stability. Immediately following his lament for the loss of Waldo, he reports, "In Providence I found Charles Newcomb, who made me happy by his conversation and his reading of his tales." Emerson then plays on the city's name of Providence to suggest that Newcomb was sent to him by divine providence, since, according to "the rhetoric of religionists, we might say that nothing seems more intended" than such fortuitous encounters with bright youth bearing the promise of new hope and vitality.[16] Indeed, after Waldo's death on January 27, Emerson resolved as early as February 15 "to bring Charles Newcomb home with me to show him to some of my men and things" (*L*, 3:13). Just as Jones Very had come into Emerson's life when he needed an arrow to fire back at the rising resistance to his Divinity School Address, a radical voice, more radical and fearless than even his own, appeared, giving Emerson another savior, this time of a more monastic sort. Whereas Very was his brave saint, Newcomb was his "Catholic Fra Carlo," his abiding spiritual guide and creative mind, to bring Waldo into a literary light that would enable him to confront his guilt. In both cases, we see an unusually vulnerable Emerson, reaching out for younger minds as a source of stability in the face of the two most traumatic events of his life.

Newcomb's Catholic predilections appealed to Emerson, who imaginatively cloaked him in priestly garb in accord with his fundamental sense that "Charles is a Religious Intellect" (*JMN*, 8:178). This connection to Catholicism promised to purge Emerson of his guilt and pay tribute to his memory beyond his own efforts in letters and his elegiac poem,

"Threnody." Further, Newcomb's connection to Fuller, whose friendship dated back to his childhood in Providence, was invaluable to Emerson, for through her, Newcomb might learn to appreciate the significance of Waldo. Fuller was an ideal source from which Newcomb might ascertain the special powers of the child for the creation of "Dolon," since she had loved Waldo "more than any child I ever knew," and "he was the only child I ever saw, that I sometimes wished I could have called mine."[17] The construction of "Dolon" was in many ways a collaborative effort involving not only Fuller's heartfelt memories and Emerson's editorial advice, but also anecdotes from Lidian. The work of writing in this case became the agent for a type of social cohesion the antebellum standard etiquette for mourning suggested should result from the transformation of individual inner pain to collective outward sympathy. Having appointed Newcomb the creative nexus of this network of mourners, Emerson thus poured himself into the young author's professional and creative development from February 1842 to September 1843. Emerson knew too well that "this age will be characterized as the era of Trade" and that "meantime, it is also a social era; the age of associations, the powers of Combination are discovered," both developments that brought liabilities of materialism and political corruption (*JMN*, 5:273). This situation, however, offered the opportunity to bring the "powers of Combination" into a creative project that he would pilot into the world of trade in the periodical press. He thus tapped into the collective as well as his own personal memory of Waldo to bring Newcomb's story to life and in turn retrieve the literary career forever lost to his son.

One "Dolon"

Like Fuller, Hawthorne was Newcomb's friend and literary model. Hawthorne's play of light and shadow, as seen in the early depictions of the love-child Pearl in *The Scarlet Letter*, bears an unmistakable influence on Newcomb's use of chiaroscuro in "Dolon."[18] Pearl is the offspring of sin but still exudes natural beauty; beams of sunlight seem magnetically attracted to her as she plays in the forest. Nature seems to also embrace Dolon, yet violent portents loom in the shadows of his ethereal play just as they morbidly tint Pearl's otherwise sunny frolic. Dolon seems to exist in a heavenly realm only to face terrible doom. Newcomb's rendition of Dolon draws on Emerson's sense of Waldo as the embodiment of natural unity and symmetry, Hawthorne's dark, even morbid, vision of the doomed angelic child, and Coleridge's conception of beauty inhering in death. Newcomb dramatized the tragedy Emerson otherwise could not comprehend, "Dear Boy too precious and unique a creation to be huddled aside into the waste and prodigality of things!" or forcibly blended "with every happy moment" to be shelved safely with the philosophical category of the transcendent "delight in the regularity and symmetry of his nature." Indeed, the shape of Dolon's character holds true to Emerson's profile of his son expressed in a letter to Caroline Sturgis as one for whom "the beautiful Creative power looked out from him and spoke of anything but chaos and interruption," whose essence exuded "the moral of sun and moon, of roses and acorns, that was the moral of the sweet boy's life, softened only and humanized by blue eyes and infant eloquence" (L, 3:10). Such melting tenderness Newcomb establishes early in his portrait of Dolon, only to stunningly violate it with chaos of biblical proportions, unleashing forces at the intersection of nature, God, and the ancient ritual sacrifices of humans.

Although Waldo's fictionalization in "Dolon" begins with a Shelleyesque fairy nymph quality, it darkens rapidly when the child of nature comes in contact with a strange man in the forest, a delusional hermit cloaked in druid's robes performing the primitive pagan rituals of the Iron Age Celtics and Gauls. The story resonates with Newcomb's affinity for Swedenborg, who posits that intellectual work is artificial and only removes one further from the forces of nature. The narrative is not uniformly somber and unremittingly dark, but rather a rambling disquisition on Nature and self via childhood's interface with the demands of the adult world predicated on school and work. Newcomb, like Emerson, was averse to such demands. The first sentence originally ran all the way to the end of the page, alarming Elizabeth Hoar, whom Emerson had asked to copyedit the piece (L, 3:66–67). Once she referred the issue to Emerson for help in how to proceed, he immediately requested Newcomb's presence at Bush for an editorial session.

Newcomb's cumulative syntax continually doubles back on itself and tends to confuse rather than clarify, thus building a narrative that initially appears a jumble of incoherence. Newcomb's prose continually drives deeper, however, as his clauses penetrate rather than evade his subject. His description of children executes this technique by casting them as the best transcendentalists. For them nature is fact and not sentiment; they do not search for facts to attach to sentiments but instead live in them. "Nature is not primarily a sentiment to children," the narrator explains; "sentiment may be a feeling in it, but it is place and not sentiment which leads them to it."[19] This was a direct challenge, if not an inversion, of Emerson's syllogism posited at the opening of his chapter "Language," in *Nature* (1836). Words are derived from nature, Emerson claims, and "natural facts are symbols of particular spiritual facts." Language to Emerson is the conduit communicating and encoding the natural world's function as an outward symbol of the paramount inward soul. For Emerson, sentiment leads him to nature because it is a valuable tool for communicating and validating the soul. "Nature is the vehicle of thought," in Emerson's formulation, because it represents "the symbol of the spirit" (*CW*, 1:18). To Dolon, nature is a place first, and not a metaphor for the spirit. Only later, when Dolon reaches maturity, does he begin to apprehend nature more in the abstract, but he never espouses a neoplatonic Emersonian appreciation of it as a figurative reflection of idealized truths inherent in the soul.

Newcomb's rhetoric of the intuitive powers of the child, a conceit rooted in Wordsworth, opposes the prominent place of the intellect—one autonomous and willfully controlled, even heroically so—in Emersonian transcendentalism. The nearly anti-intellectual Swedenborgian strands of intuition in Dolon signify not only Waldo but also point more metonymically to all children. Emerson observed this tendency, characterizing Newcomb as "hating intellect with the ferocity of a Swedenborg" (*JMN*, 16:265). Since "Fourierism was too bald a materialism to suit the higher classes of its disciples, without a religion corresponding, Swedenborgianism was a godsend to the enthusiasts of Brook Farm" such as Newcomb, "and they made it the complement of Fourierism," John Humphrey Noyes explained in 1870. Newcomb was particularly taken by Swedenborg's writings because they embraced the intuition and invisible worlds, while also preserving the significance of Christ, if not as a Trinitarian figure, then "as Jehovah himself [and] an illusive representation of the Father."[20] These reconsiderations accommodate the forces of evil within a seemingly spot-less transcendental optimism devoid of hell.

As Newcomb calls into question socially constructed notions of individualism while establishing Dolon as simultaneously ideal and natural, the narrative builds toward a violent dramatization of the capacity for sin inherent in Emerson's concept of self-reliance. Dolon begins to show more explicitly the characteristics of Waldo, especially in his "visionary and romantic" development despite his father's insistence that he "learn more decidedly."[21] Though taken by his innate romantic predilections, Emerson attempted to impose order and discipline on the intellectual growth of his son. Newcomb evokes Emerson's own tendency as a mentor to pressure his promising literary apprentices, including Newcomb himself, toward a definable professional career. This is hardly a sin for which Emerson felt any sense of deep guilt, however. Dolon's father, in fact, appears only briefly, as the boy's dwelling deep in nature becomes his surrogate father figure and paternal guide, pointing toward another distinct set of Emersonian traits more directly probing Emerson's pain and guilt. The reclusive Druid represents this other side of Emerson, far darker and more sinister, one shrouded in the seclusion of a life dedicated to contemplation of the immortality of the human spirit. Emerson cherished his solitude—when he was disconnected socially and not engaged on the lecture circuit, entertaining callers, or mentoring his apprentices—but paradoxically feared that his individualism caused his insufficient mourning of Waldo's death. That life-buoy of privacy to which Emerson alludes in the conclusion of "Experience," "the solitude to which every man is always returning," offered him "a sanity and revelations which in his passage into new worlds he will carry with him" (*CW*, 3:49). Did Emerson love his Wordsworthian poetic moment of "emotion recollected in tranquility," the sweet solitary imagination that gave him courage to face the world again, "never mind defeat; up again, old heart!" more than his own son? Ironically that locus of "sanity and revelations" proved simultaneously to be nurturing a depravity within his own heart beyond his own fathoming.[22] The loss of his son revealed that to him.

That refuge within the self for Emerson correlates with Dolon's favorite place in the woods, at "a large rock" that provides the setting of his own primitive ritual sacrifice. His connection to nature sustains and nurtures him just as it ultimately destroys him. "Genius," which Dolon possesses the way Waldo did, is defined as "youth matured with Nature in it." Clearly, Dolon, and Waldo by extension, grow precisely insofar as they are deriving energy and imagination from nature. But nature also contains a dark perversity, and so it comes "one afternoon" that Dolon encounters the Druid. Intuitively gravitating toward each other, they exchange no words but share a spiritual connection. He is revealed to be a Greek "scholar" who has gone mad and retreated into the woods, and is thus a mortal threat to Dolon. This first threat of death is tellingly followed by a reference to Emerson's transparent eyeball, figured as an emptying of the self to channel in the forces of nature: "Being" is the "raising of an eyelid, like the soul of man in Jesus." This Christianized variation of Emerson's transparent eyeball image renders Dolon infused with the divine spirit of Nature. Adults also have this capacity, for "in the absence of mind [they too] are somewhat youthlike." Dolon, the quintessential intellectual and moral offspring of Emerson, is gifted with the capacity to draw the Universal Being into his soul.[23]

At first glance, it might appear that this story was written to flatter Emerson with a highly idealized, angelic portrait of his son, and references to self-reliance as well as the transparent eyeball. But the figure of the Druid ominously points not only toward the dark forces of nature in general, but toward Emerson himself. Dolon is "in a state" of seriousness upon seeing the Druid and hearing others speak of him; apprehending him as a fact sends Dolon into a crisis that represents the first step in his "intellectual development," thus further allegorizing the Emersonian pattern of mentorship. Emerson indeed brought nature to his protégés, and each would undergo a period of intense spirituality and creativity parallel to Dolon's early growth, in which "youth matured with Nature in it." The error in so many youths, however, was blindness to the mortal threats to their careers. Similarly, Dolon begins "naturalizing the crazy man" so that he is a form of nature, a part of nature. This is precisely the aspect of the transcendental credo that threatens to destroy the individual for the sake of Nature, leaving the self stagnant and reified "like a full formed tree whose sap ceases to circulate."[24] Dolon appreciates both the sanity—figured in the Druid credo of the immortality of the human soul analogous to Emerson's concept of the infinitude of private man—and the insanity of the Druid, thus reaching full intellectual maturation. Newcomb has prepared him to die. His "Fairy faith" is now gone; Dolon exudes a "plaintiveness that is serene and possessed." The ritual killing of Dolon's boyhood is signified by his emergence into a more worldly understanding of "belief and its subjects and faith."[25]

Dolon comes to terms with the hermit's insanity in a way that Emerson found cathartic and validating. Dolon's rational and intuitive acceptance of the Druid is Newcomb's means of preparing Emerson for the story's final brutal blow signifying his murder of his own son. The scene is an unmistakable dramatization of Waldo forgiving his father for his sins and coming to terms with his unconventional system of belief, an imaginative leap, since the five-year-old boy of course was far from intellectual maturation. Dolon had achieved an understanding "of the crazy man's belief in that which had been ages before a belief . . . and of the difference between his outward and inward relation to it" through which "Dolon acknowledged the sanity and insanity of the man . . . of the difference between this man's and his own relation to the Mythology; or belief of its subjects, and of faith." That is, Newcomb is asserting that Waldo, though a child of nature endowed with the power to invite the Universal Being into his soul, was not Emerson, nor did he share in his more abstract relation with nature and understanding of "the Mythology." It might have been something of a fantasy for Emerson to imagine his own son reaching the age of intellectual maturation and reconciling his own understanding of self, nature, and myth with that of his father.[26]

The story ends with perhaps the most excruciating scene Emerson would ever read in a work of fiction, the substance of which he never alluded to in any surviving documentation. Emerson wanted to hurt more when Waldo died, and indeed this conclusion delivers the intense register of pain he desired. The third day Dolon enters the woods, the Druid is performing an ante-ritual in the cave in preparation for a sacrifice. He fittingly emerges from a dark recess, signifying Emerson's own isolated existence. He seizes the boy and plunges a knife through his breast, performing the sacrifice "earnestly, reverently, solemn, facing heaven," and with his hand over his heart lays prostrate beside the rock upon which Dolon "had fallen backward . . . and lay facing heaven." Like Fuller's Leila who does not "shrink from baptism," singing out "from slavery let freedom, from parricide piety, from death let birth be known," Dolon also does not resist the ritual, however malevolent, which cannot suppress the resurrection of his spirit.[27] Newcomb overdetermines the hermit's piety here, likely to assuage the sting of this scene for Emerson. Lawrence Buell's note about "Experience" readily applies to this scene, which "murders little Waldo all over again." Yet unlike the reasoning of "Experience," which defiantly justifies shedding dependent relationships for the sake of self-reliance with no guilt, "for there is no crime to the intellect," this gesture of heroic individualism falls hard on his conscience. Buell's commentary on "Experience" has clear implications for "Dolon": "the writer does not excuse himself for his coldness; on the contrary, he is prepared to rank himself chief among sinners," like Newcomb's murderous hermit, "as the world reckons such offenses." Just as the deranged Druid sees his murder of Dolon as a necessary divine sacrifice rather than a crime, Emerson "makes his deed of forgetting seem more monstrous by passing it off as a noncrime of the intellect."[28] The conclusion of "Dolon" thus stands as a fictional spiritual counterpart to the intellectual essay "Experience" in this regard, both registering the profound cost of self-reliance.

Emerson had adamantly pushed for the story to be published in the next issue of the *Dial*. He was more obsessed with this work of short fiction than any other during his entire career. A succession of three letters began in June 1842 with an invitation to Newcomb "to confirm with me on this paper . . . for I wish to speak to you of the two ways of ending the tale" (*L*, 3:61). The next day he wrote Fuller, proclaiming in ecstasy, "there are sentences in Dolon worth the printing the Dial that they may go forth" (*L*, 3:63). Later that month, he seems all but reborn, gushing with unconstrained enthusiasm for Newcomb and his "strange beautiful story called Dolon. I hope it will come to you in better season than some of its predecessors. But how strange that this light spirit of life and reality can so seldom survive the printers' types. . . . Instantly to a printer with these young energetic words, and let them run over the globe" (*L*, 3:65). He could not publish the story quickly enough. Why would he want to publicize, however discreetly veiled in the fiction, such dramatic anguish over Waldo's loss?

Emerson had felt the power of Newcomb's hell, in which "sin conspires with solitude, in that it makes a man sole arbiter, in himself, apart from principle, of character and conduct." Flight from the world of evil, like that of the Druid and Emerson by extension, was concomitant to flight "from the world which is good despite its evil." Both contain the one-sidedness Newcomb found "irrational and insane," since they violate the principle of Coleridgean unity. Newcomb believed that life was predicated on the inevitable exposure to evil, and that all "must expect to be exposed to evils prevalent in it." Further, he advocated for "all who are conscious of the particular or general evils in themselves" to live in the world "notwithstanding the injury which their evils may inflict on others."[29] This frank acceptance of evil in nature, the human community, and the self, almost Whitmanian in its forthright toleration, helps explain Newcomb's caustic medicine for Emerson as well as his mentor's enthusiasm for publication that followed. For encoded in his bizarre, violent tale was a vision of hell, relatively unknown in transcendental writings, one vividly imagined in such a way as to defy "visionary optimists [who] pretend to go, go beyond the fact that evil and hell are and always will be correlative words."[30] To Newcomb, as long as evil could exist, so too could hell, even in the well-meaning pious actions of a withdrawn iconoclastic thinker like the Druid of "Dolon," Emerson's dark shadow.

Spiritualism at Brook Farm

While Emerson had measured Newcomb's sparks of life by his dearth of correspondence and submissions to the *Dial*, Newcomb had been busily building a steady fire of self-culture and social capital in residence at Brook Farm in West Roxbury. Beginning in June 1841 with intermittent breaks until his departure in December 1845, Newcomb thrived on life at Brook Farm, which he found deeply satisfying. For here was an escape from the protective, often domineering, watchful eye of his doting mother, who demanded frequent and detailed letters as a means of exerting control over him from Providence. Brook Farm not only granted him freedom from his mother, it also provided him a spiritually stimulating, close-knit community like that of the Episcopal seminary in Alexandria. Without the imposition of the seminary's rigid theological doctrine, the experiment in communal living offered the advantage of a more liberating and tolerant ideological climate, given its eclectic pantheistic transcendentalism.

Newcomb was drawn to aspects of Brook Farm that Emerson found revolting. One was its theatricalism, which Hawthorne satirized as Zenobia's "wild spectral legend" in his novel *The Blithedale Romance*, highlighting where mysticism met entertainment at the real Brook Farm in performances by residents like Anna Parsons.[31] Her command performance was "A Reading of Fourier's Character," in which she held the philosopher's letter she had purportedly never read to her forehead and described the character of its author. As she spoke, someone present took notes. Such readings earned her notoriety and admiration; her performances were not taken with the sort of skepticism one might expect. Instead, "She was so perfectly sincere a person, that, while people were surprised at the accuracy of her descriptions of character, no one ever questioned the genuineness of the process by which her impressions were obtained," according to Helen Dwight Orvis.[32] Hawthorne, however, questioned the veracity of such performances in a scene in *The Blithedale Romance*, where the narrator Miles Coverdale has a premonition he finds more than coincidental that leads him to conclude correctly that the letter borne by his young associate Priscilla is from Margaret Fuller. His believing mysticism is bluntly undercut by her cold reason. "How could I possibly make myself resemble this lady, merely by holding her letter in my hand?" she asks, effectively rendering him impotent to prove his point as he confesses that "it would puzzle me to explain it."[33]

The stream of consciousness that flows from "Dolon" very much mirrors the sort of freewheeling yet psychologically probing syntax of a Parsons reading. One critic has even suggested that Newcomb's "cryptic phraseology" deceived Emerson—who had otherwise openly criticized followers like Margaret Fuller for their dabblings in mesmerism, animal magnetism, gemology, and other mystical fads—into overestimating his genius, leading him to discover meanings in the byzantine prose that really issued from his own mind.[34] Emerson, however, was not deceived, because he had clearly reinforced his belief in Newcomb's unique genius over a decade after he had first read "Dolon." Emerson indeed believed that his son truly existed in the cryptic ciphers of a man who had always believed in the powers of psychic mysticism. It is no surprise therefore that Newcomb was enchanted by Fuller's rendition of the clairvoyant Seeress of Prevoorst (the German Frederike Hauffe, daughter of a forester of Prevoorst) in *Summer on the Lakes.* Parsons was a performer, and Newcomb attempted a similar performance in the short story form as "reading" of Waldo's character. Jones Very similarly transformed himself into a conduit to channel the Holy Spirit in a way that suggests the centrality of mysticism and performance in transcendental culture. At the heart of each is a religious fervor. Parsons's clairvoyant reading of Fourier's character, for example, intuits that he "has a religious *feeling,*" despite his distrust of denominational doctrine.[35] She also exalts him as messianic, directly comparing his visionary power to that of Christ. The use of Christian elements in such transcendental mysticism was also essential to Newcomb's aesthetic. Further, Newcomb was fond of the more dramatic liturgies and rituals of Catholicism, dressed in flamboyant attire, and had a predilection for sleeping in white gloves beneath a veil. More than mere idiosyncrasies, these tastes and preferences describe the depth of his immersion in the theatricality of popular mysticism. Hawthorne also recognized veils and gloves as staples of the mesmerist's performance art.

During his residence at Brook Farm, psychic character reading intrigued Newcomb more than any other subject. Marianne Dwight's letters are saturated with references to Newcomb's fascination with this novelty in popular mysticism, which was not only of interest among the aesthetes and philosophers of Brook Farm, but also very much a mainstream phenomenon as indicated by the flattering self-portraits made to appear like phrenological profiles (according to the pseudoscientific method of identity mapping) in Fanny Fern's *Ruth Hall* and Walt Whitman's *Leaves of Grass.* It is telling of Newcomb's obsession with Parsons's character-reading prowess and renown that in nearly every mention of him in Dwight's voluminous correspondence, which details every major event and social dynamic of the commune, he is hotly pursuing her services or explanations of her art. Newcomb's interest in Parsons exceeded that of the already enthusiastic reception for her readings, and unanimous acceptance of their accuracy, by Brook Farm residents. "Your dream is entirely true," he affirmed about one of her readings, despite it lacking "one particular feeling he wished to see," which prompted him to request her consultation. "Mr. Newcomb is *very* desirous to have you send your impressions," Dwight wrote to Parsons.[36] During a brief departure from the commune, Newcomb sent a letter in Fuller's care to Parsons so that she might hold it, unopened, to her forehead and render her "impressions of him."[37] Impressed by her powers as a "seer," Newcomb said Parsons "must read the *Seherin von Prevorst* in Margaret Fuller's book."[38] Brook Farm was not without its interests, social cohesion, and indeed personal and creative growth to Newcomb, who would take his fascination in Parsons's special talent and attempt a similar technique in "Dolon," using the letters Lidian had sent him to read the character of their departed son.[39]

Brook Farm may indeed have driven a wedge between Emerson and Newcomb, but its culture of mesmerism and mysticism that fanned the embers of his interest in the practice originally encouraged by Margaret Fuller paradoxically appealed to Emerson, especially when it came to harnessing those powers for the memory of Waldo and his own emotional role in his death. The popular mysticism Emerson had chided in Fuller indeed became a force of nature in Newcomb's hands, with the capacity to do what he himself had failed to accomplish on his own: discover transcendentalism's dark side and finish the burying of his son.

Newcomb had always been something of a secret to Emerson, one he maintained sixteen years after encountering the promising youth. Emerson concurred with Caroline Sturgis's remark that " 'No one could compare with him in original genius,' though I knew she saw, as I saw, that his mind was far richer than mine, which nobody but she or I knew or suspected." Emerson took her observation not as an arguable impression, but as a revelation of a hidden undeniable truth, and thus he "rejoiced in the very proof of her perception." With regret that his talent remained hidden despite his efforts to publicize it, he observed that "now, sixteen years later, we two alone possess this secret still" (*JMN*, 14:279). The key characteristic is the emphasis not only on his singularity and originality, but also the richness and depth of vision, one powerful enough to rescue him out of his crippling emotional turmoil upon the loss of his son. Emerson found Newcomb's writing was as complex as his persona, bearing with it a series of seemingly irreconcilable features, all somehow reconciling themselves into symmetrical union. He described his pupil as at once "puny in body and habit as a girl, but with an aplomb like a general's, never disconcerted" (*JMN*, 16:265).

Those paradoxes are inscribed in Emerson's mentorship and attempted professionalization of Newcomb's career at every turn. It is telling that

Newcomb failed to produce the second "Dolon" for an edition of the *Dial* appearing in October 1842 that would feature, more than any other single issue of the journal, a showcase of Emerson's disciples' work. Contributions included eight poems from Thoreau, two from Channing, one from Cranch, and one from Ellen Sturgis Hooper. The success of this issue thus did not depend on the second "Dolon," as he had proclaimed of the prior issue for the first story, for there was an abundance of material from his other disciples to fill its pages. What troubled Emerson was that Newcomb's absence from the journal signaled his withdrawal from professional authorship, and more personally, that he would never gain further insight into the spiritual awareness he gained from the first "Dolon." "Dolon" inspired Emerson to grapple with the loss of Waldo and his self-loathing at his inadequate grief. He was attracted to the story because he saw himself as the murderous Druid, and took satisfaction in its horrifying rendition of him sacrificing his child for his ascetic, isolated life of the mind. "Dolon" thus metes out the punishment he felt he deserved. In *Billy Budd, Sailor (An Inside Narrative)*, Captain Vere's anguished tears at his miscarriage of justice that resulted in his execution of the youthful Billy Budd are also Melville's self-indictment for the loss of his son Malcolm to suicide, a death for which he felt deeply responsible and thus yearned for punishment in the space of imaginative literature. "Dolon" similarly gave Emerson the punishment he felt he deserved for espousing a system of belief rooted in principles so radically individualistic as to sacrifice his very own son.

This brutal glimpse into the mirror forced Emerson to face the brutality of his own philosophy that threatened to alienate himself from his own immediate family. "The soul is not twin-born, but the only begotten, and though revealing itself as child in time, child in appearance, is of a fatal and universal power, admitting no co-life" (*CW*, 3:45). The ironic import of that self-examination through the imaginative lens of "Dolon" was a project bent on coaxing "our Catholic Fra Carlo" from his Brook Farm lair onto the more visible stage of the literary market to bring him a material reward for the genius he never second-guessed, even years after the second "Dolon" failed to materialize and his repeated invitations had been politely yet consistently rebuffed. After returning to Providence, Newcomb moved to Philadelphia, where he resided for five years, until 1850. He sailed for Europe in 1871, and remained there the rest of his life. The evidence of his journal reveals an active mind and a prolific pen, as he was constantly immersed in philosophy, politics, art, and literature. The Newcomb we thought we knew was actually far more content, engaged, and energetically productive than Emerson could ever understand, especially from the vantage point of Concord while under pressure to fill the *Dial* with fresh writing by his promising youth.

As a mentor and marketer of transcendentalism's future, Emerson could not have been faced with a more difficult task. Working against his pedagogy was his insistence that the sublime could only be apprehended in a spontaneous and untutored state. His promotion of his followers in the publishing world, furthermore, met with the formidable obstacle of the movement's inherent antimaterialism and sharp criticism of trade. The task of professionalizing his disciples by guiding their writings into a wider market proved perplexing in light of his romantic aesthetic, which posited that literary creativity is most potent when "inflamed and carried away by his thought, to that degree that he forgets the author and the public and heeds only this one dream which holds him like an insanity" (*CW*, 3:19). Ironically, "author and public" provided much of the focus of his mentor-ships and posed a considerable amount of tension, some fruitful and some damaging, in each relationship. His challenge was profound, and his success as variable as the diverse protégés he served. Given the inherent strain in the incongruous project of professionally guiding aspiring romantic authors, why then would he have eagerly encouraged so many apprentice-ships during the late 1830s and early 1840s?

Emerson loved individual mentoring—especially the excitement of intimate conversation and shared literary challenges for mutual intellectual growth—indeed as much as he hated schoolteaching in the confines of an institution. As Mark Twain later advised never to let one's schooling inter-fere with one's education, Emerson noted that the environment was liable to impoverish instructors as well. As an instructor at his brother William's school, he confessed, "I never expected success in my present employment," for it left him "little wiser" since the routine-driven "duties were never congenial with my disposition," a temperament far better suited for the more liberal exchange of ideas that characterized his mentorships (*JMN*, 2:241). The intimate anti-institutional educational environment he would establish for his disciples was not an escapist lair, for it was freighted with the presentiment, suspense, and anxiety inherent in the project of generating new celebrity authors. Emerson's scrupulous and often relentless pursuit of this goal appears in his arrangements for publication of his pupils' works into the literary market to initiate their professional literary careers, a process complicated by serious aesthetic and interpersonal challenges.

An entry in Emerson's journal dated October 1838, a time when interest in him from Harvard's collegians was sharply rising, is telling of the perplexing situation Emerson faced as a mentor and marketer of his promising youth. "The men you meet and seek to raise to higher thought," he wrote, "know as well as you know that you're of them and that you stand yet on the ground." His followers could plainly see that both shared the same human condition and thus occupied equal footing for their point of departure to higher thought; no mysterious powers, Emerson urged, were intrinsic to him that his protégés did not already possess themselves. Yet they regarded him with awe, assuming themselves incapable of ascent into "higher thought" like his. So "whilst you say to them sincerely, let us arise, let us fly," too many in his experience stopped and stared, paralyzed. Once Emerson himself rose to higher thought, he often looked back in disappointment to see that he was being watched in awe, surveyed at a distance from those still on the ground. As in his lectures, he frequently became a spectacle to his protégés. "But once fly yourself" to encourage the onlookers to join through the potent method of pedagogical and professional inspiration by example, "they will only look up to you" (*JMN*, 7:126).

The timidity Emerson saw in his interlocutors lends a great deal of understanding to his perception of the pupils he trained who are profiled in this book. When confronted with "the first entering ray of light . . . They flee to new topics to their learning, to the solid institutions about them . . . to escape the apparition." They repel like "the wild horse who has heard the Whisper of the Tamer [and] the maniac [who] has caught the glance of the Keeper" (*JMN*, 7:126). The dilemma Emerson faced, and at times solved triumphantly, pitted him with the challenge of inspiring by example. Leading his disciples to the sublime in self and nature, a realm both terrifying and beautiful, Emerson's efforts designed to provoke his followers into action prompted some to only stare back at him in paralyzed admiration, others to retreat in panic, and a select few to rise to the occasion.

Undeterred by the economic turbulence of the Panic of 1837, the protégés weathered formidable mitigating circumstances complicating their career aspirations, the most powerful of which were economic turmoil, distrust of institutions, the movement toward demodernization, and the subsequent construction of quasi-institutions. The latter is epitomized in Emerson's informal apprenticeships he conducted for entry into professional transcendental authorship. During this age, the pursuit of poetry as a career demanded flexibility and the capacity to reinvent oneself, for this escape from conventional professions was itself an embrace of a new kind of profession, whose very lack of established guidelines actually made it more demanding. Emersonian transcendentalism subverted plans for employment in the Unitarian ministry for which many had trained. Christopher Cranch exemplifies how an alliance with Concord's circle could force one from the pulpit. Many felt they needed to be retrained vocationally given their Emerson-inspired ethical epiphanies. "For the privileged," however, "prolonged transition to adulthood [marked by the acquisition of a job with career potential and a future] enables a lengthy period of educational and occupational exploration," according to the journal *Work and Occupations* regarding the timing of career acquisition.[1] Such privilege was not safeguarded, however, as in the case of Channing, who wantonly jettisoned his ties to his well-to-do relatives. With the exception of Ward, Emerson's protégés were not gainfully employed when they first approached him. Apprenticeships with Emerson were thus understood as serious career commitments, in many ways the most spiritually authentic and thus intense of vocational options, demanding a prolonged and unusually challenging transition to the literary profession.

Transition to career acquisition among Emerson's protégés was rapid in the case of Margaret Fuller, who edited the *Dial*, took a high-profile post with the *New-York Tribune*, and became America's primary war correspondent during the Italian revolution of 1848. At the opposite end of the spectrum was her dear friend, Charles Newcomb, who retreated from Emerson's pressure to publish. After sending Emerson his bizarre yet electrifyingly innovative Gothic short story allegorizing the death of Emerson's son Waldo, he stubbornly refused to respond to entreaties from Emerson to revise his work into a more presentable form for the *Dial*. Emerson virtually begged Newcomb for more submissions for years after the first installment of "Dolon" went into print, never receiving the second part of what was intended to be a diptych. His varying attempts at stirring the youth into action took on an almost comical series of shifting rhetorical strategies and tones in his correspondence. The thought of making Newcomb into a successful professional author was remote indeed, given how difficult it had been to secure his work in the *Dial*, a venue even a writer so averse to professionalization should have found comfortable considering a vast portion of its narrow readership consisted of his best friends. In other cases, the poetry of Ellery Channing and Henry Thoreau did not take flight as Emerson had hoped, despite his concerted efforts to publicize and promote them in both book and periodical markets. While Very located his source of heavenly authority as far from Emerson as one could imagine, others such as the young Cranch and Thoreau during the early days of their poetic apprenticeships transformed Emerson himself into a messianic fount of wisdom.

Margaret Fuller stands out along with the man she nearly married, Samuel Ward, as the most thoroughly self-actualized of the protégés. Ward's childhood friend Channing, as recalcitrant as he was, seemed oddly stuck in a state of arrested development, having convinced himself early in his relationship with Emerson that his initial unfinished poetics cast his aesthetic mold for life. Channing never achieved his dream of winning fame measurable by sales and income from his writing. He may have been perhaps the most strident about maintaining his individualism, an eccentricity he wore on his sleeve through his inflexible definition of his poetic identity.

The disciples expanded not only Emerson's aesthetic principles and business practice, but also the social and institutional fabric of New England in the 1830s and '40s. The case of Jones Very raised the very real need to revise centuries-old Puritanical blasphemy laws on the Massachusetts statute books that threatened his liberty and well-being. He and his situation were volatile enough to cause a thorough reassessment of such superannuated and oppressive laws. Ward alerted Emerson to the power of trade and the free market; Fuller awakened the feminist in him; Thoreau connected him as he had never been before to living rather than abstracted nature; Channing prompted his rethinking of the democratic function of poetry in the young Republic; Newcomb enabled him to imaginatively process the death of his young son through the power of gothic allegory and thus confront the darkest side of himself he rarely faced. Quite gently and subtly, Cranch proved to Emerson that a transcendentalist need not be a poet, but could also be an accomplished painter, humorist, and writer of children's novels. Cranch also provoked Emerson's rethinking of relational influence by emphasizing the immortality of aesthetic commingling of thought through his numerous bifurcated and reunited waterfalls that consistently appear in his landscape paintings.

The emotional struggle of Emerson's most difficult pupils, particularly Channing and Very, would arise from Emerson's tendency to transform them into abstractions, or icons through which he might better wage larger ideological battles. Channing became what Lawrence Buell has called the "poster-boy example" of Emerson's ideal of the "Verses of the Portfolio," and thus a metonym for his reformulation of the role of poetry to fit the populist and democratic character of the new nation.[2] Jones Very's uncommon zeal became useful to Emerson in warding off the siege led by Norton Andrews in retaliation against his Harvard Divinity School Address. With his "brave saint" thus mobilized in opposition to the conservative Unitarian backlash, Emerson drew from Very not only his fierce zeal, but also a sense of confidence in the larger contingency of Very's cohort of Harvard collegians. Ward served a different purpose to Emerson by expanding his horizons into the world of art and Boston's high society. Ward, like Newcomb, was more independent than Very, and thus served less as a corrective measure to an immediate or urgent issue in Emerson's life or social crusade within greater culture. Instead, Ward alerted Emerson to the power of capital—its acquisition, management, and allocation—he had always secretly admired.

An Emersonian apprenticeship promised a vocational oasis in the occupational wasteland of hidebound theology for ministers in training (Newcomb, Very, Cranch) and a release or refiguring of the stultifying convention of professions and trades (Channing, Ward). Indeed, many of the disciples reached an epiphany of vocational self-discovery in which they came to realize that they had been laboring under a mistake, a grand illusion that had been preventing their full spiritual development. Cranch affirmed his abandonment of the Unitarian ministry by burning a series of his own sermons that he eventually regarded as mocking tokens of his false pretensions to a professional identity that never suited him. Very unceremoniously removed himself from Harvard's ranks by embarking on a frenzied mission to convert by forcible baptism a variety of unwilling participants, from Elizabeth Peabody to his own professors and local clergy. Thoreau tossed a bouquet of flowers through a window to Lucy Brown wrapped in a poem he had written with the full knowledge that she would show it to Emerson and bring him in contact with his master. Channing hastily drifted west to embark on a dubious farming venture in Illinois to cultivate his career in transcendental poetry. Charles Newcomb deviated from vocational expectation by abandoning his Episcopal divinity school training for residence at Brook Farm, where he could give full vent to his eccentricity and sporadic writings.

All were acts of vocational rebellion representing divergent approaches to transcendentalism that challenged and expanded Emerson's own philosophical and aesthetic principles. The idealist in him had a taste for rebels and distaste for the coarse and corrosive aspects of commerce; the successful professional author and lecturer in him harnessed the admirable aspects of commerce for their promotional agency and guidance in the publishing world. Emerson called for action, production, and a more reliable, less volatile temperament among his youths. Eccentricity, he argued in "Experience," neutralizes the promise of genius. Still in the role of motivator, only in this instance warning in the lashing rhetoric of a jeremiad homily of the shortcomings among his promising youth, he declared that "temperament is the iron wire on which the beads are strung." A "defective nature," he urged, squanders "good fortune," like that of the generous financial patronage and aesthetic instruction his youths received from him. The pragmatic bent he found missing in many of them prompted him to ask, "What use is genius, if the organ is too convex or too concave and cannot find a focal distance within the actual horizon of human life?" The risk of an aborted literary mentorship increases dramatically if "the man does not care enough for results to stimulate him to experiment" and exert himself toward a finished product to make him proud, the fruit of his mind, spirit, *and* ambition. He counsels the economy of the self here as a token of the business practice he hoped to instill in his followers, whose talent he eagerly awaited to yield dividends, "so readily and lavishly they promise, but they never acquit the debt; they die young [as in the premature passing of Ellen Sturgis Hooper, Fuller, and Thoreau] and dodge the account; or if they live they lose themselves in the crowd." If not losing themselves in the crowd, they might disappear into the void by joining Brook Farm, or "Education Farm," as he mockingly called it, where "the noblest theory of life sat on the noblest figures of young men [including Cranch and Newcomb] and maidens, quite powerless and melancholy" (*CW*, 3:30, 34).

It is easy to misread such venom as a dismissal of his disciples. Emerson, however, was acutely aware that he had much to owe this youth movement not only for the establishment of his reputation but also for his own stimulation and intellectual growth. Indeed, the above-cited passages from "Experience" mark some of Emerson's very best writings about the limitations and liabilities of the ideal transcendental poet he had upheld in "The Poet." Youth not only characterized his followers, it sounded the keynote of transcendentalism from its origin. Emerson derived his best thoughts from his own vocational crisis suffered in youth, which led to the formulation of his powerful theory justifying his own break from the Unitarian Church for a professional career as "scholar" and "poet." More than pawns in the struggle to justify his break from the church, these were real people whom he would grow to love. They would commune with him, shape the best writings of his career, at times exasperate him, go to New York City to become a star—as Fuller became Greeley's "star"—and take their calling of Emersonian transcendentalism so seriously that at least one literally went mad in the process. This cohort of youths changed their lives when they were first exposed to Emerson in the late 1830s. This book has told the tales of just how the triumphs and tragedies of those lives unfolded.

Hooper's Poetic Tribute to Emerson

Among the many common threads connecting Emerson's protégés were their literary tributes to their mentor. Like many of her fellow protégés, Ellen Sturgis Hooper penned a poetic ode to Emerson. Regarded as one of the best of the Concord poets, she criticized the rampant materialism of the age like many in the cohort. Like Cranch, she noted an alarming emotional coldness in the romantic ideal, exposing the isolating effects of the individualism touted by the transcendental philosophy. Such charges she directs toward Emerson in her otherwise laudatory poetic assessment of her mentor, who deeply influenced her literary development until her early death at the age of thirty-six.

Hooper's "To Emerson" casts her mentor as a champion decorated with the "laurel for the victories" won on a "bloodless field." The lack of death or suffering on Emerson's battlefield seems appealing. Yet "bloodless" also functions as Hooper's description of his passionless, disembodied philosophy. Speaking as the collective voice of the protégés, she intimates that intellectual development occurs in relation to a monumental Emerson who is figured as "the mountain where we climb to see / The land our feet have trod this many a year." The third and crucially qualifying stanza of the poem confirms the secondary connotation of the symbol of the battlefield as a token of his bloodlessness in the first stanza. The indictment becomes explicit when she accuses him of being cold and lacking in passion: "It may be Bacchus, at thy birth, forgot," specifically the gift of Dionysian wine, music, and ecstatic dance that frees revelers from self-conscious fear and care. She finds his emotional coldness contrary to romantic ideals, particularly in how he "doth miss the heat which often breeds excess" and which is Bacchus's "gift to man." She uses his own phrase to describe him as an arid " 'dry lighted soul.' "[3]

Hooper's characterization of Emerson as lacking in Dionysian passion runs counter to the protégés' first impressions of their mentor. Indeed, "the heat which ofttimes breeds excess" was not lacking so much as it was in excess, according to most. Such excess is pictured in Cranch's caricature of a manic Emerson splashing through a rainstorm, reveling in a "perfect exhilaration. Almost I fear to think how glad I am" (*CW*, 1:10). Cranch's tableau reflects the centrality of romantic ecstasy in his adviser's ethos, as he drew the caption from *Nature* immediately preceding the famous transparent eyeball passage. Indeed, this was the figure, reveling in the mystical power of nature, who would inspire the break from expected vocations. Hardly the dry, distant mountain peak of Hooper's severely qualified tribute, he sparked his followers' liberation from self-consciousness, fear, and care with such intensity that it led to a false sense of security, in some cases, like Channing's or even Thoreau's, resulting in a lack of realistic planning for a professional career. Initially appearing to the disciples as the bold Bacchanalian Harvard Divinity School Address icon releasing them from conformity and duty, Emerson inevitably shifted his tone thereafter toward more practical and serious Apollonian considerations designed to gain his youth a foothold in the publishing world. What Hooper assumed of Emerson was thus partly true. His liberating gusto—so powerful that Margaret Fuller regarded it as a controlled substance she did not trust herself around ("I ought to go away now these last days I have been fairly intoxicated with his mind. I am not in full possession of my own. I feel faint in the presence of too strong a fragrance")—sobered in the face of the pressures of the publishing world and the reality of the reading public's role in determining name recognition.[4] Emerson was always alert to the need for careful editing of first drafts for a calculated effect, even if it meant humbly compromising artistic ideals to win a readership. Newcomb, for example, had little or no interest in this aspect of authorship; although Channing sought a popular audience, he resisted altering his craft to reach it.

The seriousness of Emerson's pressure toward professionalization that usually followed his exuberant adoption of his protégés is rooted in his surprisingly pragmatic slant on the concept of the ideal. His message of composure, both personal and aesthetic, and clear-headed management of the literary market to his disciples corresponded directly with his sense in his writings—especially in his essay "Experience" and his elegy "Threnody" to his son—that the soul is immortal, but its earthly manifestations are inconsistent and require vigorous cultivation. As Lawrence Buell points out, "everyone in theory is godlike, but in practice alive only by fits and starts," implying that authors must be especially careful to capture, record, and package those passing divine moments for a paying audience.[5] It was not simply, as William M. Moss has argued, that Emerson "warmed" toward those who "initially inspired [him] to enthusiasm" only to have "each later [bring] disappointment."[6] To read him as cold and aloof, as Hooper and the older embittered Channing did, looking back in anger at his own missed opportunities, is just as misguided as judging him only for his ecstatic moments. Although his charisma magnetically drew in his followers and continues to account for his lasting appeal in the twenty-first century, Emerson is at his strongest as a thinker not merely when he is exulting in the ideal. Instead his power resides in the "struggles of one who *would* be liberated," as Buell describes, "convinced of the right to liberation, but contending against the limits from which no human being can hope altogether to shake free."[7] Yet Emerson's treatment of his protégés, as the case studies of this book repeatedly show, was not nearly so hopeless. By investing faith, influence, and capital in their struggle to succeed in the market, Emerson offered his followers a method of transcending the forces of capitalism—the most frequently cited obstacle to liberation in his work—by paradoxically harnessing its power for self-fulfillment. Indeed, Emerson locates the ideal not in a detached abstraction, but in social practice and the market, despite its more obvious failures. As Richard F. Teichgraeber has usefully observed, Emerson believed that progressive and innovative social practice in the market can play a role in fulfilling American promise.[8]

Emerson identified America's promise in the protégés who sought him out and competed to win a prized apprenticeship under his guiding hand. In this sense, Emerson may have been grossly misunderstood by some of his promising youths who were blinded by his liberating charisma and thus failed to connect his ideals to social practice that might be transformed into practical professional functions in the publishing world. Indeed, Cranch, Channing, and Thoreau all fit this description; only Cranch and Thoreau emerged from their early apprenticeships to realize the application of the Emersonian ideals to individuated and practically grounded professional identities. Fuller always understood how to transform her lessons from Emerson into the journalism that became her life's work. Cranch beautifully transformed Emersonian principle into spectacular art. Later in his career, Thoreau used the lyceum circuit as a means of meeting pressing financial needs, especially in seeing to the welfare of his mother and sister when they fell on hard times. Emerson's relationship with Ward and his affinity for the principles of Adam Smith suggests that the Concord sage had never completely rejected the market so much as he discovered how the spirituality of individuals could be a deciding and shaping force within capitalism's transformational growth from the late 1830s throughout the 1840s.

Emerson's guidance of his protégés' careers resolutely refutes stereotypes of him as economically disinterested, emotionally aloof, and philosophically abstract to the point of irrelevance. To return to Hooper's tribute to him, the last stanza reveals her own approach toward Emerson *after* the height of Emerson fever. Her tone sets her apart from that of his earlier disciples who had responded exuberantly to his electrifying Harvard Divinity School Address. She regarded him as a tonic from the hurry of the "day's heat and blinding dust," whereas most others replaced their prior *cool* and *dry* occupations with the passion of literary transcendentalism. Indeed, an apprenticeship with Emerson promised an enlivening rather than a sedate "place to cool our souls in thy refreshing air." Zealous figures like Jones Very hardly turned to Emerson to "find the peace [they] had lost before" but overflowed with enthusiasm, reveling in their liberation from precisely the corpse-cold Unitarianism Emerson himself assailed. In Very's case, spiritual release did not render him peacefully anesthetized so much as it drove him into a zealous mania that embroiled him in intense controversy and eventual incarceration in a mental institution. The pattern of experience among Emerson's protégés that effectively deconstructs Hooper's cold and dry portrait instead renders a fiery figure magnetically leading Harvard's youth to frenetically redirect their lives' ambition. They drew toward him, if not always with the best professional foresight. All felt their previous ambition was misplaced. Emerson offered them a portal to their creative transcendental endeavors.

Emerson was not so much a peaceful oasis for his promising youths as an outlet for their passionate ambition. Perhaps Hooper's poem better describes Emerson's function in the larger culture—especially among hurried businessmen and industrialists looking for reflective solace—rather than his direct effect on his protégés. But even a banker by trade like Samuel Gray Ward never regarded Emerson as a complete escape from the rampant materialism and frenetic commercialism that characterized the antebellum market revolution. Ward of course discussed art and literature extensively with Emerson, but never to the exclusion of business, markets, finances, and investments, inspiring in one letter Emerson's blistering critique of the shortcomings of the city of Philadelphia based primarily on its tepid market and flaccid professional acumen.[9] The aloof side of Emerson that Hooper responded to was nonetheless real, but spoke nothing of the equally real socially engaged and passionate Emerson. His distanced side rankled Cranch, who found that the romantic idealism often left one cold and alone, a feeling he expressed in his poem "Enosis." "The Consolers," Ward's own poetic tribute to Emerson, intones precisely this dilemma in which he found himself isolated and alone, like a bare tree in winter, struggling to sustain himself according to a form of self-reliance that only left him in a stark and barren state. The poem dramatizes how his encounter with Emerson awakens him to the regenerative power of nature, and directs him toward the source of vitality that enables his branches to sprout fresh leaves.

Hooper's tribute also testifies to how each protégé sought something different in Emerson and thus came away with varying personal and professional results. Known as perhaps the darkest of the transcendental poets—all three of her children committed suicide as adults—Hooper's chilly rendition of Emerson points to something in her disposition opposite of the ebullient conviction of Fuller, Thoreau, Channing, Very, Newcomb, Cranch, and Ward. Thus portraits of Emerson in the disciples' writings function as two-way mirrors of both mentor and protégé, reflecting the dispositions and ambitions of both. Hooper remains something of an enigma among the protégés, and further research of her training under Emerson might well reveal still more insight into his progressive gender views that were so instrumental in the formation of Fuller's feminism.

Emerson's Pattern of Patronage and Investment

Emerson's patronage has been described as an arbitrary process of consecrating aspiring authors followed by his realization, much to his chagrin, that he had drastically misjudged their talent. Carlos Baker explains that "Emerson was so eager to find evidence of good new young American poets—Thoreau, Very, and Ellery Channing were among his prime examples—that he characteristically overestimated their powers and always did his level best to get them into print."[10] Yet such explanations beg the question of why he would proceed to arrange for the publication of works by writers whose stature had diminished considerably since first encountering them. Essential to understanding Emerson's undying support for his protégés' professional development is the fact that he did not unilaterally "discover" any of them. In Jones Very's case, Elizabeth Peabody's intervention was critical; she was also responsible for initiating Emerson's relationship with Fuller. Channing depended on Ward for his introduction, while Thoreau relied on Emerson's sister-in-law, Lucy Brown, for his. Newcomb came by way of Fuller, and Cranch through the good word of William Ellery Channing (the elder and divine) and James Freeman Clarke. Fuller had enthusiastically promoted Ward to Emerson with the love of a woman prepared to be the bride of the young art critic and connoisseur. Acting as intermediaries on each other's behalf, the protégés conspired to choose Emerson rather than passively waiting for him to select them for apprenticeships. Furthermore, although Emerson deeply admired and even looked up to these disciples for the unique talent they brought to the circle, he never abandoned his own core values and aesthetic paradigm for theirs. Despite his deep respect for Very's authentic dealings in interpersonal relationships, for example, Emerson should not be misapprehended as a Veryite, since he held serious misgivings about Very's Christian paradigm of obedience and attendant proselytizing, both of which employ rhetoric less tolerant and liberating than Emerson's in the Divinity School Address.

Although he certainly was enamored of his followers at specific stages in their training, he was never so taken by them that he lost sight of his pragmatic and rational preparation of their professional futures. Much of Emerson's maneuverings should be understood as fully aware and calculated. Joel Myerson's research on Emerson's income puts to rest any suggestion that he was an incompetent professional advocate, a romantic philosopher ill-suited to the practical concerns of the business world. Emerson pored over his accounts and was a crafty negotiator of his publishing contracts, almost all of which worked to his advantage by deviating from the standard half-profits arrangement most authors quietly accepted. He took bold yet calculated risks with his contracts, and like any good financier amassed a career marked by greater risk in the early going and more conservative measures aimed at wealth management later. "This is no empyrean Emerson," Myerson urges, "it is someone well versed in the ways of the financial and publishing worlds" who amassed his wealth not only through royalties from writings, but because of his astute business acumen, evidenced by eleven "account books" he copiously maintained "down to the fraction of a penny."[11] This deep understanding of the market based on the management of his own career did not necessarily transfer to his followers, for its microeconomic system and methodology was invisible to some. Further, he was often guilty of applying to fledglings like Thoreau standards for navigating the literary market that worked for him as a seasoned well-known author.

Yet many of Emerson's maneuverings in the publishing world on his disciples' behalf that appear negligible were actually quite astute. Emerson's refusal to review Thoreau's *A Week on the Concord and Merrimack Rivers* immediately upon its release, for example, was not a token of his capricious rejection of his apprentice and embarrassment at being called into the limelight to advocate his work. Instead, the public's awareness of his status as Thoreau's mentor would have made his review appear grossly biased. Thoreau, of course, was his dearest intellectual progeny, and their highly visible relationship had been roundly mocked by James Russell Lowell in "A Fable for Critics." Though it appeared cruel, Emerson's refusal to review his protégé in this case was an act of kindness. His anticipation of the skeptical reception awaiting a quick, favorable review reveals a patron alert to the damage his fame could do to his pupil's career, suggesting a more nuanced understanding of the delicate business of promotion in the literary marketplace than previously assumed. Further, his decision points to his profound sensitivity to the mechanism of his own fame and the effect of his celebrity status on the careers of his followers.

By no means an apologist for crass materialism or the avaricious pursuit of capital, Emerson's care in protecting the best financial interests of reckless romantics like Very, Newcomb, and Channing was part of his radicalism. He addressed in "The American Scholar," "The Poet," "Literary Ethics," and *Representative Men* an audience not of materialists, but "the class of intellectuals who would serve as missionaries to him," as Robert Milder aptly describes it.[12] This was a band of radicals he actively recruited as a collective generation (if not individually enlisting them per se), and it was in his best interest to shepherd their careers to at least a first step into the literary market. This first step was a tense and precarious moment, one acutely sensitive to political and aesthetic ramifications of his own career's impact on that of his disciple. Thus Emerson was exceedingly careful in mediating the extremes of his radicalism through the public profiles of his disciples. He knew those radical tones could be muted, as his own works could be construed as "an endorsement of the existing order" rather than "a subtle indictment of its short-comings."[13] It is precisely this restraint that Emerson sought to cultivate in his own work and that of his disciples, for the advantages in appealing to a broader audience were profound.

In both his own and his disciples' careers, the pattern of high-risk investment followed by conservative management was not only visible in Emerson's editorial strategy for Very's *Essays and Poems*, Channing's *Poems*, and the myriad pieces he shepherded into the periodical press. The pattern also reveals itself in his journal. "Steady, steady," he counseled himself, feeling a riot brewing in "the odium, and aversion of faces to be presently encountered in society" in the wake of the Divinity School Address controversy. He resolved to remain "no partisan, a singer merely for the love of music, his is a position of perfect immunity: to him no disgusts can attach; he is invulnerable." Invulnerable, but not hostile. Andrews Norton had been baiting him into a public brawl, and Emerson responded by expounding on the virtue of composure in his journal with an eye toward the preservation of his literary reputation. "All that life demands us through the greater part of the day, is composure, an equilibrium, a readiness." His refusal to jump into the fray mirrored the characteristic poised and sober negotiation of the literary market that typically followed his more wild and intuitive public gestures, such as the Divinity School Address and the adoptions of Very, Channing, and Newcomb. Unlike Norton and Very, Emerson exercised calculated restraint rooted in the principle that one must neither act rashly nor suffer the losses of compromised public expression "in irregular, faltering, disturbed speech too emphatic for the occasion," a pitfall he studiously avoided, and which the stammering and ever-defensive Very—whose cheeks flushed and eyes watered in the face of his controversy—did not. "This is not beautiful," and thus not conducive to maintaining the value of one's authorial brand name in the market (*JMN*, 7:63–64).

Elsewhere in his journal Emerson remarked on the dangers of authenticity and spontaneity slipping into rant and absurdity. Indeed, this was the trap in which Very found himself during his more zealous pontificating. He had struggled to carry out his frank comments about his neighbors' spiritual shortcomings "with a sustained, even-minded frankness and love, which alone could save such a speech from rant and absurdity" (*JMN*, 7:131). Careers suffer when expression is rash and lacking in poise; "let them split wood and work off this superabundant irritability" rather than allow it into the public forum of discourse in either the spoken or written word (*JMN*, 7:63–64). Thus Emerson saved his passionate volleys, his swift intuitive radical thrusts for his initial investments in radicals like Very, Newcomb, and Channing, and even in his own nonlinear career decision to leave the ministry for the literary market. This first intuitive move lays the vital groundwork for a romantic authorial persona, which Emerson knew was the most salable and marketable, "since I think we love characters in proportion as they are impulsive and spontaneous" (*JMN*, 7:67). It is not enough, furthermore, in Emerson's view to don such a public image and expect remuneration, "to make a claim on the community for all my wants" without working "hard all day" and spending "my time in the best manner I could," knowing "I must have benefitted the world in some manner that will appear and be felt somewhere." This formula shows us Emerson's sense of responsibility, even necessity, to see to it that at least one of the works of each of his disciples was published so that they "will appear and be felt somewhere" (*JMN*, 7:109). Logic, poise, and rationality then take over in the management of his assets for survival and growth, the second of this two-step process that divulged itself in a later journal entry.

In late 1842, Emerson meditated on the nature of wealth, first recording the insight that "the world is too rich for us. We have hardly set our hearts on one toy, say a house and land, before a poetic reputation seems the high prize," in a chain of shifting interests in which "each of many things draws us aside from the other." On one hand the world offers too much to choose from, not the least of which are "so many promising youths" to adopt and nurture, to invest in and educate. But two journal entries later, he reflects on a world whose riches have been usurped by the same capitalists who win them every time, lamenting how "there are men who always seem to hold marked cards in their hand. Prices fall or rise, markets may change or not, they are always holders of the game, and winners." The insight appears to be a standard rejection of the market. However, the two pages immediately following consist of book sales figures and account ledgers tallying binding and printing costs for his poems. Preceding the economic "marked card" metaphor, Emerson muses on the nature of ambition, which has provocative implications for both his own and his disciples'. "Self help is good," especially the pecuniary Franklinian acquisition of wealth, but "abandonment . . . to the great spirit, without hurry to do or be anything" free from frenetic acquisitiveness offers "content with saying, 'it is good to be here.'" That poetic release into irrational passion, into the intuitive heart of "the great spirit," then gives way to Emerson positioning himself at the poker table of laissez-faire capitalism, observing how "the holders of the game" are its perennial winners, ending finally by taking stock of his own hand, as it were, with his ledger accounts. In this progression we see Emerson the stockbroker, who wanted to hold the winning cards, grappling with the poet and poet maker in him, advocating wild abandonment, denouncing "hurry to do or be anything," and complaining of the competing interests in an ever-widening market that conspires to rob us of our loyalties (*JMN*, 7:483–84). Such loyalties need not always be poetic, but are contiguous with his market concern of the ledger, which was very much economic.

No matter how resistant his pupils were to professional authorship, Emerson never abandoned them, but did his best to put them on the path toward success with a first significant publication. Further, this series of journal entries also evokes precisely the type of professional poet he had hoped Cranch, Channing, and Very would become. Abandonment and loss of self to "the great spirit" could thus be managed directly into the market. Emerson was acutely aware of his competitors as figured in the card players of his journal entry; his detailed accounting of his own holdings aids him in competing directly with them (*JMN*, 7:483–84). It is to Emerson's credit that he applied this latter sensibility to showcase Very's work in the most appealing light possible in *Essays and Poems*, as testified by Rufus Griswold's inclusion of Very's verse two years later in the highly influential *Poets and Poetry of America* (1842). Whether or not it was worth a fit of insanity, Very's poetry finally became an asset to his biography and vice versa, especially since he had safely withdrawn from society and the literary market into a peripheral role with the Unitarian ministry. As a supply minister, Very preached with both the kinetic and effusive qualities of his poems as well as their more regrettable Hebraistic and derivative intonations. This was still Jones Very, as indeed his best sermons, much like those that won him acclaim, stirred with a unique blend of ecstasy and mysticism. His sermons, safely voiced from the pulpits of a rotating series of other men's churches, masked his madness. They met neither offense nor scandal in the culture. Even Emerson, perhaps his best and most appreciative reader, expressed frustration and betrayal at his withdrawal from professional letters for the clergy they had both so boldly renounced earlier, ironically misreading Very's later career as his retreat into "the thin porridge and cold tea of Unitarianism" (*JMN*, 9:339).

It is ironic that a reckless romantic like Very would be such a *producer*, with output that dwarfed that of Channing and Newcomb. It is also ironic that his high point of spiritual ecstasy would mark not only his most prolific period as an author, but by all accounts his most effective. These poems would be recognized as his most powerful by his contemporaries and generations of readers thereafter, especially in his 1913 centenary commemoration held in Salem's North Church, where manuscripts of his verse, sermons, and letters were on proud display. Just as Thoreau was fully immersed in self-culture at Walden Pond, so too was Very immersed in the work of capturing the utterance of the muse. His prolific streak arose not simply out of his mystical religious frenzy, but because he was directly responding to Emerson's directive, "I beg you, let not a whisper of the muse go unattended to or unrecorded."[14]

Democratizing Patronage and Pedagogy

Both the romantic poet listening closely to the muse and the ambitious professional seeking an advantage can be heard in Emerson's advice. His voice is not that of a pedant demanding his pupil's unwavering devotion. At his best, Emerson urged his pupils on to new heights by encouraging them to trust their inner vision rather than his authority. In June 1838, just one month after delivering the Harvard Divinity School Address, Emerson gave a lecture titled "Literary Ethics" at Dartmouth. In it, he asserted that "the infinitude and impersonality of intellectual power" is accessible to the true scholar. Solidifying the democratic view of genius, the infinitude of intellectual power in this lecture begins to resemble the Oversoul or the Divine Being recast as the source of literary greatness. In his mentorships, Emerson encouraged the channeling of this "intellectual power," exhorting his charges to become "its minister" and usher its divine truth to the world. The protégés' responses ranged from the pragmatic and efficacious social reform of Fuller's writings in the New York periodical press to Very's monstrous folio of sonnets he purportedly channeled directly from the voice of God. However disparate, both Fuller and Very were motivated by Emerson's point that the "whole value of history, of biography" is to demonstrate what humans can be and can do, according to the lecture. In this way, Emerson anticipated the 1960s human potential movement insofar as he sought to cultivate extraordinary untapped reserves of power, creativity, joy, and fulfillment. The best function of biography, he argues, is that great lives of Milton, Shakespeare, and Plato demonstrate what we are capable of. Their lives inspire us to tap into our own wells of inspiration, our "infinitude of intellectual power" (*CW*, 1:101–3). A great thinker resides in each individual, according to Emerson, who offers a distinct democratic slant on the more authoritarian theories of genius popular at the time, particularly those forwarded by Carlyle, that posited the importance of modeling, and even worshiping, heroic and great men.

In a literary sense, Emerson seems to have been particularly interested in the component of human potential that necessarily expressed itself through publication. To him, publication was the author's breach—after long, deep rumination beneath the surface—into the bright, bold daylight like Melville's playful and powerful White Whale. Emerson's message by his own example to his followers was that they too might find their own unique vision and burst through the waters as he had, harnessing the new mechanisms of mass media and print culture to reach a national audience. This was a key reason why he was so adamant about publishing the writings of his followers not just in the *Dial*, but in other periodicals with wider distribution, or even better, in book form. Such patronage he deemed essential, yet some like Channing turned his support into a crutch. Patronage became increasingly diffuse and diverse in the 1830s and '40s, embracing a growing range of intermediaries that made themselves indispensible to the broadening spectrum of vocations, including authorship. "Astronomers come [to Paris] because there they can find apparatus and companions," Emerson once observed of the bourgeoning networks of intermediaries supporting professional advancement. These included "Chemist, geologist, artist, musician, dancer, because there only are grandees and their patronage, appreciators and patrons" (*JMN*, 14:61). He preferred to play the role of patron in the fashion of a facilitator of necessary materials, much less a patrician protector providing permanent shelter from the competitive risk of the free market. In this sense, patronage to Emerson should be a staple for production; an individual's "workbench is home, education, power, and patron."[15] Among his protégés, Emerson could "look on that man as happy, who, when there is a question of success, looks into his work for a reply . . . not into patronage" (*CW*, 6:120).

Emerson tended to associate the sort of patronage common to the era as incarcerating and usually demanding some sort of aesthetic compromise necessarily restricting the full expression of genius. He admired Michelangelo's frescoes in the Sistine Chapel, for example, precisely for how they rebel against the strictures of his patrons: "We appreciate the taste which led Michelangelo, against the taste and against the admonition of his patrons, to cover the walls of churches with unclothed figures" (*W*, 10:223). The antithesis of this model has its late-twentieth-century dramatic expression in the confidence man Paul Poitier, of John Guare's *Six Degrees of Separation* (1990). Paul's primary occupation is to seek out and win wealthy patrons among the elite denizens of brownstone New York. He wants physically to touch the hand of God on the ceiling of the Sistine Chapel, but feels he can only do so through the right connections. He produces nothing other than deceitful performances in search of the ideal patron, brokering his success solely on his fraudulent identity as a Harvard graduate and son of the film celebrity Sidney Poitier. Emerson anticipated, and resisted, such corrosive effects of the development of patronage into a situation rendering the intermediary—advisers, publicists, and promoters—supreme and producers meaningless.

Emerson's style of patronage offered none of his protégés the effortless success that Guare's Paul assumes a celebrity endorsement inevitably brings. In several cases, Emerson's emphasis on productivity and efficiency were for the most part drastically underestimated by his protégés. Although he espoused the powers of inner reflection and solitary contemplation, he had a fundamental aversion to the pointless waste of "a vast deal of time spent in thinking of what we have done, and in fruitless imaginations concerning what we are to do" (*JMN*, 3:83). Highly sensitive to the wasted time and effort intellectuals could be liable to, Emerson observed, "the difference between men," and indeed a determining factor in the success of his protégés, "seems chiefly to appear in the different use they make of time. One holds it cheap, another costly. One consults his ease, the other his improvement. The difference is infinite" (*JMN*, 3:101).

According to his bold and intellectually mercenary principle of self-reliance, Emerson advised his disciples to avoid conforming their minds to exalted figures. He instead urged his charges to swell with the signal works of Western civilization rather than bow down to them with excessive reverence. His democratic sense of the use of great men became a point of contention with his friend Thomas Carlyle, who had encouraged Emerson to "take an American hero, one whom you really love, and give us a history of him" (*CEC*, 381). Just as Thoreau balked at Horace Greeley's lucrative offer to serialize profiles of America's great men in the *New-York Tribune*, particularly blanching at the prospect of idolizing his mentor in the first installment, Emerson rebelled against Carlyle's suggestion. *Representative Men* not only includes no Americans, its profiles of Plato, Swedenborg, Montaigne, Shakespeare, Napoleon, and Goethe sharply criticize each thinker's philosophical and aesthetic shortcomings and expose flaws in the social implications of their work. Emerson had perceived something debasing and oppressive in Carlyle's model, which approached the cult of personality commonly attached to political authoritarianism in the next century. "Men ought to be thankful to get themselves governed," Carlyle insisted, "if it is only done in a strong and resolute way" (*CEC*, 396). Indeed, Carlyle's politics in the slave debate proved reprehensible, forming the most abhorrent face of his understanding of the social function of heroes and great men. It is to Emerson's credit that he rejected Carlyle's thinking on the issue.

Emerson's demystification of heroes in *Representative Men* affirmed his approach toward mentorship. If he had played the role of heroic man in the works that had so effectively appealed to young intellectuals, he certainly disowned that role in his mentorships. Addressing their generation collectively, he was larger than life. Individually, he inspired not with messianic charisma, but as a professional advocate, critical sounding board, and literary adviser. When he assumed this pragmatic collaborative role, the least ambitious protégés like Newcomb struggled to adjust and retreated. His assessments of the shortcomings of each major figure in *Representative*

Men exhibits precisely the Emersonian habit of mind that would champion his young apprentices at one moment and coolly rebuke them at another. Hardly the act of whim or the token of an inconsistent mind, this was fully intentional and integral to his approach toward biography and human relationships alike. As Robert Richardson points out, Emerson "thought that the use of great persons is to educate the present generation, not to stun it with superiority [because] he had no wish to intimidate readers and hearers by describing the unmatchable perfections of his subjects."[16] This insight also explains Emerson's use of his own heroic presence in the culture to mentor and market his youths, to encourage them to fly rather than to stun them with his impossible feats. No messianic figure can achieve for them and produce literature in their stead, he firmly believed. "Is it not the lesson of our experience," he asks rhetorically in *Nature*, "that every man . . . write history for himself?" (*CW*, 1:107).

Representative men, like Emerson himself, are thus useful only insofar as they serve a student-centered education that avoids degenerating into "the love and cherishing of these patrons" who are iconic charismatic leaders. Ironically, most students approach their education in precisely the way that serves them the least. "The student of history is like a man going into a warehouse to buy cloths or carpets: he fancies he has a new article," Emerson explains through his metaphor of the consumerist ideology that so aptly describes the liabilities of his own youth movement's discovery of novelty in him. "If he go to the factory, he shall find that his new stuff still repeats the scrolls and rosettes which are found on the interior walls of the pyramids of Egypt" (*CW*, 4:4). Indeed, there is something more timeless yet beyond the novelty of literary celebrity that gave rise to Emerson fever, a source of inner spiritual power toward which he had hoped to direct his followers.

Expanding on this notion of the consumerist tendencies of youth seeking knowledge, Emerson laments the understanding of the mentor's role as mechanically providing "direct giving of material or metaphysical aid." The trouble, he argues, is that "the boy believes there is a teacher who can sell him wisdom." Such "direct serving" expected of mentors, he suggests, misses the deeper lessons a truly effective guide can offer. "Man is endogenous, and education is unfolding," rather than static and remunerative, like the knowledge-as-capital for which many acolytes hunger. "The aid we have from others is mechanical, compared with the discoveries of nature in us," he urges in a line directly echoed in Ward's poem "The Shield" (*CW*, 4:5–6). Herein lies the key to ideal patronage and mentorship in Emerson. His greatest function was to point his followers toward the source of power in nature that could best develop the strengths and talents they already possessed.

Although his protégés in many cases stood by passively and watched his ascent while he awaited theirs, Emerson was convinced that "activity is contagious" and that "we catch the charm that lured them." He believed that effective literary patronage amid the runaway capitalism of the antebellum era was not passive philanthropy or the dilettantish doling out of charitable donations. He instead adopted a more productive approach toward assistance by casting himself as an intimate aesthetic counselor rather than a distant wealthy donor. He never gloated on his role as financial supporter, but regarded it as a necessary staple of professional development. To Emerson, literary patronage at its best was a vigorous leading by example; "Men are helpful through the intellect and affections. Other help I find a false appearance" (*CW*, 4:8). The best Emerson could do was to "inspire an audacious mental habit." He thus sought successors of the representative men profiled in his essay, acknowledging the tendency in himself of scanning the horizon for his own intellectual heirs. But producing successors always was predicated on the assumption that these mentorships would necessarily, even naturally, come to an end. "The soul is impatient of masters and eager for change," a pattern corresponding to the change of seasons in nature. Through the presence of death in nature, furthermore, great figures come and go. "Rotation is her [i.e., nature's] remedy" for the tyranny of one figure over an age just as it is in mentorships.

If the human soul moves like nature, it necessarily craves change. Emerson's relationships cooled less because he suddenly deemed their work atrocious in a jarring turnabout from his welcoming adoration. His gradual separation from his subjects appears more a function of his understanding that once his youths extracted their full use of him, they must, by virtue of the soul's desire for change, grow apart from him for their own good. "We touch and go and sip the foam of many lives," he wrote, describing his theory of the intellectual equivalent of free love. Indeed, the more ideas we can encounter that move us, the larger we are as individuals. No single mind, furthermore (including his own), deserves to be exalted above the rest, for "when we are exalted by ideas, we do not owe this to Plato, but to the idea, to which also Plato was debtor" (*CW*, 4:11). For this reason above all others—especially those that might point to his modest temperament or shy, aloof demeanor—Emerson loathed hero worship of himself as well as great figures of classical literature and philosophy.

Condemning the notion of a messiah as tantamount to depleting independent thought to the point of "intellectual suicide," Emerson found that "all heroes become bores," as they are increasingly reified into unmoving monuments divorced and abstracted from their original visions. Antebellum culture consumed its heroes in ways he actively counseled his protégés to avoid. More than any disciple, Thoreau may have felt the adverse effects of overexposure to Emerson, particularly at the end of his poetic apprenticeship. At that stage in his mentorship, he felt as Voltaire did of Jesus when he cried, " 'Let me never hear that man's name again.' " "Thus we feed on genius," Emerson laments in *Representative Men*, endlessly invoking the iconoclastic figures of the age with a kind of mindless repetition (*CW*, 4:16). In this way, Emerson's departure from his disciples was not so much the casting of his disapproving judgment (except for Thoreau's and Channing's poetry) as the deliberate removal of himself from a position of authority over his pupils.

As a whole, Emerson's protégés emulated their mentor, sharing a desire to pull off a spectacular professional stunt like his for full immersion in the infinitude of their souls and nature's Universal Being. Their intellectual ambition led to the professional stunt of risking their careers on a visionary belief so radically divorced from conventional occupations that its death-defying feats dramatizing immortality dwarfed milder pursuits locked in safety and routine. Nothing could have been more irresistible, however veiled the exigencies of the literary marketplace were beneath this ethereal allure. Emerson knew this dynamic well, and with care attempted to learn from each disciple, despite his own risks at affiliating with a known madman like Very, or in squandering his time with an unknown like Newcomb. His patronage was never passive, but vigorous and deliberately inclined toward developing his young writers for a place in the publishing world.

Among the more surprising discoveries in Emerson's mentorships is his insistence that labor—its methods, its risks, its rewards—must constitute the foundation of a literary identity. Emerson always admired the work of the sailor, especially since it was a model for making a living as well as carrying out one's literary career. In the sailor's juggling of the demands of life at sea, Emerson found an apt metaphor for effective literary work as well as sound business practice: "The sailor, the man of his hands, man of all work; all eye, all finger, muscle, skill, and endurance; a tailor, a carpenter, cooper stevedore, and clerk and astronomer besides. He is a great saver, and a great quiddle by the necessity of his situation." All the vocations, particularly the authorial trade, could learn from the sailor's example. Emerson had hoped to instill in his protégés not only a renaissance man's wholeness that comprehends so many of the otherwise subdivided professions. He also wanted each pupil to be fastidious, "a great quiddle," like the sailor, a "saver" who exercises a prudent and watchful economy in the efficiency of his labor and the management of his resources. A sailor, of course, exercises such habits by "the necessity of his situation" at sea, the woodland equivalent of which Thoreau established in his spartan economy at Walden Pond (*JMN*, 4:103). Emerson wished to see his disciples achieve such economic independence by scrupulously managing not only their accounts, but also their unwieldy creative surges of productivity into the most effective series of publications for the advancement of their careers. But did the fastidious saver repudiate the romantic dreamer? Hardly. The sailor must be a romantic to find himself on the open sea in the first place, just as Thoreau found himself in the woods because of his impulse to go fishing in the pebbly stars and drink in the infinitude of nature. Likewise, the romantic urges of the Emersonian protégés thrust them into a professional open sea, and it was Emerson's desire to see them manage their resources for survival.

Never neglectful of his responsibility, Emerson was fully committed to the moral challenge of training his fledglings to fly. With his philosophy so diversely comprehended by his protégés, who had such radically dissimilar motives for coming to transcendentalism to begin with, Emerson should be admired for his care, patience, and generosity in mentoring and marketing his youths. For he was saddled with a commitment in each relationship that carried all the sweet sadness of parenting, a topic he drifted toward in a telling diversion in *Representative Men* that aptly allegorizes his unique challenge. Drawing from the world of microbiology, Emerson saw the predicament with his protégés in the way "a microscope observes" a "dot appear" on an insect, "which enlarges to a slit and it becomes two perfect [organisms]. The ever-proceeding detachment appears not less in all thought and in all society." Like his protégés in the early stages of their apprenticeships, "Children think they cannot live without their parents. But long before they are aware of it, the black dot has appeared, and the detachment taken place. Any accident"—like the many that befell Emerson's promising youths as they entered the market with hopes of becoming professional authors—"will now reveal to them their independence," just as Ward's youthful soldier in his poem drops the paternal inheritance of his shield in battle, and Cranch paints the mighty waterfall diverging around an obstacle (*CW*, 4:17).

However distant many of the relationships became, Emerson accompanied them in spirit in their later ventures, leaving his impression in the best way a mentor can, by pointing them to the source of inspiration in nature to realize their personal and professional autonomy. All were better for having worked with Emerson in varying degrees of aesthetic and professional growth, and all expanded and enriched Emerson's own thought, spurring him to new heights. Their accomplishments were remarkable in light of the exceedingly self-conscious atmosphere that attends a circle of contemplative philosophers bent on cultivating inner intuition. Such an environment can bring an air of unreality about human relationships, and Emerson was all too aware of how it conditioned his mentorships. Such self-awareness was integral to grappling with the power of markets and souls in the fraught and dramatic training of Emerson's promising youths, aimed finally at enabling his protégés to realize their independence from him. In this way Emerson bestowed the ultimate gift—the power to write one's own Bible.

NOTES

Introduction

1. Much of Emerson's radicalism has been obscured by the later decades of his celebrity and subsequent twentieth-century canonization. As Robert D. Habich notes, "All of Emerson's early biographers faced a similar challenge: how to represent a figure whose subversive individualism had been eclipsed in later years by his celebrity, making him less a representative of his age than a caricature of it"; Habich, *Building Their Own Waldos: Emerson's Early Biographers and the Politics of Life Writing in the Gilded Age* (Iowa City: University of Iowa Press, 2011), xiii.

2. During the early 1840s, likely around 1843 when Thoreau was twenty-six, Emerson had urged him to destroy the verses, presumably by burning them; Franklin Sanborn, *Henry D. Thoreau* (Cambridge: Houghton Mifflin, 1892), 286–87.

3. For an excellent discussion of Whitman's use of Emerson's endorsement, see Jay Grossman, *Reconstituting the American Renaissance: Emerson, Whitman, and the Politics of Representation* (Durham: Duke University Press, 2003), 97.

4. After Whitman had safely established his career, he still retaliated against Emerson for rejecting him. Whereas Whitman earlier took every opportunity to pair his name with Emerson's, decades later in *Specimen Days and Collect* the poet aggressively distanced himself from the man, but not without a good measure of self-aggrandizement in the process. "Bloodless intellectuality dominates him," he alleged, crediting himself for exploring and mapping land that Emerson had discovered. Whitman indicted Emerson for killing the passion in his pupils, so that his "final influence is to make his students cease to worship anything—almost cease to believe in anything outside of themselves." Emerson's protégés were thus "well-washed and grammatical, but blood-less" to Whitman—a claim overwhelmingly refuted by the myriad reckless romantics profiled in this book—suggesting a regional pattern in which "fires . . . glow deep . . . as in all New Englanders, but the façade hides them well, they give no sign"; Whitman, *Specimen Days and Collect* (Philadelphia: David McKay, 1882), 321. Ironically, passion

was precisely what Emerson called for in his Divinity School Address, and was deemed dangerous by clerics for his own attack against the cold doctrine of conservative Unitarianism, a target virtually interchangeable with the cold, emotionally repressed New England character Whitman assails. At the time Whitman himself had caught Emerson fever, confessing, "I was simmering, simmering, simmering. Emerson brought me to a boil," quoted in John Townsend Trowbridge, *My Own Story, With Recollection of Noted Persons* (Boston: Houghton Mifflin, 1903), 367.

5. Richard F. Teichgraeber convincingly argues that Emerson's status as "transatlantic star" during the 1840s "bears no resemblance to that provincial figure we encounter in the received account" forwarded by William Charvat and a host of others; Teichgraeber, *Sublime Thoughts/Penny Wisdom: Situating Emerson and Thoreau in the American Market* (Baltimore: Johns Hopkins University Press, 1995), 177. David S. Reynolds documents the magnitude of Emerson's celebrity as a published author, lecturer on the lyceum circuit, and subject in the popular press; Reynolds, " 'A Chaos-Deep Soil': Emerson, Thoreau, and Popular Literature," in *Transient and Permanent: The Transcendentalist Movement and Its Contexts*, ed. Charles Capper and Conrad Edick Wright (Boston: Massachusetts Historical Society, 1999), 294. In the 1840s, Emerson commanded between three and five times the average fee for his lectures. By 1850 he was attracting standing-room-only crowds in New York City, and by the Gilded Age, he outshone even the brightest of stars such as Mark Twain and Harriet Beecher Stowe, as the *Springfield Republican* declared him "the most widely known, the greatest, and the most attractive of all the present lecturers" (295).

6. More than any of Emerson's protégés, Ellery Channing felt the most moved to document the sting of this pattern and thus has left the best record of its psychological and professional effects, as Kathryn B. McKee shows in " 'A Fearful Price I Have Had to Pay for Loving Him': Ellery Channing's Troubled Relationship with Ralph Waldo Emerson," in *Studies in the American Renaissance, 1994*, ed. Joel Myerson (Charlottesville: University of Virginia Press, 1994), 251–69.

7. William Moss, " 'So Many Promising Youths': Emerson's Disappointing Discoveries of New England Poet-Seers," *New England Quarterly* 49.1 (1976), 47.

8. Caleb Crain, *American Sympathy: Men, Friendship, and Literature in the New Nation* (New Haven: Yale University Press, 2001), 192.

9. Emerson did include Thoreau's "Haze," "Mist," and "Smoke" in *Parnassus* (Boston: Houghton Mifflin, 1884), 47–48. These poems, which were selected to the exclusion of "Sympathy," reflect Thoreau's self-definition as a naturalist, which became increasingly scientific during the 1850s, and thus show Emerson's respect for his refined powers of perception of organic phenomena.

10. Christina Zwarg, *Feminist Conversations: Fuller, Emerson, and the Role of Reading* (Ithaca: Cornell University Press, 1995).

11. Besides a host of full-scale histories of transcendentalism, few group biographies of particular social subdivisions of the movement have appeared. For the social matrices of Brook Farm (more an institutional history than group biography per se), the Peabody Sisters, and the Emerson-Thoreau partnership see, respectively, Sterling F. Delano,

Brook Farm: The Dark Side of Utopia (Cambridge: Belknap Press of Harvard University Press, 2004), Megan Marshall, *The Peabody Sisters: Three Women Who Ignited American Romanticism* (Boston: Houghton Mifflin, 2005), and Harmon Smith, *My Friend, My Friend: The Story of Thoreau's Relationship with Emerson* (Amherst: University of Massachusetts Press, 1999). Minor transcendentalists that I examine appear in the following biographies: Edwin Gittleman, *Jones Very: The Effective Years* (New York: Columbia University Press, 1967), De Wolfe Miller, *Christopher Pearse Cranch and His Caricatures of New England Transcendentalism* (Cambridge: Harvard University Press, 1951), Frederick T. McGill, *Channing of Concord: A Life of William Ellery Channing II* (New Brunswick: Rutgers University Press, 1967).

12. In a recent study of neglected theological figures associated with transcendentalism, David Robinson notes that other unknowns such as the majority of the promising youths of this book are often mentioned as "part of the movement. But I sometimes think that we do not carry this analysis much further. In this case, their identification as 'Transcendentalists' becomes a screen which obscures the particularity of their lives or works from us"; Robinson, "'A Religious Demonstration': The Theological Emergence of New England Transcendentalism," in *Transient and Permanent: The Transcendentalist Movement and Its Contexts*, ed. Charles Capper and Conrad Edick Wright (Boston: Massachusetts Historical Society, 1999), 69. This book attempts to restore their memories within the context of the movement as well as that of their relationships with Emerson during the formative years of their literary careers. In doing so, this research responds historically to Ronald Bosco's challenge to "study Emerson further for the influence his writing and thought have exerted on the professionalization of literary study and, one might add, creative writing in America"; Bosco, "We Find What We Seek: Emerson and His Biographers," in *A Historical Guide to Ralph Waldo Emerson*, ed. Joel Myerson (New York: Oxford University Press), 284. Long before creative writing became institutionalized in American higher education, it most certainly was professionalized, with training occurring mainly through informal mentorships such as those between Emerson and his followers.

13. This book draws on the methodology of Michael Robertson's *Worshipping Walt: The Whitman Disciples* (Princeton: Princeton University Press, 2008) by historically profiling each of Emerson's principal followers. The key difference lies in my concern with the professional consequences of Emerson's relationships with his disciples with close attention to his aesthetic and financial impact on the trajectory of their careers. Unlike Emerson's protégés, none of the Whitman disciples in Robertson's study approached the poet with the intention of being adopted by him for sustained training in an apprenticeship aimed at professional authorship. Instead, they sought out Whitman as more of a religious icon, viewing *Leaves of Grass* as the Emersonian disciples had seen *Nature*, "a religion to live and die by," according to Thomas Harned, qtd. in Robertson, *Worshipping Walt*, 5. Whitman zealot Paul Zweig's comment that "we respond to his poem . . . as followers of an impassioned saint speaking radical new words" certainly resonates with the starry-eyed collegians spellbound by Emerson's radical Harvard Divinity School Address (6). Whitman's disciples, like Emerson's, were

overwhelmed upon meeting their idol with "a curious state of exaltation and excitement as to produce a partial wakefulness, the general feeling not wearing off for a fortnight," but did not expect any patronage or tutelage from Whitman himself as Emerson's youth had (6). Unlike Emerson, Whitman was known neither for assisting fledgling literary careers nor for expanding established ones, as Emerson had done for Carlyle through editing and publicity. Thus Robertson's objective lies not in the exigencies of the literary market, but in exploring why "the disciples think that Whitmanism might become an organized religion, possibly rivaling Christianity" and why this group was "ready to regard Whitman as a successor to Jesus, Kronos, Buddha," even Emerson. Whitman "promoted an individualistic spirituality that, to many people later in the century, seemed to find its highest expression in *Leaves of Grass*" (9, 11).

14. Frederic Jameson, *Valences of the Dialectic* (London: Verso, 2009), 30–31. See also Gustavus Stadler's discussion of genius in Emerson in *Troubling Minds: The Cultural Politics of Genius in the United States, 1840–1890* (Minneapolis: University of Minnesota Press, 2006), particularly the chapter "The Geography of Genius in Emerson, Fuller, and Douglass," 1–32.

15. For more on the radical pedagogy of the Temple School, see Geraldine Brooks, "Orpheus at the Plow," *New Yorker* (January 10, 2005), 58–70. Brooks writes that "if a pupil misbehaved, he would present his own hand, and instruct the miscreant to apply the ferule, saying that the fault lay chiefly with the teacher, who had not inspired the pupil to sufficient self-discipline," noting that the guilt instilled by such a measure meant "Alcott's classes were orderly" (62). The most penetrating research into Alcott's pedagogy that usefully reflects on applications for contemporary American education is Martin Bickman, *Minding American Education: Reclaiming the Tradition of Active Learning* (New York: Teachers College Press, 2003).

16. Lawrence Buell, *Emerson* (Cambridge: Belknap Press of Harvard University Press, 2003), 291.

17. Jürgen Habermas's comments are helpful here in describing the processes of deinstitutionalization, which help explain the romantic reaction against the development of capitalism. Habermas argues that the public sphere is incapable of providing meaningful concrete confirmation of social structures and their subjective identities within them, in "The Public Sphere," *New German Critique* 3 (1974): 18–34. The anthropological protest against modernity is inclined toward that which is presumably more real. For Jackson, this was specie, or hard currency, for Emerson, this was the intuition and nature. Social theorist Arnold Gehlen has also argued that deinstitutionalization occurs when normative codes for social behavior lose their plausibility. This brings the taken-for-granted background structure into the foreground, where institutions are self-consciously rearranged. Brook Farm was precisely such a gesture, in which normative codes of acquisitive behavior were radically reconceived in communal living. Emerson did the same with conventional codes of vocational expectations. Gehlen identifies a salient feature of modernity in that the foreground of choice is growing, while the background pattern of stable, reliable institutions diminishes. Bryan S. Turner, "Social Systems and Complexity Theory," in *Talcott Parsons Today: His Theory and*

Legacy in Contemporary Sociology, ed. A. Javier Trevino (Lanham, Md.: Rowman and Littlefield, 2001), 95.

18. Henry David Thoreau, *Walden*, ed. J. Lyndon Shanley (Princeton: Princeton University Press, 2004 [1854]), 98.

19. Turner, "Social Systems and Complexity," 95.

20. Charles J. Woodbury, *Talks with Ralph Waldo Emerson* (New York: Baker and Taylor, 1890), 27.

21. Richard Poirier, *Poetry and Pragmatism* (Cambridge: Harvard University Press, 1992), 69.

22. "The Emerson Mania," *English Review* 12 (September 1849), 132.

23. Christopher Cranch, "Transcendentalism," *The Western Messenger* 8 (January 1841), 406.

24. For more on Emerson's treatment of the topic of scholarly and poetic vocation as a method of forging a new kind of public intellectual in antebellum America, see Buell, *Emerson*, 40–41. The issue of vocation is also central to Peter S. Field's chapter "The Transformation of Genius into Practical Power" in his monograph, *Ralph Waldo Emerson: The Making of a Democratic Intellectual* (Lanham, Md.: Rowman and Littlefield, 2002), 131–66, and Mary Kupiec Cayton's "The Calling" in *Emerson's Emergence: Self and Society in the Transformation of New England, 1800–1845* (Chapel Hill: University of North Carolina Press, 1989), 137–64.

25. Qtd. in Robert D. Richardson, *Emerson: The Mind on Fire* (Berkeley: University of California Press, 1995), 301.

26. Emerson refused the offer to join Brook Farm mainly because it would interfere with his literary production ("when I am engaged in literary composition I find myself not inclined to insist with heat on new methods") and because of its inclination toward institutionalization. In regard to the latter, he was particularly repulsed "as it respects the formation of a School or College." Although a "concentration of scholars in one place has great advantages," Emerson explained, education was more effective in isolated mentorships like the sort that took up so much of his time and energy: "I do now keep school for all comers, & the energy of our thought & will measures our influence"; *L*, 2:370–71.

27. Buell, *Emerson*, 40.

28. Robert D. Richardson, *First We Read, Then We Write: Emerson on the Creative Process* (Iowa City: University of Iowa Press, 2009), 71.

29. Henry Ware, Jr., "God's Personhood Vindicated," in *The American Transcendentalists: Essential Writings*, ed. Lawrence Buell (New York: Random House, 2006), 151.

30. Mary Kupiec Cayton has argued that "many modern American professions can claim Emerson as forebear—he was the first professional intellectual, one of the first media heroes, the first modern American poet and writer, even a primitive ego psychologist of sorts." Though the claim accurately suggests "he intended to be none of these" since he was "antiprofessional in orientation," it risks ignoring his very real work as a literary intermediary, agent, marketer, and editor of his followers' and friends' writings

as well as his own; Cayton, *Emerson's Emergence*, 159. Indeed, his arrangements in the literary market for booking his own lectures, and his meticulous recordings of his costs and earnings on each trip were certainly professional activities. He certainly did not advocate narrow specialization or confining his work to an institution or bureaucracy, and in this sense should be considered antiprofessional. But his bent in all his relationships with his protégés, which they sometimes resisted, was to encourage greater professionalization through publication and the development of a marketable authorial identity.

31. Qtd. in Richardson, *Mind on Fire*, 91.

32. "Historic Notes of Life and Letters in Massachusetts," *Atlantic Monthly* 52 (October 1883), 532.

33. Jameson, *Valences of the Dialectic*, 14.

34. Gilbert Haven and Thomas Russell, *Father Taylor, the Sailor Preacher* (Boston: B. B. Russell, 1872), 330.

35. Quoted in Oliver Wendell Holmes, *Ralph Waldo Emerson* (Cambridge: Riverside Press, 1884), 150.

36. Buell, *Emerson*, 37.

37. Robert Sattelmeyer, "Ellery Channing in the 1855 Massachusetts Census," *Thoreau Research Newsletter*, 2.2 (1980): 8.

38. For details on Emerson as "Carlyle's editor," see Teichgraeber, *Sublime Thoughts*, 217.

39. Andrews Norton, "The New School in Literature and Religion," *Boston Daily Advertiser* (August 27, 1838), 12.

40. Teichgraeber, *Sublime Thoughts*, 20.

41. Teichgraeber, *Sublime Thoughts*, 12; *CW*, 62.

42. Buell, *Emerson*, 305.

Chapter 1. Emerson's Hero

1. Leslie Eckel also supports the significance of Fuller's belief in the power of journalism to reach the entire nation (together with her cosmopolitanism and commitment to foreign languages and literatures) and thus effectively reinscribes her "into a recognizably American tradition of internationalist thought"; Eckel, "Margaret Fuller's Conversational Journalism: New York, London, Rome," *Arizona Quarterly* 63.2 (Summer 2007), 27. For one of the most thorough treatments of the daily newspaper industry in which Greeley operated, and his unique approach of harnessing the latest technological innovations such as "the Lightning," "the new four-cylinder rotary press of Richard M. Hoe," for the production of his liberal mass media platform, see Robert Chadwell Williams, *Horace Greeley: Champion of American Freedom* (New York: New York University Press, 2006), 61. Greeley served his progressive agenda by both reaching a broad audience through cutting-edge technology and employing a preponderance of progressive liberals on his staff, many of whom were directly connected to Emerson and his ideas.

2. Cornelius Mathews, qtd. in Margaret Fuller, *Papers on Literature and Art* (London: Wiley and Putnam, 1846), 141.

3. Qtd. in Ronald J. and Mary Saracino Zboray, "Transcendentalism in Print: Production, Dissemination, and Common Reception," in *Transient and Permanent: The Transcendentalist Movement and Its Contexts*, ed. Charles Capper and Conrad Edick Wright (Boston: Massachusetts Historical Society, 1999), 356.

4. Qtd. in Philip F. Gura, *The Transcendentalists: A History* (New York: Hill and Wang, 2007), 152.

5. Elizabeth Palmer Peabody, *Reminiscences of Rev. Wm. Ellery Channing, D.D.* (Boston: Roberts Brothers, 1880), 406–7.

6. Ralph Waldo Emerson, "Thoughts on Modern Literature," *The Dial* (October 1840), 137. For more on the proliferation and diversification of literary genres that occurred in the average antebellum bookstore, see Ronald J. Zboray, *A Fictive People: Antebellum Economic Development and the American Reading Public* (Oxford: Oxford University Press, 1992), and Richard F. Teichgraeber III, *Sublime Thoughts/Penny Wisdom: Situating Emerson and Thoreau in the American Market* (Baltimore: Johns Hopkins University Press, 1995), 155–74.

7. Emerson's critique of the commodification of the reform movement appears throughout his writings. He asserted that "genius is the power to labor better and more availably" and thus ample potential exists to improve upon the literary market's profusion of commodities, many driven by reform special interests, such that "Each 'cause' as it is called—say Abolition, Temperance, say Calvinism, or Unitarianism— becomes speedily a little shop, where the article, let it have been at first never so subtle and ethereal, is now made up into portable and convenient cakes, and retailed in small quantities to suit purchasers"; *CW*, 1:211. Instead, Emerson did not want insubstantial packaged treats, but writing of far richer moral fiber and nutrition for the vitality of the whole man.

8. Judith Mattson Bean, "Texts from Conversation: Margaret Fuller's Influence on Emerson," in *Studies in the American Renaissance, 1994*, ed. Joel Myerson (Charlottesville: University Press of Virginia, 1994), 228.

9. Bean, "Texts from Conversation," 232.

10. Margaret Fuller, *The Letters of Margaret Fuller*, 6 vols., 1839–41, ed. Robert N. Hudspeth (Ithaca: Cornell University Press, 1983–94), 2:32 (hereafter *LMF*).

11. *LMF*, 2:68–69. "Do not read when the mind is creative, and do not read thoroughly," Emerson advised, "and don't try to get what isn't meant for you." He warned, "reading long at one time anything, no matter how it fascinates, destroys thought as completely as the inflections forced by external causes. Do not permit this. Stop if you find yourself becoming absorbed, at even the first paragraph." The use of reading to spur on writing involved the notion of divining, or creatively abstracting from whole works their meaning through singular passages or chapters. Thus one should not "read by the bookful" as an escapist consumer might, but to "learn to divine books, to *feel* those that you want without wasting much time over them. Remember you must know only the excellent of all that has been presented"; qtd. in Charles Woodbury, *Talks with Ralph Waldo Emerson* (New York: Baker and Taylor, 1890), 27–29. For a thorough analysis of the implications of Emerson's

approach to reading for the creative process, see Robert D. Richardson, *First We Read, Then We Write: Emerson on the Creative Process* (Iowa City: University of Iowa Press, 2009).

12. *LMF*, 2:116.

13. *LMF*, 2:160.

14. *LMF*, 2:161.

15. Gura, *The Transcendentalists*, 150–79.

16. *LMF*, 2:146.

17. "The extension of the privileges of women is the basic principle of all social progress," Fourier wrote; quoted in Pamela M. Pilbeam, *French Socialists Before Marx: Workers, Women, and the Social Question in France* (Montreal: McGill-Queen's University Press, 2001), 76.

18. *LMF*, 2:181.

19. *LMF*, 2:188.

20. Charles Capper, *Margaret Fuller: An American Romantic Life, The Public Years* (Oxford: Oxford University Press, 2007), x.

21. Ralph Waldo Emerson, J. F. Clarke, and W. H. Channing, eds., *Memoirs of Margaret Fuller Ossoli*, 2 vols. (Boston: Phillips, Sampson, 1852), 1:213, 236–37 (hereafter *Memoirs*).

22. Buell, *Emerson*, 21.

23. Fuller, *Papers on Literature and Art*, 138. For more on this principle of the periodical press as a vehicle for social justice, see Aleta Feinsod Cane and Susan Alves, eds., *"The Only Efficient Instrument": American Women Writers and the Periodical, 1837–1916* (Iowa City: University of Iowa Press, 2001).

24. Margaret Fuller, "Our City's Charities," *The Essential Margaret Fuller*, ed. Jeffrey Steele (New Brunswick: Rutgers University Press, 1995), 388.

25. Fuller, "Our City's Charities," 388.

26. Fuller, "Our City's Charities," 389.

27. *Memoirs*, 1:306.

28. Meg McGavran Murray's *Margaret Fuller: Wandering Pilgrim* (Athens: University of Georgia Press, 2008) aptly observes that Emerson's heresies in the Divinity School Address inspired Fuller's refusal of Christ (187). Murray usefully points out that nature for Fuller thus functions like Jesus by providing access to the divine, whereby the ego vanishes in a fusion with "the currents of Universal Being" (93). Elsewhere, Emerson appears the exorcist of Fuller's spirits she conjured in her mystical dabbling in mesmerism, animal magnetism, and gemology. Here Murray finds Fuller "deliberately countering Emerson" with "the magnetic aura" of "Mother Power" in *Woman in the Nineteenth Century*, casting the formation of her feminism in contrast to Emerson's aversion to her mystical inclinations (119). David Robinson points out that such tension did not give rise to her feminist views so much as reflect their different temperaments; Robinson, "Margaret Fuller and the Transcendental Ethos," in *Woman in the Nineteenth Century*, ed. Larry J. Reynolds (New York: Norton, 1998), 245. Fuller's feminist call for spiritual and professional development of women by unleashing them in the

marketplace was instead modeled after Emerson's vocational liberation called for throughout his work, especially in "The Poet."

29. Emerson represents a hegemonic white male patriarchal barrier to Fuller's professional development in Dorothy Berkson, "'Born and Bred in Different Nations': Margaret Fuller and Ralph Waldo Emerson," in *Patrons and Proteges: Gender, Friendship, and Writing in Nineteenth-Century America*, ed. Shirley Marchalonis (New Brunswick: Rutgers University Press, 1988), 3–30. In the process of revising old scholarship that posited that Fuller was romantically in love with Emerson, Berkson overstates the claim that any passion for him in her letters was strictly rhetorical and not genuine (6–8). Jeffrey Steele's "Introduction" to *The Essential Margaret Fuller* (New Brunswick: Rutgers University Press, 1995) has Fuller consistently in opposition to Emerson, and usually forging her views by confronting or challenging his (xviii, xxxiii–xxxiv). Paula Kopacz, "Feminist at the *Tribune*: Margaret Fuller as Professional Writer," *Studies in the American Renaissance, 1991* (Charlottesville: University Press of Virginia), depicts Emerson as eviscerating Fuller's feminist strains in her writing and regarding them as "unsettling masculine qualities" (119). Kopacz claims that his *Memoirs* were a spiteful distortion of her life that occluded the significance of her achievements as a literary critic (119). Susan Belasco, "'The Animating Influences of Discord': Margaret Fuller in 1844," *Legacy* 20 (2003), usefully complicates the picture by pointing toward Fuller's transformation from transcendentalist to social critic as a function not only of gender-driven crisis and conflict, but in "defining the proper role of the scholar in a society in need of reform" (76).

30. Robinson, "Fuller," 245.

31. Capper, *Margaret Fuller*, xiii. Fuller promised to write Goethe's biography "if I had four or five years to give to my task. But I content myself with doing it inadequately rather than risk living so long in the shadow of one mind"; letter to Emerson, June 3, 1839, *LMF*, 2:69. She was likely to have written Goethe's biography if she had access to better materials as Robert Hudspeth notes; *LMF*, 2:70.

32. Carole Moses, "The Domestic Transcendentalism of Fanny Fern," *Texas Studies in Literature and Language* 50.1 (2008): 90–119.

33. *Memoirs*, 1:155.

34. *Memoirs*, 1:304.

35. *LMF*, 2:111.

36. Margaret Fuller, *"My Heart Is a Large Kingdom": Selected Letters of Margaret Fuller*, ed. Robert N. Hudspeth (Ithaca: Cornell University Press, 2001), 124.

37. *Memoirs*, 1:304.

38. *Memoirs*, 1:280.

39. *Memoirs*, 1:201.

40. Emerson complains that "instead of Man Thinking, we have the bookworm. Hence the book-learned class, who value books, as such; not as related to nature and the human constitution, but as making a sort of Third Estate with the world of the soul." Books, he argues, are put to "right use" when they inspire action, for to Emerson, "the one thing in the world, of value, is the active soul"; *CW*, 1:56. Fuller clearly

emerges in the correspondence and *Memoirs* as such an active soul, preventing him from falling into the detached scholarly existence of the bookworm.

41. *Memoirs*, 1:234.

42. *Memoirs*, 1:160.

43. In 1893, Martha Louise Rayne reflected on Fuller's era that "fifty-three or fifty-four years ago . . . in Massachusetts, one of the most highly civilized and advanced communities in the world, there were but seven industries open to women who wanted work." Along with domestic service and needle trades, "they might keep borders, or set type, or teach needlework, or tend looms in cotton mills, or fold and stitch in book binderies." By 1893, more than 300,000 Massachusetts women were earning their own living in more than 300 occupations, "receiving from $150 to $3,000 every year"; Martha Louise Rayne, *What Can a Woman Do?; or, Her Position in the Business and Literary World* (Petersburgh, N.Y.: Eagle, 1893), iii–iv. These reports are relatively standard, yet appear to have overlooked the significant presence of women in editorial positions like Fuller's. Patricia Okker notes, "more than six hundred nineteenth-century American women periodical editors [represented] a rich and varied tradition" in the trade; Okker, *Our Sister Editors: Sarah J. Hale and the Tradition of Nineteenth-Century American Women Editors* (Athens: University of Georgia Press, 1995 [rpt. 2008]), 6. At first glance it appears that Fuller was not the pioneer female editor she was touted to be, but in her era there were far fewer women editors than Okker's numbers for the entire century indicate.

44. Qtd. in Zwarg, *Feminist Conversations*, 190. See also Catharine Castro Mitchell, *Margaret Fuller's New York Journalism: A Biographical Essay and Key Writings* (Knoxville: University of Tennessee Press, 1995), and John Matteson, *The Lives of Margaret Fuller* (New York: Norton, 2012), 273–306.

45. Eric Cheyvitz, *The Trans-Parent: Sexual Politics in the Language of Emerson* (Baltimore: Johns Hopkins University Press, 1981), 102.

46. Fuller, *Papers on Literature and Art*, 140.

47. *LMF*, 2:183.

48. *LMF*, 2:99.

49. *LMF*, 2:104.

50. *LMF*, 2:99.

51. Caleb Crain, *American Sympathy: Men, Friendship, and Literature in the New Nation* (New Haven: Yale University Press, 2001), 192.

52. See Buell, *Emerson*, 295.

53. *LMF*, 2:40.

54. *LMF*, 2:32.

55. *LMF*, 3:40.

56. *LMF*, 4:456–57. For more on Fuller's literary journalism and her understanding of the periodical press as an instrument not only for educating the masses but also for promoting her work (despite its other function as an outlet for adverse criticism), see Robert Scholnick, "'The Ultraism of the Day': Greene's *Boston Post*, Hawthorne, Fuller, Melville, Stowe, and Literary Journalism in Antebellum America," *American Periodicals* 8.2 (2008), 163–91.

57. Steven Fink usefully points out that "the source of both the strengths and weaknesses" of "The Service" lies in its "experimental use of language and structure to create a transcendentalist essay." As with "Persius," the "organizing principle," Fink explains, "is associational rather than narrative or expository; it is built around image clusters and extended metaphors"; Fink, *Prophet in the Marketplace: Thoreau's Development as Professional Writer* (Princeton: Princeton University Press, 1992), 26–27.

58. Margaret Fuller, "Emerson's Essays," in *The Essential Margaret Fuller*, ed. Jeffrey Steele (New Brunswick: Rutgers University Press, 1995), 378, 381.

59. *Memoirs*, 1:312.

60. Margaret Fuller, "Farewell," in *The Essential Margaret Fuller*, ed. Steele, 403–4. Emerson was instrumental in Fuller's support of national education, which represented a crucial revision of Thomas Carlyle's *On Heroes, Hero-Worship, and the Heroic in History* (1841). Emerson democratized Carlyle's elitist claim that outstanding individuals possess powers inaccessible to the common man, who should be content to be ruled by them given their superiority. Instead Emerson supports democracy and universal education in his contrary claim that "there is one mind common to all individual men. Every man is an inlet to the same and to all of the same. He that is admitted to the right of reason is made a freeman of the whole estate. What Plato has thought, he may think, what a saint has felt, he may feel; what at any time has befallen any man, he can understand"; *CW*, 2:3.

Chapter 2. Henry David Thoreau

1. "Sometimes one of those great cakes slips from the ice-man's sled into the village street, and lies there for a week like a great emerald, an object of interest to all passers," Thoreau notes in "The Pond in Winter," *Walden*, ed. James Lyndon Shanley (Princeton: Princeton University Press, 2004), 296–97. The commodified ice block interestingly transforms here into a wondrous and absurd jewel dislodged from its seat in nature for scrutiny in the marketplace.

2. Raymond R. Borst, ed., *The Thoreau Log: A Documentary Life of Henry David Thoreau* (New York: G. K. Hall, 1992), 25 (hereafter *Log*).

3. Henry David Thoreau, *The Collected Poems of Henry Thoreau*, ed. Carl Bode (Baltimore: Johns Hopkins University Press, 1964), 352 (hereafter *CP*). For more on Thoreau's passion for Lidian Emerson, see Robert Sattelmeyer, " 'When He Became My Enemy': Emerson and Thoreau, 1848–1849," *New England Quarterly* 62.2 (June 1989), 201. As with Lucy Brown Jackson, Thoreau professed to Lidian that "when I love you I feel as if I were annexing another world to mine," viewing her from a sliding perspective from romantic lover to filial endearment, "Whether art thou my mother or sister—whether am I thy son or thy brother" (199).

4. *Log*, 25–26.

5. Harmon Smith, *My Friend, My Friend: The Story of Thoreau's Relationship with Emerson* (Amherst: University of Massachusetts Press, 1999), 5.

6. *Log*, 29–30.

7. Thoreau, *Walden*, 107. Ronald Bosco astutely observes, "Although following Oliver Wendell Holmes, modern scholars and cultural critics have cited Emerson's lecture on 'The American Scholar' as America's declaration of intellectual independence, I believe Emerson made the first call for America's intellectual independence in *Nature*"; Bosco, *Creating Waldens: An East-West Conversation on the American Renaissance*, with Joel Myerson and Daisaku Ikeda (Cambridge, Mass.: Dialogue Path Press, 2009), 31. *Nature*, more than any of Emerson's works, attracted the vast majority of his disciples to make a similar professional declaration of independence from conventional pursuits and dedicate their lives instead to literary transcendentalism. *Nature* functioned as the impetus for Thoreau, Channing, and Very to commit not only their vocational identities, but the very fabric of their lives, to an Emersonian apprenticeship.

8. Smith, *My Friend, My Friend*, 7.

9. Emily Dickinson, *Selected Letters*, ed. Thomas H. Johnson (Cambridge: Belknap Press of Harvard University Press, 1986 [1862]), 171. Emily Dickinson, *Final Harvest: Emily Dickinson's Poems*, ed. Thomas H. Johnson (Boston: Little, Brown, 1961), vii. For more on Dickinson's poetic apprenticeship under Higginson, see Brenda Wineapple, *White Heat: The Friendship of Emily Dickinson and Thomas Wentworth Higginson* (New York: Random House, 2009).

10. Wineapple, *White Heat*, 116.

11. Elizabeth Hall Witherell, "Thoreau as Poet," in *The Cambridge Companion to Henry David Thoreau*, ed. Joel Myerson (Cambridge: Cambridge University Press, 1995), 67. This position, which asserts that Thoreau's poetic apprenticeship sharpened his skills in a way that lent unique power to his later prose, is also consonant with older research by Paul O. Williams. Williams sees Thoreau's penchant for myth, sensitivity to reconciling opposites into idealized unity, and his lyrical and ecstatic interludes that pepper his prose as the shaping forces of his poetic development; Williams, "Thoreau's Growth as a Transcendental Poet," *ESQ: A Journal of the American Renaissance* 19 (1973): 189–98. I build on Williams and Witherell by showing where Emerson's method entered into Thoreau's repertoire for verse, and how it ultimately was better suited to his prose. Further, I consider the professional pressures of living up to the ideal of the Emersonian poet that prompted Thoreau's adoption of Channing's more liberal and alternative understanding of the poet's function.

12. *CP*, 81.

13. *Log*, 27.

14. *CP*, 76.

15. Robert Sattelmeyer aptly covers this aspect of Thoreau's early foray into a literary career in "Thoreau's Projected Works on the English Poets," in *Studies in the American Renaissance, 1980*, ed. Joel Meyerson (Boston: Twayne, 1980), 239–57.

16. Robert Sattelmeyer, *Thoreau's Reading: A Study in Intellectual History* (Princeton: Princeton University Press, 1988), 35.

17. Walter Harding, *The Days of Henry Thoreau* (New York: Alfred A. Knopf, 1967), 116.

18. Henry David Thoreau, *Journal*, ed. John C. Broderick, Robert Sattelmeyer, et al. (Princeton: Princeton University Press, 1981–2002), 4:188.

19. *CP*, 82.

20. Thoreau, *Journal*, 1:140.

21. *CP*, viii.

22. For an excellent study of the significance of Thoreau's surveying in his career and aesthetic vision, see Patrick Chura, *Thoreau the Land Surveyor* (Gainesville: University Press of Florida, 2010).

23. Ralph Waldo Emerson, "Thoreau," *Emerson and Thoreau: The Contemporary Reviews* (Cambridge: Cambridge University Press, 1992 [1862]), 427.

24. Thoreau, *Journal*, 1:5.

25. Thoreau, *Journal*, 1:6.

26. Lawrence Buell, *Emerson* (Cambridge: Belknap Press of Harvard University Press, 2003), 297.

27. Joel Myerson, "Eight Lowell Letters from Concord in 1838," *Illinois Quarterly* 38 (Winter 1975), 28.

28. Qtd. in Joel Myerson, *The New England Transcendentalists and the* Dial: *A History of the Magazine and Its Contributors* (Cranbury, N.J.: Associated University Presses, 1980), 234.

29. Qtd. in Harding, *Days of Henry Thoreau*, 66.

30. Qtd. in *CP*, 349. Scholars had originally assumed that Channing's marginalia in his copy of the 1849 *A Week on the Concord and Merrimack Rivers* could be trusted, until Henry Seidel Canby noted that Thoreau did not meet Ellen until the next month after composing the poem, and that therefore, its subject must have been her brother; Canby, *Thoreau* (Boston: Houghton Mifflin, 1939), 110. A host of scholars since have supported this view, with Perry Miller extrapolating rather recklessly and without further evidence that Thoreau's persistent interest in friendship represented not a philosophical inquiry in the manner of Emerson, so much as it calls "attention to the androgynous character of Thoreau's monomaniac discussions of friendship"; Miller, *Consciousness in Concord* (Boston: Houghton Mifflin, 1958), 82.

31. Thoreau, *Journal*, 1:142.

32. Thoreau, *Journal*, 1:141.

33. Both Harding, *Days of Henry Thoreau*, 117, and Franklin D. Sanborn argue that likely around 1843 when Thoreau was twenty-six, Emerson urged him to destroy the poems, presumably by burning them; Sanborn, *Henry D. Thoreau* (Boston: Houghton Mifflin, 1892), 286–87. Witherell notes that precisely when Emerson ordered the burning is conjectural. She suggests that the directive likely occurred after the *Dial* had ceased publication, and points to damning lines, "I look in vain for the poem whom I describe"; *CW*, 3:21, in Emerson's 1844 essay, "The Poet," which Emerson shared with Thoreau, as a likely occasion; Witherell, "Thoreau as Poet," 68.

34. Sanborn, *Henry D. Thoreau*, 286.

35. Roland Barthes, "The Death of the Author," *Image, Music, Text* (New York: Hill and Wang, 1978), 146. For a thorough study of the sources excerpted in Thoreau's journal, see Sattelmeyer, *Thoreau's Reading*, 25–53.

36. "The initial version of this poem, in run-on form, but with verse lines occasionally indicated by capitalization, appears in pencil in notebook 1833, used in the years

1833–1836," report editors Ralph H. Orth et al., in Ralph Waldo Emerson, *The Poetry Notebooks of Ralph Waldo Emerson* (Columbia: University of Missouri Press, 1986), 918 (hereafter *PN*). See *JMN*, 6:246, for the original run-on form of "The Snow-Storm."

37. Robert D. Richardson, *First We Read, Then We Write: Emerson on the Creative Process* (Iowa City: University of Iowa Press, 2009), 75.

38. Ralph Waldo Emerson, *Poems* (Boston: James Munroe, 1847), 25.

39. Sattelmeyer, *Thoreau's Reading*, 26.

40. *PN*, 31, 914.

41. *PN*, 910.

42. *CP*, 366. Thoreau was also deeply influenced by Wordsworth at this time, as he borrowed and extended many features of *Lyrical Ballads* in his own verse. Thoreau's poems were thus "exploratory and miscellaneous, and they do not show the same kind of absolutely confident and single-minded formal invention that marks the work of Whitman or Dickinson," according to Lance Newman, " 'Patron of the World': Henry Thoreau as Wordsworthian Poet," in *Modern Critical Views: Henry Thoreau—Updated Edition*, ed. Harold Bloom (New York: Infobase, 2007), 108. Thoreau's poetry has vanished from the critical horizon because it does not so resolutely throw off the yoke of the Fireside Poets for a natural democratic verse better suited to the new republic. Emerson's high esteem for Wordsworth's power—he maintained that "the fame of Wordsworth is a leading fact in modern Europe"—instead encouraged Thoreau's liberal borrowings from the British poet's prosody and treatment of natural subjects; qtd. in Newman, "Patron of the World," 108.

43. *CP*, 230.

44. *CP*, 378.

45. For more on how the rhetorical structure of the jeremiad functions as a broader organizing principle throughout the history of American literature, see Sacvan Berkovich, *The American Jeremiad* (Madison: University of Wisconsin Press, 1980).

46. Emerson's prospectus for the "Verses of the Portfolio" department in the *Dial* appears under the title "New Poetry," *The Dial* (October 1840): 220–23, and intones a democratization of verse echoing that of Wordsworth's in his preface to the *Lyrical Ballads*, quote on 221. Sattelmeyer astutely recognizes the unfinished, process-oriented approach to poetry was considered a strength by more radical romantic thinkers at the time, as this approach embodied the paradox that the highest art exuded artlessness. The "rough and untutored qualities . . . in the ballad and particularly early Scottish poetry seems to have presaged a focus in his collection," and also informed his aesthetic preferences and frame of reference in his own poetry writing, because this type of "verse constituted a kind of virtue in some Romantic theory"; Sattelmeyer, "English Poets," 251.

47. *CP*, 78.

48. *CP*, 68.

49. Thoreau, *A Week*, 378.

50. Meredith L. McGill, "Common Places: Poetry, Illocality, and Temporal Dislocation in Thoreau's *A Week on the Concord and Merrimack Rivers*," *American Literary History* 19.2 (2007), 358, 362.

51. James Russell Lowell, "Review of *A Week on the Concord and Merrimack Rivers*," *Massachusetts Quarterly Review* (December 1849), 47, 51.

52. Robert N. Hudspeth, *Ellery Channing* (New York: Twayne, 1973), 44.

53. Edward Waldo Emerson, *Henry Thoreau as Remembered by a Young Friend* (Mineola, N.Y.: Dover, 1999 [1917]), 53. Edward Emerson recollected Thoreau saying, "'Boys if you went to talk business with a man, and he persisted in thrusting words having no connection with the subject into all parts of every sentence, wouldn't you think he was taking a liberty with you, and trifling with your time and wasting his own,'" 53. His lesson is notable, for it models the concision demanded of language during business transactions, anticipating the unvarnished power of the agrarian's utilitarian call to his teams in the field, which he extols in *A Week*.

54. *CP*, 105.

55. William Ellery Channing, *Thoreau: The Poet-Naturalist* (Boston: Roberts Brothers, 1873), 226.

56. *CP*, 172.

57. Channing, *Thoreau*, 220–25.

58. Channing, *Thoreau*, 242.

59. Channing, *Thoreau*, 221–25.

60. Qtd. in Channing, *Thoreau*, 237.

61. Channing, *Thoreau*, 229. For more on Channing and Thoreau's relationship, see the chapter on Channing in this book, as well as Hudspeth, *Ellery Channing*, and Frederick T. McGill, *Channing of Concord: A Life of William Ellery Channing, II* (New Brunswick: Rutgers University Press, 1967).

62. Thoreau, *Journal*, 1:337–38.

63. David Robinson, *Natural Life: Thoreau's Worldly Transcendentalism* (Ithaca: Cornell University Press, 2004), 18.

64. Thoreau, *Journal*, 1:143. I am amending Robinson's assertion that this passage represents Thoreau's "active or willed pursuit," by suggesting it also reflects his acceptance and stillness. Both forces created the tension at the heart of his vocational crisis, as he struggled to reconcile the accepting stillness of the romantic poet with the willed pursuit of the professional author. The result is a seemingly self-contradictory tension that proved less fruitful in verse than in prose. Thoreau managed to achieve positive gains from will-less surrender, especially in the lyrical prose reveries that animate *Walden*.

65. Sattelmeyer, "English Poets," 239.

66. Thoreau, *A Week*, 116–17.

Chapter 3. Christopher Cranch

1. Leonora Cranch Scott, *The Life and Letters of Christopher Pearse Cranch* (Boston: Houghton Mifflin, 1917), 52.

2. Scott, *Life and Letters*, 41. The line is quoted from Cranch's unpublished auto-biography, which his daughter Leonora liberally excerpted for *Life and Letters*. He originally wrote it at the request of his son-in-law, Colonel H. B. Scott. Leonora elected not to publish it in its entirety, for "a man does not see himself at his best; cannot therefore do justice to himself in an autobiography," as she noted in her preface, vi.

3. Scott, *Life and Letters*, 40.

4. Joel Myerson, "Transcendentalism and Unitarianism in 1840: A New Letter by C. P. Cranch," *CLA Journal* 16 (March 1973): 366–67.

5. Myerson, "Transcendentalism," 39.

6. Poe's treatment of Cranch was quite charitable considering how he had savaged the rest of Emerson's protégés. He found him "one of the least intolerable of the school of Boston transcendentalists" and "undoubtedly one of the least absurd contributors to 'The Dial,'" who seems "to possess unusual vivacity of fancy and dexterity of expression." Poe described him as "well educated and quite accomplished . . . a musician, painter, and poet, being in each capacity very respectably successful" (71). Joseph M. DeFalco, editor of *Collected Poems of Christopher Pearse Cranch, 1835–1892* (Gainesville, Fla.: Scholars' Facsimiles and Reprints, 1971), represents the commonly held view of Cranch as "one of the few transcendentalists who possessed a keen sense of humor," a statement that nonetheless neglects the wit of Ellery Channing and Henry Thoreau, and even the private Emerson (vii).

7. DeFalco observed in 1971 that "many assign Cranch the pejorative label of 'dilettante,'" particularly Perry Miller in an early biographical profile. Merely because he was "a lover of arts and certainly had diverse talents," DeFalco argued, it is a "gross misrepresentation to consider him a mere dabbler because of his lighter moods," especially since "the profession of art was a serious matter for Cranch; for almost half a century he labored to achieve success in poetry and painting" (vii). This observation sounded a keynote in Cranch criticism for the next three decades, and it has lately become a critical commonplace, and even a straw man, used to discuss his work. The stigma of the dilettante aesthete who never fulfilled his professional promise largely because he failed to specialize appears in works such as William R. Hutchinson's *Transcendentalist Ministers: Church Reform in the New England Renaissance* (New Haven: Yale University Press, 1959), which casts him as a "painter and dilettante" who had a "happy but unproductive career" (198). Such a position not only misses the seriousness with which he took poetry, painting, and children's writing. It also overlooks the financial profits and critical accolades he enjoyed from each. His expertise and authority in these areas made him a sought-after and consistent contributor of hundreds of pieces to the most respected magazines in America, including *Harper's* and the *Atlantic Monthly*, from 1837 to 1892. Further, most of the defenses of Cranch overlook that after his initial struggle to choose between poetry and painting in the early 1840s, his career divides itself into four distinct phases after leaving the ministry. First he pursued poetry through his 1844 *Poems*, then moved on to painting, then to children's writing, and finally back to painting. Throughout all of these phases he was a steady contributor to the periodical press, mainly on the subject of painting.

8. Scott, *Life and Letters*, 50.

9. David Robinson, "Christopher Cranch and the New England Transcendentalists," in *At Home and Abroad: The Transcendental Landscapes of Christopher Pearse Cranch (1815–1892)*, ed. Nancy Stula (New London, Conn.: Lyman Allyn Art Museum, 2007), 63.

10. Scott, *Life and Letters*, 24–26, 35.

11. Nancy Stula conversely claims that "preaching and painting were not separate activities" for Cranch, "but simply two sides of the same coin: celebrations of God in nature." Although the conflation is tempting, the spirituality and the artistry of transcendental painting profoundly differ in degree and kind from Unitarian preaching and thus did not function as such simple interchangeable cogs in Cranch's life. Cranch's vocational and spiritual crisis is obscured by the too-easy assumption that "the forest became Cranch's pulpit. He continued to write and pray, but after 1841 he began to see painting as an authentic form of religious expression"; Nancy Stula, "Christopher Pearse Cranch: Painter of Transcendentalism," in *Transient and Permanent: The Transcendentalist Movement and Its Contexts*, ed. Charles Capper and Conrad Edick Wright (Boston: Massachusetts Historical Society, 1999), 554; Nancy Stula, "Transcendentalism: The Path From Preaching to Painting," in *At Home and Abroad*, ed. Stula, 23.

12. Perry Miller has argued oppositely that the objective of transcendentalism was to create a substitute "living religion without recourse to . . . the obsolete jargon of theology"; Miller, *The Transcendentalists: An Anthology* (Cambridge: Harvard University Press, 1950), 8.

13. Christopher Pearse Cranch, "Transcendentalism," *Western Messenger* 8 (January 1841), 406.

14. Cranch, "Emerson," *Collected Poems*, 459.

15. Scott, *Life and Letters*, 50–51.

16. Julie Norko usefully notes that Cranch's struggle to abide by his vocational duty troubles and intensifies Van Wyck Brooks's older portrait of him as a mere entertainer and dabbler. She claims, more problematically, that he either "ignored or unsuccessfully reconciled his sense of duty with his natural inclinations"; Julie Norko, "Christopher Pearse Cranch's Struggle with the Muses," in *Studies in the American Renaissance, 1992*, ed. Joel Myerson (Charlottesville: University Press of Virginia, 1993), 210. I instead find an intensely conflicted crisis pitting Cranch not between dutiful work and natural play, but between the ministry and transcendentalism. Once he embraced transcendentalism, his vocational conflict was between poetry and painting.

17. F. DeWolfe Miller, *Christopher Pearse Cranch and His Caricatures of New England Transcendentalism* (Cambridge: Harvard University Press, 1951), 31. Eric Cheyfitz also notes, "The figure of the transparent eye-ball, Emerson's central metaphor in *Nature* for eloquent transcendence, is, like the hermit with saucer eyes, comically grotesque"; Cheyfitz, *The Trans-Parent: Sexual Politics in the Language of Emerson* (Baltimore: Johns Hopkins University Press, 1981), 63. Cranch's aesthetic hinging on the ridiculous and the profound has been observed by James M. Cox, who describes the caricature

of Emerson "as a monstrous eyeball on two spindly legs"; Cox, "Circles of the Eye," in *Emerson: Prophecy, Metamorphosis, and Influence*, ed. David Levin (New York: Columbia University Press, 1975), 59. The caricatures signify Cranch's coming into his vocational awareness, at once frightened by the distorted perceptions the transcendental perspective offers and laughing at its release from inhibition into profound reverie. Jonathan Bishop explains that "it is difficult to distinguish, either in principle or among particulars, the exciting truth from the trivial illusion, the authentic insight from its near self parody," which he finds correlates directly to the parody inherent in Emerson's original sentence; Bishop, *Emerson on the Soul* (Cambridge: Harvard University Press, 1964), 1, 15. This double portrait of Emerson as one of self-parody and authentic insight not only allegorizes Cranch's own philosophical struggle to reconcile himself to leaving the ministry for an unconventional, and potentially silly, career choice that appealed to him for its prophecy. It also instantiates his own affinity for self-expression through a quintessentially Emersonian dialectic for a sense of the sublime colored by the bizarre, grotesque, and humorous, elements that would later figure prominently in his children's fiction and illustrations.

18. Henry David Thoreau, *The Maine Woods*, ed. Joseph J. Moldenhauer (Princeton: Princeton University Press, 1972), 71.

19. Christopher Cranch, Versos of Drawings, bMS Am 1506 (24) 6b. Houghton Library, Harvard University.

20. Christopher Cranch, Versos of Drawings, bMS Am 1506 (24) 6b. Houghton Library, Harvard University.

21. Christopher Cranch, *Illustrations of the New Philosophy by C. P. Cranch, 1835*, bMS Am 1506 (24) 5. Houghton Library, Harvard University.

22. Christopher Cranch, *Illustrations of the New Philosophy by C. P. Cranch, 1835*, bMS Am 1506 (24) 5. Houghton Library, Harvard University.

23. Christopher Cranch, *Illustrations of the New Philosophy by C. P. Cranch, 1835*, bMS Am 1506 (24) 5. Houghton Library, Harvard University.

24. Qtd. in *Collected Poems*, x.

25. Cranch, *Collected Poems*, 457.

26. Perry Miller appears to have established more than a half century ago this understanding of Cranch's early verse as "resolute attempts to turn Transcendental metaphysics into poetry," in *The Transcendentalists*, 385. David Robinson's recent assessment of "Correspondences" as "a poetic version of Emerson's philosophical doctrine of correspondence" is a clear echo of Miller. Robinson, however, spins the poem's rather prosaic lyricism into a merit rather than a defect, dubiously crediting his "form of verse so closely tied to the structure of the sentence" for breaking down "generic boundaries between poetry and prose . . . in an anticipation of Walt Whitman's *Leaves of Grass* some fifteen years later"; Robinson, "Christopher Cranch," 65. Cranch's poem would never be mistaken for the buoyant and dynamic free verse of Whitman, however. Although the poem does draw from Emerson, Cranch also transposed Dwight's Swedenborgian philosophy into his verse.

27. Christopher Pearse Cranch, *Poems* (Philadelphia: Carey and Hart, 1844), 41–42; *CW*, 1:19.

28. For more on John S. Dwight's discussions of Swedenborg that appeared in the *Harbinger* see John Humphrey Noyes, *The History of American Socialism* (Philadelphia: J. B. Lippincott, 1870), 546–49.

29. Cranch, *Poems*, 51.

30. Scott, *Life and Letters*, 58–60.

31. Madeleine B. Stern, *The Life of Margaret Fuller* (Westport, Conn.: Greenwood Press, 1991 [1942]), 213.

32. DeWolfe, *Cranch and His Caricatures*, 13.

33. Lawrence Buell, ed., *The American Transcendentalists: Essential Writings* (New York: Modern Library, 2006), 445.

34. David Robinson, "Christopher Pearse Cranch, Robert Browning, and the Problem of 'Transcendental' Friendship," in *Studies in the American Renaissance, 1977*, ed. Joel Myerson (Charlottesville: University Press of Virginia, 1977), 145–53.

35. Joel Myerson, *The New England Transcendentalists and the Dial: A History of the Magazine and Its Contributors* (Cranbury, N.J.: Associated Presses, 1980), 136.

36. Myerson, *The New England Transcendentalists and the Dial*, 137–38.

37. For more on Cranch's militant defenses of Emerson, see Francis B. Dedmond, "Christopher Pearse Cranch: Emerson's Self-Appointed Defender Against the Philistines," *The Concord Saunterer* 15 (1980): 6–19. Dedmond provides a far more careful treatment of his early rebellious writings in the wake of the Divinity School Address than their flip dismissal led by Perry Miller, who takes Cranch seriously only beginning with the publication of *The Bird and the Bell with Other Poems* in 1875, "after [he] had ceased to pretend that he was a militant Transcendentalist, [and] after he had amused himself with travel and with sketching" (385). To underestimate Cranch's early writings is to miss his significant contribution to transcendental periodical publishing. He not only published more poems in the first two *Dial* issues than any other author, he was also a leading contributor to Clarke's *Western Messenger*, initiating a career-long presence in the major elite magazines of the day. Robert D. Habich remarks that "Cranch's importance to the magazine is difficult to overestimate. He would twice serve as editor in Clarke's absence, and for two years he provided a steady stream of essays and verse"; Habich, *Transcendentalism and the Western Messenger: A History of the Magazine and Its Contributors, 1835–1841* (Cranbury, N.J.: Associated University Presses, 1985), 84. Unlike Miller, Habich admires the bravery in Cranch's early defenses of transcendentalism. Clarke had taken Cranch seriously enough to devote the lion's share of the November 1837 issue of the *Messenger* to his writings. Far from being pretentious poses, "Mr. Emerson's Oration," in addition to no fewer than six other prose pieces published in the November 1837 issue of the *Messenger*, support Habich's claim that "it took courage to defend Emerson and his circle" during this hostile melee (84). Future research on Cranch would profit from assessing his vast contribution to and influence on the nineteenth-century American periodical press throughout his career.

38. Marianne Dwight, *Letters from Brook Farm, 1844–1847*, ed. Amy L. Reed (Poughkeepsie, N.Y.: Vassar College Press, 1928), 114, 117.

39. Scott, *Life and Letters*, 60.

40. Scott, *Life and Letters*, 62.

41. Scott, *Life and Letters*, 61.

42. Cranch, *Poems*, 77.

43. Hazen C. Carpenter, "Emerson and Christopher Pearse Cranch," *New England Quarterly* 37.1 (1964), 31.

44. Scott, *Life and Letters*, 181.

45. DeWolfe, *Cranch and His Caricatures*, 20.

46. DeWolfe, *Cranch and His Caricatures*, 64–65.

47. Scott, *Life and Letters*, 281.

48. Ralph Waldo Emerson, *Poems* (Boston: James Munroe, 1847), 126.

49. Cranch, *Poems*, 25.

50. Cranch, *Poems*, 33, 22, 21, 60.

51. Cranch, *Poems*, 38–39.

52. Cranch, *Poems*, 39.

53. Cranch, *Poems*, 78–79.

54. Cranch, *Poems*, 41.

55. DeWolfe, *Cranch and His Caricatures*, 16.

56. DeWolfe, *Cranch and His Caricatures*, 84–85.

57. Cranch, *Collected Poems*, 189.

58. Christopher Pearse Cranch, "On the Ideal of Art," *The Harbinger* 1 (August 23, 1845): 170–71.

59. Washington Allston's *Moonlight* (1819) was the most exalted American painting among the transcendentalists. In *Summer on the Lakes* (1844), Margaret Fuller eulogizes Allston upon his death in 1843. Her impassioned ode points to his iconic status among Emerson's circle, along with an unsigned poem in the *Dial* titled "Allston's Funeral," which invokes the unforgettable moonlight of his signature painting: "The summer moonlight lingered there/ Thy gently mouldered brow to see,/ For art in thee had softened care,/ As night's mild beams the dying tree"; *Dial* 4.2 (October 1843), 259. Allston was the favored painter of the movement from the start, as his art was the subject of prominently placed criticism by Fuller and poetry by Samuel Gray Ward in the first issue of the *Dial*, in "A Record of Impressions Produced by Mr. Allston's Pictures in the Summer of 1839," *Dial* 1.1 (July 1840), 73–83, and "To W. Allston, on Seeing His 'Bride,'" *Dial* 1.1 (July 1840), 83. Allston had trained Fuller's friend and traveling companion Sarah Clarke, who contributed several sketches of their journey through the Midwest for *Summer on the Lakes*. Emerson greatly admired Clarke's work and even owned one of her paintings, according to Susan Belasco Smith, ed., *Summer on the Lakes in 1843* (Champaign: University of Illinois Press, 1991), x.

60. Cranch, *Poems*, 52.

61. Stula, *At Home and Abroad*, 34.

62. Scott, *Life and Letters*, 281.

63. Christopher Pearse Cranch, Letter to RWE from CPC, October 13, 1874, MS Am 1280, 712, Houghton Library, Harvard University.

Chapter 4. Samuel Gray Ward

1. Qtd. in Eleanor M. Tilton, "The True Romance of Anna Hazard Barker and Samuel Gray Ward," in *Studies in the American Renaissance, 1987*, ed. Joel Myerson (Charlottesville: University Press of Virginia, 1987), 70.

2. For more on the romantic dimensions of the Ward-Fuller-Barker love triangle as a montage of Emerson's philosophical concept of friendship, see Caleb Crain, *American Sympathy: Men, Friendship, and Literature in the New Nation* (New Haven: Yale University Press, 2001), 198–208.

3. *LMF*, 3:88–89.

4. Margaret Fuller, *"My Heart Is a Large Kingdom": Selected Letters of Margaret Fuller*, ed. Robert N. Hudspeth (Ithaca: Cornell University Press, 2001), 5.

5. Lawrence Buell, "Transcendental Friendship: An Oxymoron?" in *Emerson and Thoreau: Figures of Friendship*, ed. John T. Lysaker and William Rossi (Bloomington: Indiana University Press, 2010), 22; Crain, *American Sympathy*, 177–237; David Robinson, "'In the Golden Hour of Friendship': Transcendentalism and Utopian Desire," in *Emerson and Thoreau*, ed. Lysaker and Rossi, 55.

6. Robinson, "In the Golden Hour," 55.

7. Joel Myerson, "Margaret Fuller's 1842 Journal: At Concord with the Emersons," *Harvard Library Bulletin* 21 (1973), 328.

8. Qtd. in Joel Myerson, *New England Transcendentalism and the Dial: A History of the Magazine and Its Contributors* (Teaneck, N.J.: Fairleigh Dickinson University Press, 1980), 217.

9. Elizabeth Palmer Peabody, *Reminiscences of Rev. Wm. Ellery Channing, D.D.* (Boston: Roberts Brothers, 1880), 406–7.

10. Elizabeth Palmer Peabody, *The Letters of Elizabeth Palmer Peabody: American Renaissance Woman*, ed. Bruce A. Ronda (Middletown, Conn.: Wesleyan University Press, 1984), 247.

11. David Baldwin, "The Emerson-Ward Friendship," in *Studies in the American Renaissance, 1984*, ed. Joel Myerson (Charlottesville: University Press of Virginia, 1984), 305–6. Baldwin's is the most thorough study of the Emerson-Ward relationship. However, it draws on much older research, the conclusions from which are virtually unrevised. In particular, Baldwin argues rather one-sidedly that Ward shared little with Emerson, diverging from him in his views on culture and society, while his "business and financial side removed him even more from Emerson's idealism" (304). Emerson commented upon hearing that Ward took over the high-powered executive position in foreign trade vacated by his father that his friend was "very happy in his new position, which he justifies"; qtd. in Baldwin, 304. Baldwin takes this as evidence of Ward's rejection of Emerson's contemplative life and Emerson's subsequent "annoyance at Ward's defection" (304). Such was clearly not the case, however, as Emerson remained

intimate with Ward, as evidenced by the enduring and lively correspondence in which the mentor is captivated by, and even envious of, his protégé's lofty social and financial standing. An overemphasis on their divergences, furthermore, neglects more recent portraits of Emerson's alliance with commerce and industry that would suggest the mentor deeply admired rather than resented his pupil's financial skills. Indeed, Emerson's image as the detached isolated idealist totally unconnected with the exigencies of commercial trade has been debunked by Joel Myerson in "Ralph Waldo Emerson's Income from His Books," in *The Professions of Authorship: Essays in Honor of Matthew J. Bruccoli* (Columbia: University of South Carolina Press, 1996), 135–49, and more recently, R. Jackson Wilson, "Emerson as Lecturer: Man Thinking, Man Saying," in *The Cambridge Companion to Ralph Waldo Emerson*, ed. Joel Porte and Saundra Morris (Cambridge: Cambridge University Press, 1999), 76–96, which is an updated version of his analysis of Emerson's use of antimaterialistic tropes for his own self-promotion in the literary marketplace in *Figures of Speech: American Writers and the Literary Marketplace, From Benjamin Franklin to Emily Dickinson* (Baltimore: Johns Hopkins University Press, 1990). For an excellent discussion of Emerson's accommodation of certain key capitalist values in his dialectic, see John Patrick Diggins, "Transcendentalism and the Spirit of Capitalism," in *Transient and Permanent: The Transcendentalist Movement and Its Contexts*, ed. Charles Capper and Conrad Edick Wright (Boston: Massachusetts Historical Society, 1999), 229–50. The foundational work in this field remains Richard F. Teichgraeber III, *Sublime Thoughts/Penny Wisdom: Situating Emerson and Thoreau in the American Market* (Baltimore: Johns Hopkins University Press, 1995).

12. Thomas Carlyle, "Signs of the Times," in *Critical and Miscellaneous Essays*, ed. Ralph Waldo Emerson (Boston: Phillips, Sampson, 1855 [1829]), 195.

13. Ralph Waldo Emerson, *Letters from Ralph Waldo Emerson to a Friend, 1838–1853*, ed. Charles Eliot Norton (Boston: Houghton Mifflin, 1899), 11.

14. Qtd. in Tilton, "The True Romance," 59.

15. Qtd. in Baldwin, "Emerson-Ward Friendship," 305.

16. Emerson, *Letters to a Friend*, 40.

17. Emerson, *Letters to a Friend*, 13.

18. Emerson, *Letters to a Friend*, 37.

19. Emerson, *Letters to a Friend*, 40.

20. Baldwin, "Emerson-Ward Friendship," 315.

21. Charles Eliot Norton, ed., *Letters to a Friend*, 6.

22. Thomas Wentworth Higginson, "Walks with Ellery Channing," *Atlantic Monthly* 90 (1902), 28.

23. "If the *Dial* had continued longer, it is quite possible that Ward would have contributed more"; Myerson, *History of the Dial*, 218. Ward's steady literary efforts are a commonly overlooked trait of this neglected Emersonian disciple, who was one of the most consistent contributors to the *Dial*. His writing, however, appears to have been dependent on the journal, as it rather abruptly stopped with its cessation. Thus Ward's professional authorial identity was primarily that of an informal staff writer for

the *Dial*, with limited forays into the book market with his Goethe translation, and the broader periodical press.

24. Myerson, *History of the Dial*, 28.

25. Emerson qtd. in Crain, *American Sympathy*, 211.

26. Emerson, *Letters to a Friend*, 24.

27. Emerson, *Letters to a Friend*, 30.

28. Emerson, *Letters to a Friend*, 63.

29. Qtd. in Charles Capper, *Margaret Fuller: An American Romantic Life, The Public Years* (Oxford: Oxford University Press, 2007), 283.

30. Capper, *Margaret Fuller*, 284.

31. Emerson, *Letters to a Friend*, 65.

32. Emerson, *Letters to a Friend*, 64–65.

33. Emerson, *Letters to a Friend*, 47.

34. Emerson, *Letters to a Friend*, 51–52.

35. Emerson, *Letters to a Friend*, 58–59.

36. Emerson, *Letters to a Friend*, 61.

37. Qtd. in Myerson, *History of the Dial*, 218.

38. Samuel Gray Ward, "The Shield," *Dial* 1.1 (July 1840), 121.

39. Ward, "The Shield," 121.

40. Ralph Waldo Emerson, *Poems* (Boston: James Munroe, 1847), 32.

41. Christopher Cranch, *Poems* (Philadelphia: Carey and Hart, 1844), 77.

42. Samuel Gray Ward, "The Consolers," *Dial* 4.4 (April 1844), 469.

43. Samuel Gray Ward, "Notes on Art and Architecture," *Dial* 4.1 (1843), 107–8.

44. Ward, "Notes on Art and Architecture," 113, 111.

Chapter 5. Ellery Channing

1. Qtd. in Frederick T. McGill, Jr., *Channing of Concord: A Life of William Ellery Channing, II* (New Brunswick: Rutgers University Press, 1967), 34.

2. Robert Sattelmeyer, "Ellery Channing in the 1855 Massachusetts Census," *Thoreau Research Newsletter*, 2.2 (n.d.), 8. Ralph L. Rusk, *The Life of Ralph Waldo Emerson* (New York: Columbia University Press, 1949), 233.

3. Ralph Waldo Emerson Papers, Houghton Library, Harvard University. William Ellery Channing, Poems (unsigned) to RWE [n.p., n.d.], MS Am 1280, 627 (hereafter Emerson Papers, Houghton Library). Eleanor M. Tilton notes the poem's existence in the Emerson Papers insofar as it corresponds to an October letter from Emerson to Ward, identifiable through its "Spensarian stanzas." She does not, however, take account of the poem as a whole, or in the context of Channing's professional circumstances that conditioned its production. Tilton's is the only mention of the poem's existence; the poem has not been published, as she correctly notes that it does not appear in Channing's *The Collected Poems of Ellery Channing*, ed. Walter Harding (Gainesville, Fla.: Scholars' Facsimilies and Reprints, 1967).

4. McGill, *Channing of Concord*, 21.

5. Emerson Papers, Houghton Library, MS Am 1280, 627.

6. Hal Menge [Ellery Channing], Review of John Greenleaf Whittier's "Mogg Megone," *Boston Mercantile Journal* (April 22, 1835), 59.

7. Hal Menge [Ellery Channing], "Paul, A Sketch," *Mercantile Ledger* (July 14, 1835), 37.

8. Robert N. Hudspeth, *Ellery Channing* (New York: Twayne, 1973), 120.

9. McGill, *Channing of Concord*, 87; Hudspeth, *Ellery Channing*, 32.

10. *Proceedings of the Massachusetts Historical Society* (Boston: Massachusetts Historical Society, 1932), 250.

11. See Kathryn B. McKee, "'A Fearful Price I Have Had to Pay for Loving Him': Ellery Channing's Troubled Relationship with Ralph Waldo Emerson," in *Studies in the American Renaissance, 1994*, ed. Joel Myerson (Charlottesville: University Press of Virginia, 1994), 252, for the standard critical emphasis on Channing's faults as seen by Emerson. McKee usefully unveils Channing's overriding bitterness toward Emerson in Francis B. Dedmond, "The Selected Letters of William Ellery Channing the Younger (Parts One-Three)," in *Studies in the American Renaissance, 1989–1990*, ed. Joel Myerson (Charlottesville: University Press of Virginia, 1990), 115–218, 257–343, 159–241. I build on McKee's fine readings of those letters to suggest that Emerson's mentoring of Channing was not as inhumane as Channing suggested—especially in statements made to the sympathetic Franklin Sanborn, who tended to coddle Channing later in life—but was always done to advance his professional career. Further, my argument adds to McKee's by highlighting detours in Emerson's own poetic career as the source for much of his alternately frustrated and defensive responses to Channing's unfinished verse.

12. See Lawrence Buell, *Emerson* (Cambridge: Belknap Press of Harvard University Press, 2003), for a discussion of Emerson's Americanization of Wordsworth's argument in the preface to *Lyrical Ballads* that unaffected peasant speech makes for better poetry (110).

13. Emerson Papers, Houghton Library, MS Am 1280, 627.

14. Emerson Papers, Houghton Library, MS Am 1280, 627.

15. Emerson Papers, Houghton Library, MS Am 1280, 627.

16. Emerson Papers, Houghton Library, MS Am 1280, 627.

17. Dedmond, "Selected Letters," 2:165.

18. Hyatt H. Waggoner, *Emerson as Poet* (Princeton: Princeton University Press, 1974), 108. Emerson's contemporary critics disliked his poetry for many of the same reasons critics do today. John Michael, for example, has observed that "virtually every critic writing on Emerson's poetry" has felt obligated "to note just how disappointing his worst poetry can be," particularly in light of passages from his "least compelling essays [that] seem more poetic" than his verse; Michael, "Death, Love, and Emerson's Poetry," in *Emerson for the Twenty-First Century: Global Perspectives on an American Icon*, ed. Barry Tharaud (Newark: University of Delaware Press, 2010), 385, 387.

19. Terence Whalen, *Poe and the Masses: The Political Economy of Literature in Antebellum America* (Princeton: Princeton University Press, 1999), 7.

20. Lance Newman, "'Patron of the World': Henry Thoreau as Wordsworthian Poet," in *Modern Critical Views: Henry Thoreau—Updated Edition*, ed. Harold Bloom (New York: Infobase, 2007), 109.

21. Ralph Waldo Emerson, "New Poetry," *The Dial* (October 1840), 220.

22. Emerson, "New Poetry," 220.

23. Lawrence Buell, ed., *The American Transcendentalists: Essential Writings* (New York: Modern Library, 2006), 388.

24. Emerson, "New Poetry," 227.

25. Ellery Channing, "The Youth of the Poet and the Painter," *The Dial* 4.2 (October 1843), 180.

26. "Historic Notes of Life and Letters in Massachusetts," *Atlantic Monthly* 52 (October 1883), 530.

27. Ellery Channing, "The Youth of the Poet and the Painter," *The Dial* 4.3 (January 1844), 273.

28. Channing, "The Youth of the Poet and the Painter," 185.

29. Channing, "The Youth of the Poet and the Painter," 275.

30. Qtd. in Carlos Baker, *Emerson Among the Eccentrics: A Group Portrait* (New York: Viking, 1996), 235.

31. My emphasis on "The Youth of the Poet and the Painter" as an emblem of Channing's vocational crisis and declaration of independence builds on the useful yet brief overview of the story's function as a group portrait of the young transcendentalist authors in Hudspeth, *Ellery Channing*, 57–61. Hudspeth focuses instead on the humor of the Uncle Dick character in Channing's "Youth of the Poet and the Painter." The story has received surprisingly little serious critical attention, even in discussions of Channing's professional career and conception of authorship in the literary market.

32. Whitman, *Leaves*, 17.

33. McKee, "A Fearful Price," 258.

34. Despite such evidence of these two sides of Channing, he continues to be portrayed as a headstrong narcissist. Francis Dedmond quotes Frederick McGill's description of him as an unruly infant who "shook his tiny fist at the universe whenever it said No to his desires" and was given to temper tantrums. But McGill clearly says that between his tantrums, which infants generally throw, "he was a happy child"; McGill, *Channing of Concord*, 3. Dedmond also dismisses Hudspeth, who renders a picture of Channing that accentuates his companionable attributes and his jocular, refreshing wit. Conversely, Dedmond openly admits to selecting only those letters that highlight "the troubled man . . . frustrated literary artist [and] . . . unpredictable friend"; Dedmond, "Selected Letters," 1:116.

35. Dedmond, "Selected Letters," 3:335.

36. Rufus Griswold, ed., *The Poets and Poetry of America, with an Historical Introduction* (Philadelphia: Carey and Hart, 1847), 334, 6.

37. Thoreau, *Journal*, 8:39. Baker alternately describes this tendency of Channing's to "ask for a paradox, an eccentric statement, and too often I give it to him" as a "contagion" and "disease of their common affliction" that worked to "moderate his

considered observations of society"; Baker, *Emerson Among the Eccentrics*, 330–31. But at close examination of the hyperbole of assault against New England debt-ridden farmers, and New Yorkers captive to the whims of the fashion industry in "Economy" of *Walden*, for example, it appears that Channing was more an asset than a liability, as the eccentric statement in Thoreau rose to the level of poetry, "I have always been regretting that I was not as wise as the day I was born," and high comedy, "As for the pyramids, there is nothing to wonder at in them so much as the fact that so many men could be found degraded enough to spend their lives constructing a tomb for some ambitious booby, whom it would have been wiser and manlier to have drown in the Nile, and then given his body to the dogs"; *The Writings of Henry David Thoreau: Walden*, ed. J. Lyndon Shanley (Princeton: Princeton University Press, 1971), 109, 64.

38. Thomas Wentworth Higginson, "Walks with Ellery Channing," *Atlantic Monthly* 90 (1902), 30–31.

39. Henry David Thoreau, *The Correspondence of Henry David Thoreau*, ed. Walter Harding and Carl Bode (New York: New York University Press, 1958), 124, 145.

40. Ethel Seybold's tentative claim that Channing "may have contributed" to Thoreau's retreat to Walden Pond is far more affirmative than she implies, given the depth of their relationship at the time; Seybold, "Thoreau: The Quest and the Classics," in *Bloom's Modern Critical Views: Henry David Thoreau—Updated Edition*, ed. Harold Bloom (New York: Infobase, 2007), 21. Seybold also claims that the young romantic thirst for rural retreat and solitude had become so hackneyed in Emerson's view that he lamented its central role in the plot of Channing's "Youth of the Poet and the Painter." Emerson's misgivings were rooted less in the natural retreat as a romantic cliché, however, than in the eccentric tone shifts of the narrative from somber vocational soul searching into the burlesque satire of the Uncle Dick character. Further, the opposition between the domestic and the rural was hardly so uncomplicated, as Channing's roles in *Walden*—from suggesting it in the first place and helping raise the beams of the house to his frequent appearances in the narrative—are decidedly domestic and social rather than rural and isolated.

41. Thoreau, *Walden*, 145–46, 156, 173.

42. *The Hawthorne Centenary Celebration at the Wayside*, ed. Thomas Wentworth Higginson (Boston: Houghton Mifflin, 1905), 183–84.

43. *The Hawthorne Centenary Celebration at the Wayside*, 184–85.

44. McGill, *Channing of Concord*, 72.

45. Qtd. in McKee, "A Fearful Price," 270.

46. Margaret Fuller, "Margaret Fuller's 1842 Journal: At Concord with the Emersons," ed. Joel Myerson, *Harvard Library Bulletin* 21 (July 1973), 340. Walt Whitman, *Specimen Days and Collect* (Philadelphia: David McKay, 1882), 321.

47. Whitman, *Specimen Days*, 321–22.

48. Thoreau, *Journal*, 3:256.

49. Higginson, "Walks with Ellery Channing," 28.

50. Dedmond imagines Channing "would be upset" that so many of his friends had "lovingly preserved" his most scandalous letters from that ten-year span; Dedmond,

"Selected Letters," 1:116. Some of that material undoubtedly was intended to remain private. It does not, however, uniformly malign him. Franklin Sanborn, with whom he lodged during the last few decades of his life, functioned much in the way Horace Traubel did for Whitman, as his companion and biographer. Were he so averse to leaving a record of his legacy, he would never have lodged with Sanborn, the self-professed last of the transcendentalists who staked his authority on his relationship with Channing.

51. Channing's financial dependence on Ward lasted for decades, as indicated by his letter of May 20, 1853, acknowledging, "Forthwith I am completely in your debt. [With] Your generous gift of 200.00 . . . you have saved me from bankruptcy," and I consider you "the most generous and honorable of all the persons I have known"; Samuel Ward and Anna Hazard Barker Ward Papers, MS Am 146, Houghton Library, Harvard University.

52. Emerson's way of doing literary business at the time was to bring his works out at his own expense, placing his writing under tremendous pressure since he risked greater losses under such contracts, which also promised richer profits. Emerson could afford to shun the safer but less lucrative half-profits arrangements that set the industry standard literary contract, because the ample crowds that gathered for his lectures suggested that an audience for his books existed. He recorded in his account book his greatest intellectual and capital investments: "The plates of 'Emerson's Essays, First Series,' in the hands of Munroe, and Co., are my property. Also the stereotype plates of 'Emerson's Poems.' Also the copyrights of the above named books and of 'Emerson's Essays, Second Series' 'Nature; Addresses and Lectures'"; Ralph Waldo Emerson, Account Book, "Journal I, 1849," Houghton Library, Harvard University.

53. Emerson's account books list innumerable occasions when his role of mentor and publicist transformed into that of employer. He hired "H.D. Thoreau for surveying the town-line in my Walden woodlot" on one occasion, and paid on December 27, 1842, $2.52 in "cash to H. D. Thoreau on expenses for the Dial" for his work as managing editor. On May 5, 1843, he paid "$7.00 cash to H.D. Thoreau for William Emerson," presumably for tutoring William's son while boarding with him on Staten Island; Ralph Waldo Emerson Account Book, "Journal I, 1849," Houghton Library, Harvard University.

54. Ralph Waldo Emerson, "Account Book 1840–44" (November 25, 1843, June 5, 1844), Houghton Library, Harvard University.

55. Kenneth Walter Cameron, "A Garland of Emerson Letters," *Emerson Society Quarterly* 10 (1958), 38.

56. Channing, *Collected Poems*, 100.

57. Channing, *Collected Poems*, 288–91.

58. Channing, *Collected Poems*, 98, 100.

59. Channing, *Collected Poems*, 471–73.

60. Channing, *Collected Poems*, 473.

61. William Ellery Channing, Letter to RWE from WEC, December 20, 1874, MS Am 1280, 631, Houghton Library, Harvard University.

62. Channing, *Collected Poems*, 940.

63. Channing, *Collected Poems*, 941.

64. Franklin B. Sanborn, ed., *Poems of Sixty-Five Years by Ellery Channing* (Philadelphia: James H. Bentley, 1902), xxxvi; Walt Whitman, *Leaves of Grass*, ed. Malcolm Cowley (New York: Penguin, 1988 [1855]), 85.

65. Sanborn, *Poems of Sixty-Five Years*, 445.

Chapter 6. Jones Very

1. Helen R. Deese usefully characterizes Very's spirituality, which remained surprisingly consistent from his early poems to his later sermons, as Unitarian pietism driven by a combination of affectation, devotionalism, modified asceticism (anti-materialism that does not neglect the body or nature), and ecstatic mysticism; Deese, "Selected Sermons of Jones Very," in *Studies in the American Renaissance, 1984*, ed. Joel Myerson (Charlottesville: University Press of Virginia, 1984), 9.

2. Joel Myerson, "Ralph Waldo Emerson's Income from His Books," in *The Profession of Authorship: Essays in Honor of Matthew J. Bruccoli*, ed. Richard Layman and Joel Myerson (Columbia: University of South Carolina Press, 1996), 144.

3. Deese, for example, observes that "we tend to think of Emerson as the editor of Very's poetry" and thus neglect to acknowledge that his "fascination with Very up to this point [of their first meetings] had nothing whatever to do with his talents as a poet"; Deese, "Introduction," *Jones Very: The Complete Poems*, ed. Helen Deese (Athens: University of Georgia Press, 1993), xix. Edwin Gittleman originally noted that Emerson had regarded Very as a personality, a lecturer, and writer of essays, and not a poet, until November 1838, when he received clippings of his two most recently published sonnets, "In Him we live, and move, and have our being" and "Enoch"; Gittleman, *Jones Very: The Effective Years* (New York: Columbia University Press, 1967), 258. But to argue that Emerson had dissociated Very from poetry misses that Very's "personality" became the embodiment of Emerson's own privately held thoughts about vocation, which rebelled against the conservative Unitarian clergy and favored the independent scholar, a figure contiguous with the idealized poet that would recur throughout his writings as the icon of a fulfilling and daring alternative vocational identity. I find that Emerson's early attraction to Very depended on his capacity to imagine him as his ideal poet, much as he had initially applied the same criterion to his judgments of Channing and Thoreau. Emerson's interest in Very's poetry is in this sense an extension of his earliest fascination with Very the man, who I argue functioned as a key foot soldier in Emerson's war against historical Christianity and personalized God of the conservative Unitarian ministry. Thus Very was already Emerson's "brave saint" long before Emerson began editing the youth's essays and poems into a salable volume.

4. Deese, "Introduction," xi.

5. Robert D. Habich usefully traces a long foreground to Andrews Norton's rage at Emerson that sparked the Harvard Divinity School controversy. He specifically discovers in Norton a "pattern of response to anarchy and authority," most of which were battles waged against Harvard administration, "that dissolves the black-and-white

distinctions between Norton and Emerson into more accurate shades of gray"; Robert D. Habich, "Emerson's Reluctant Foe: Andrews Norton and the Transcendental Controversy," *The New England Quarterly* 16.2 (June 1992), 211.

6. Very, *Complete Poems*, 138.

7. In Emerson's published writings, the acceptance of poverty in exchange for higher principles is perhaps best illustrated by "Man Thinking" of "The American Scholar" who willingly forgoes material comforts for his intellectual life. In his private notes, he similarly shows a willingness to accept trying circumstances in order to gain personal success, which in the following example is not just spiritual, but monetary: "'I'll bet you fifty dollars a day for three weeks, that you will not leave your library and wade and freeze and ride and run, and suffer all manner of indignities, and stand up for an hour each night and read in a hall,' and I answer, 'I'll bet I will.' I do it, and win the $900"; *JMN*, 15:457.

8. R. Jackson Wilson, among others, has argued that Emerson cared more for his own career at the expense of those of his followers, describing the arc of his career as quitting the Church for the market. Wilson cites the promise of liberation in the Divinity School Address as a fraud designed to sell his name as a literary commodity, arguing that Emerson's idealized brave heroes boldly breaking from the past become instantly strait-jacketed into vocations confining them to language, "to the production of poems, essays, books, and lectures—to being a figure of speech" only, rendering them ineffectual trifles who would "do nothing to challenge any specific feature of existing social and political arrangements"; Wilson, *Figures of Speech* (Baltimore: Johns Hopkins University Press, 1989), 205. His formulation forgets not only that Jones Very took his message to the streets in the context of Abner Kneeland's imprisonment for blasphemy in Salem, which in effect protested against this reactionary theocratic measure. Thoreau and Fuller would notably respond to Emerson's call for the "thousands of young men . . . now crowding the barriers for a career" in works now hailed as landmarks in literary activism on behalf of civil disobedience, anticapitalism, and feminism, rendering them hardly ineffectual prisoners of language, but instead, agents of social change whose work was instead aided by the ever expanding literary marketplace; *CW*, 1:69.

9. See Melville's "Bartleby, the Scrivener, A Story of Wall Street," in *The Piazza Tales and Other Prose Pieces, 1839–1860*, ed. Harrison Hayford, Hershel Parker, and G. Thomas Tanselle (Evanston and Chicago: Northwestern University Press and Newberry Library, 1987), 13–46, for an example of a patron (the story's narrator) who learns from his mentally imbalanced underling. The lawyer's waffling on how to treat Bartleby echoes the often criticized fluctuating attitudes Emerson expressed toward Very, ranging from exultation to exasperation, from ardent support to cool dismissal.

10. "The Life and Services to Literature of Jones Very: A Memorial Meeting, Dec. 14, 1880," *Bulletin of the Essex Institute* 13 (January–June 1881), 32. *JMN*, 15:340.

11. Jones Very, "Letter of Jones Very to Henry W. Bellows," Bellows Papers, Massachusetts Historical Society, qtd. in Deese, "Introduction," lvi.

12. Gittleman, *Jones Very*, 123.

13. Carolyn Porter, *Seeing and Being* (Middletown, Conn.: Wesleyan University Press, 1981), xiv.

14. Gittleman, *Jones Very*, 123.

15. Very's affinity for Emerson's image of transparency appears in his later sermons as well. "Man's spirit should be open to receive nature, but transparent also in transmitting to others the feelings thus stirred. Christian duty is thus urged in the same breath which celebrates mystical communion," in Very's formulation, according to Deese, "Selected Sermons of Jones Very," 14.

16. Very, *Complete Poems*, 70.

17. Jones Very to Rufus Ellis, December 24, 1838, Manuscript Letters, Special Collections Department, University of Iowa, Iowa City, Iowa.

18. Very, *Complete Poems*, 93–94.

19. Very, *Complete Poems*, 131.

20. Very, *Complete Poems*, 98–99.

21. Qtd. in Gittleman, *Jones Very*, 188–89.

22. Julius Ward, "Jones Very: The Finest Sonnet Writer in America," *Boston Sunday Herald* (May 16, 1880), 130.

23. Gittleman, *Jones Very*, 189.

24. Qtd. in Carlos Baker, *Emerson Among the Eccentrics: A Group Portrait* (New York: Viking, 1996), 122.

25. Elizabeth Palmer Peabody, *The Letters of Elizabeth Palmer Peabody*, ed. Bruce A. Rhonda (Middletown, Conn.: Wesleyan University Press, 1984), 406.

26. Peabody, *Letters*, 408.

27. Very, *Complete Poems*, 73.

28. Peabody, *Letters*, 407.

29. Peabody, *Letters*, 408.

30. Very, *Complete Poems*, 94.

31. Peabody, *Letters*, 409.

32. Amos Bronson Alcott, *The Journals of Bronson Alcott*, ed. Odell Shepard (Boston: Little, Brown, 1938), 516–17.

33. Qtd. in Gittleman, *Jones Very*, 331–32.

34. Qtd. in Gittleman, *Jones Very*, 359.

35. Qtd. in Ellen Tucker Emerson, *Life of Lidian Jackson Emerson* (Boston: Twayne, 1980), 78.

36. Robert Sattelmeyer's observation about Thoreau's "misguided appraisal of his literary vocation" equally applies to Channing and Very, but not Fuller, whose success in New York City defies "the deeply ambivalent effects of Emerson's patronage"; Sattelmeyer, "Thoreau's Projected Work on the English Poets," in *Studies in the American Renaissance, 1980*, ed. Joel Myerson (Boston: Twayne, 1980), 239.

37. Emerson's assertion that embracing vocation was a matter of surrender to intuitive constitutional predilection rather than proscribed rational choice shaped Very's understanding of himself as God's medium. Very's sense of vocation also reflects key components of Charles Fourier's doctrine of passional attraction stipulating that each

person is *divinely* attracted to the work and the persons that are properly his. The Holy Spirit "shall teach you all things" as a mentor might, in such a way that geniuses, according to Fourierist and Brook Farm denizens, frequently were considered messiahs in their own right, as one orator spoke of "Fourier, the second coming of Christ"; Marianne Dwight, *Letters from Brook Farm*, ed. Amy L. Reed (Poughkeepsie, N.Y.: Vassar College Press, 1928), 90. Very's messianic self-image is rooted in precisely this progression of vocation, from learning or receiving the Holy Spirit to channeling it to the world. Figures like Anna Parsons had become notable for telepathy and the channeling of human impression. Very was engaging in a species of this kind of mysticism, offering himself as a medium for communication with God. Parsons was known for her "reading of Charles Fourier's character"; Dwight, *Letters from Brook Farm*, 181–91. Transcendental interest in telepathy also surfaced in the Seeress of Prevoorst tale in Margaret Fuller's *Summer on the Lakes*. Charles King Newcomb adored Parsons, who recommended her to Brook Farm resident Marianne Dwight. Dwight, however, soured on the telepathy business, judging Fuller's Seeress boring and Kerner's original testimony of the mystic improbable and unbelievable. Clearly the movement was afoot, yet not all transcendentalists uniformly embraced it.

38. Jones Very, *Essays and Poetry* (Boston: Little, Brown, 1839), 126.

39. David Robinson, "The Exemplary Self and the Transcendent Self in the Poetry of Jones Very," *ESQ: A Journal of the American Renaissance* 24 (1978): 206–14.

40. Very, *Complete Poems*, 92.

41. Andrews Norton, "The New School in Literature and Religion," *Boston Daily Advertiser* (August 27, 1838), 12.

42. "An Address delivered before the Senior Class, in the Divinity College, Cambridge, Sunday Evening, 15th July 1838, by Ralph Waldo Emerson," *Boston Morning Post* (August 31, 1838).

43. Anne C. Rose, *Transcendentalism as a Social Movement, 1830–1850* (New Haven: Yale University Press, 1981), 85.

44. Julian Hawthorne, *Nathaniel Hawthorne and His Wife* (Boston: James R. Osgood, 1884), 1, 221.

45. Peabody, *Letters*, 221.

46. Nathaniel Hawthorne, "The Hall of Fantasy," *The New World* 6.5 (February 4, 1843), 148.

47. Walt Whitman, *Leaves of Grass*, ed. Sculley Bradley and Harold W. Blodgett (New York: W. W. Norton, 1973), 52.

48. Peabody, *Letters*, 407.

49. Qtd. in Gittleman, *Jones Very*, 343.

50. For a provocative, yet problematic, retelling of Very's infatuation with Lidian Emerson, see Gittleman, *Jones Very*, 346. Gittleman's Freudian reading of the relationship is far fetched, yet his initial claims that "for three days in the middle of June 1839" during Very's editorial work with Emerson to prepare *Essays and Poems* for publication, Lidian "most likely was the one who stimulated Very's show of manliness at the expense of his divinity." Specifically, "her feminine ways and sensitivities, devout thoughts and

encouragements, innocently roused in Jones Very human feelings he long ago learned to despise," an insight Gittleman regrettably funnels into his neo-Freudian explanation: "Thirty-seven-year old Mrs. Emerson unwittingly made the twenty-six-year-old poet conscious once again of the natural self he thought he had exorcised for his mother's sake," 346.

51. Peabody, *Letters*, 226.

52. Deese, "Introduction," xxi.

53. Octavius Pickering, *Reports of Cases Argued and Determined in the Supreme Judicial Court of Massachusetts*, 24 vols. (Boston: Little, Brown, 1854), 20:220.

54. Robert D. Richardson, Jr., "Emerson as Editor," in *Emersonian Circles: Essays in Honor of Joel Myerson*, ed. Wesley T. Mott and Robert E. Burkholder (Rochester, N.Y.: University of Rochester Press, 1997), 108.

55. Deese, xxi.

56. Very, *Essays and Poems*, 147.

57. *Dial* 2 (July 1841), 130–31.

58. Very, *Essays and Poems*.

59. Richardson, "Emerson as Editor," 108.

60. Richard F. Teichgraeber III, *Sublime Thoughts/Penny Wisdom: Situating Emerson and Thoreau in the American Market* (Baltimore: Johns Hopkins University Press, 1995), 178–79. For a list of the British editions of Emerson's works see Joel Myerson, *Ralph Waldo Emerson: A Descriptive Bibliography* (Pittsburgh: University of Pittsburgh Press, 1982), 117–20, 151–54. For sales figures of these editions, see William J. Sowder, "Introduction," *Emerson's Impact on the British Isles and Canada* (Chapel Hill: University of North Carolina Press, 1966), 1–28.

61. Teichgraeber, *Sublime Thoughts*, 187.

62. Wilson, *Figures of Speech*, 205.

Chapter 7. Charles King Newcomb

1. Lindsay Swift, *Brook Farm: Its Members, Scholars, and Visitors* (New York: Macmillan, 1900), 198–202. Scant mention of Newcomb appears in the updated history of Brook Farm by Sterling F. Delano, *Brook Farm: The Dark Side of Utopia* (Cambridge: Harvard University Press, 2004). Swift's portrait of Newcomb as a peripheral eccentric is rehearsed by Delano with no mention of his role in abetting Emerson's philosophical apprehension of evil. Other criticism does not account for why Emerson would be so riveted to Newcomb and "Dolon." Charles Capper, for example, highlights instead "Fuller's superior handling of Newcomb" insofar as she refused to pressure him to advance his career; Capper, *Margaret Fuller: An American Romantic Life, The Public Years* (Oxford: Oxford University Press, 2007), 535n.23. Emerson never apologized for his series of letters exhorting the youth to greater literary production, and felt fully justified in applying pressure to publish, despite Newcomb's shy temperament. William M. Moss cites one of eight otherwise genuinely encouraging letters reflecting Emerson's exasperation at the prospect of editing "Dolon," in " 'So Many Promising Youths': Emerson's Disappointing Discoveries of New England's Poet-Seers," *New England*

Quarterly 49.1 (1976), 66–67. Although Emerson is frustrated in the letter, it does not represent evidence of his "rejection" of Newcomb, as he continued to support him through the publication of the story and after. I build on Joel Myerson's assessment that Emerson took deep satisfaction in shepherding "Dolon" into print, since he "knew that Newcomb would have remained unpublished and unknown had it not been for the *Dial*"; Myerson, *New England Transcendentalists and The Dial: A History of the Magazine and Its Contributors* (Cranbury, N.J.: Associated University Presses, 1980), 80. Judith Kennedy Johnson's editing of *The Journals of Charles King Newcomb* (Providence: Brown University Press, 1946; hereafter *Newcomb Journals*), makes a vigorous argument against Emerson's influence on Newcomb beyond the first decade of their relationship, in a strenuous attempt to distance him from his alleged mysticism or even transcendentalism. Johnson emphasizes their departures rather than convergences, especially in Emerson's "disappointment in Newcomb's unwillingness to speak to an audience" (23–24). Johnson's study clearly attempts to remake Newcomb's image into one more appealing to her utilitarian postwar American audience.

2. Rhoda Newcomb's interpretation of Coleridge is "among the most important of the many gnarled and intertwined Transatlantic roots of American Transcendentalism," according to Joel Pace and Chris Koenig-Woodward, "Coleridge and Divine Providence: Charles King Newcomb, Rhoda Newcomb, and Ralph Waldo Emerson," *Wordsworth Circle* 32.2 (2001), 141. For more on Coleridge's philosophical influence on Emerson, especially the source of his sense of reason as moral sentiment, see Neal Dolan, *Emerson's Liberalism* (Madison: University of Wisconsin Press, 2009), 139.

3. Robert Sattelmeyer, " 'When He Became My Enemy': Emerson and Thoreau, 1848–49," *New England Quarterly* 62.2 (June 1989), 194–95.

4. Newcomb, *Journals*, 13.

5. Newcomb, *Journals*, 14.

6. Qtd. in Pace and Koenig-Woodward, "Coleridge and Divine Providence," 140.

7. Rhoda Newcomb, "Coleridge," *Providence Daily Journal* 16 (December 3, 1845), 286.

8. Pace and Koenig-Woodward, "Coleridge and Divine Providence," 140.

9. Samuel Taylor Coleridge, *Biographia Literaria* (London: Rest Fenner, 1817), 11.

10. Newcomb, *Journals*, 273.

11. Lidian Emerson, "Lidian Emerson's 'Transcendental Bible,' " in *Studies in the American Renaissance, 1980*, ed. Delores Bird Carpenter (Charlottesville: University Press of Virginia, 1980), 91–92.

12. Emerson felt most comfortable expressing sentimentality in poetry rather than in his essays and lectures, according to Julie Ellison, "Tears for Emerson: *Essays, Second Series*," in *The Cambridge Companion to Ralph Waldo Emerson*, ed. Joel Porte and Saundra Morris (Cambridge: Cambridge University Press, 1999), 156–58. His private letters reporting Waldo's death, however, show an abundance of heartfelt anguish, raw pain and authentic rather than stylized or literary sentimentality. This problematizes Ellison's categorization of Emerson's sentimental correspondence among "Novels,

poems, and family letters [that] tend to self-consciously dramatize sympathy" as distinct from his "essays, treatises, and speeches," in which he "fretfully resists sentimental genres," particularly the ever popular child's death-bed scene (149). The language of the letters bears out an Emerson oddly at a loss for words, as his syntax is jagged and discordant, certainly with no intention to execute the sort of lyricism he employed in "Threnody."

13. Ann Schofield, "The Fashion of Mourning," in *Representations of Death in Nineteenth-Century U.S. Writing and Culture*, ed. Lucy E. Frank (Burlington, Vt.: Ashgate, 2007), 160. For more on mourning as genteel public performance to display moral correctness, see Karen Halttunen, *Confidence Men and Painted Ladies: A Study of Middle-Class Culture in America, 1830–1870* (New Haven: Yale University Press, 1982), 124–52.

14. Qtd. in Halttunen, *Confidence Men*, 130–31.

15. Sharon Cameron, "Representing Grief: Emerson's 'Experience,' " *Representations* 15 (Summer 1986): 15–41. Cameron usefully asks why Emerson seemed "to mourn the loss of his affect rather than the loss of his child" (16). Yet Emerson eventually found in Newcomb's "Dolon" the medium through which to grieve.

16. Cameron, "Representing Grief," 16.

17. Fuller, *Memoirs*, 2:62–63.

18. Though they shared walks and intimate thoughts throughout the early 1840s, their divergent politics seem to have soured Newcomb and Hawthorne's friendship. As residents at Brook Farm they were closest; "Hawthorne would smile with me, in incessantly renewed wonder, on finding our sense reflected where we never thought of seeing them in any shape," Newcomb reminisced. By 1870, however, the publication of Hawthorne's diaries precipitated Newcomb's spite, directed specifically toward *The Blithedale Romance*, which he felt profaned their sacred shared experience while at Brook Farm. Newcomb lashed back in his journal, describing Hawthorne as "chronically and chiefly self-conscious" and "self-centered," an author who is "a sensationalist, in a simple sort, in sentiment and sense," whose "novels are unreadable because of his blended aimlessness and morbidity"; Newcomb, *Journals*, 149–51.

19. Charles King Newcomb, "Dolon," *Dial* 3 (July 1842), 112–13.

20. John Humphrey Noyes, *History of American Socialisms* (Philadelphia: J. B. Lippincott, 1870), 538–39.

21. Newcomb, "Dolon," 117.

22. William Wordsworth, *Lyrical Ballads: William Wordsworth and Samuel Taylor Coleridge*, ed. R. L. Brett and A. R. Jones (New York: Routledge, 1991), xlviii; *CW*, 3:49.

23. Newcomb, "Dolon," 118–20.

24. Newcomb, "Dolon," 121.

25. Newcomb, "Dolon," 123.

26. Newcomb, "Dolon," 122.

27. Fuller, "Leila," 466–67.

28. Lawrence Buell, *Emerson* (Cambridge: Belknap Press of Harvard University Press, 2003), 129.

29. Newcomb, *Journal*, 240.

30. Newcomb, *Journal*, 262.

31. Nathaniel Hawthorne, *The Blithedale Romance* (New York: Oxford University Press, 1998 [1852]), 107. Another passage in this novel where mysticism wins the spotlight is the description of Priscilla's childhood, during which her "gift of second sight and prophecy" becomes notorious as the trends of mesmerism and clairvoyance are in their ascendancy. Indeed, "the story of Priscilla's preternatural manifestations, therefore, attracted a kind of notice of which it would have been deemed wholly unworthy a few years earlier" (187). Holgrave, the young daguerreotypist in Hawthorne's *House of the Seven Gables*, is similarly representative of the fascination with mesmerism and supernatural powers.

32. Marianne Dwight, *Letters from Brook Farm, 1844–1847*, ed. Amy L. Reed (Poughkeepsie, N.Y.: Vassar College, 1928), xiv.

33. Hawthorne, *The Blithedale Romance*, 52.

34. Johnson, *Journals of Newcomb*, 90.

35. Dwight, *Letters from Brook Farm*, 191.

36. Dwight, *Letters from Brook Farm*, 60.

37. Dwight, *Letters from Brook Farm*, 50.

38. Dwight, *Letters from Brook Farm*, 24.

39. Dwight, *Letters from Brook Farm*, 24.

Conclusion

1. Jeylan T. Mortimer, et al., "Tracing the Timing of 'Career' Acquisition in a Contemporary Youth Cohort," *Work and Occupations* 35.1 (February 2008), 47.

2. Lawrence Buell, ed., *The American Transcendentalists: Essential Writings* (New York: Modern Library, 2006), 388.

3. Buell, *American Transcendentalists*, 479.

4. Joel Myerson, "Margaret Fuller's 1842 Journal: At Concord with the Emersons," *Harvard Library Bulletin* 21 (July 1973), 339.

5. Lawrence Buell, *Emerson* (Cambridge: Belknap Press of Harvard University Press, 2003), 126.

6. William M. Moss, "'So Many Promising Youths': Emerson's Disappointing Discoveries of New England's Poet Seers," *New England Quarterly* 49.1 (March 1976), 47.

7. Lawrence Buell, *Emerson* (Cambridge: Belknap Press of Harvard University Press, 2003), 124.

8. Richard F. Teichgraeber III, *Sublime Thoughts/Penny Wisdom: Situating Emerson and Thoreau in the American Market* (Baltimore: Johns Hopkins University Press, 1995), 8.

9. Ralph Waldo Emerson, *Letters from Ralph Waldo Emerson to a Friend, 1838–1853*, ed. Charles Eliot Norton (Boston: Houghton Mifflin, 1899), 46–49.

10. Carlos Baker, *Emerson Among the Eccentrics: A Group Portrait* (New York: Viking, 1996), 144.

11. Myerson, "Ralph Waldo Emerson's Income from His Books," 136. Beyond his account books, Emerson's faith in the free market surfaces in his refusal of George Ripley's solicitation of his support for the Brook Farm experiment in communal living. In refuting the collectivist agrarian ideal, Emerson advocated four tenets of capitalism on the authority of Edmund Hosmer, a successful and well-respected gentleman farmer. Work is more productive: 1) when done separately, with few concessions for mutual aid; 2) with the aid of a skilled foreman to "buy cheap and sell dear," "without any scrupulous inquiry on the part of the employer as to his methods"; 3) with incentives to individuals for greater production than their peers; and 4) with direct individual compensation that "makes them work," rather than through the aggregate benefit of "the whole produce of the farm," which they already know is for them; O. B. Frothingham, *George Ripley* (Boston: Houghton Mifflin, 1882), 317.

12. Robert Milder, "The Radical Emerson?" *The Cambridge Companion to Ralph Waldo Emerson*, ed. Joel Porte and Saundra Morris (Cambridge: Cambridge University Press, 1999), 60.

13. Mary Kupiec Cayton, "The Making of an American Prophet: Emerson, His Audiences, and the Rise of the Culture Industry in Nineteenth-Century America," *American Historical Review* 92 (1987), 613.

14. Qtd. in Edwin Gittleman, *Jones Very: The Effective Years, 1833–1840* (New York: Columbia University Press, 1967), 258.

15. Ralph Waldo Emerson, *The Complete Works of Ralph Waldo Emerson*, ed. Edward W. Emerson (Boston: Houghton Mifflin, 1892), 12:82.

16. Robert D. Richardson, *Emerson: The Mind on Fire* (Berkeley: University of California Press, 1995), 415.

INDEX

accretion method of composition, 83, 85

aesthetics, 8, 15, 101, 154, 240, 257

Alcott, Bronson, 6, 82, 92, 144–45, 173, 196, 223, 236; and Emerson, 60; and Fruitlands, 197; and Temple School, 7, 26

Allston, Washington, 63, 133–34, 159, 164, 306

"American Scholar" (Emerson), 13, 16, 22, 24, 26, 37, 43, 48, 97, 114, 151, 154, 214, 235, 274

America's promise, 1, 3–4, 10, 270, 272

"Among the Worst of Men that Ever Lived" (Thoreau), 93

anticonsumerism. *See* materialism

anti-institution. *See* institutions

antimaterialism. *See* materialism

antinomianism, 207, 226

apprenticeship, 263, 265, 270–73, 286; Emerson's pattern of, 4–6; Emerson's style of, 23; for followers, 7, 24. *See also* mentoring; patronage

"Arched Stream" (Channing), 193–94

associationism, 144–45

authenticity, 19, 181, 210, 214, 217, 221, 275

authority, 20, 26, 58. *See also* institutions

authorship, 5, 24, 28, 178; Channing and, 142, 174–75, 177–78, 184, 186–88, 190–94, 201–2; Emerson and, 10, 74, 153, 157, 161, 184, 186, 191–92, 263, 269–70, 276–77, 285; Fuller and, 35–37, 39–40, 43–44, 50, 55, 62–65, 139; Newcomb and, 142, 258–59; Thoreau and, 68–72, 76, 80, 85–86, 93, 96; Very and, 142, 206–8, 214–15, 227; Ward and, 142, 152, 154, 158–59, 166–67. *See also* literary market

"Bacchus" (Emerson), 129, 182

bookishness, 55, 72, 95

Brook Farm, 14–15, 36, 46, 118, 120–22, 145, 186; and Newcomb, 241, 250, 255–59

Brown, Lucy Jackson: and Thoreau, 66, 68–71, 85

Buell, Lawrence, 7, 16, 21, 25, 41, 48, 79, 121, 140, 186, 188, 254, 265, 269–70

capitalism, 7–10, 20, 26–27, 37, 94, 276. *See also* economics; literary market